STUDIES IN

THEATRE HISTORY

AND CULTURE

Edited by Thomas Postlewait

EMBODIED MEMORY

THE THEATRE OF GEORGE TABORI

BY ANAT FEINBERG

University of Iowa Press

Iowa City

University of Iowa Press,
Iowa City 52242
Copyright © 1999 by the
University of Iowa Press
All rights reserved
Printed in the United States of America
Design by Richard Hendel
http://www.uiowa.edu/~uipress
No part of this book may be
reproduced or used in any form or by
any means, electronic or mechanical,
including photocopying and recording,
without permission in writing from the
publisher. All reasonable steps have
been taken to contact copyright holders
of material used in this book. The
publisher would be pleased to make
suitable arrangements with any whom
it has not been possible to reach.
Printed on acid-free paper

Library of Congress
Cataloging-in-Publication Data
Feinberg, Anat, 1951–
Embodied memory: the theatre of
George Tabori / by Anat Feinberg.
p.   cm. — (Studies in theatre history
and culture)
Includes bibliographical references and
index.
ISBN 0-87745-686-0 (cl.)
1. Tabori, George, 1914–   —Dramatic
works.   2. World War, 1939–1945—
Literature and the war.   3. Holocaust,
Jewish (1939–1945), in literature.
4. Tabori, George, 1914–   —Stage
history.   5. Jews in literature.   I. Title.
II. Series.
PS3539.A145Z6   1999
812'.54—dc21   99-16497

99   00   01   02   03
C   5   4   3   2   1

An early version of chapter 3 appeared
in *Theater gegen das Vergessen: Bühnenarbeit
und Drama bei George Tabori*, ed. Hans-
Peter Bayerdörfer and Jörg Schönert
(Tübingen: Niemeyer, 1997). A version
of chapter 4 appeared in *Verkörperte
Geschichtsentwürfe: George Taboris
Theaterarbeit*, ed. Peter Höyng (Tübingen:
Francke Verlag, 1998). An early version
of chapter 6 appeared in *Journal of Beckett
Studies* 1–4 (1992). A version of chapter
14 appeared in *Staging the Holocaust: The
Shoah in Drama and Performance*, ed.
Claude Schumacher (Cambridge:
Cambridge University Press, 1998).

FOR DANIEL

CONTENTS

George Tabori is a unique figure on the contemporary stage. Hungarian-born, Jewish, holder of a British passport, he is an intriguing presence who writes his plays in English then produces them (and the plays of others) in the German-speaking theatre of Germany and Austria. He began his long and astonishingly productive career in the United States, in Hollywood and later in New York — over twenty years in all; but his career only took off when he came to Germany, aged fifty-five, and began producing theatrical events which were both highly original and provocative.

This is the first study of the man and his theatre in English and the first book on Tabori which makes use of his enormous private archive. My aim is to introduce Tabori and his plays and productions to an English-speaking audience. There has been a growing interest in the work of this extraordinary writer and theatre subversive, and quite a number of his plays have been produced in the United States and in Britain. Rather than providing a chronology, I chose to concentrate on certain preeminent aspects of his work, foregrounding his singular contribution to contemporary theatre and to the so-called Theatre of the Holocaust.

Chapter 1 introduces Tabori the man and examines the innumerable stations in his well-traveled and travailed life. It includes a brief mention of all those plays and productions which are not addressed extensively in the book.

Chapter 2 is devoted to Tabori's theatrics and describes the major elements of his stage theory, as compared to other stage avant-gardists. Chapters 3 to 6 focus on Tabori's early productions in Germany. It was in Bremen and in Munich in the 1970s that he tried to implement his ideas of an alternative theatre-making, presenting spectators with his most adventurous and radical productions. This is not only the most exciting phase of his career as innovator, but also the period in which he approximated the works of his most cherished writers such as Franz Kafka and Samuel Beckett.

Chapters 7 to 10 concentrate on Tabori's unorthodox, at times iconoclastic, productions of Shakespeare, which he directed mostly in his own Kreis Theatre in Vienna in the late 1980s. Chapters 11 to 15 are devoted to the so-called Holocaust Plays or the Theatre of the Holocaust. While introducing the reader to Tabori's best-known plays, among them *The Cannibals* and *Mein Kampf*, I have tried to focus attention on the way in which Tabori's theatre becomes a locus of remembrance (*Gedächtnisort*), offering a unique and engaging memory-work (*Erinnerungsarbeit*).

I would like to take this opportunity to thank all those who contributed in deed, advice, and comment to the making of the book. First and foremost, to George Tabori, who granted me access to his enormous and invaluable archive and patiently filled in the gaps over cups of coffee. Special thanks must go to Dr. Renate Rätz and the staff of the Archiv der Akademie der Künste in Berlin for wonderful cooperation, not too common in archives these days. My thanks go to the Gustav Kiepenheuer Bühnenvertriebs GmbH in Berlin and to the Press Department of the Burgtheater in Vienna for providing me with stage scripts, unpublished material, documentation, and illustrative material. The Alexander von Humboldt Stiftung gave me a generous stipend, which helped me embark on this study.

Many thanks go to Detlef Jacobsen, the veteran among Tabori's actors, who provided me with much insider's information and was always ready to help and advise. Peter von Becker helped me establish the first necessary ties. I wish to thank all those on both sides of the Atlantic who were on the watch for any press material on Tabori, knowing how grateful I am for any report, especially to Steven Bloom, Hildegard and Jochen Bußmann, Sibylle Ehrlich, Thomas Faltin, Gundula Ohngemach, Klaus Rürup, and Claudia Stein. Rabbi Joel Berger patiently helped me in all matters Hungarian. Tamar Doron-Harris played an important role in all stages of this manuscript. I am grateful also to the editor of the Studies in Theatre History and Culture series, Thomas Postlewait, for many insights and editorial suggestions.

Special thanks go to my dear friend Jeanette Malkin, who provided me with invaluable critical comments and encouraging words. Finally, I would like to thank my husband, Robert, and my son, Daniel, for accompanying me so lovingly during the years of this journey.

EMBODIED MEMORY

It has been a long life and I have been lucky. Eighty percent of my family perished during the war, but I always enjoyed a narrow escape, by pure chance, not because I wanted to. George Tabori

FAMILY CONNECTIONS

George Tabori (György Tábori) was born in Budapest on 24 May 1914. This was, or so it seemed, a time of innocence, and the Danube, that much eulogized main artery of the Habsburg monarchy, "was free of charge."[1] A month later Archduke Franz Ferdinand was shot in Sarajevo, and in midsummer Europe was plunged into a merciless war.

Cornelius Tabori was not present when his second son, György, came into the world, as he happened to be one of the journalists accompanying the crown prince on his fatal journey. Women were there to welcome the newborn, along with plenty of laughter, two themes that were to play a major role throughout Tabori's life. A splendid storyteller with a penchant for weaving his own experiences into fiction, Tabori describes his birth thus: "I didn't want to be born. I felt fine in my mother's womb. She and I — we were together, all by ourselves. But one day, on May 23rd, 1914, my mother had a fit of laughter and the contractions began. I had in mind to get out into the cold world already, it was 23:30, but my grandmother joined in and said: tomorrow is Sunday. Wait another half hour, then you'll be a Sunday-boy. So I returned to the womb and emerged on Sunday."[2]

It was Sunday, not the Sabbath, which crowned the week

for the assimilated Tabori family. The origin of that family name goes back to a Jewish ancestor who was known in the ghetto as Josef the Deaf (*der Tauber* [*sic*]),[3] who changed his name to Tabori when he moved to the town of Tabor in what was then Bohemia. Max Tabori, the paternal grandfather, was the director of the post office in Szolnok, a provincial town on the bank of the river Tisza, which in 1880 numbered some 1,100 Jews, who were engaged mainly in trade and crafts. Max Tabori had three sons and three daughters.[4] George, who never met him, learned that his grandfather was "a terrible tyrant" who never forgave his son Cornelius (born 1879) for his rebellious flight to Budapest.[5]

Determined to become a writer like one of his uncles, Cornelius arrived in the big city (in which 25 percent of the inhabitants were Jews) with no money save one golden forint, which was immediately stolen from him. He soon made a name for himself as a reporter on criminal matters and was eventually appointed assistant editor of the oldest Hungarian daily, *Pesti Napló*. Troubled by the social malaise of modern urban society, by the poverty and misery around him, he helped organize large-scale relief for thousands of the destitute, especially children. He wrote extensively about it and even made films depicting life in the slums and the fate of the homeless, which he then screened and accompanied by lectures in Holland, Belgium, and Switzerland. He made it a custom to visit criminals in prison and to talk with jailbirds and was known as Mr. Fix-It, for his goodwill and helpfulness.

During the war he reported from the front and chronicled the wretchedness of the refugees in various parts of the monarchy. His experiences swayed him politically to the left. In 1919 he supported the revolution headed by Béla Kun — a Hungarian Communist of Jewish origin — only to find himself blacklisted after it was crushed in the summer. From then on he had to settle for all kinds of odd jobs. He worked as a freelance writer for various newspapers and was for over fifteen years press chief to the Hungarian Foreign Traffic Association, acting as guide to foreign writers and artists who visited Hungary. One of the celebrities he met was Thomas Mann, who came to Budapest in 1923 to lecture "about occult problems." Cornelius Tabori, who was interested in psychological research and in the paranatural, recorded Mann's visit in *My Occult Diary*, which he kept for over forty years.[6]

An autodidact, well-read and widely traveled, he was the first journalist to be admitted to the secret archives of the Habsburgs after the First World War. The list of his publications is extraordinarily variegated: over fifty books, thousands of articles and hundreds of lectures, children's books, accounts of criminal cases, historical studies (e.g., about the 1905 revolution in Russia, which he eyewitnessed), a guide to Hungarian hotels and restaurants, translations of novels and nonfiction books by English and American authors.[7]

A picture taken on their honeymoon shows Cornelius Tabori as a handsome, well-dressed young gentleman with a beret and an elongated slim cigar in his mouth; Elsa Tabori, née Ziffer (born 1889), is an elegant young woman with a stylized hairdo in the fashion of the times, a soft gaze, and full lips. Elsa's family came from Slovenia, which was then part of the Habsburg monarchy. Her father was a physician who also practiced in various fashionable health resorts, such as Bad Ischel. The first son of Cornelius and Elsa Tabori, Paul (Pál), was born in 1908; their second, George, followed six years later.

"I have a mother tongue, Hungarian, a father tongue, English, and an uncle tongue, German," says Tabori with a grain of irony.[8] He wrote all his works in English, but directed his and others' plays mostly on German stages. When I asked Tabori, then eighty-three, in which language he really feels at home, he hesitated, then smiled. "I wonder . . . " he muttered. "I rarely have an opportunity to speak English. I speak English with my children in New York. I have never really learned German, systematically I mean. And my Hungarian is old-fashioned; it's the language spoken there before the war."

In fact, he grew up in a bilingual household. His parents spoke Hungarian; the nanny spoke German. Elsa Tabori spoke perfect German, as did her mother and her sisters. Grandma Fanny spoke only German — "the middle class in Hungary favored German, the aristocracy spoke French" — and used to tell George stories while he fell asleep. "These were always Shakespeare stories, and no matter how many corpses there were at the end, she always said that they lived happily ever after."[9]

A photo taken around 1910 shows the Tabori clan taking a swim at a summer resort: over twenty men, women, and children, in old-fashioned bathing suits and curious headcovers. It is a moving snapshot of happy days, for many would perish in the Holocaust. Cornelius and his brothers — Uncle Geza, the textile merchant, and

Uncle Alex, the bookshop owner — were murdered in Auschwitz. Aunt Martha, Elsa's sister, and Aunt Gisela were murdered, as were male and female cousins. "Crazy Aunt Piroschka," an ardent admirer of G. E. Lessing's *Nathan the Wise*, committed suicide in a telephone booth after bidding her Aryan husband farewell.[10] The daughter of Aunt Bella was found with her head severed on a Budapest street after she was blown up by a grenade. Residing in London, Paul Tabori used his wide contacts to obtain whatever news he could about his parents, particularly after Cornelius had been arrested. He firmly believed that his father was denounced by members of the fascist Hungarian Arrow Cross.[11] The final news came on the shining Victory May Day. It contained a list of names of those deported via the death camps Csepel and Horthy-Liget. Cornelius Tabori was the last name on that list. A brief official note from the Red Cross followed: Cornelius Tabori was murdered in Auschwitz. A few months later, in winter, Paul found his mother in Budapest: Elsa escaped the deportation by the skin of her teeth and survived the war in hiding.

George grew up in a house steeped in culture, with books lining the walls and frequent visits by writers, liberal intellectuals, and artists of all sorts. Both parents were avid consumers of culture, took their boys to circus and theatre performances, and introduced them at a young age to the magic of motion pictures. As part of their broad-based education, the Tabori boys played musical instruments: Paul played the piano, George the saxophone ("The neighbours were mad at me"). Cornelius Tabori was determined to bring up his sons in the spirit of enlightened humanism, to imbue them with the best of the European heritage. "Seduced by the promises for a liberal cosmopolitanism,"[12] he envisaged them as citizens of the world, free of nationalistic sentiments or prejudices. When young George came home from school one day and reported that Rumanians were homosexual, his father slapped his face: there is no such thing as The Rumanians, or for that matter any homogeneous collective group, he contended. There are only individuals, each with his or her own peculiarities.

The Tabori boys were to make up for what their father had missed. "I spent sixteen years of my life at school and university. Because my father had been unable to finish university studies, I had to pass a dozen examinations in subjects which did not interest me in the least," admits Paul in his "personal record" *Restless Summer* (1946),[13] which he dedicated to his brother, George ("This is your book. Perhaps you should have written it"). Apart from eighteen months in Hollywood, Paul resided in London, where he worked as foreign correspondent, broadcaster (in the Hungarian section of the BBC), screen and television writer and assistant at Korda Film, editor, and translator.

"I was the golden boy in the family," recalls George. "I could speak nicely when I was 18 months old; I recited poems and was the darling whom everybody loved." [14] No less gifted was brother Paul, who, as George himself admits, had a decisive influence on him from the start. At thirteen Paul was known in literary circles as a surrealist poet and a competent translator. He rendered poems by Christian Morgenstern and Hugo von Hofmannsthal into Hungarian and translated from English westerns and adventure books. "Whenever I was praised at school the teacher added: 'But your brother Paul did it even better.'" [15]

A precocious child, well-bred and inquisitive, Paul had a vivid imagination. "He was a pathological liar and consequently a great poet," alleges George, who, following in Paul's footsteps, founded a liars' club in which the members let their imagination loose and had to lie ingeniously and convincingly. It was from Paul that George heard for the first time of Bertolt Brecht and the new Expressionist venues in drama. Paul had been to Berlin, where he obtained a degree in English and German philology. There he attended rehearsals run by Erwin Piscator and returned with news from the wide world and exciting stories about celebrities like Fritz Kortner and Hans Albers. In the late 1920s, he sojourned in seventeen countries — like George later — and when he returned to Budapest he took a doctorate in economics and political science, married, and "began to plot to get away as soon as possible." [16] When Paul settled in London for good in 1937, he was twenty-nine years old, a much-acclaimed journalist and author of several novels. He soon became a leading figure in the expanding community of European artists in exile and was eventually appointed chairman of the Writers in Exile section of the International PEN (Poets, Essayists, Novelists). [17]

The two brothers were very close, sharing interests from literature to traveling, from "celluloid beauties to those of flesh-and-blood," as Paul notes. They kept in touch despite the war and the thousands of miles separating them. Both were ardent letter-writers, and they corresponded regularly and frequently. Their correspondence — long letters and telegrams, all in English — is a fascinating and moving document of an intense and honest relationship. It includes personal hardships as well as reflections on political and social developments. The dialogue is often fueled by dissent and difference of opinion. "Our premises are fundamentally different," writes George to his brother in 1949 on the issue of postwar liberalism; he continues: "I can't tell you how sorry I am about this, but we have, after all, known for some time, although we never discussed it in so many words, that there is a wall between us. I only pray that before it turns into a barricade, you'll come over to my side . . . liberal and socialist phraseology is being used to cover up the systematic resurgence of Nazism." No less intense, poignant, and all-too-often biting is the dialogue on literary matters. The two brothers record their struggle with publishers and their frustrated hopes. They exchange manuscripts and are uncompromisingly harsh in their criticism of each other's oeuvre. "Your system of doing a hundred stories in the hope of selling two is immoral to yourself," George reproaches his brother.[18] He excuses his harsh tone by applying the same unrelenting standards to his own writing, as well as by expressing his high opinion of Paul's talent: "I remember the early Paul, who had the gift and the patience to become one of the finest lyrical poets in Hungary, or, if you like, one of the finest short-story writers in England."

There must have been a sense of rivalry between the siblings, vying for recognition in the same field, even if there is no explicit note of envy in their correspondence. A letter written by Paul in 1953, when George was settling in New York after working with Hollywood moguls and experiencing his first flop as playwright (*Flight into Egypt*), offers some insight into the complex relationship between the brothers. "In the last few years I've felt that we have been drifting apart, and though I could not put it into words, it has given me a good many sleepless nights and much heartache. . . . Somehow I flatter myself that we could have been friends even if we had not been brothers. It is always in my mind that two-thirds of our family has been exterminated and perhaps it is not unreasonable to feel that we should draw together, hold together, for the world is dark and terrible, and we all need what little warmth there is left. This is, in a way, an appeal that things between us should change and that we should start afresh."[19]

Paul Tabori died in London on 9 November 1974. He left one son, Peter, and some one hundred film and television scripts, innumerable translations from Hungarian, and over thirty books in Hungarian and English. These include biographies (*Alexander Korda*, 1959; and *Maria Theresa*, 1969), various studies (*The Social History of Rape*, 1971; *Crime and the Occult: A Forensic Study*, 1974), and many novels, among them *Bricks upon Dust* (1945), *Solo* (1948), and *Hazard Island* (1973).[20]

PEREGRINATIONS

A Hungarian proverb says: there's no defense against one's family. Tabori quotes it when he recounts how his family was determined to prevent him from becoming a writer.[21] In his close circle there were already too many literary figures, some more, others less successful: an uncle, two aunts, his father, and brother Paul. "In our family . . . literature has been a hereditary disease," writes Paul in *Restless Summer*, addressing his brother, George (to whom the book is dedicated); he elaborates: "It goes back to our distant great-grandfather, the one who had all the trouble with the Austrian Secret Police because he persisted in translating Rousseau, Diderot and the other young revolutionary firebirds."[22] George wrote his first novel when he was fifteen; this work, which was unfortunately lost, was soon followed by other experimental writings, among them a libretto for Uncle Zoltán, an opera tenor, and a play which was nearly produced in Budapest.[23]

It was his mother who vehemently opposed the idea of having yet another writer in the family. "My father had set a bad precedent for me to follow from her point of view. . . . In our family journalism turned out to be a very poor paying profession. For four generations our family had been made up of writers and as one of my great-uncles put it, 'none of us could ever buy a fur coat for his wife.'"[24] Soon after his matriculation, in autumn 1932, George was sent to Germany. His father had good connections among foreign hoteliers and managed to obtain a job for his son as a practical trainee at the glamorous Adlon hotel in the heart of Berlin. When the German nationalist Herr Kretschmar resigned as general director, to run the small Hessler hotel and its adjacent café frequented by artists, George followed him to Kantstraße. A jack-of-all-trades, he cleaned ashtrays, tried his hand as a cook, tapped beer in high glasses, played the waiter, and manned the reception desk.

Those were exciting months for eighteen-year-old Tabori. Berlin was the capital of culture in central Europe, a place of pilgrimage for those who, like the Taboris, considered their hometown, Budapest, to be a somewhat sleepy, provincial city. Captured by the pulsating metropolis, he met a medley of people — artists, aristocrats, and simple workers. During the time in Berlin and the three months in 1934 when he worked at the Four Seasons hotel in Dresden, he had some personal, rather harmless encounters with devout Nazis. One of them, a waiter with whom he shared a room, "a goggly-eyed *Schrumpfgermane*," [25] expounded his fiery tirades to his foreign colleague, whom he denounced for being a Marxist. On 30 January 1933 Tabori was present as Adolf Hitler waved to the raving masses, with hundreds of torches parading in front of the Reichskanzlei. "He appeared rather lonely to me, even if I didn't have pity for him. I thought, how weird, power makes you lonely. The decisive thing was that most people, like me, didn't know what all this really meant." [26]

At the end of 1935, after a short interval in Budapest, he followed Paul to London. This was George's act of defiance and self-assertion, ironically, quite similar to his father's rebellious flight from home.[27] His English was deficient and awkward. He had been tutored by an American cousin, a violinist who stayed for a while in Budapest, but when the British failed to understand him, he realized that his English, "a mixture of Brooklyn and Texan English, was ghastly." [28] Truly, Tabori's acquisition of English — his command of this foreign language to a degree that enabled him to write novels in English less than ten years after setting foot in London, indeed all his works from that point onward — is undoubtedly one of his most impressive achievements, reminiscent of Joseph Conrad's or Vladimir Nabokov's virtuosity. He worked hard to acquire this dexterity, reading feverishly, translating anything that came his way, from westerns to Aldous Huxley. An exemplary autodidact, then and later, when he decided to devote himself to theatre-making, he approached the task with studiousness and determination. Some twelve years later, in a CBS interview, he said: "English is a language I adopted at the age of twenty-five, and the world I chose to write about is also a recent acquisition. In both cases, the learning was a painful process . . . Munich, Guernica and Dunkirk and Belsen were my university — with a first-rate faculty." [29] In later years he would occasionally mention his original wish to become a physician and applied the metaphor of sickness and healing to theatre. He compared his role as play-maker (not director!) to that of the medic, the shaman, who painstakingly and patiently attends to the needs of the sick.[30]

Those London days were challenging and difficult for both brothers. They stayed for a while in a friend's house, completely unfurnished except for two mattresses. George packed and delivered books for three pounds a week, translated daily news from English into Hungarian for a press agency, worked for a travel agency conducting deluxe tours to the Continent. The war put an end to all this.

The last time George was at home, in Budapest, was for Christmas in 1939. He happened to be in Vienna on a business trip, reporting on economic matters for an English newspaper. A letter he received from an actress friend in Budapest — "it was a cry for help" — prompted him to go home, although he risked being recruited to the Hungarian army or not being allowed to leave the country. "I went to the theatre in Budapest. She was playing in a Noel Coward. She saw me, as I was sitting in the front row, but she took no notice of me. I was amazed. After the show I looked for her. I embraced her. She was very pregnant by her husband, and I stayed in Budapest until her daughter was born."[31] This is a typical Tabori anecdote; he recounted it to me and left much unsaid.

That was the last Christmas at home, "with tastes, smells, touchings,"[32] an interval of warmth, oblivious to the harsh events outside. It was the last time he saw his father and so many family members who were to perish. A few years after the war, in a letter to Paul, George painted a moving portrait of his father, who decided to stay in Hungary: "His choice was between emigration or patching up things for the sake of the family. It was a terrible choice and he chose the second alternative, and it tortured him all his life. He played with the idea of suicide for several years, and had a tragic contempt for himself."[33]

Cornelius Tabori was arrested for the first time in 1941, presumably because his son was working for the "enemy" as a BBC broadcaster. For years Paul would torture himself, feeling responsible for his father's death.[34] In 1944 Cornelius was one of fifty leading journalists whom the Nazis caught in their first dragnet. He was sent from camp to camp and finally to Auschwitz.[35] The last picture of Cornelius Tabori, taken shortly before his deportation, on a street in Budapest, shows a short, spectacled man, dressed in suit and tie, with a yellow star on his dark jacket. In a letter he sent from prison to his wife, Elsa, he wrote: "There are no tyrants; only tyrannical moments, and they will pass. There is no evil in man save in his attitudes; and they shall be changed. Love life and its people; and death shall be like the peasant's good night to a tired day." That, says his son George, "was advice from a man who knew he was going to be burned to death."[36]

Tabori's first visit back to Hungary after the war was in the 1980s. There he met one cousin who survived as well as a few old and some new friends like writers István Eörsi, Péter Nádas, and Péter Esterházy.[37] He visited the house in which he grew up, but soon realized that his native country was no longer home for him. Budapest had radically changed, the Hungarian language had changed, and so had he. There was something about Vienna, where he settled in 1987, which reminded him of the old Hungarian capital, he told me, adding softly: "Or is it only an illusion?"

"Chance reigns over my life," remarks Tabori,[38] like a good many Holocaust survivors, whenever he speaks about his peripeteiac life. One of the times he profited from chance was in London during an air raid: he was on his way to the bakery when his shoelace became untied. A V-2 bomber flew over as he was bending down to tie it properly. The bus nearby was demolished, as was the bakery.

Coincidence determined Tabori's life, including his peregrinations across the Balkan and the Middle East during the war. In 1940 he went to Bulgaria as the Balkan correspondent of a Hungarian newspaper. Once Bulgaria fell into the hands of the fascists, he moved to Istanbul, which was still neutral. There he worked as a reporter for the United Press and the Swedish paper *Aftonbladet*. Tabori has fond memories of Istanbul: the city on both sides of the Bosphorus was colorful and lively, at long last he earned some money, and he had good connections with British officials stationed there. One of them, Basil Davidson, called on him to organize all the Hungarians in the city to work for the British. In early 1942 Davidson informed George that he had to leave Istanbul instantly. George was to find out the reason months later: the Germans knew of his contacts with the English, and Davidson was hoping to spare Tabori's parents harassment in Budapest by smuggling George from Turkey.

Before he crossed the Bosphorus under cover of darkness, he wrote a farewell letter in which he confessed he saw no way out of the political misery except to commit suicide. The train took him south, to the Syrian border, where he showed the soldiers official papers he had been given by the British. His name in those papers was George Turner, first lieutenant. But the Australian soldiers on the other side of the border, in Syria, were suspicious. They detained the newcomer and interrogated him. A telephone conversation with the commanders in Istanbul finally settled matters. Tabori, alias Turner, was told to take a taxi to Jerusalem. "By cab to Jerusalem? I asked, as the journey covered hundreds of kilometers! It doesn't matter, we pay for it, he [the officer] replied. So I took a cab to Jerusalem. When I finally arrived there, I dialed a number which I had been given, in order to receive further instructions." In hindsight, the attempt to smuggle him out of Turkey so as to save his family in Budapest seems senseless. "All this was silly," says Tabori. "The Germans surely knew about everything!"[39]

Tabori/Turner joined the BBC radio station operating under the auspices of the Political Warfare Department, located in a monastery on the Mount of Olives, overlooking Jerusalem. He was one of the journalists who prepared and broadcast the daily 20-minute programs for the population in Hungary. Every evening as he went on the air, propagating antifascism and resistance, he pretended he was speaking from a hiding place in Hungary; in order to make it all convincing, his broadcasts were occasionally disrupted.

Years later, after the war was long over, he found out that nobody in Hungary had ever heard those programs. When he met Basil Davidson in London in 1952 he sought the answer for this riddle. The programs had never been transmitted, confessed his interlocutor. It was all a well-contrived show. "The English didn't really need us," Tabori explains in retrospect. "Detaining us in a concentration camp wouldn't have looked nice, though it was a tennis club. So they staged the whole thing."

It was in Jerusalem on 12 September 1942 that the 28-year-old Tabori married Hannah Freund, the first of his four wives. They met in professional circles: known as Sergeant Higgins, she was running the BBC office coordinating the radio programs and was involved, like most of her colleagues, in work for the British Secret Service. "She was very blonde, very beautiful, and very Zionist," recalls Tabori. Born in 1919 in Darmstadt,[40] Hannah emigrated to Palestine with her sister, in the framework of Youth Aliya organized by the Zionist organization in Germany. She was enrolled in a youth village, where (along with academic subjects) she learned the skills required for agricultural work in the restored Jewish home country. "She combined the worst-best qualities of both Jew and German, a living illustration of the alarming similarities between these two people," writes Tabori.[41] For him she was the typical "Eierjecke[s]"[42] — a Jewish immigrant from Germany, product of German-Jewish *Bildungsbürgertum*, who became a hardworking country woman in Palestine, and it was from Hannah that he first heard the names of Arnold Schönberg, George Grosz, and Alfred Döblin.

A pro-British rabbi, "that is, also a traitor," married them, with two agents from the Secret Service as witnesses, after civil marriage proved to be impossible for professional reasons.[43] In a letter to Paul (1 October 1942) George describes their honeymoon (using the German term *Flitterwochen*) as a fiasco: he had a modest boil that "started to gather momentum" and had to be lanced; she broke a finger, suffered an electric shock, and finally was bogged down by a nasty cold. Very much in love with Hannah, he found the first separation from her — due to a professional trip she had to make — "rather painful." "We are staying in a good deal, reading and eating chocolate," he tells Paul;[44] Hannah, taking up correspondence too, prepares her sister-in-law Kate for their eventual meeting: "Please do not have any expectations regarding myself. I have been living among the 'savages of this country' for years and years; when I want food I yell: yyueöäää, when I want to drink, I produce a sound . . . xssszzuuuuu!"[45]

The marriage lasted through common and separate journeys in several countries with many ups and downs for nearly ten years. Though she was an ardent Zionist, Hannah followed her husband to London and later to America. The couple divorced when George was already living in New York with actress Viveca Lindfors, who was to become his second wife.[46]

"YOU ARE REMINDED THAT YOU ARE A JEW"

No doubt the most perplexing question about his year in Jerusalem is Tabori's total indifference to Jewish life and to the zealous Zionist activities that were sweeping the country overtly and covertly. Hannah was animated by the dream of making Eretz Israel harbor and home for the Jews, even though she worked for the "enemy," the British (tellingly she concludes a letter to Paul in Hebrew with *Shalom uvracha!*). On the other hand, George's letters from

British Mandate Jerusalem show not the slightest interest in, let alone sympathy for, the Jewish/Zionist struggle. "I like it here — Jerusalem is a lovely city, rather serene and quite clean," he writes from Café Europe, a meeting place for intellectuals and artists, upon his arrival in April 1942.[47] He lived for a while in a flat overlooking the Mount of Olives ("every day for breakfast I walked down Calvary, and wrote a play called *Unterammergau* which I later burnt");[48] later he moved into the beautiful building of the American School of Archaeology "amidst mummies, potters, and elderly ladies." And yet there is neither Holy Land sentimentalism nor biblical nostalgia in his letters from Jerusalem, such as may be found here and there in Paul Tabori's book *Palesztina* (in Hungarian, 1947), which he wrote after six months of extensive touring on behalf of Reuters in the Middle East and the Balkans (autumn 1945 to April 1946). "I never thought blue skies, blue sea can look and feel so utterly desolate," he confides in Paul, and a short trip across the country he undertook with Hannah "was rather a flop because of a weather which suddenly turned disgustingly cold."[49]

It is uncanny that Tabori could live in Palestine and remain indifferent to the promise of a Jewish homeland even as masses of Jews — including his own family — were being humiliated and persecuted in Europe. The strangeness of Tabori's neutrality calls for an explanation, and it turns out to be one of the most complex, unresolved aspects of his personality. This seminal issue has in fact escaped serious consideration because of the oversimplified, partly philo-Semitic attitude of critics and admirers in Germany, for whom Tabori came to be the Honoric Jew, *Alibijude*, or as some have put it, a *Versöhnungsjude* (a reconciliatory Jew).[50]

Matters were complicated from the outset. Cornelius Tabori, like so many mid-European Jews, "did get seduced by promises for a liberal cosmopolitanism . . . , gave up his Jewishness . . . and had us boys baptized, although circumcised."[51] The Tabori boys went to a Protestant school in Budapest, attended Catholic religious instruction, and went regularly to confession, where both, endowed with a lively imagination, fabricated the most outrageous sins. While their mother, Elsa, was Catholic, Cornelius, according to his son Paul, was an agnostic who consciously avoided discussing matters of faith.[52] George was seven years old when he first heard of his Jewish heritage, but he never set foot in a synagogue and of course did not celebrate Bar Mitzvah. During the year he stayed in Eretz Israel he made no effort to learn Hebrew. "I know *shalom, toda raba* [thanks a lot]," he replied when I inquired about his Hebrew; yet later, when I used the untranslatable *davka* (implying that a statement is the opposite of what would be expected), he knew exactly what it meant. Even though Yiddish words and expressions abound in his texts, and despite what is widely assumed, he does not know Yiddish. I suspect he encountered Yiddish and picked up some of its delicious expressions during his stay in the United States, particularly during his years in New York.[53]

Is it that Hitler made him into a Jew, as some assimilated Jews ("I hate that word 'assimilated'"), survivors of the Holocaust, maintain? "My Jewish consciousness evolved before the Holocaust," Tabori replied to a question I posed to him; he repeated, "even before the Holocaust," but he did not elaborate. Modeled on Cornelius, Uncle in *Cannibals* comes to realize: "You do not become a Jew. You are reminded of being one." In an interview for the volume *Jüdische Portraits* Tabori explained: "It's like this: one doesn't gradually become a Jew and one isn't a Jew from the outset. One is reminded by the others that one is a Jew. This makes one really Jewish. I myself wasn't conscious at first of being a Jew. Perhaps it was an unconscious knowledge. But Fascism in Germany and in Hungary prodded me to realize that I am a Jew. At some point I accepted this role. This was my most important experience."[54]

But if this was so, how did he keep himself so aloof in Jerusalem, playing the foreigner according to the rules set by his British superiors? Despite all the psychological explanations and speculations, this puzzle remains unsolved. It is surely related to Tabori's ambiguous feelings toward Israel. Since 1942, he has visited the country three times, though never attending an Israeli production of his plays. He scribbled in his scrapbook notes and names of people he met and wrote a comedy entitled *Shalom*, depicting the love of a Jewish woman and an Arab. The script was due to be filmed in 1960, but this did not materialize.[55] Earlier, in May 1949, he listened on the radio to "Israel's admission into the UN" and reported to Paul that "it was quite exciting."[56] During the Six-Day War (1967) he admitted to his children: "I began to feel bloody high-minded and proud when they [the Israeli soldiers] were raving across the desert and took Jerusalem. It hasn't been in Jewish hands since 78 BC."[57]

Notably, these signs of empathy find expression only in Tabori's intimate writing, his letters. Elsewhere, in interviews and articles, he voices criticism of Israel. Less than a month after the euphoria following Israel's 1967 victory, he writes to a friend that "Auschwitz was in a way the last Judaic gesture. Salvation through suffering. . . . the alternative is what Israel is doing now. It is all very admirable and practical, but it may also be the end of Jewishness."[58]

Tabori discerns a far-reaching metamorphosis in the Jewish self-image, engendered and cultivated in the sovereign Jewish state: "The Jews are no longer the victims, they now have power. But power corrupts," he argues.[59] In his autobiographical essay "Unterammergau," he speaks sarcastically of success, which is bound to corrupt, and describes the Jewish state as an "absurd theatre," "the last of the Jewish jokes." He scorns the rabbis trying to run it as a religious state (according to the *Halacha*) and shows no affinity for Zionism or for military strength. "Israel is not so much a land as a family. I'm not such a family man," he remarks — somewhat apologetically and yet confidently.[60]

Though he was aware of his Jewishness, however vaguely, Tabori's return to Europe and nearly twenty-year stay in Germany did much to build his Jewish identity. "I have suppressed the Jewish in me up to a certain point in time. . . . I didn't want people to tell me, you are such and such. I wanted to determine myself, when I felt a Jew, and when not," he admits. "After Auschwitz, at the latest, I had to face the fact that I am Jewish."[61]

Living in Germany it is impossible to evade one's Jewishness in general, and the German-Jewish question in particular; Tabori's works since the 1970s attest to this. A letter to the Jewish community of Vienna (1988) shows that Tabori considered himself a Jew in private, but resisted official affiliation: he sent a personal donation, but refused to become a member.[62] None of his children — the three he adopted when married to Viveca Lindfors — was born Jewish, yet he makes a point of informing brother Paul that John, his eldest, is "studying Hebrew and will go to a kibbutz in summer"; and he lovingly teases his daughter Lena about her Jewish boyfriend — "Why don't you keep away from Jews?"[63]

"I MISSED ALL THE BIG STORIES"

Tabori's year in Jerusalem was followed by another in Cairo (1943), where he worked for British Intelligence. Tabori alias Turner tuned into the Yugoslavian radio in order to map out the inner conflicts and the struggle for power between the Communist Marshal Tito and the fascist Dragoljub Mihailovic. During the period when Hannah was still in Jerusalem, he shared a room (under a bordello) with a British Jew, named Kaufmann. A passionate sinologist, Kaufmann was in charge of posting the trainees — a medley of antifascists from all over the Continent — behind enemy lines. George, who had no direct contact with his parents and had to content himself with scraps of information via Paul, was hoping to be sent to Hungary. "I'll tell you when you'll be sent," Kaufmann told George one evening in response to his incessant nagging: "Never!" "And why?" "Because I like you," was Kaufmann's reply.[64] Tabori revisited some of his unusual experiences as an agent in British Intelligence in his play *Requiem for a Spy* (1993).[65]

During those months — oscillating between the dull, at times absurd, routine of intelligence work and the exotics of a multicultural crew of exiles all stuck in the desertscape of Palestine and Egypt — Tabori took up writing again. In 1942–1943 he wrote two novels; one "got lost," as he puts it, the other, *Beneath the Stone the Scorpion*, was published in London and New York in 1945, his first novel in print.[66]

Beneath the Stone is the story of a brief yet loaded encounter between a German officer and an English captive, in a small Slovenian village near the Hungarian border. In a letter to Paul, George described the theme: "the perverted and frustrated love of the Germans for the English."[67] Written during the war, this early work already shows traces of the taboo-breaking that Tabori later became known for. The German, von Borst, is no Nazi monster, no stereotypic representative of the master race, but a sophisticated self-reflecting gentleman, who seeks to find out the truth about the purported English agent and his mission by gaining his confidence. The surprising turning point occurs at a seemingly cozy dinner, staged in hopes of squeezing a confession from Fowler, when Gestapo agent Hirtenberg drops in. Von Borst learns that his colleague, unscrupulous, sly, and cynical, has already found out all about the Englishman's doings. Tabori's political thriller, tinged with the moral seriousness of a Graham Greene or Arthur Koestler work, is also marked by the buoyancy and epigrammatic witticism of Ferenc Molnár's comedies. It ends on a melodramatic, edifying note: von Borst helps Fowler to escape and then puts an end to his own life. Despite Tabori's later claim that the novel was greeted by a storm of indignation in the Anglo-American press,[68] the original reviews in the *New York Times* and *New Yorker* commend the novel, "an elegant thriller," for its original approach and applaud Tabori as "master of imagination" who successfully depicted the dark, tense atmosphere of Borst's agonizing introspection.

A subsequent novel was written even before the first was out, aboard the crowded ship that took Tabori back to England at the end of 1943. *Companions of the Left Hand* takes place in September 1943,[69] more or less when it was being composed. Its protagonist is the prominent author of buoyant comedies Stefan Farkas, reminiscent in his literary prowess of Molnár, the successful Hungarian-Jewish novelist and playwright (who also wrote *A Fárkas*, the legend of the wolf). Self-centered and spoilt by success, the middle-aged writer arrives at the small Italian village of San Fernando with Blaise Pascal's *Pensées*, hoping for harmless adventures that might nurture his next comedy. Against his will, Farkas is drawn into local commotion and dispassionately observes the uprising against the fascists in the village, but insists on maintaining the foreigner's privileged position of neutrality. When German troops brutally crush the uprising, he reluctantly consents to serve as go-between. But this time things get out of his control; the action overtakes the cynical observer of the provincial spectacle. The head of the rebels shoots Farkas and kills himself, rather than submitting to the enemy. In his final hour, Farkas recalls his past and realizes that he has found the title for his next play: "Companions of the Left Hand" — a phrase taken from the Koran and referring to the bad ones, who will be standing on God's left-hand side when the Day of Judgment comes. Only a few years after its successful publication in 1946, Tabori conceded to his brother that *"Companions* was nearer to reality [than *Original Sin*, his third novel], but romanticized hopelessly the revolutionary, and betrayed a sneaking sympathy for the villain."[70]

Tabori remained in London until 1947, when he was granted British citizenship. He worked for the Hungarian department of the BBC and devoted much of his free time to writing. His third novel, *Original Sin*, was published in 1947 and received rather lukewarm critiques.[71] Nearly half a century later, the German translation (1992) won showers of praise; theatre director Peter Zadek wrote: "Like the wonderful Joseph Conrad, Tabori understands how to describe people's repulsive traits so sensuously that they fascinate us even as they disgust us."[72]

Original Sin is a psychological thriller set against the hot desert wind and the pestering flies of Cairo, with bizarre figures coming and going between whisky, soothing showers, and spooky rooms. Tristan Manasse, owner of a small guest house, finds the body of his wife, Adela, in the bathtub. The murderer is none other than himself — "But pray, who is without murder in his heart?" — and the novel evolves as a kind of journey into the innermost crevices of Manasse's soul. Did jealousy engender the murder, or did Manasse put an end to his wife's life so as to spare her the ludicrous anguish of her pathetic role as the mistress — one of many — of the much younger menial servant Zouba? Moreover, there are suggestions that the murder was a repetition of an earlier sin and that Manasse murdered his wife to answer for another crime: having abandoned his dying father for the sake of licentious gratification. "No murderer ever knows the true motive, the reason why he crossed the gulf between the desire and the deed," says Tabori's narrator-murderer.[73]

"I lived or passed through some twelve countries since 1939, and the funny thing is that nothing ever happened to me; I wasn't invaded, bombed, machine-gunned, and I missed all the big stories there were to miss," Tabori complains in his typically self-deprecating manner to his brother in February 1943.[74] As it turns out, those years of ceaseless peregrinations provided him with stories, anecdotes, and impressions he would extensively draw upon in the future. Among them is the lost collection of stories *Pogrom* (see chapter 11), the novels *Basra* ("a muddled attempt to inject real issues into a wholly artificial framework," as he observed critically only a few years after receiving a nice advance of $1,500 for it)[75] and *Eye for Eye*,[76] the play *Flight Into Egypt* (premiered in 1952), and the novel *The Caravan Passes* (published in 1951).[77]

The Caravan Passes, written in Santa Monica, California, between 1947 and 1950 and taking its title from a levantine proverb ("The dogs bark, but the caravan passes"), offers a broad and vivid panorama of life in a Middle Eastern city at the twilight of British colonialism. The Rumanian physician Varga finds himself entangled in political and familial machinations when he is called to help the fatally sick Governor El Bekkaa. He operates on the despicable tyrant, but fails to be present at the postoperative crisis because of a rendezvous with a British nurse. Betrayal and guilt are leitmotifs here as in Tabori's previous novels. Like Manasse, Varga has a scorpion hidden under a stone: he dissuaded his beloved from having their child. When he dies at the hand of a governor's brutal bodyguard, Varga realizes that "every life, his life, all life, which is not holy, is criminal"; he has been a "Conradesque wreck" that carried his guilt "from one port to the other."

"I WAS SUPPOSED TO STAY THREE MONTHS AND I STAYED TWENTY YEARS"

The war was barely over when Carol Brandt, a literary agent working for Metro-Goldwyn-Mayer, came to London to do "cultural spying." Hollywood's expanding film industry required talented scriptwriters. Brandt, the "beautiful vulture," to quote Tabori, managed to catch Evelyn Waugh — "an immensely nasty, spiteful Englishman, who hated everything connected with America" — and George Tabori. "I was supposed to stay three months and I stayed twenty years," he writes.[78]

A stranger in paradise, he was enchanted at first: he stayed in a luxurious villa in sun-flooded Santa Monica, with a swimming pool at his disposal, all his expenses paid, "T-bone-steak and little-thin-hot-cakes and all the things which had been unavailable for years."[79] After the three months were over, he realized he was in a trap: though he was a foreigner on a short-term assignment, the authorities refused him permission to leave the country until he paid taxes on the fat income of $500 a week. He stayed to pay his debts and remained in Los Angeles until 1950. None of the film scripts he wrote for MGM and later for Warner Brothers was ever produced. The glittering scene, the glamorous facade, he soon realized, could not hide a puritan mentality, a callous "salad system" that exploited its writers, who worked simultaneously (yet unaware) on the same scripts, wasting whatever talent they had. "Hollywood was a big bordello and I was not a good whore," recalls Tabori, who nevertheless succumbed, supplying the required eighteen pages per week, "no matter what was in them." "It's not enough to be a Hungarian, you also need the third act" was one of the premises of expatriate writers in Hollywood, he soon learned.

But the truth is more complex. Characteristically, Tabori beguiles his audience with charming anecdotes, "fictionalizing" his own experiences and presenting a hybrid of fiction and memoir which makes it difficult to reconstruct the facts of the narrative. In contrast to Tabori's own account, media and film expert Michael Töteberg maintains that Tabori was not at all driven by his agent into the clutches of the film industry and that much of what went awry was of his own choice and doing.[80]

"I've got to get out of here; it's almost impossible to do any serious work, the more money one makes, the less one seems to have. . . . So I'll try to do some whoring and write a few pieces for the magazines," George wrote to Paul from Hollywood.[81] In his plays (*The 25th Hour* or the unpublished "The Household Traitor"), he describes Hollywood as Necropolis and debunks it as the epitome of the deceptive American Dream.

Tabori's engagement in the film industry yielded six film scripts and two television scripts. Notably, all of these date to his post-Hollywood period, although admittedly connections with directors such as Alfred Hitchcock and Joseph Losey go back to his L.A. days. Together with Will Archibald he wrote the film script for *I Confess* (1953), directed by Hitchcock — "an inspired sadist," "the greatest gourmandizer and gourmet in Hollywood."[82] A year later he was in charge of the story for Anthony Asquith's *The Young Lovers*, "a kind of Romeo-and-Juliet story set in the Cold War."[83] This was followed in 1958 by *The Journey*, directed by Anatole Litvak, a politically nuanced love triangle with perplexing similarities to *Casablanca*.[84] Tabori's film script *No Exit* (1962), based on Jean-Paul Sartre's *Huis Clos*, was directed by Tad Danielewski and featured Tabori's second wife, Viveca Lindfors; it won the Silver Bear award in Berlin. Less successful was *The Stronger*, directed by Jeff Young, Tabori's film version of August Strindberg's play.[85] *Parades*, directed by Robert J. Siegel, premiered in 1974.

The only one of his film scripts that Tabori was pleased with in retrospect is the psycho-thriller *Secret Ceremony*, which was directed in 1968 by Joseph Losey, with Mia Farrow as a rich young heiress who sees in the ravishing Elizabeth Taylor her surrogate mother. This was one of many mutual projects Tabori and Losey pursued, but the only one that was successfully accomplished. Friendship apart, Losey was not always happy with Tabori's scripts. "He showed me a disastrous screenplay," he remarked after reading Tabori's rendition of Georges Simenon's *Les inconnus dans la maison*. Similarly, John Osborne's judgment of Tabori's script "Black Comedy" was devastating: "silly beyond words, forced, facetious and fake profound."[86]

Yet Tabori did not give up writing for the screen. *Insomnia* (1974), his first television script, which he also directed, is a parody of Beckett's *Happy Days*:[87] an elderly woman puts up a lonely foreigner, possibly a *Gastarbeiter*, for a night. The night passes with their mutual hunting of mosquitoes, recollections, trivial and funny misunderstandings, anecdotes, and short spells of dream-filled sleep. The morning finds the two in the same bed; they go their own way.

Frohes Fest (Happy Holiday, 1979), his second television play,[88] a studiously low-budget production, is a hilarious parody, albeit artistically flawed, of the German Christmas cult. Chattanooga Kid, the purebred Indian (a predecessor as it were of Copperface in Tabori's *Weisman and Copperface*), comes to Bavaria just before Christmas. Armed with a video-camera, he keenly observes the goings-on like a lay anthropologist. He interviews passersby in an attempt to fathom the charm of the holiday and encounters rude, funny, and grumpy answers. Ultimately he is overwhelmed by three Santa Claus figures, who beat him, pull his clothes off, and leave him naked in the snow.

Notwithstanding his disenchantment with Hollywood and his frustration as a writer, the three years in California were of invaluable significance in Tabori's artistic development. He learned firsthand the many faces of commercial writing, success and fame, thwarted hopes, the price of intellectual prostitution, and the pain of rejection. Residing in Los Angeles in a garage-turned-studio that he rented with Salka Viertel, wife of the prominent German director Berthold Viertel, he not only met celebrities such as Charles Chaplin ("a fabulous story-teller"), Charles Laughton, and the legendary Greta Garbo ("a health freak . . . , a mixture of the divine and the philistine"),[89] but also ran into the community of German writers and artists living in American exile. Those encounters engendered scores of anecdotes, which Tabori readily recounts over and over again and which his listeners, mainly the Germans, are avid to hear. Without doubting the authenticity of these anecdotes, many questions remain unanswered: not only the question of whether or not these contacts had a decisive influence on Tabori's development as an artist, as Peter Höyng notes,[90] but also the more pedestrian question: how much of these piquant stories is fact and how much fiction?

The Nobel Prize–winning German exile Thomas Mann briefly mentions five meetings with George Tabori in 1948, in connection with the planned filming of *The Magic Mountain*.[91] Tabori writes in great detail of his acquaintance with Mann. They once shared a lecture platform, and Mann invited him for coffee and cakes afterward. "He told me that if I was going to make a success of lecturing in the USA, I should always start with a joke," he writes in "Unterammergau." A mutual visit to Lion Feuchtwanger in his villa overlooking the Pacific Ocean followed, and Tabori quotes Mann's deliciously derisive comment on Feuchtwanger's perfect setting and the worthless literature he produced ("pure shit").[92] As for the film script based on Mann's novel, in which Garbo was due to play Madame Chauchat, the project was abandoned by the spring of 1949. Hollywood would not tolerate a movie about sick people, Tabori explains in retrospect.[93] But was this the only reason? A letter to Paul dated 12 May 1949 makes clear that Tabori pursued the matter further and staunchly looked for other options: "Erika [Mann] told me that the Kordas [Alexander and Zoltan, who had bought the film rights] decided to drop their option on "Magic Mountain." Mann liked my synopsis. Couldn't you take up this matter over there? It could be a magnificent picture, I'm sure. Klaus [Mann] may have to be included in any writing project, but he's drunk or suicidal most of the time, so he won't be too much trouble. . . . Anyway, if and when you do see the Manns in London, talk to Erika or Mrs Mann about it (The old man does not like sordid financial details, who does?)."[94]

Doubtless of pivotal weight was Tabori's casual encounter with another German exile, Bertolt Brecht. There were three meetings altogether, each one relating to Joseph Losey's production of Brecht's *Galileo* ("but Brecht was really the director"), with Charles Laughton in the title role.[95]

At that point Tabori knew only a little about Brecht, who had written his major plays in exile after leaving Germany in 1933. He had read *The Threepenny Opera* and seen *Mahagonny* in Berlin and admittedly did not notice Brecht's celebrated charisma when he attended the preliminary staging of *Galileo*, to which he was taken by his friend Losey.[96] "He [Brecht] sat like a tailor on the pinewood floor, wearing luxurious jeans, his cigar stinking like the pest. He only said one or two things to me and then went off with a Swedish blonde, who later described him as a Magnificent Rabbit."[97] The next time they met was at Laughton's villa; the host and the playwright were translating the play: "I helped them a little with the famous 'self-judgment speech,' and the occasion changed my life.

These two bums have, not by persuasion but by mere presence, made me change from prose to drama."[98]

Notably, it was neither Brecht's dramatic theory nor his didactic plays, the *Lehrstücke*, that impressed 33-year-old Tabori, but these two theatre celebrities' mere *presence* — a key concept in modern performance theory from Konstantin Stanislavsky to Joseph Chaikin. From then on Tabori had an active hand in the introduction of Brecht's drama in the United States. He did "a free translation" of *The Resistible Ascent of Arturo Ui*,[99] which was staged in 1963 in New York by Tony Richardson with Christopher Plummer in the lead role. The production — "totally different from that of the Berliner Ensemble, more naive and more primitive, but on a certain level better and more authentic than that of Ekkehard Schall"[100] — was no success, "as Brecht was still suspect" as leftist agitprop. Tabori also translated into English *Señora Carrar's Rifles* and *Mother Courage*, which he had first read at Laughton's instigation.[101] He directed *Mother Courage* himself at Castleton State College in Vermont in 1967, only to find out that if one rigorously follows Brecht's detailed instructions in the *Modellbuch* one ends up with a pale imitation, whereas if one takes liberties (for instance, by moving the wagon one meter to the left or to the right) the entire scene does not work.

No doubt his most valuable contribution to the dissemination of Brecht's works in the United States was the production entitled *Brecht on Brecht* which he directed with Gene Frankel (Theatre de Lys, New York, 14 November 1961). This was a collage made up of excerpts from Brecht plays, songs, and biographical episodes as well as Brecht's mesmerizing taped testimony when he was investigated by the House Un-American Activities Committee (HUAC) in Washington in 1947. The idea for *Brecht on Brecht* was born when Tabori's wife, actress Viveca Lindfors, approached Lucille Lortel asking to present the episode "The Jewish Wife" out of *The Private Life of the Master Race* as a matinee under the auspices of the American National Theater and Academy (ANTA). Lortel, who ran the series, suggested instead that Tabori "put together some songs, poems, scenes," which he immediately did. Six actors, including Lindfors, Eli Wallach, Anne Jackson (all members of the Actors Studio), and Lotte Lenya, Kurt Weill's famous widow, rehearsed against a simple set designed by Wolfgang Roth, who had worked with Brecht in Berlin. Four weeks later the collage was premiered. What was originally conceived as a one-time matinee ran for months. "The effect was chilling and wonderful," recalls Lindfors. "We were six actors sitting on the stage on high stools. There was a large picture of Brecht hanging behind us. . . . We were a hit, and G.T. and I were doing it together."[102] And Tabori remembers: "This was an attempt to define Brecht through his work, not through what critics had to say."[103]

Brecht on Brecht was taken to London and premiered under the auspices of George Devine at the Royal Court. Viveca Lindfors learned to her amazement that she had to stay behind, as Lotte Lenya was taking over her part. "That's right, Viveca. It's either me or you," the aging Lenya informed her. Tabori let his wife down: "They don't want to do the production unless Lotte is in it."[104] Later, in an homage to Lenya entitled "The Last of the Great Old Heartless Hustlers," he admitted that this nearly destroyed his marriage. "She [Lenya] was already a legend. . . . I was half in love with her, out of vanity, for she liked my translations. I admired her without restraint, which she accepted with gracious cool."[105] Ironically, the London production was a flop and closed within a few weeks.

As a result of his involvement with Brecht's plays, in 1968 Tabori and his wife were invited by Helene Weigel to participate in the Brecht-Dialogue in East Berlin, a meeting of writers, directors, and actors on the occasion of Brecht's seventieth birthday. "It was a glorious experience, an inspiration for both G.T. and me," writes Lindfors in her memoirs.[106] "I thought it was the best theatre I had even seen," Tabori notes about the Berliner Ensemble. But when his turn came to relate his impressions, "just after Strehler," he tore up his manuscript and started crying. "I learned a lot and I learned one thing: that this wonderful theatre of yours is not my way," he confessed. Later, he was to distance himself from the normative interpretation, the perfectionism, the virtuosity, the super-aesthetics propagated by Brecht and his ensemble. His theatre pursued the symbiotic relationship between stage and reality; and it purposely set out to involve the spectator both intellectually and emotionally. "I told Weigel that I no longer understood *Verfremdung*, the Brechtian coolness," he recalls as he recounts how he was in tears watching Weigel as Mother Courage.[107]

The only Brecht performance he directed after that experience in Berlin was the staging of Brecht's early play *He Who Said Yes / He Who Said No* at the Staatstheater in Kassel (9 May 1981). "In a way, the production epitomized Tabori's ambivalent relationship to

Brecht, for he used the *Lehrstück* critically, undermining its intentions," observes Martin Kagel.[108] Among the innumerable unpublished manuscripts in the Tabori archive is "The Brecht File," a quasidocumentary he wrote about Brecht in America, which ends with Brecht's interrogation by HUAC.[109] "Actually I did it in order to be near him again," he told his publisher and friend Maria Sommer.[110] The manuscript was never filmed.

"LOVE IS THE ART OF THE IMPOSSIBLE"

London 1950: Viveca Lindfors had a stopover on her way to Zurich, where she was cast in Leopold Lindtberg's film *Four in a Jeep*. Her agent fixed an appointment for her to meet the Hungarian author of a script she had just read. "He was thin, tall, and elegant and picked me up in his chauffeur-driven Bentley."[111] This was the first meeting between the film star, freshly married to director Don Siegel, and George Tabori. Months later she discovered that George was broke when he tried to impress her, that being short of money, very often in debt, was in fact a hallmark of his personality. "I've got nothing but debts and memories," he quips, yet insolvency never stopped him from spending extravagantly.

Something sparked between Tabori and the beautiful, temperamental Swedish actress, who had made a career in Hollywood (albeit incomparable to that of her compatriots Garbo and Ingrid Bergman). However, two years elapsed before they met again. She was very pregnant with her third child when she ran into Tabori in Los Angeles in August 1952 and invited him and his wife, Hannah, for the evening. She gave birth the same night, a few hours after the couple had left.

Kristoffer was the only child she had with her third husband, Don Siegel — in those days a novice in Hollywood, later a successful and prosperous director known for *Dirty Harry*, *Escape from Alcatraz*, *The Verdict*, etc. Three months after Kristoffer's birth, when she was playing the lead in John Van Druten's *I've Got Sixpence* in Boston, her love affair with Tabori was no longer avoidable. He had flown in from California and was waiting for her at the stage entrance on opening night. "I went with him to his room at the hotel to drop off his bags, and never left. It was wild," she writes in her memoirs. It took a while before both settled their divorces. Tabori moved in with Viveca and her children even before legal proceedings were over. He soon found himself the father of Viveca's three children from her previous three marriages. Ten-year-old John was born in 1942 when she was married in Sweden to cameraman Harry Hasso; Lena, almost nine, was daughter of the much older Swedish lawyer Folke Rogard; and baby Kristoffer was son of Don Siegel. Bruised by their mother's volatile temperament and her tempestuous love life, the children were "out to get a father for themselves and one that would not drop them the moment their mother left him. Or vice versa," maintains Lindfors.[112] Tabori proved to be this kind of father. They all call him "Dad" and they all adopted the last name Tabori. John, "the Hamlet in our family" as Tabori puts it, is in the computer industry. Lena, the one Tabori is closest to, heads a publishing house in New York. And Kristoffer has made a name for himself as a theatre and film actor. Tabori's relationship with all three endured his separation from Lindfors in the early 1970s, after nearly twenty years together. The children knew about his love affair with Ursula Grützmacher long before their mother did and even met her. Tabori never had a child with Viveca or with any other woman.

"Being with Viveca is such an adventure and it is so liberating an experience that it justifies leaving work behind any time," Tabori writes to Paul.[113] Yet the relationship (the couple married in July 1954) was not frictionless and moved along with sharp twists and turns. The couple shared professional interests — struggling mutually and individually for work (meaning income) and recognition. Tabori wrote the female leads of his early plays with his wife in mind; the two undertook common theatre projects (like *Brecht on Brecht* and the Berkshire Theatre Festival), which more often than not ended in discord or failure, with disappointment and recriminations. "Every time we work together, it turns out to be a disaster. Why do I insist upon it, why this constant yearning?" admits Lindfors in her autobiography, written with arresting raw power and courageous sincerity.[114]

"We will build a fire around our love," he used to reassure her, but the fire could not sustain the passion. She broke down when George left her to live with Ursula Grützmacher, a young German who was to become his third wife and the translator of most of his works into German. Lindfors's memoirs, *Viveka . . . Viveca*, written in 1977, reveal her immense love for him and the enormous pain she suffered when he left her.[115] In 1987, when he was finally given the chance to run his own theatre, Der Kreis, in Vienna, he offered her a role. Though nothing came of it, she acknowledged in her reply that his decision to go back to Europe, finding "a place to put all your talent and creativity," was "the right choice." "It's the Hungarian in you ... the gypsy, the survivor," she added.[116]

As it soon turned out, the relationship with Ursula Grützmacher, Uschi I, did not last too long. A few years after she was forced to come to terms with the presence of Uschi I, Lindfors was introduced to Uschi II, actress Ursula Höpfner, with whom Tabori visited the United States. "She looks like Lena," he warned his ex-wife, who regarded with a jaundiced eye the "fragile and beautiful" woman George was gently protecting in his arm, even younger than "their" daughter Lena. Tabori's marriage to Uschi I was long dead when Viveca finally accepted the fact that George had not left her for Grützmacher. In a letter to Lindfors, in April 1979 (by then Viveca had a new companion and Tabori was already living with Uschi II), he insists on "reaffirm[ing] my version, even if you can't accept it. I did not leave you because of Uschi. I left to do *Pinkville* in Berlin and then got a grant from the Academy there. Uschi was part of the pattern but the work was prime."[117]

Was the pattern "change a place, change a woman," as Lindfors surmises? Not quite; but Tabori hardly made a secret of his various love affairs. Love is the prime mover in his *Weltanschauung*, the source of anguish and great happiness. "Love is the art of the impossible. Between the longing and the fulfillment there falls a shadow."[118] He is the advocate of Eros, Don in Heaven (thus the title of his self-portrait),[119] who succeeded in seducing women "only because I was always available." His alter-ego, nicknamed "Dirty John," explains: "My success was not due to my looks . . . , not to charm, / or annual magnetism, ha-ha, / but to a cursed bodily condition, which condemned me to a permanent thirst." A true *charmeur*, sensitive, imaginative, and erudite, with a fatherly manner, he always attracted women, often much younger than himself. Hungarian playwright István Eörsi, friend and colleague, declares George a first-rate authority in matters of Eros, describing how during a rehearsal Tabori had a string of young women following in his footsteps, ready to comply with his whims, strip themselves naked if he so wished.[120]

In spite of their separation, intermittent irritation, and rancor ("the offenses which you inflict on others in an unexpected and painful way"),[121] Ursula Grützmacher remained the sole translator of Tabori's works. She explicitly asked for this role, and he readily consented: after all, she does such a superb job, always finding the right tone, that some people believe the texts were originally written in German.[122]

In 1985 Tabori married Ursula Höpfner, Uschi II, his junior by thirty-five years. She participated — often in the lead role — in nearly all his productions beginning with the experimental Theater-labor he ran in Bremen and accompanied him through thick and thin to Munich, Hamburg, and finally Vienna. She proved to be the exemplary Tabori actress: adventurous, uncompromising, ready to invest herself, curious to participate in unconventional theatre, combining spontaneity and discipline, and drawing on her tremendous physical skills and declamatory dexterity. Her presence on the stage is impressive and her performances, even when flawed, are remarkable. Sharing her life and work with Tabori, she nonetheless succeeded in asserting her individuality and maintaining critical distance, as when she probed his theatrics and challenged some of its essentials in her unpublished study "Der Begriff der Authentizität aus der Sicht eines Theatermachers" (The Notion of Authenticity from the Point of View of a Play-Maker). In a eulogy he wrote when she was voted Best Actress of the Year 1995, in his autobiographical essays, and in interviews, Tabori mentioned Ursula Höpfner's devotion, her "little secrets," which he "gratefully accepts."[123]

DISCOVERING THE STAGE

Tabori's career in the theatre began with Elia Kazan's production of *Flight into Egypt* at the Music Box on Broadway (premiered 18 March 1952). The play addresses the plight of refugees and exiles. Franz and Lili Engel and their young son, Bubi, are trapped in the corruption and decadence of a fetid hotel in Cairo. For six years Franz has been waiting for a visa. Significantly, Tabori's drama does not depict the horrors of the war itself, but its ramifications in the postwar period; nor is his tragic protagonist a Jew. After his shop is bombed, Franz flees his native Vienna — the rubble, the despair, and the burden of memories. Earlier he had been sent to Buchen-wald for hiding his family's Jewish maid; in this concentration camp he suffered an injury — not from the Nazis, but from an American air raid — that permanently disabled him.

Waiting for the verdict of American officials (a situation similar to that in Gian-Carlo Menotti's memorable opera *The Consul*, which premiered only two years earlier), Lili can hardly pay the bills, is cheated and harassed, and finally succumbs to her husband's hunchbacked Egyptian physician (there is no shortage of invalids and the maimed in Tabori's oeuvre). Confined to a wheelchair, Franz makes heroic if pathetic efforts to persuade the American officials that he will not be a public burden, but the immigration visa is denied. He commits suicide, ironically freeing his wife and son to return home.

Tabori's debut as a playwright received lukewarm to unfavorable reviews. *Time* wrote: "Just as he chokes his story with too many themes, Tabori ultimately deadens it with too much theater," and critic Walter Kerr found himself "curiously unmoved" despite the "harrowing intensity" of the lead performances (by Gusti Huber and Paul Lukas).[124] Viveca Lindfors (still married to Siegel), who had been offered the part of Lili Engel and had to decline due to her pregnancy, found the performance "disappointing and lacking in point of view . . . the excitement I had felt reading the play was gone."[125] Tabori had taken nearly a year to write the play, later revising and rewriting it during the rehearsals and even the previews — a procedure that became a hallmark of his theatre work. He was open to comments by Kazan as well as by established dramatists such as Arthur Miller, Tennessee Williams, and Lillian Hellman, for he soon realized that writing for the stage is totally different from writing a novel or film script. "[Theatre] is the most technical medium of them all," he wrote Paul.[126]

Tabori underplayed his disappointment at the closing of the play after a few weeks ("It was at this time that I realized, with a shock, that the production of a play could be infinitely more interesting than the play itself"),[127] retrospectively attributing the flop to a basic breach between Kazan's interpretation and his own dramatic concept. "It's an ironic tragedy, and Kazan made a melodrama of it and forgot all about the humor."[128] More interesting than the flippant remark, and not altogether compatible with the idea of an "ironic tragedy," is Tabori's Brechtian attitude, as he formulated it in a letter to the *Saturday Review*: "I did not want to 'please,' I wanted to irritate, disturb, and shock; to leave the audience in a state of tension; to send them home unpurged, with a memory of pain."[129]

Even more devastating were the reviews of Tabori's second play, *The Emperor's Clothes*, which premiered at the Ethel Barrymore Theatre under the direction of Harold Clurman (23 February 1953). Bruce Atkinson and his colleagues sealed the fate of the production on opening night thus: "theatrically an in-&-outer and artistically a might-have-been." [130] Deriving its name from Hans Christian Andersen's tale about the small boy who dared cry out that the parading emperor had no clothes on, Tabori's play depicts the relationship between a man and his loving son, focusing on the disparity between the idealized father image and the prosaic truth. The action takes place in Budapest in 1930, in the atmosphere of an incipient police state. The boy Ferike, carried away by his vivid imagination, admires Sherlock Holmes and the Scarlet Pimpernel. More than anyone else, he worships his father, a schoolmaster who has been blacklisted for his liberal opinions. The boy's fantasies culminate in an encounter with the police, who interrogate and grill the father until he is ready to make shameful compromises. By the end of the play, however, he emerges as a real hero and regains his son's admiration.

The play has distinct autobiographical elements. The oppressive atmosphere of a police state brutally crushing persons to extract the truth, at best a trivial and unimportant one, is a clear allusion to the McCarthy hysteria. Many of Tabori's liberal or left-wing colleagues in the film and theatre industry fell victim to the ferocious witch-hunt, and Tabori himself, though no Communist, was blacklisted for being a "fellow traveler." It was a bitter experience for him to witness Kazan's fallibility: "his" director became a cooperative witness in front of the Un-American Activities Committee, denouncing some of his closest friends.

The other autobiographical theme in *The Emperor's Clothes* goes back to Tabori's childhood. In his extensive unpublished interview with Ursula Höpfner, Tabori explicitly refers to Paul as the model for the boy in the play.[131] Paul idealized his father as a "great revolutionary" yet brought upon him all sorts of trouble — an episode fictionalized and embedded in "the truth of the organ-grinder" in *Mein Kampf.* In one of the most moving letters George sent his brother, he seeks to shake Paul free of all the romantic illusions he has cultivated about their father: "Father is a moot point, of course. He wasn't a friendly liberal as you would like to see him, but a defeated socialist. . . . He played with the idea of suicide for several years, and had a tragic contempt for himself, because he knew he had the makings of Lincoln Steffens. He tried to make peace with himself by getting involved . . . , by being a man of charity who knew that personal help was a sorry substitute for institutionalised help." [132]

Tabori's third play was never produced. The unpublished "Jealousy Play" is the story of a woman who, upon finding out that her husband had an affair, betrays him with a young black actor. Tabori wrote the female part for his wife and the lover's part for Sidney Poitier, who was at that time making his living by selling hamburgers from a stand in Harlem. "G.T. used his [Poitier's] background, his language, his life story to its fullest in the play," writes Lindfors. [133] But producer "Saint" Subber did not like the various versions Tabori presented him: "Don't you dare tell us Americans what's wrong with this country," he exclaimed. Tabori, who never ceased handling hot topics, encountered further misunderstanding when he directed the sex scene between the white woman and the black man at the Actors Studio. A curious discussion ensued, he recalls: "People objected to the whole idea, and Lee [Strasberg] said, I don't understand it. Monroe was there too, she was a beginner then, and she said, I like it, and I asked, why, and she said, because it's complicated." [134]

It was Viveca Lindfors who introduced Tabori to the Actors Studio. A theatre and film actress of repute, she began attending sessions in the spring of 1953, and "for the next four years I 'lived' there." [135] George, who never had formal theatre training, soon joined her and became a permanent guest at Strasberg's exclusive theatre workshop. Notably, he did not attend the writers' sessions, but preferred to observe theatre-in-the-making, the closed biweekly meetings at which actors performed, improvised, experimented, and widened their experience through listening to each other's critiques. It was during these sessions, as well as in various workshops he conducted later with professional and lay actors, that Tabori acquired his theatrical savvy. He resolutely discarded all sorts of predefined principles or ready-made recipes, advocating instead fresh practical experience — an ongoing process of training and learning that would enrich the individual as an actor and as a human being. Though the influence of Strasberg's Studio and his Method is undeniable, Tabori is very ambivalent about "Dear Lee." [136] "I didn't like him personally," he told me. He elaborated: "He treated us all like kids. He had basically some six or seven working principles which he formulated in his excellent book [*A Dream of Passion*] and he had some excellent actors in his Studio, but when I asked for his opinion on *The Emperor's Clothes* and provoked him for three hours to speak out, he just muttered, it's no good, but wouldn't explain."[137]

Again, in a letter to Paul dating back to the early 1950s, we gain more insight into Tabori's autodidactic dramatic training. He is aware that "instinctive approaches are terribly dangerous in drama, and unless one has direct theatrical experience — acting or directing — one must go to the few, very few, sources that can be useful." He dismisses out of hand "the so-called academicians" and finds equally useless the works of famous dramatists. The only guides from which he personally profited are John Howard Lawson's "book on technique" (*Theory and Techniques of Playwrighting*, 1936), Brecht's *Organon*, and a book by a Hungarian named Egry. Self-critical and clearsighted as he is, he admits: "The trouble with both of us is, I believe, that we have a very excitable imagination which gets easily agitated . . . but unless we watch out it ends in coitus prematurus."[138]

Truly, Tabori was always keen to learn, always prepared to reconsider an idea, rewrite a scene, revise, and reshape a dramatic production. And he admits that he learned most from his actors. "It's not enough to write a play, you've got to actually do it." In the midsixties he worked with the Free Southern Theatre, the first mixed group of white and black actors in New Orleans, which performed for all-black audiences in churches and pubs.[139] In 1966 together with his wife, Viveca, he founded the Strolling Players, a small troupe that toured university campuses for two months annually, with an ambitious program.[140] Later, in Germany, he ran his own experimental group, the Theaterlabor in Bremen (1975–1978; see chapter 3), and worked with a group of professional and amateurs in Munich; finally, he ran his own theatre, Der Kreis in Vienna, with an adjacent workshop modeled on the Actors Studio. For Tabori theatre is "a learning process about human encounters, about the nature of freedom and necessity."[141]

Neither the critical reviews nor the commercial failure of his plays tore Tabori away from writing for the stage. There are four more plays in his "American" phase, none of which brought him the hoped-for breakthrough. *Brouhaha*, a comedy directed by Peter Hall at the Aldwych in London (premiere 27 August 1958), received such devastating reviews that it closed soon after the opening.[142] In New York, some six years after his successful Brecht collage, his double bill *The Niggerlovers* was premiered, directed by Gene Frankel. The two short plays (*The Demonstration* and *Man and Dog*) are, in Tabori's own words, "sort of mini-Brecht, and very Newyorkish and contemporary."[143] He depicts the dialectics of victims and victimizers against the background of multiethnic, multicultural New York. "Both pieces fit into the so-called 'new wave' type of writing for the theatre. They are highly theatrical, thin of plot, excessively vulgar and hold the attention of the eye rather than the mind," wrote critic James Davis.[144] *Man and Dog* is the last Tabori play written with Viveca in mind as the female lead. A man kills his beloved bitch because she has prevented him from living as he wished. "I played her, Stacy Keach played him," Lindfors recalls. "In the end of the play, her master shoots her. It upset me as if it were a personal warning toward me, but I dared not ask him [Tabori]."[145]

Tabori's plays teem with animals: Mitzi in *Mein Kampf*, the chicken in *I Pagliacci*, a peacock in *The Fasting Artists*, a siluroid in *The Sinking of the Titanic*, a rat in *Voyeur*. In his sarcastic article "Protestations of an Ever-Young Pig," bearing the motto "Some of my best friends are swine" and signed "Miss Piggy," Tabori protests against the physical abuse and semantic misappropriation of animals. "'Human' is forever celebrated (by humans, of course), while 'animal,' with the rare exception of lambs, butterflies or nightingales, is denounced as reprehensible or even criminal." Reminiscent of Joseph Beuys's campaign against cruelty to animals, Tabori writes: "We are, we and my friends, sick and tired of this agelong abuse of animal (and vegetable) rights, and not only of the verbal sort."[146]

Of all animals and pets, he has a soft spot for dogs, and dogs have always accompanied him, in Hollywood, New York, and Vienna. "The only time I saw G.T. cry was when our dog, Lady, died," recounts Lindfors.[147] "Dogs are wonderful people," Tabori says. "They never lie. Dogs behave as women should."[148]

The play with which Tabori took his leave from America was his antiwar *Pinkville*, premiered at the American Place Theatre on 17 March 1971. Eight years after the Living Theater's provocative performance of the antimilitary play *The Brig*, Tabori's Vietnam play shows the process of dehumanization and brutalization that war entails. Welding together colloquial language, songs, and a series of episodes, and following Brecht's parable play *Man Is Man*, Tabori depicts how good-natured people relinquish their individual struggles to become bloody murderers. Rehearsals took place while legal proceedings were being levied against Lieutenant William Calley, who was in charge of the My Lai massacre. Musician Stanley Walden, in charge of the production's sophisticated music, maintains that the play failed in America because "it was un-nationalistic to have such an attitude in those days."[149] Yet this seems to be an inadequate explanation in view of the success of several antiwar plays and films, not least the film (1970) and stage adaptation (Easthampton, New York, 1971) of Joseph Heller's memorable *Catch-22*.

By the time *Pinkville* was staged in New York, Tabori was more a visitor there than a resident. *Cannibals*, his striking play about Auschwitz prisoners who cook and intend to consume a dead inmate in hopes of surviving, was mildly received on Broadway (17 October 1968). Yet this play won Tabori entry into the German theatre world after its exciting, if controversial, reception in Berlin (13 December 1969; see chapter 11). Maria Sommer, proprietress of the Gustav Kiepenheuer Bühnenvertriebs GmbH, was piqued by the review of *Cannibals* she read in the New York–based German-language paper *Aufbau*, got hold of the stage script, and passed it on to Albert Bessler, chief dramaturg of the Schiller-Theater. "Germany offered him [Tabori] contracts, money, security, a theater of his own, and a kind of respect that G.T. felt he had never received in this country," writes Lindfors.[150] Their marriage was failing, a new young lover (Uschi I) was waiting in Berlin, and, above all, at long last there was genuine interest in his writing and a prospect for continued theatre-making.

THE SECOND CHANCE

Tabori came to Germany with one suitcase and 150 dollars and, unknowingly, came to stay. Surprised that the Germans were interested in staging a play about Auschwitz in the first place, Tabori joined director Marty Fried (his sometime son-in-law, Lena's first husband) and went to Berlin.[151] "I was curious to find out how a German audience would respond to a Black Mass whose texture was humor, not piety." At fifty-five, he was at an unexpected crossroads in his career. A DAAD (Deutscher Akademischer Austauschdienst) grant and offers to stage others of his plays enticed him to stay.

"Moving back to Europe had always been his wish," attests Viveca Lindfors,[152] yet tearing himself away from America after more than twenty years was difficult "on every level," he avows. Tabori was attached to his children, knew scores of people from all walks of life — more acquaintances and professional colleagues than intimate friends — and liked the colorful, pulsating life of Manhattan. Like so many Americans in those years, he sought the help of a psychotherapist (two, in fact) and attended group dynamics sessions (observing rather than participating).[153] He did not hide his skeptical irreverence toward psychotherapy ("perhaps the idea of therapy is to drive one out [of] one's wretched mind"),[154] and in particular psycho-babble, and yet he was interested in the relevance of psychology to the stage, and sought ways to utilize some psychological "techniques" in acting. It is from Frederick Perls, the founder of *Gestalt*-therapy, whose demonstration session he once attended ("I wasn't particularly impressed"), that Tabori heard the aphorism which was to become his own credo: "Don't push the river. It flows."[155]

"I have always loved this land [America], the landscape and the people too," Tabori confesses.[156] Yet he had the distinct feeling that his work, whether poorly or well received, was always considered bizarre, "almost exotic." He felt himself a stranger in a country full of foreigners. Neither Germany nor Vienna became "home" to him, but it was in the rediscovered European milieu that he acknowledged and came to terms with his existential foreignness and even consciously cultivated it. Whenever asked, he would retort that his home (*Heimat*) could not be geographically defined, that he was an existential sojourner (although he hates traveling) and in that sense homeless. He readily repeated his subversive formula — "my home is the stage, bed and books"[157] — a definition that soon acquired the aura of exotic nonchalance.

His second chance, in Germany, was not smooth sailing. Although he was hardly ever short of work, always involved in one theatre project or another, he was for years a peripheral figure in German theatre, esteemed mostly by experiment-oriented critics, connoisseurs, and insiders. Contrary to Lindfors's stipulations, he never made big money in Germany, nor did he enjoy financial security; as in the past, he was permanently in debt. Yet it is true that in Germany, for the first time, he was free to devote himself entirely to theatre-making: write (and rewrite!) for the stage, direct, work with actors and learn from them, try things out, dismiss them, experiment further, and gradually, in reciprocity between practice and theory, formulate the essentials of his theatrics. It was in Germany that he matured as a playwright, found his tone, his themes — prominent among these the German-Jewish issue — and worked them out.

Tabori set out on his theatre experimentations in Germany immediately after the remarkable reception of *Cannibals* in Berlin. His first project was *Pinkville*, which he pursued with students of the Max-Reinhardt-Acting-School in a church in suburban Berlin. Making use of the setting, he embedded the political themes with religious associations and images; Jerry, the protagonist, carried the cross in this ritual-influenced performance. A wild satire on the American way of life followed with *Clowns*, a domestic drama showing life in a family as a cauldron of anger, lust, rivalry, and loneliness. The production which premiered at the workshop of the Zimmertheater in Tübingen (8 May 1972) was a hyped-up show of mime and slapstick. Its elements included a medley of musical associations from J. S. Bach to *I Pagliacci*; an actor playing a dog; a huge bed/ trampoline center-stage; a huge penis and a multifunctional "Thing" as metaphors for anxieties, phobias, and sexual neuroses. Written and rewritten during rehearsals with a devoted team, this hybrid show debunks the myth of the intact, harmonious family.[158]

Tabori's final station before embarking on his Theaterlabor in Bremen was Bonn, where he directed James Saunders's version of *Kohlhaas* (premiered 8 April 1974). The group of ten young actors, all eager to experiment and shape the performance through teamwork, rehearsed for twelve weeks: "eight for the play, four for ourselves." In his first German production of the work of another playwright, Tabori did not refrain from taking substantial liberties with the text: abridging and pruning the original and interspersing the story of Kohlhaas's struggle for justice with the remarks or commentaries of the actors/spectators. Heinrich von Kleist's story is seen from the point of view of the victim; the actors are the prisoners with naked chests, blindfolded and chained. The performance oscillated between stark realism and the oppressive, the nightmarish. Kafka's spirit seems to hover over it: "The four Ks — Kleist, Kafka, Kohlhaas and Josef K. — are kinsmen in essence and in attitude," maintains Tabori.[159] Three years later he presented his original stage version of Kafka's *Metamorphosis* (1977), followed by a memorable performance of *The Fasting-Artists* (1977; see chapter 3).

These were, however, sporadic experimentations with changing troupes, which only underlined Tabori's unusual approach to theatre-making, unparalleled among German directors and not particularly encouraged by the established mainstream theatres. Thus, when he was offered the directorship of a group of his own under the auspices of the municipal theatre in Bremen, he seized the rare opportunity. It was at the so-called Theaterlabor that he made — together with a team of dedicated young actors eager to engage in alternative theatre-making — some of his most radical and memorable experiments. These were followed by further explorations and highly unconventional productions in Munich (with some actors from the Theatre Lab) of Kafka, Hans Magnus Enzensberger, Beckett (see chapters 4, 5, and 6), and Shakespeare. Tabori has always enjoyed a heavy dose of magnetism. The self-confessed outsider with the looming face, ever-young and indefatigable, in jeans and full hair falling hippielike down his neck, fascinates many of those he meets. Bewilderingly well-read, he uses a vast range of references from literature, history, art, psychology, and science; added to this is his ingenious manner of telling stories and jokes or bowling you over with a casual *aperçu*. Generous, attentive, and patient, he became an endearing mentor for the young, a kind of *paterfamilias* for his actors.

This period was marked by both professional and financial insecurity, friction with theatre authorities and officials, controversial reception of his work, and some vicious reviews. Nevertheless, and despite the uneven artistic results, I find this period the most inspiring and significant phase in Tabori's stage experimentations. It is for this reason that I devote a substantial part of this book to a comprehensive elucidation and analysis of productions from 1975 to 1980.

The 1980s saw a proliferation of Tabori's theatre engagements. He worked with various troupes, often integrating his own loyal actors, and in diverse established theatres, premiering and reinterpreting others' texts. In 1984 he directed the world premiere at the Schaubühne in Berlin of István Eörsi's political play *Das Verhör* (The Hearing), about persecution in Communist Hungary.[160] A few months later he bowled over the audience at the Kammerspiele in Munich with an original and powerful rendering of Herbert Achternbusch's *Mein Herbert* (My Herbert), an autobiographical drama of a love-hate relationship between mother and son, with both parts played by women![161] At the same time, he conducted experimental projects such as the performance *Death & Co.*, based on texts by Sylvia Plath, which he undertook with students of the Hochschule der Künste in Berlin (February 1982), and tried his hand in the production of opera. It was likewise in that phase that he established himself as a playwright of note with *The Voyeur* (1982), *Jubilee* (1983), and *Peepshow* (1984).

Commissioned by the municipal theatre of Bochum, *Jubilee* was meant to mark the fiftieth anniversary of the National Socialists' rise to power in Germany; it turned into an extraordinary experience of remembrance (see chapter 14). A cabaretlike grotesque, *The Voyeur* pits two subalterns: a Jewish Holocaust-survivor named Dryfoos (!) and a neighboring Puerto Rican family. The play, which is part of Tabori's New Yorker trilogy dating back to the late 1960s,[162] depicts the tortuous relationship between the Jew, a victim turned victimizer, and black Americans, the new underdogs, culminating in murder and a casuistic trial. Avoiding a didactic tone, Tabori's message is nonetheless unequivocal: nobody may claim a monopoly on suffering, and under no circumstances should the infliction of suffering recompense for wrong endured.

Peepshow, premiered in Bochum (6 April 1984), is an anecdotal quasi-autobiography (Tabori: "personally motivated and privately defamiliarized") of a would-be-writer, foregrounding Eros and Thanatos. Willie, Tabori's alter-ego, a self-ironizing oedipal erotoman, discovers the bliss and curse of sexual excitement in a wild scenario, at times hilariously funny, a collage of quotations from and references to the Bible, Shakespeare, and Beckett as well as self-referential intertextuality (primarily Tabori's *Man and Dog*, *Talk Show*, and the novella *Son of a Bitch*).[163]

Among the fascinating productions of that period is Tabori's staging of Harald Mueller's *Totenfloß* (Deathraft, premiere 29 November 1986) — one in a long list of productions of this "Play of the Year 1986" — which had much in common with his Kafka, Beckett, and Enzensberger experiments. The story of four ostracized individuals trying to flee a futuristic environment contaminated by radioactive fallout and chemical toxins, in the hope of reaching the supposedly clean and "bodyempty" Xanten down the river Rhine, evolves into an apocalyptic stage vision in which playfulness and subtle humor alleviate the sense of catastrophe. Here again Tabori discloses his interest in human behavior under extreme conditions, *Grenzsituationen*. Rather than addressing the political-ecological issue raised by Mueller's topical play (those were the days of Chernobyl, after all), he focused on existential and psychological ramifications, namely, the question "How does one live when one dies?"[164] Stage and setting are reminiscent of the minimalist yet highly effective scene of his earlier experimental productions: an unlocalized, timeless scene, at times a laboratory of catastrophes, at times a gym hall. Ropes hung across the stage and the walls were pasted with white cloth, while children's paintings and photos could be seen at the rear. Ankle-high water covered the stage, with the odd shoe aimlessly floating about, a fire hose jutting out. The only stage requisite was a piano on wheels, which served alternately as bed, house, raft, or dreambox.[165] "Tabori avoids stumbling into the science fiction demonic, he creates a kind of postmodern Hades . . . , eerie poetic images," accurately observes critic Armin Eichholz.[166] For instance: Kuckuck, the aging wanderer who tries to save the singing of birds from oblivion, uses a lollypop, instead of a fish, to determine whether the river is polluted; the "end-of-all-times quartet" move closer together, embrace, show compassion as they lie vulnerably on the piano-raft; Checker, the domineering leader, kills the underdog Itai, blind and debilitated, with a kiss (not with a knife, as in Mueller's text); the three men look hypnotized at some shoes they retrieve from the water — an extraordinary silent moment of remembering the Holocaust. Time is dislocated in Tabori's staging of *Totenfloß* — images surge up and are washed away, as it were; the dystopia, like the dream of deliverance, is a flight of fancy and a ghastly imaginary constellation.

One of the few occasions when Tabori confronted a contemporary German political issue was his *Stammheim-Epilog* (The Stammheim Epilogue), ironically subtitled "Kleine Nachtmusik" (A Little Night Music), which premiered in Hamburg on 31 January 1986, immediately following the screening of Reinhard Hauff's film *Stammheim*. Tabori's forty-minute sequel begins where Hauff's film about the Baader-Meinhof group ends, with improvisations on the detainees' last night. What started off in the first draft as a mosaic of quotations was discarded in the course of rehearsals in favor of a virtually silent show, a kind of "combined painting" which focused on the private human side rather than on the strictly political polemics or on the debate whether the Red Army Faction members committed suicide or were killed on orders. The actors, most of whom participated in Hauff's film, perform slow-motion rituals of dying. While Meinhof tears a towel to strips and braids it into a rope, Baader plays with a pistol, Raspe takes an overdose of tablets, Ensslin busies herself with a rope, and Möller putters about with a knife and ketchup. Each rehearses death, and each dies alone, smearing him/herself with dead-white or blood-red stains.

Simultaneously another element of this combined painting emerges, visually and acoustically: one of the film actresses plays on the piano "Schröder's Death," a composition by the Hungarian Laszlo Vidowsky with endless up and down scales. This sound gains metaphorical meaning (Tabori: "Metaphor for censorship, for the struggle between power and art, for coldness, death, apocalypse"[167]) as two "assistants" pull the strings out one by one, sever the musical line, and ultimately choke the life out of the piano. No sound is heard, only the striking of the hammers operated by the mechanical keys; the pianist departs after a minute of silence, while the Stammheim judge-turned-executioner gleefully approaches the prisoners.

The silent play ends with a collagelike requiem composed of quotations from Brecht's *Die Massnahme* (The Measure Taken) statements made by the terrorists-turned-victims, Meinhof's letters to her children ("you needn't be sad that you have a mummy who's in prison"), etc.

Designed as an epilogue to Hauff's film, the performance was also meant to provoke a discussion about the RAF, truth and legend. Yet the first night ended with physical rather than verbal exchanges, much to the dismay of the organizers. Tabori, whose contribution received mixed reviews, saw this as confirmation of his assumption that "theater is one number bigger than the cinema; cinema is in the final judgment harmless, theatre, by contrast, is dangerous."[168]

A "mini opera" is how Ulrich Schreiber describes Tabori's stage rendering of Gertrude Stein's *Doctor Faustus Lights the Lights* (premiere 4 June 1983),[169] a text she wrote in 1938 as an opera libretto, but which was never set to music. Musician Stanley Walden provided extensive live and prerecorded jazzlike music ("not only a simple collection of melodies, but a genuinely composed piece of music theatre").[170] Working with him, Tabori created an "opera for actors," an extravagant phantasmagoria of expressive dancing, mime, and melodious *Sprachgesang* which blurred the borders of the fictitious and the real. In the atelier of an abandoned locksmith plant, with pipes and retorts creating a setting reminiscent of a Stanley Kubrick film, the actors performed the story of Faust's discovery of electric light and his descent to hell after killing his boy and his dog (Tabori's obsession with dogs!). Tabori was fascinated by Stein's acute awareness that — as he put it — "words, like things, become ill and die, they taste rotten in our mouth before they putrefy."[171] Consequently he renounced an "interpretation" of the text, that "serious pursuit of explanation" which typifies to his mind the established theatre. Instead he opted for a joyful performance conveying the polysemy of the text and playing upon the evasiveness and ambiguity of words (light as enlightenment or stage-light, for instance). With the conscious relinquishing of an all-inclusive interpretation, the spectator has "the chance to be a co-author, not the consumer of the true and the beautiful," as Tabori explained in the program for the enthusiastically reviewed show.[172]

The transition from miniopera to opera proper was only a matter of time for someone with an insatiable curiosity, eager to try his hand in all dramatic forms, ready to fail, "always fail, fail better," as he repeatedly quotes Beckett. "Actually I understand nothing about opera," he told an interviewer while rehearsing yet another opera, in 1994. "I do it only in order to learn," he confessed. "For me the whole thing is a learning process, the singers have to tell me what they need. I do the same with actors. I am an interested spectator, I decide certain things myself, but we do it together."[173]

Observers and critics who saw Tabori's production of *Moses und Aron* (1994) speak of "a non-staging [*Nicht-Inszenierung*]" of his silent presence during rehearsals.[174] Yet Tabori's idiosyncratic stamp is unmistakable in all eight opera and music productions — notably, most of them twentieth-century works — he directed between 1986 and 1998.[175]

His debut as opera director was Ruggiero Leoncavallo's *I Pagliacci*, at the small Vienna Kammeroper (8 May 1986). Tabori was clearly out to challenge hackneyed opera clichés — he mentioned in this context Peter Brook's unorthodox staging of *Carmen* — and yet, like Brook, he never questioned the operatic genre as such. Tabori did away with the ubiquitous Sicilian folklore, colorful costumes, and rich setting. In keeping with his original rendering of Beckett's *Godot* (1984), he likewise staged *I Pagliacci* as a rehearsal. The nearly bare stage had black wrapping papers covering the walls and two open doors at the rear disclosing the artists' wardrobe. The actors could be seen getting ready for the show, as the coach with a twirled Leoncavallo mustache played some tunes on the piano.

Seeking to dismantle the conventional barrier between stage and audience, Tabori placed the opera chorus in the front row of seats, among spectators. Along with the audience, the chorus witnessed a drama of love and jealousy which at times brought *Othello* to mind (spurred on by a Iago-like Tonio, Canio strangles his wife, Nedda, instead of stabbing her to death). The comic intermezzo which kindles Canio's jealousy, that play-within-play, was a puppet show, with hand puppets — small faces, big mouths — quarreling with each other. Incensed with jealousy, Canio pulls the curtain down and challenges his purportedly unfaithful wife. Tabori foregrounds the ambiguity of Leoncavallo's opera, the dualism of life and art: no sooner are Nedda and her lover dead than they stand up. "Go home all of you," proclaims Canio, eyeballing his double audience, the stage one and the real one, "*La commedia è finita!*"

Typically, Tabori claims that he hardly directed his cast, mostly singers at the start of their career who were thus open to experimentation; that he merely animated them to discover the role in themselves. "The real danger is that I enjoy the singing so much," he adds.

The much-applauded *Pagliacci* was followed by an unparalleled éclat when Tabori's staging of Franz Schmidt's oratory *The Book of the Seven Seals*,[176] performed in the baroque church of Salzburg on 28 July 1987, raised a cultural-religious storm. "The sensation was premeditated," wrote one of the reporters, and he was right.[177] The commission was an explosive combination of a postromantic oratory by an Austrian with overt National Socialist sympathies,[178] a famously controversial Jewish director, and the devoutly Catholic milieu of Salzburg. Tabori described the work as "MGM-Catholicism" and chose to accompany the musical performance with mimetic counterpoint;[179] his *Gegenbilder* and chimeral icons neither interpret nor illustrate the Revelation of the Gospel according to John, but offer the listeners a series of associative images of the apocalyptic vision. Some forty white mummy-puppets were placed on a modern tower of Babel, a 22-meter-high multiplatform tower, erected in the middle of the church with a maze of ropes connecting it to the surrounding walls. The actors, in evening dress, smoking jackets, or jeans, blood-stained or smeared with dirt, relate to the puppets and to each other, acting out their anxieties and need for love in a trance that culminates in a carnal orgy. Finally they merge with the mummies, become, as it were, "human garbage." No wonder that devout Catholics were offended by this blasphemous spectacle, accusing Tabori of prurience and tactlessness. They were supported by conservative groups that launched a fierce campaign against Tabori and the actors, ultimately leading to the cancellation of the production.[180]

It was also in Salzburg, four years later (1991), that Tabori directed Bruno Maderna's short opera *Satyricon* as a *dolce vita* spectacle, a provocative farce on contemporary hedonism, lewdness, and gourmandizing.[181] Udo Zimmermann engaged Tabori for the Maderna opera-persiflage and invited him in 1994 to direct Schönberg's *Moses and Aaron*, which Tabori had always wanted to do. At eighty, somewhat apprehensive of the formidable task, he worked for the first time with a chorus of 160 singers; surprisingly perhaps, the choir, representing the "pre-Jewish people,"[182] became the protagonist of the production. Wavering between Moses, the idealistic theoretician, and pragmatic Aaron, the choir ultimately holds sway over both; it demands and gets an image of God as a projection of human wishes and conflicts. Once the cathartic dance (with naked maidens) is over, the choir retires. Left on the stage are piled-up chairs and a bunch of shoes.

Finally, mention should be made of Tabori's chilling production of *The Emperor of Atlantis* in the framework of the *Berliner Festwochen* (1 October 1987). The one-act opera, composed in Theresienstadt by Schönberg's disciple Viktor Ullmann to a libretto by inmate Peter Kien, got as far as a dress rehearsal in the concentration camp before the artists were sent to the gas chamber. Tabori restores the opera to its original context; it is a barely disguised allegory of Nazi Germany, where Death has abdicated and condemned the people to live forever, miserable or maimed: art out of and in human-made hell (as in his *Cannibals*). Set in a framework of blood-red bars surrounded by barbed wire, and performed by singers wearing striped uniforms and yellow and black stars of David (as well as the pink triangle of the interned homosexuals), Tabori's production replicates as it were the original performance in Theresienstadt, which Ullmann never got to see. The sense of reality is intensified by the projection of clips from the cynical film *The Führer Offers a Town for the Jews*. The seven singers, white-faced and sunken-eyed — accompanied by a thin accompaniment of strings, banjo, saxophone, and harmonium, which gave the score a cabaret coloring à la Kurt Weill — gave a harrowing performance, which won them and Tabori complimentary reviews in Germany and far beyond.[183]

The year 1987 was important for Tabori. His farce *Mein Kampf,* presenting a fictitious encounter between Hitler and the Jew Shlomo Herzl in a Viennese flophouse for men, was a sensational hit (see chapter 15), placing Tabori at the forefront of contemporary German (!) drama. After seven different productions in the first season, 1987/1988, the play enjoyed 22 productions in Germany, Austria, and Switzerland in 1990/1991 (with 452 performances), and 23 productions (with 383 performances) in the following season. With 45 different productions of 7 of his plays, Tabori became in the 1991/1992 season one of the most frequently produced playwrights on the German-speaking stages and advanced in the following season to the ninth position (seventh in Germany), ranking immediately after Goethe and Schiller! Indeed, *Mein Kampf* became Tabori's *billet d'entrée* to the big institutionalized theatres which he had for years disdainfully rejected as the "cathedrals."

Only four weeks after its premiere, celebrating his seventy-third birthday, Tabori's own theatre Der Kreis (The Circle) was inaugurated with a production of Eugene O'Neill's *The Iceman Cometh,* directed by Martin Fried. The small theatre with its adjacent backyard rooms in the heart of Vienna — around the corner from Sigmund Freud's last Austrian home — was the fulfillment of Tabori's longtime dream of running his own theatre, determining the repertoire, and abandoning the star-oriented casting system in favor of teamwork and adventurous productions. The Circle — "a beautiful, feminine and democratic form, a sign for some of our utopian dream" [184] — brought together veteran Tabori actors (Detlef Jacobsen, Rainer Frieb, Ursula Höpfner) and professionals of varying experience in German and Viennese theatres. Tabori managed to win over such renowned actors as Angelica Domröse, Hildegard Schmahl, Hilmar Thate, Michael Degen, and Hanna Schygulla. The invigorating contradictions behind everything Tabori did and wrote, along with his refreshing antiauthoritarian approach to theatre-making, won them over for one or more productions. In parallel, a workshop modeled on the Actors Studio was open to actors and interested students free of charge. Sessions were conducted by Tabori, Martin Fried, and Walter Lott, all of whom had attended Strasberg's legendary Studio. It was here, at the Kreis, that Tabori sought to explore a theatre aesthetics determined by personal relations, experimentation, and improvisation. The actors practiced "warm-ups" and "sense memory" while Tabori encouraged them to tap into their reservoir of experiences, recall, relive, react, and integrate the personal and authentic into the performance. He had of course done it all before, with diverse actors in different places and over three years at his Theaterlabor in Bremen. But in Vienna he was for the first time his own boss, answerable to no one, in charge of budget, repertory, and scheduling along with all sorts of petty administrative matters — an arduous and time-consuming task, as he was soon to find out.

Not surprisingly, this enterprising, "utopian" project, this risk-taking "dangerous" theatre-making in the "catacombs," was only partly successful. In his capacity as director Tabori seized the opportunity to explore the plays of Shakespeare in his own, idiosyncratic way (see chapters 7–9) and to stage plays of topical political interest; for instance, during the Waldheim scandal he staged a dramatized version of Peter Sichrovsky's interviews with children of prominent Nazis, *Schuldig geboren* (Born Guilty, premiered 19 September 1987). Tabori's troupe also premiered (in one of the halls at the Vienna fairground!) Thomas Brasch's play *Frauen, Krieg, Lustspiel* (Women, War, Comedy, premiered 10 May 1988) — a hybrid theatrical mediation mixing dreams, recollections, intertextuality, and playfulness, to expose the male-concocted myth of war and valor as seen through women's eyes.[185]

Besides a new production of *Cannibals* (directed by Martin Fried), only one other Tabori play was staged at the Kreis, *Masada* (1988).[186] Amidst the expanse of ruins (the last Jewish stronghold) — sandy mounds, stones, miniature tin soldiers, barbed wire, abandoned shoes, and candles clearly alluding to the Holocaust — two survivors of the mass suicide reflect on questions such as the right to live, the guilt of the survivor, the duty to bear witness. In a static, almost Beckett staging, a female survivor, relative of the leader Eleazar, mourns the dead. Her counterpart, Jewish historian Josephus Flavius (in modern dress), whose *War of the Jews* is the source of Tabori's text, tries to talk himself out of feeling guilty over his defection to the Romans. The Masada episode, eulogized in modern Jewish historiography and assimilated in the national mythopoetics of the state of Israel,[187] treats of major Taborian themes such as self-assertion through passivity, voluntary death, and the moral superiority of the victim. The concluding line of the epilogue makes the larger historical context explicit: from the top of Masada one can see "Libya,

Egypt, Tunisia, Algiers; to the east Jordan and Saudi Arabia, to the north Iraq, Libanon and Syria. In the west one can see on clear days Auschwitz."

In the summer of 1990, some three years after its inauguration, the Kreis closed.[188] The company of some thirty actors and administrators disbanded with an essaylike farewell letter by Tabori, which sought to be dispassionate, at times philosophical, and always free of sentimental indulgence: "*Partir c'est mourir un peu*, but not in the theatre: the curtain falls, the dead rise, bow, and are ready to die again the following evening."[189] Rumors about hardships and friction had long before made their way to the local press. Tabori refused to draw a balance-sheet of his shortlived undertaking, which doubtless surpassed his initial plans in both size and commitment. "If you begin to speak about the outcome and about money, you are already in a bordello," he said in his nonchalant manner, adding that he had never been so deeply in debt and so often ill as in Vienna.[190] Reflecting on the entire undertaking, he repeated his Beckettian conviction that one always fails, fails better. Significantly, he took the blame upon himself and diagnosed with a grain of irony three major mistakes: "The first was that I came to Vienna with the utopia of running a laboratory and not a production-machine . . . ; the second was, not to back out; . . . my third mistake was to believe that such work is still relevant."[191] It boils down to the question whether it is possible to run a commercially viable yet artistically uncompromising alternative theatre in the "catacombs," or whether experimental theatre is only feasible under the auspices of the financially secure institutionalized stages (i.e., in the "cathedrals").

Ironically, Tabori himself forsook his own utopian vision; or perhaps it would be fairer to say that it was a combination of circumstances and *Realpolitik*. For following the overwhelming success in 1987 of *Mein Kampf* at the Burg, just when he embarked on his alternative theatre-making at the Kreis, he was again and again courted to direct at the Burg. He resisted the temptation at first, but ultimately succumbed to Claus Peymann's offers to direct *Othello* with Gert Voss (10 January 1990; see chapter 10) and soon after premiered his own *Weisman and Copperface* (23 March 1990). Some of his actors and colleagues at the Kreis felt he had betrayed their common ideals, bailing out and leaving them in the lurch. The local press used the word *fremdgehen* (being unfaithful to one's wife) whenever it discussed Tabori's involvement with the Burg. The question whether Tabori deserted the Kreis in frustration because he realized its limitations or whether the Kreis disbanded because he neglected his duty remains open to speculation.

"ALL OVER AGAIN. CURTAIN": TABORI'S LAST PLAYS

Thus Tabori was back at the cathedrals he had railed against. He was continuously engaged at the Burg, apart from the odd production: Maderna's short opera *Satyricon*, *Delirium* (1994), a lyrical collage based on texts by Hans Magnus Enzensberger, and *Nathans Tod* (1991), a highly original and subversive, albeit artistically debatable, variation on Lessing's appeal for tolerance, *Nathan the Wise* — indeed an anti-Lessing piece in which evil has the upper hand ("Tabori's Satan the Wise").[192] He never made a secret of his ambivalent feelings toward the foremost theatre in Vienna. The glamorous theatre house located on the part of the Vienna Ring named after its anti-Semitic lord mayor Karl Lueger is in Tabori's eyes "a coproduction of Jesuits and Disneyland," "a Magic Mountain," so called after Mann's novel in which he analyzes "the relationship between pathology and art."[193] Tabori never kept to himself his critical opinion of and occasional conflict with Burg intendant Claus Peymann. Nonetheless, in May 1997, upon his eighty-third birthday, he was made an honorary member of the Burg; when Peymann announced a year later that he was going to take over the artistic direction of the Berliner Ensemble, Tabori made known that he intended to follow suit and move to Berlin.

The facts speak for themselves. From 1990 until 1999 Tabori directed fourteen productions, mostly at the Akademietheater, the second house of the Burg. Four were productions of plays by other authors — *Othello* (1990), Kafka's *A Report for an Academy* (1992; see chapter 4), Elfriede Jelinek's *Stecken, Stab und Stangl* (1997), and Beckett's *Endgame* (1998; see chapter 6).[194] The others were premieres of new texts of his own. Indeed, the last phase of Tabori's artistic career is distinguished less for its theatrical and stagecraft experimentation characteristic of his work at the Theaterlabor or at the Kreis than for its productivity. Tabori came up with a new play every year, at times recycling older materials, at times — as with *The 25th Hour*[195] — revising an existing text or, in the case of *Unruhige*

Träume (Restless Dreams), producing a collage based on fragments by Kafka. For director Johann Kresnik he wrote the libretto *Red Roses for You*, about Rosa (the Red) Luxemburg.[196]

Two of the later plays are actually double, even triple bills. The evening entitled *The Mass-Murderess and Her Friends* (1995) was a theatrical discourse on aging and the ludicrousness of dying.[197] It was comprised of a melancholy episode about the aging Don John, Dirty John, the notorious womanizer, now half blind and half deaf,[198] and, in the second part of the evening, a blithe playlet about the murderous career of Madame la Mort (a variation on Frau Death in *Mein Kampf*!), who slyly wriggles out of the electric chair.

The triple bill *The Last Night in September* (1997) — his "last play" though regrettably not his best[199] — is a kind of extended parting: aging Ernst bids his four wives farewell before he takes the lethal pill (actually he doesn't: nobody dies on the stage, says the stagehand who makes off with the pill). Survivors Dr. Grisby and Dr. Hollunder tear themselves away from their past as they shut their eyes to the suffering of the new victim of political malaise; finally, Tabori pays homage to Shakespeare and lets the curtain fall with the bard's bust illuminated on the forefront of the empty stage. While *Requiem for a Spy* (1993) draws on Tabori's experiences with the British Secret Service,[200] his *Weisman and Copperface* (1990) and *The Ballad of the Wiener Schnitzel* (1996; see chapter 14) take up a major topos of his theatre-making, namely, the dialectics of victim and victimizer. *Weisman and Copperface* (subtitled " A Jewish Western"), undoubtedly one of Tabori's finest plays, pits two subalterns, the Jew and the American Indian: two cantankerous pariahs squabbling about hegemony and justice, voicing rival claims to victimhood and vying over the monopoly on suffering in a play recalling cinematic topoi from *High Noon* to *Blazing Saddles*.[201]

"How can one be happy without trying too hard?" — a long-standing Tabori preoccupation he took up in such plays as *Sigmunds Freude* (1975)[202] — is the question underlying *Babylon Blues* ("The Babylon Schmaltz," in one of the earlier drafts) (1991),[203] a highbrow fun show — or as one critic put it, "an intellectual entertainment"[204] — scintillating at times, trite and full of platitudes at others. Structured along aleatory jazz principles, it is a kind of all-out jam session: Albert Einstein is delighted to have discovered the ultimate formula, Kafka dies contented in Milena's arms, Beckett's tramps are happy that Godot has finally come, Oedipus — not blind! — shrugs off his guilt feelings, Goethe and Schiller ruminate on success or failure, mentioning tennis stars Boris Becker and Steffi Graf. Supervising this brisk-paced flight of fancy — revue, requiem, and cabaret all in one — is Master Zvi, a wise Torah student ("Talmid Chacham"), sitting on the waters of Babylon with his dog, pondering the nature of happiness — Tabori's alter-ego (Tabori himself crossed the stage occasionally disguised as a stagehand). More than twenty anecdotal scenes make up this resourceful collage (admittedly, Tabori's favorite play), with quotations and malapropisms as well as references and parodied allusions to major works and seminal figures of Western civilization. The end finds the master sitting at the waters of Babylon, telling Jewish jokes in Hungarian: this too is a moment of happiness, simple, wise, comforting.

The jewel among the latter plays is, to my mind, *The Goldberg Variations* (1991), a text and a production (with the unforgettable duo Gert Voss and Ignaz Kirchner in the leading parts) that surely merit a detailed study far beyond the scope of this book.[205] *The Goldberg Variations*, an exemplary *mise-en-abyme*, is as it were the rehearsing process of a show (Tabori subtitled an early draft "A Rehearsal"[206]), a pastiche made up of various Old and New Testament episodes, from the Creation and the Fall in paradise through the sacrifice of Isaac and the Golden Calf to the Crucifixion. Director Mr. Jay (*J* for Jehovah? for Jesus? for "Jew" marked out by the Nazis? like the single-lettered Kafka protagonist K.? or an intertextual allusion to Tabori's own Jay Jay in *The 25th Hour*?) is in charge of the creation of the world and also the production,[207] and he is dissatisfied with both. Everything goes wrong. "Fail. Always fail. Fail again, fail better," Jay's assistant, Holocaust survivor Goldberg, cites Beckett. This congenial duo embodies the dyadic tension between theatre-makers, master and assistant, father and son, while echoing other couples, from slapstick masters Stan Laurel and Oliver Hardy to Beckett's tramps or Tabori's own pairs Weisman and Copperface or Shlomo Herzl and Hitler. *The Goldberg Variations* (Bach's composition accompanies the play) beautifully blends together philosophical deliberation ("God is dead — Nietzsche" is projected as epigraph to the performance, followed seconds later by "Nietzsche is dead — God"), biblical travesty (the rock band Hell's Angels is responsible for the worship of the Golden Calf), Judeo-Christian polemics, backstage comedy, and theatre argy-bargy. It is strewn with anecdotes, jokes, and strokes of wit ("Okay, man is not god, but what if

God is not God either?"), cut-and-thrust repartee, visual puns, and melancholy banter — a delicious *jeu d'esprit*. A mock-Passion brings the play/rehearsal to an end. Three crosses are erected (Mr. Jay: "Only two. The kid is bringing his own"); the lamb, a soft toy, is nailed to the cross; a terrible howl is heard. The crosses are lifted. "So, all over again. Curtain," exclaims Goldberg. The show can begin.

"There comes a point when one has to stop being an idiot savant," Tabori told an interviewer when he turned seventy-four.[208] He made up his mind to do theatre just one year longer, no more. That was in 1988. Since then he has been uninterruptedly involved in writing and directing plays, operas, and radio plays and has even been involved in filming.[209] His periodical announcement, usually on the eve of a new premiere, that this is the very last engagement is now taken with a smile. In recent years he has been showered with ovations and honors — he has relished it all. His many awards include the Mülheim Prize for Dramatists (twice, in 1983 and in 1990), the Josef Kainz Medal of the City of Vienna (1988), and the Peter Weiß Prize (Bochum 1991). No doubt Tabori's crowning glory was being the first non-German dramatist to receive the highly prestigious Georg Büchner Prize (Darmstadt, 10 October 1992).[210]

Well over eighty, no longer swift in his movements — "a camel with an upright gait"[211] — with a stroke and various operations behind him, Tabori is still full of ideas, insatiable curiosity, and his redeeming sense of humor. He still has a passion for chess, often playing, as Beckett did, against himself.[212] The weather- and life-beaten face, framed by the disheveled mane and the bushy sideburns, still radiates liveliness and warmth. A soft gaze emanates from his shrunken eyes when he smiles, and one is tempted to discern wisdom and benevolence in them. "You are old and young — Romeo and Methusalem / Occident and Orient / Joseph K. and Nathan the Wise," writes actress Hanna Schygulla in her portrait "Dear George." Like so many who met Tabori, she cannot hide being charmed by this cryptic man who seems to contain endless contradictions.[213]

Tabori speaks of old age with humor and self-irony. "Life is an incurable disease," he quips.[214] His London-based doctor, Barrington Cooper, points out his patient's composure in times of serious illness and an astonishing, incomprehensible anxiety about minor complaints.[215] Stoically aloof though fully conscious of his attentive audience, Tabori envisages (or perhaps it would be more appropriate to say stages) his own, ideal death — "like being born, only the other way round"[216] — and even imagines his (un-Jewish!) cremation. Shortly after his eighty-third birthday, in the summer of 1997, he launched his memoirs, devoting the first part to his family. His favorite autobiography is André Malraux's, because "he lied so well."[217] When we sat in his small habitual café in Vienna, facing each other yet very close because of his poor hearing, he conjured up stories and anecdotes, jumping from Hollywood to Vienna and back to Budapest, shuffling times and places. He sipped his black coffee slowly, with relish, and ordered another. "I never did sports. I smoke. And I drink lots of coffee," he said in his soft mumble. "I decided to live until the year 2000. It's a nice, round date." He smiled, amused at himself, almost like a capricious child. Then he looked at me and, like one who had come upon a revelation, said softly, "I have just found out, did you know, that Eörsi too is Jewish . . ."

*Now that, as Ronsard would sing,
I am old and gray and full of sleep,
I think I have earned the right to
celebrate the sanctity of life, which
I now find (it has not always been
so) more artful than art, more
theatrical than the theatre.*

George Tabori, "Unterammergau"

An ardent storyteller, Tabori sheds light on his approach to
the theatre through two childhood recollections. He was
three years old when he first visited the circus. The drums
rolled, a girl in tights climbed fifty feet up to a platform, and
he wet his pants. The artist then performed a *salto mortale*,
missed the cross bar, and crashed through the net. "For
many years I thought this was how it was meant to be each
performance" — the anticipation, the exciting show, the
highlight of the flying trapeze, and the impending crash;
"each night, to lie there in a puddle of blood and sand."[1]

Three years later Tabori paid his first visit to the theatre,
to see Edmond Rostand's *L'Aiglon*. The six-year-old in a
sailor suit was captivated by the "moment of magic" as the
houselights were dimmed and the curtain was slowly raised.
In the intermission, however, his father robbed him of several of his illusions. The production was awful, the high-
brow Hungarian said, then added sarcastically, "But don't
give up, son, the scenery may still collapse." Years later, Tabori would realize that his father's casual pronouncement
was a highly accurate description of the theatrical experi-

ence: "Catastrophic expectation as the essence of the performing arts; the silent assumption that in spite of all our best-laid plans, something will go wrong, that Othello may, in fact, strangle his lady."[2]

It is not the studiously preconceived and meticulously produced performance that Tabori has pursued all his life, but a theatrical experience which is densely intertwined with life, marked by its dynamic and absorbing nature. Spontaneity, experimentation, and inventiveness are its hallmarks, as well as a gambling with the fortuitous, the immediate, sensuous, and authentic. It is the "dangerous theatre" that Tabori has always advanced, maintaining that "if it be true theatre, it should operate without a net."[3]

WHAT MAKES THE THEATRE SICK?

Like his avant-garde contemporaries, Tabori has resisted the dominant modes of drama and the practice common in mainstream theatres. He was scarred when he came to Germany in 1969 to embark upon an extraordinary artistic journey. Having observed and personally experienced the ups and downs of theatre-making on and off Broadway, he was thoroughly disillusioned: "America is a sick country that has lost its innocence and must find a new identity," he maintained. And he explained that the American theatre system was badly structured and its aesthetic misconceived and overall depressing.[4]

Tabori's encounter with the German stage both as a spectator and as a director crushed some of the hopes he may have entertained while making his first steps in Germany at the end of the 1960s. In a letter he wrote to Rolf Michaelis, one of the leading theatre critics in Germany, he compared the American theatre to its German counterpart: "The difference between the American and German theatre can best be expressed, I feel, with a sexual metaphor: The American theatre is like a quick visit to a bordello, the German theatre is like a marriage. Both experiences have their charms and horrors."[5]

In the following years Tabori was to make further comparisons between the two theatre systems, each of which mirrored a very specific mentality. The absence of an overall judgment about the two national theatres is noteworthy, reflecting Tabori's impressionistic approach, which seems to be nurtured by changing attitudes and moods. On many occasions he praised the German theatre system as "the best thing Germany has to offer" or as "the best in the world," even if the price paid for this accomplishment was much too high.[6] At the same time, in a 1987 interview entitled "Why Does the German Theatre Make Us Sick, Mr. Tabori?" he diagnosed a series of pathological symptoms of the German stage, suggesting the superiority of the Anglo-American theatre, in which freedom and anarchy encourage experimentation and in which the actor is "the main thing."[7]

Indeed, it seems that the harsh criticism Tabori leveled against the American stage softened with age or with ongoing experience on the other side of the ocean. Ironically, it is none other than the German theatrical system which has served him as a negative paradigm, a model of the stagnant and ailing stage — reminiscent of Brook's Deadly Theatre — which he has indomitably challenged: "Most evenings at the theatre are 'unhappy' occasions, on account of their boredom, their vulgarity, or what is worse, their good taste. The old magic is gone."[8] The absence of magic, that magic which held him spellbound as a child, is, in his opinion, among the gravest symptoms of the malaise prevailing in the theatre. An avid theatregoer, Tabori found himself again and again confronted with productions devoid of imagination, liveliness, and human warmth. Ostentatious paraphernalia did not hide the hollow core of many productions; in fact, the trappings only made the hollowness more obvious. Ultimately, it was Tabori's direct engagement with the heavily subsidized official German theatre, which seemed willing to indulge all his whims, that afforded him a closer and more penetrating look into the ailing body. "These theatres are pathologized," he consequently argued; "people become sick or are already sick without knowing it."[9] Tabori was struck by the prevalence of alcoholism among actors, by the excessive frequency of physical indisposition, and by the high rate of accidents. He detected signs of lassitude, cynical resignation, or indifference among theatre professionals. Above all, he was alarmed by the disconcerting languor of the actor, who to his mind is and should be the soul of any theatre experience. In a letter he wrote to the artistic director of the Kammerspiele in Munich, he described what he had observed: "The average German actor . . . is lonely, isolated, unmotivated or even cynical. He is par excellence a burnt child . . . , whose main method of surviving the system is by falling sick."[10]

Tabori considers the institutional theatre system — "a late capitalist enterprise"[11] — responsible for this desolate state of affairs. In turn, this system itself is the product of a fundamentally erroneous approach to theatre-making, an approach firmly rooted in the German mentality, which he describes in his seminal essay "Hamlet in Blue" as being chronically and thoroughly diseased.[12]

The problem begins with the structure: the official theatre fosters a hierarchic, "feudal" order and stringent discipline.[13] The indisputable authoritative power of artistic managers and directors (*Intendanten*) leaves no room for the personal initiative of the actors, for their own imagination and free choice. "Discipline . . . may help to get a quick result, but it is a form of violation. Self-awareness is twisted into self-control," he asserts.[14] While concentrating on the production, directors neglect the actor, who is the prime factor in the theatre; striving for perfectionism, they attain an immaculate show, which is nonetheless a deplorable waste of energy. "Perfect theatre is dead theatre," claims Tabori. "Perfectionism is blasphemy. It was not given to us humans, maybe not even to God, to judge by the looks of the world."[15]

In fact, Tabori holds directors responsible for the undemocratic, strained, and inhumane atmosphere in the big theatres. He charges them with the cultivation of a personality cult and speaks of a "late capitalist directing mania,"[16] which is part and parcel of the prevailing mentality. Empowered by the system, most directors abuse their authoritative prerogative and act as if they were omniscient deities; they impose their views on the actors, order them around, and instrumentalize them. Under this category of "godfathers" (*Gott-Väter*), Tabori includes not only the ubiquitous director of any establishment theatre in Germany, but also enterprising figures like the late Fritz Kortner or Gustav Gründgens, the highly acclaimed Peter Stein, and even purveyors of new theatre modes like Ariane Mnouchkine.[17] While holding directors responsible for this pernicious overbearing attitude, Tabori does not ignore the servility and submissiveness of so many actors, who thereby support the abuse of directorial authority: "One must not ignore their [the actors'] fear of freedom. With all their brave talk of participatory democracy, they want Daddy to tell them *exactly* (their favourite word) what to do, why and how. They become frightened when one asks them to offer something of themselves."[18]

What all this amounts to is the lack of a truly innovative and experimental spirit in the theatre, the total absence of joy. Rehearsals are rarely taken as an opportunity to try things out (*Probe*, the German word for rehearsal, is related to *ausprobieren*, which means trying out), but as *repetition* in the "ghastly French sense." Working under harassing deadlines and the coercion to prove oneself successful, there is no time left for questions or the fruitful exchange of ideas, no room for exercises and improvisations. Naturally, there is no incentive for workshops like the exemplary Actors Studio, in which practical problems were mutually addressed and professional matters discussed at leisure.

Thus, German theatre is mainly concerned with extrinsic matters — the spectacular dimensions of a performance at the expense of the human spirit. Stage paraphernalia and an arsenal of tricks, gags, and sensational effects breed "a new monumentalism" which Tabori interprets as a sign of escapism: "The more beautiful the set, the greater the effects, the less interesting I find it"; he adds, "When I'm particularly paranoid, I'm reminded of the monumentalism of the convention at Nuremberg, which as a spectacle proved to be grandiose."[19]

During his first years of work with German actors, Tabori came to see a close connection between this adverse approach to the theatre and what he considers to be the German mentality. The obsessive concern with the external aspects of production stems, in his opinion, from the actors' inability or reluctance to focus inward and look right into themselves. It is likewise linked to the German fear of intimacy, the apprehension about emotions and passions. "'Emotion' is a dirty word around here," Tabori observes. "'Psychology' is another dirty word here, and 'therapy' makes some . . . fairly froth."[20]

The portrayal of German actors as an emotionally crippled lot is part of Tabori's elaborate discussion of what he calls the German mentality. This is surprising, if not paradoxical, for Tabori has gone out of his way to stress that all generalizations are by nature misleading, that it is wrong, for example, to speak of "The Germans." And yet, in "Hamlet in Blue" he offers an anamnesis of postwar German society. Adopting the well-known thesis of the Mitscherlichs about the inability of the Germans to mourn,[21] he carries the argument further. "What Mitscherlich [*sic*] has found in his countrymen is indifference, apathy, a compassion for themselves rather than for their victims. They would like to feel regret but do not quite know how. Their inability to grieve has escalated into a general inability — unwillingness that is — to feel."[22]

This emotional block, this paralysis of feeling, which Tabori defines as the "Hamletism of the Germans," goes hand in hand with the overrating of the intellect or rationalism and the celebration of impartiality (*Sachlichkeit*) over sensuality (*Sinnlichkeit*). Sensations are dull, emotions suppressed, "All [is] dead." The cultivation of the rational and cerebral promotes discipline and coercion, which in turn curtail the vitality of the theatre.

Even so, the German theatre system is just an illustrative instance, admittedly the most salient, of a civilization sick to the core. Tabori often depicts the maladies of modern society in his plays and deploys sickness metaphorically — as does Susan Sontag in her *Illness and Metaphor* — to describe the malaise of our civilization. There is "no cure for life, which is a miserable disease, and death is perhaps the only cessation of unhappiness." [23] This seemingly defeatist attitude runs like a leitmotif in Tabori's work. Sickness is perceived as an existential state, the *condition humaine*, and as such it embraces patients and doctors alike. "We are not the doctors, we are the disease," he fondly quotes Alexander Herzen.[24] Only by accepting sickness as a given can one maintain hope for improvement, an amelioration which can be only partial, of course. The wise and honest doctor is the one who offers no more than help for self-help. Under the heading "Consultation Hours" in his essay "Time to Play" ("Spiel und Zeit"), Tabori offers a metaphorical reflection on living and art, which, to his mind, are inseparable: "We are all sick, on both sides of the footlights, suffering from every disease in the book, especially affective atrophy and the schizoid lust for reification. Any cursory observation of theatre-makers or theatre-goers confirms the diagnosis." [25] Tabori points out the inclination to rationalize everything, the avoidance of genuine communication, the deep-seated suspicion toward proximity and human warmth, and the atrophy of the senses as the major symptoms of a cankerous civilization. His job — a "pretty hopeless one" — is to help people help themselves; as he puts it, "It is my Hippocratic task to thaw our sensorium by helping us to see, to hear, to smell, and to feel better." [26]

Uncompromising in his sober and critical scrutiny, fully aware of the hopelessness of his undertaking, Tabori sets out to challenge the malady "at home," in the theatre. His hope lies with the actor, "the last harbinger of Humanism," who, once restored to a pivotal position in theatre-making and liberated from all constraints, will bring about the long-overdue "radical Aristotelian purge," [27] affording the spectator insight into the collective and individual ailment. Tabori's theatre seeks a therapeutic shamanistic appeal, and as such it may be associated with major theatrical avant-garde experiments, which strive to create truly inspiring images and to challenge taboos and socially conditioned patterns of thought.[28] Tabori's venture leads him away from the inert and sluggish system and its institutional theatres — the "cathedrals" — to the "catacombs," from the monumental to the "poor theatre," from the abstract concept to the living actor. And he describes this adventure in a key passage in his essay "Unterammergau or the Good Germans" (July 1978):

> I was like Prospero, sick and tired of the tricks of magic, of snow-capped palaces of all the theatre-cathedrals; my way from then on was to the catacombs, i.e., funky little rooms where we might offer ourselves, at close quarters so that we might be seen precisely, not bigger and better than those looking at us; . . . What began to die for me that morning was not only the Hero and Heroine, the Great Mime, the Star and other Supermen or Women, but also eloquence, rhetoric, arias, points, elegant choreographies and arrangements, gorgeous sceneries; not the Poor Theatre (Grotowski was just another Magnificent Magician, with his Holy Brotherhood of Superactors, until he apparently discovered life), but the Difficult Theatre that is so simple to do, provided one is prepared to discover, without democratic bathos, the actor within every man, and find new ways to develop the skills of a *Mensch* [sic] rather than the tricks of the actor.[29]

EROS AND THE THEATRE

Tabori's aesthetic owes much to his years in America. His meeting with Bertolt Brecht, "a revolutionary thinker,"[30] in 1947 — as two European exiles in California — was decisive, prompting his shift from prose to drama. Elia Kazan's production of Tabori's stage debut *Flight into Egypt* (New York premiere in 1952) for the first time allowed him insight into practical stage-work and taught him, to his great surprise, that the production of a play can be endlessly more interesting than the play itself. His work as the translator or adapter of Brecht, his involvement with various troupes, mostly from the fringe, the professional experience he shared with his wife, actress Viveca Lindfors — all impressed on him the hardships and disappointments of theatre-making in the context of a commercialized mass-culture. It was in Lee Strasberg's renowned Actors Studio that he found an appropriate and compelling way, indeed a Method of making genuine and good theatre. Strasberg, both an innovator and a traditionalist, who tried to resolve the old dialectics of external and internal techniques by overcoming the gap between being and acting, between the actor and the role, was to become Tabori's prime mentor. Not only did he learn the secrets of the profession at the Actors Studio, he also came to understand the immense challenge of merging performance and reality into a unique moment of presence. In his obituary to "Dear Lee" Tabori acknowledges the enormous influence Strasberg — that "winking Jewish owl" — had on him: "You are always around me, treading on my toes, sniffing your notorious Nasaltics."[31]

No less weighty were Tabori's earlier experiences in Hollywood, both as a hired scriptwriter for the colossal film industry and as a perceptive observer of the extravagantly glamorous facade of the place he later named Necropolis. The central question which he was to ask himself time and again was what, if any, is the function of the theatre in an age of film, television, mass media? How is it possible, if at all, to create a genuine and meaningful performance in the face of what the Postmodernists call the "inauthenticity of representation"?[32]

In "Time to Play" Tabori delineates this essential dilemma, unaware of how closely he is treading on Postmodernist territory with its incredulity toward the narrative of scientific progress:[33] "In our computerized culture, which is able to reproduce mechanically all things from Mozart to the floating kidney, the theatre remains irreproducible and therefore unique, producing life rather than reproducing art; our last abode, perhaps, of applied humanism, where in the living labor of a play we may reveal our diminishing freedom to remain human and true to ourselves, not as pretty shadows in a cave, but as a three-dimensional presence exuding gall, sweat, and tears."[34]

The age of the worldwide electronic network, of reproducibility and perfectionism — that age which has seen a "democratization of taste," condemned by some, welcomed by others — calls for "a new aesthetic."[35] At the heart of his neo-Romantic aesthetic, Tabori reinstates the human being, "not the hero." And he goes further, insinuating the unique and obviously superior position of the theatre among the arts as the only form of creative engagement which breathes and secretes life. Instead of the inert or the reproducible,

Tabori — like other innovators such as Brook, Chaikin, or Richard Schechner — calls for the "presence" of the actor, who produces life instead of reproducing art. In both his essays and his practice, Tabori adamantly insists on unique, authentic experience as opposed to the fossilized work of art. The theatre is, notably, the place where the unique becomes manifest, every evening anew.

Singularity and presence are essential to Tabori's theatrics: no performance is an exact repetition, each show offers a variation on the theme, generating a new theatric experience and remolding reality. In the words of Antonin Artaud, each performance is "a kind of event" (*une sorte d'événement*).[36] The supremacy of the theatre lies in its being the only abode in which we can "freeze time and frame it into an immortal Now that is never out of joint."[37]

The theatre has no place, no justification, in a highly mechanized age, in times of "outrageous crimes and deafness," unless it addresses itself consciously to the recipients, seeking to explore the human, and emanates humanism. Tabori underscores his view by quoting Alexander Pope's famous verse, "The proper study of mankind is Man,"[38] though study, as he understands it, is never abstract, always concrete and daring. Like Brook, he believes that one cannot act ideas, a claim which in turn brings to mind Artaud's directive that "metaphysics must be made to enter the mind through the body."[39] For Tabori, this indefatigable, never-ending quest for truth, or, to be more precise, "the truths" in human beings, is the only object of art.[40]

Sweeping away the concept of "art for art's sake," Tabori states: "Acting, as in Hamlet's great monologue, is a synonym for Being, and Being is an affirmation of the self."[41] Genuine acting is never an imitation of life, but an extension of life — "not another country, but, say, an extension of the bathroom,"[42] — and it is in fact the actor's business to bridge the growing gap between art and life. The actor creates not a sterile illusion of realism, but a pulsating presence adhering to its own immanent laws, marked by spontaneity and authenticity. Drawing on the parallels between Frederick Perls's *Gestalt*-technique and the ideal working method of the actor, Tabori maintains that at the end of such an honest quest for truth(s), at the end of the long journey inward, "one may find that being and playing, self and role, life and art, are opposites to be unified in a pattern or *Gestalt*."[43]

It was by no means an ingratiating gesture that Tabori entitled his Büchner Prize acceptance speech "This Embarrassing Word: Love."[44] The 78-year-old recipient of the prestigious prize reassessed his life and long history in the theatre in terms of love. Love had always been his main concern, he said, and what he did professionally was comparable to an act of love — the act, like the notion, encompassing a variety of sensations and affections ranging from longing and jealousy to hatred and violence.

Indeed, Tabori's vision of theatre-making is wanting if one overlooks the seminal role Eros plays in it. "Theatre-making should be pure Eros. It should be life-affirming . . . I mean, the life instinct instead of taking on all this necrophilia."[45] Not only is the theatre experience, like every act of love, a manifestation of humanity, but as in love-making any attempt to fake it, pretend, or simulate is bound to be exposed sooner or later. "Don't play-act" (*mach kein Theater*) is Tabori's maxim, along with "everything is allowed." A good rehearsal or a genuine performance, like sexual intercourse, cannot be repeated because it is carried out or, better, happens "as if each act were done for the first time."[46] Structured like good coitus, it opens with a prologue, leading to intensification, to the climax, and finally to the coda.[47] Genuine involvement in love as in theatre-making entails a willingness to risk all, to forgo invulnerability. It likewise requires free rein of the imagination, promoting unconstrained involvement and dissolving the disparity between being and acting.

Moreover, Tabori's Eros-suffused theatre accentuates the sensory and sensuous aspects of performance: it advocates the reactivation of the body and the sensitization of the skin and the senses, it presses for the exciting exploration of nonverbal communication, of a mute but pulsating proximity. All this implies, of course, utmost dedication and a high degree of concentration, the willingness to expose oneself and give of oneself even at the price of vulnerability and pain. It brings to mind Jerzy Grotowski's call for the unconditional involvement, the self-sacrifice of the "holy actor."

Tabori's actor, like a lover, strips naked, figuratively and in many productions literally too — a demonstration of human power *and* helplessness. As with the Living Theatre and other avant-garde experiments, nudity is also a form of protest, an affront to repressive taboos, and, in the words of Tabori, "the act of tearing off the figleaf." Indeed, "true art or true love is apocalyptic, the shameless revelation of that which is prohibited, which is between the thighs, where truth lies, in contrast to the lie, the figleaf." [48]

The genuine actor is an honest provocateur, a sorcerer who persistently tries to tickle out whatever has been repressed or concealed. The theatre Tabori believes in is one dedicated to the pursuit of truth, to the exploration of the self and of human relationships: "The truth is a 'tiger wrapp'd in a player's hide,' or less fancifully, it is pain, frequently unbearable pain. To this beast, this pain, I must say Yes, and the stage is one good place for saying it." [49]

DEMOCRACY AND RESPECT IN THE THEATRE

Tabori's focus on the actor goes hand in hand with his plea for a "poor theatre." Well acquainted with the work and writing of major theatrical innovators, he indeed refers to Grotowski's famous maxim as well as to Brook's "empty stage." [50] Opting for the "catacombs," Tabori signals his preference for a spatial arrangement which accords with the demands of the theatrical event and produces a direct and immediate physical impact — a circus tent, an abandoned plant, a workshop studio. [51] It is the bare stage, free of signifiers, uncircumscribed, which offers the ideal space for experimentation. A great admirer of Shakespearean theatre, Tabori extols the "wooden O," the *platea*, with its reliance on and appeal to the imagination; quoting Shakespeare's contemporary Lope de Vega, he defines his ideal stage as "two boards and a passion." Whenever there are scenery or props, they are used sparingly, never as decorative elements, always as signifiers in relationship to the actor using them. Tabori does not create artefact-spaces (*Kunsträume*), as Rolf Ronzier points out, [52] but tries to establish real spatial arrangements utilizing real and elementary materials: scaffolds, a bed, a table, sand.

Ideally, the necessary set and costumes would emerge in the course of working on a production, as an integral component of the performance. Such was the case in most productions at Tabori's Theaterlabor in Bremen, where the actors and those who were assigned responsibility for stage design worked as a team. Underlying this decision-making process was Tabori's belief in the urgent need to democratize the theatre on every possible level. This is an ideal he always sought to realize, particularly whenever he was given the opportunity of running his own theatre, the lab in Bremen or, later, his Kreis in Vienna. Admittedly, Tabori chose the name Kreis, or the Circle, because it is "the most democratic form; because it is spatial, non-hierarchical, and every person is equidistant from the others. The circle is also something like an embrace, and yet open." [53] Seeking to eliminate the crippling hierarchy obsessed by the compulsion to produce, he encouraged the exchange of ideas and delegated responsibility to each and every member of the group. Even though theatre-making was not a collective ritual, as it had been in the Living Theatre, Tabori advocated joint experimentation and personal initiative. Intensive ensemble work (such as he saw and admired in the Berliner Ensemble, such as Stanislavsky cultivated much earlier) was, in his opinion, the only theatre form that could be meaningful in an age in which "the star is dead."

"The Hero is dead, and the Star is dead, because people will no longer tolerate such presumption to pseudo-divinity, acting out fairy tales." [54] Tabori experimented with collage productions because this seemed to be the ideal mode for teamwork, in which all these actors could nonetheless assert themselves, fulfill their ego needs, and relish their own solo performances. "A group, to me, is not a closed cell or a sect united by solidarities issuing from substance and context, but a living organism based on respect — in the original sense of the word, i.e., a learning experience in which each must develop the ability to truly look and listen." [55] Not surprisingly, Tabori occasionally refers to free jazz as a model for his idea of inspired and inspiring theatre work: a team collaborates without the control of an authoritarian director; one of the players begins, the others listen, accompany, or answer with a counterpoint; another member picks up the tune and improvises; solo parts and ensemble sections are intertwined.

Tabori's defiance of the supreme position of the director is strikingly rebellious, especially when measured against the German theatrical tradition. "The German word *Regisseur* [director] reminds me of *Regime* and *Regierung* [government]. I'm not a *Regisseur*. I call myself a playmaker [*Spielmacher*]," he explains. Rejecting the role of the "godfatherly," all-knowing, and bossy director, ubiquitous in the "cathedrals," he considers the director *primus inter pares*; at best a coach, whose role is to create a conducive working atmosphere in which the actor can transpose the "energy of fear" into creative energy.[56] Tabori's understanding of the director's role is radical, even in comparison to prominent revolutionaries such as Grotowski or

Brook in his later phase. A director, he argues, can best help the actor by indirection, and minimal intervention or guidance should be the norm.

During rehearsals, Tabori was often inclined to sit apart and silently observe the actors scrambling to find their way in the maze, attempting to mold the performance. Occasionally he would interject a comment, always in a gentle and quiet voice, almost like one unsure of his right to intrude or offer his opinion. Gundula Ohngemach, who participated in one of his experimental Beckett productions and later observed the rehearsals of *Jubilee*, believes that Tabori conducts his work with the actors in the spirit of the principle *primum non nocere* — don't hurt anyone.[57] "Use it" and "do as you like" are Tabori's favorite, minimalistic, stage directives. His intention is, unmistakably, to stimulate the actors to try things out, to seek a possible answer on their own rather than look up to the director for a redemptive formula. He animates and encourages them never to give up, to try other avenues by improvising or adopting a radical perspective such as a "nonsense reading" of a text. Occasionally he would suggest a basic physical gesture to serve as a catalyst for improvisation.

Not surprisingly, many actors who have worked with Tabori express embarrassment, disagreement, or frustration with his newfangled approach to directing. Theatre professional Gisela Stein, who worked with him in the early 1970s, approached his publisher, Maria Sommer, with tears in her eyes. Stein unleashed her anger and frustration: "I can't work with such a man, the things he demands from me, 'touch me,' 'heal me,' this is all alien to me and I don't want it. A director must tell me: 'take the glass this way and drink that way' — the rest I do myself."[58]

Fifteen years later, again working with Tabori, Gisela Stein came to appreciate his discreet and hesitant way of "directing," the immense freedom he allows his actors. Similar expressions come from other stage veterans who, having worked with authoritarian directors, were puzzled by Tabori's permissive directorial strategy. Thomas Holtzmann, Vladimir in Tabori's highly acclaimed *Waiting for Godot*, recounts how Tabori sat aside, always with gaping eyes, "embarrassingly afraid of us," and hardly intervened. Holtzmann's assessment some years later: "We [the actors] actually arranged the proceedings by ourselves." Hanna Schygulla describes having to accustom herself to Tabori's unique way of directing when she played the leading part in *My Mother's Courage*, how perplexed she was by the vocabulary of pregnancy and childbirth he used to describe the creative theatrical process.[59] It was the way he let "the imagination work, like a muscle," which she particularly came to cherish, because it widened the scope of her own imaginative incentive. A similar comment is made by Gert Voss, Tabori's leading male actor in recent years: "George is basically no director in the usual theatre sense, but an animator, or animatus, who kindles and liberates the actors' imagination. I think there is no quality more beautiful and courageous in any theatre-man. In his rehearsals there is never the anxiety of having to prove oneself. He stimulates one to seek, not to produce results."[60]

Even more ambivalent are the reactions of novices who worked with Tabori. Many admit to having been skeptical at first, puzzled by the absence of a directing hand, perturbed by the unexpected freedom they did not know how to use. Much of the training and technical skills they had acquired proved inexpedient, even cumbersome. They had to overcome their own resistance to Tabori's psychotherapeutically oriented method and to learn to withstand the criticism of their colleagues. In retrospect, most of these actors speak positively about their experiences with Tabori, and for some it certainly was a professional turning point, an irrevocable break from traditional working habits. Tabori opened the actors' eyes to the environment and sensitized them; he brought home to many the values of honesty and authenticity; he imbued them with the gusto and excitement of open-ended exploration; he convinced them that introspection was a prerequisite for and a part of theatre work. Perhaps his most important contribution to them — as human beings and as actors — was helping them gain confidence in themselves.

Some critics have accused Tabori of playing the guru or inspiring mystical reverence, accusations which, ironically, echo criticisms leveled against Tabori's mentor, Strasberg.[61] Others, like director Claus Peymann, described Tabori as "a tyrant of the first order," whose "gentle method" is but a deceptive strategy.[62] For Tabori, who deems the title director a misnomer, rehearsing a play with a group of actors — preferably a steady troupe — is a dynamic and organic process of creation or "writing with other means."[63] The script he brings along — at times merely notes, fragments, or a list of episodes — is considered the starting point for a collective quest, a work-in-progress. Like other theatre innovators, Tabori too champions the belief that the process of producing is much more important than the final product. Indeed, the close collaboration with the actors, which produces its own dynamics, accounts for the numerous versions of many of Tabori's plays.

Among the various delineations of the director's role scattered throughout his writings, one is of particular interest. It coincides with the launching of his own theatre Der Kreis in Vienna in 1987. Tabori defines the role of the director/manager in the following words: "An artistic director of a Circle guides, does not direct; he tries to be an attentive listener/observer, perhaps a tour guide with a map, who tries to accompany the others through the dark wood toward the light." [64] The emphasis lies on accompanying, or coaching, and Tabori deliberately uses the word "try" to indicate that he is by no means sure that his path is the decisive or correct one.

Thus, the director's primary role is to coach attentively, never to demonstrate by setting an example for imitation, [65] let alone to tame the actors like an animal-trainer or enforce an interpretation on them. Tabori's redefinition of the director's role owes a great deal to his close observation of Strasberg's work at the Studio. It also marks his attempt to conflate theatre-making and psychotherapeutic techniques, especially along the lines of Jacob Moreno's psychodrama and Perls's *Gestalt*-therapy. Over and above all, it attests to his great respect for the actors and their artistic profession. "Raping actors who have different ideas is morally questionable," he asserts. "One should not treat actors like children or idiots." [66]

THE ACTOR IS THE CONCEPT

Stripping away all the conventional elements and gags not vitally necessary for a performance, and minimizing directorial intervention, Tabori entrusts the performance to the actor. This is his understanding of Lope de Vega's image of "two boards and a passion": the passion does not depend on external stimuli such as a given text, but solely on the actor. "Texts are silent, they need a voice, our voice, all voices imply disloyalty to texts other than their own," Tabori declares, redirecting attention to the speaker rather than to what is said. [67] His celebrated premise — less original in content than in its rigorous application — is that the actor is both producer and product. Moreover: "The actor is more 'interesting' than the role he plays, producing more productive than the product." [68]

In his essays Tabori expounds these principles, echoing other theatre avant-gardists. The actor is first and foremost a human being, obliged to the existential imperative of being true to himself or herself. The ultimate goal of a genuine actor is not to slip into a role or be submerged in the other, but to own up to individual humanity. The key to acting, to being, lies *ipso facto* with the actor. Tabori adopts Strasberg's image of the actor being an instrument. "The actor is his own piano," he says in his introduction to the German edition of Strasberg's *A Dream of Passion*. The actor's reality — experiences, dreams and passions, the conscious and the subconscious — are the source of theatrical creativity. Everything within the self is fit for use, and only that which one "is" should be employed.[69]

The encounter with the secret recesses of the self makes the actor aware of the wide scope of human experience and of latent potential. The actor becomes aware of the difficulties, even neuroses, which, once acknowledged, can fuel one's self-presentation within the framework of the role. Instead of following Stanislavsky's dictum that the actor should identify with the role, Tabori approaches the role from the opposite venue: the role should slip into the actor, allowing greater scope for self-expression: "Every person has elements of the role in him, and these are to be discovered."[70] Tabori's admiration for Brecht does not inhibit or bar him from speaking against the principle which advises the actor to maintain a distance from the role.

The pivotal and autonomous position of the actor entails dismissing any thought of using the actor as a vehicle or medium to transmit a message. The role is subordinated to the idiosyncrasies of the actor, and the success of the presentation (not representation) depends on the authenticity of the performer. In Tabori's words, "For me, Mr. Schmidt in the group, if one approaches him correctly, is more interesting than Hamlet, because he is ever so much more variable. Hamlet is final, completed, and cannot be altered. There is simply much more in a human being than there is in a role."[71]

Acting then is a higher, more crystallized form of being; the theatre, as with Grotowski or Brook, is a terrain of self-discovery, and rehearsing is always a fresh encounter with the subliminal, a never-ending exploration of the body as a source of expressiveness. Tabori underpins his precepts with fine lexical nuances. He prefers the English "to act" to the German *schauspielen*, since the latter connotes pretending; for rehearsal, he prefers the German *Probe*, which suggests testing or trying out, rather than the French *répétition*. In fact, the idea of rehearsing anything is arguably out of place in his theatrics, as theatre work is perceived as an ongoing learning process, in which the actor continuously examines technical skills, reassesses the "magic box of tricks," and seeks to further develop and improve through permanent training, like a musician or a dancer. The particular text, or the traditional role, is thus only another stimulus, a catalyst for exploration. Tabori urges the actors, as Brecht did, to always start at "point zero,"[72] to relate to the given and to master the environment creatively, to be simultaneously introspective and attentive to one's fellow actors. Since it is the actor who "is the concept," any preconceived interpretation should be discarded and all dogmas met with resistance. The actor becomes, as in Strasberg's Studio, "best judge" or codirector.[73] Furthermore, Tabori insinuates that it is vital to question matters and reconsider solutions unremittingly, to allow for the dynamic process of experimentation and shaping to go on. "It begins with chaos . . . an empty stage," he states. "The more one binds oneself conceptually, the more one blocks the creativity of the actor. . . . In the course of the work, other matters turn up and blow up the concept."[74] A production is thus a work-in-progress, which does not end with the premiere, as the first night is merely a public rehearsal. Work goes on after the critics have passed judgment, and the performance, being a singular and authentic experience, is continuously revised and reshaped.

SMELLING WITH THE EYES,
LISTENING WITH THE NOSE

A key notion in Tabori's theatrics is that of pinching (*kneifen*): it suggests the presence of the actor, utmost concentration at any given moment. "The pinch is my alphabet, the beginning of a syntax," Tabori writes.[75] The roots of this key notion go back to an unforgettable experience of adolescence, a summer afternoon in a pine forest, where Tabori tasted the first intimations of erotic love. "It is like a dream," he reminisces, "and I pinch myself, as peasant-wisdom will have it, to come alive, to myself, with a sense of reality never felt before." Pinching signifies the heightened awareness of a compelling moment, "the cue for living or coming alive through an experience of pain without which there can be no pleasure,"[76] the wish to arrest a unique moment. The emphasis is not on intellectual cognition, but on sensory perception. Here indeed we hit upon an essential element in Tabori's *Weltanschauung*, to which I alluded before. According to Tabori, one of the severest problems of modern civilization and its theatre — and here the German theatre sets a prime example — is its insensitivity, sensory numbness, and, consequently, emotional atrophy. Overrationalization and emotional torpor are accompanied by resentment and disregard of the body, of all that is corporeal and sensory. Impartiality (*Sachlichkeit*) is celebrated at the expense of sensuality (*Sinnlichkeit*). The remedy lies in resensitization, and it is the responsibility of the director, "that would-be doctor," to help the actor recover and resuscitate the senses and reactivate them, to assist in breaking up physical and emotional rigidity. Tabori relates this to "pinching" and speaks of "smelling with my eyes, listening with my nose, seeing with my ears, waking up from the non-life we call living and presence, not in the past or the future, but in the presence."

The prerequisite for resensitization is a radical change of attitude: the actor must realize the value of sensory knowledge, the advantages of visceral truth over elaborate reasoning. Practical training comprises a variety of exercises ranging from Strasberg's Method, via Richard Boleslavsky and Yevgeny Vakhtangov, back to Stanislavsky's System. Along with relaxation and concentration exercises, which are the essentials of the warm-up procedure, Tabori introduces various exercises which refamiliarize the performer with each part of the body, helping to explore kinetic energy. Then come breathing exercises, diverse sensory exercises with objects as stimuli, and exercises destined to expand the actor's sensual imagination and creative associations. Besides individually oriented exercises, there are also interactive games which sensitize the actors to their partners or to the spatial environment. And there is, of course, intensive work with "affective memory," with sensory recall techniques, designed to stimulate the actor's body and mental awareness through recollected sensations and emotions — which, according to Strasberg, secured the vitality and verisimilitude of the performance.

For Tabori, remembering always means recollecting a tactile perception. That truth which is viscerally felt or intuitively surmised is rarely misleading. And yet it would be wrong to accuse Tabori, as some have done, of wallowing in emotions, cultivating private whims, or indulging in fetishism. For him the dissociation of the rational from the irrational, of the thought from the felt, is artificial and wrong; not unlike T. S. Eliot's rejection of the "dissociation of sensibility," he maintains that feelings "are merely strong thoughts."[77]

Along with the reanimation of the senses and the discovery of kinetic energy, Tabori also incites the actor to acknowledge and assimilate the irrational, "which is part of each one of us."[78] Seconding Artaud's appeal for irrational spontaneity and the release of repressed urges, he encourages the actor to give vent to innermost drives and to resist mendacious sociocultural norms. Acting then has a therapeutic effect; in Tabori's words: "Theatre and acting are a form of therapy."[79] As baring wounds allows them to heal, so the painful process of self-discovery brings hope. The goal is twofold: to heal the actor-patient from the maladies of repressive conventions and to restore performance to its original form as an uncurbed and direct act of creativity.

No wonder, then, that Tabori's writing and practical work at the theatre abound with references to prominent therapists, from Freud to Jacob Moreno to Wilhelm Reich and Frederick (Fritz) Perls. Though at times he has made extensive use of therapeutic techniques — particularly during his experimental phase in Bremen and Munich — Tabori has always considered psychotherapy a means and not an end in itself.

The kinship between theatre and therapy is ancient, he maintains, and he claims that the catharsis principle of the Greeks had "a therapeutic effect on the public and most certainly on the actor." Moreover, Stanislavsky's psycho-technique had much in common with practical therapy, while therapists like Freud, Moreno, or Perls availed themselves of theatrical modes.[80] Seeking to enable the actor to act out inhibitions and fears, that which has been subdued and repressed, Tabori deploys elements from therapeutic techniques, modified and upended, in his theatre work. The underlying principle is that of "role potential," which enables the patient/protagonist to act out the conflicting aspects of the self, the "auxiliary egos," thereby exploring and releasing long-repressed drives which had drained psychic energy. This procedure was essential to Moreno's group psychotherapy, known as psychodrama, in the 1920s and was also a distinct feature of Perls's *Gestalt*-therapy. Whereas Moreno defined the role of the individual in relationship to the group and developed a methodology for social psychology (sociometry), Perls's holistic approach had a pronounced existential bent. Conducted within group sessions, the therapy progressed primarily along individual lines. The therapist, following the principle of "selective authenticity," monitored the patient to uncover and act out those "unfinished matters" (*unerledigte Geschäfte*) of the past, which impede the gratification of needs and desires in the present. The technique emphasizes direct and subjective expression or presentation, body language, and mimicry. Likewise, the dream-work of *Gestalt*-therapy leads the protagonist to identify with diverse dream elements, including animate and inanimate objects, in the hope of unearthing the repressed.

Exposed to *Gestalt*-therapy in its heyday in the United States of the 1960s, Tabori was apparently attracted by its emphasis on the existential "here and now"; by the wholeness and immediacy of experience (dissolving the dichotomy between body and soul and considering "being" as process); by phenomenological rather than causal thinking. Last but not least, he was indubitably drawn by the theatrical aspects of this therapeutic method.

Through verbal and nonverbal improvisations and the vivid acting out of sensations and conflicts, in the footsteps of these therapists, Tabori sought to heighten the actor's awareness and to gain an accurate perception of inner and outer events. Rather than monitoring the actor authoritatively as Perls did, Tabori assists the actor in discovering and working through conflicts, to articulate inhibitions and anxieties, and he encourages the actor to explore unknown inner territories sensitively and actively, to experience past events by making the past vividly present. "Perls tries to guide us to the centre, where the fragments of the Self may be united in a whole," Tabori writes in his article "Why Fritz?"[81] His own approach may best be described as a process of breaking down the self, or deconstructing, so as to reconstruct or recontextualize it as a healthy creative whole.

When asked how acting and being can be intertwined organically, Tabori answered by pointing out the need to avoid the "hole" (*Loch*). The rift can be avoided by pursuing the middle (*die Mitte*). The best explanation of what it means to act from the middle is formulated, as so often with Tabori, impressionistically, in broad and somewhat vague terms. Acting from the middle is closely related to Perls's technique:

> Like an ideal director, Perls prompts his patient, the actor, to find himself so as to recognize the connection between being and acting, the authentic, namely, as well as the phony, or whatever else

you may call it — and somehow get to the middle. This sounds odd, but concretely it is like this: the actor either functions from the middle or what he does is wrong. If you do not tune a Stradivarius, it will be off-key. Getting to the middle — which technically means using whatever it is, voice training, or body exercises — is itself the challenge, which is often approached anarchically or amateurishly. The means are beyond any aesthetic or style, whether it be Kabuki or theatre-making with Bob Wilson or Claus Peymann. If that which the actor does is wrong, then only external, technical, mechanical means are being deployed. This is unsatisfactory: one feels that it is fake and strained. [82]

The "middle" is perhaps best understood simply as the authentic, a pivotal concept which lies at the heart of Tabori's theatrics, as Ursula Höpfner has noted.[83] Notably, Tabori's elucidation of this key concept, authenticity, is likewise vague and unsatisfactory. A precise and unequivocal definition is strikingly missing, even though Höpfner pressed her interlocutor and husband against the wall and refused to let go. In the absence of a clear-cut definition of authenticity, the best one can do is to locate it as the "middle" between freedom and structure, the delicate balance, so to speak, between spontaneity and constraint, which are dialectically vital for an imaginative and genuine performance. In other words, the point is to reject chaos, simplification, and sentimentalization on the one hand and to beware of formalism and restrictive conventions on the other; to weld together Apollonian decorum with Dionysian vitality.

THE AUDIENCE

"The theatre is the only art form which cannot exist without the presence of an audience," states Tabori.[84] Despite his paramount concern for the actor as the soul of the performance, Tabori makes it clear that in his theatrics creative exploration cannot be sustained without the presence, at one point or another, of spectators. Like many avant-garde directors, he seeks to break down the standard physical separation between performers and spectators, preferring the "catacombs" to the "cathedrals" because of the immanent proximity. Tabori attributes the conventional separation of stage and auditorium partly to the anachronistic architecture of the nineteenth century, which entertained "feudal relationships," and partly to the modern malady with its dread of the intimate and the direct. If the theatre is to remain alive and lively, it must serve society by serving itself, namely, in "setting the lively actor and attentive spectator at the center of a common experience," and this can only be accomplished when the gap between the audience and the stage is bridged.[85]

Tabori has adamantly stood (particularly during his experimental phase) for the elimination of the spatial frontiers between stage and audience, and he has given credit to the audience for being the "co-author" of the theatrical enterprise.[86] Nevertheless, he never went as far as some avant-garde groups such as the Living Theatre or the Performance Group, which turned the performance into a Happening, calling for an unreserved involvement of spectators.

Tabori's attitude to the audience, like his attitude to the actor, is marked by great respect and high regard. In his opinion, spectators are often abused, manipulated, or ignored by theatre professionals. At the same time, he recognizes in contemporary humankind, overwhelmed by electronic media, an innate need for participation and involvement. This longing to take part in the performance, to be in the act — an impulse which goes back to the ritualistic origins of drama — is evident in the astounding popularity of talk shows and game shows on radio or television. The theatre is unique in that it is the only medium in which a real-life meeting can take place. The premise underlying such an encounter is the equal status of the participants, actors, and spectators, as autonomous and free-thinking beings.

In his unpublished notes to *Sigmunds Freude*, one of his more radical experiments, Tabori describes the desired approach to spectators. They are participants in the show who, seated in a comfortable and relaxed manner — unlike the formal and detached seating arrangements in commercial theatres — should enjoy the atmosphere of "a party, a feast." "We must treat our spectators not as dodos, schoolboys, or *Scheißbürger*, but as playmates in a great kindergarten. Our grand gesture to them should be what the French call 'the courtesy of the heart,' to keep a balance between distance and intimacy."

The key to the rapport between audience and actors seems to me to be in finding the "middle," as in the dialectic tension that marks authentic acting. However, Tabori leaves this issue undefined, even more obscure, in fact, than the question of the actor's authenticity. His remarks about the audience are few and far between, and his actual productions dispense with the idea of the spectator as co-author and active participant, particularly as his productions become less experimental and as he is lured back to the "cathedrals" in later years. It is hardly surprising, then, to find most of the innovative and unorthodox remarks concerning the role of the audience in his earlier writing. It is there that he rules out those passive onlookers who remain aloof as they watch the show. Even though the element of fun and entertainment is significant, Tabori aims, like Brecht, to awaken the concern and involvement of the spectator. While Brecht sought to sharpen the audience's social and political awareness, Tabori, "never working with a raised forefinger,"[87] hopes to provoke each spectator to turn the perspective inward, to contemplate psychological and existential issues.

"In order to change the spectator's consciousness, one must allow him to participate in the process of discovery-making, i.e. the experience of sharing the newness of a moment," he maintains in his essay "Hamlet in Blue." The ideal production would be one in which the situation remained unresolved; all questions posed but hardly any answered. In such presentations (in the works of Beckett or Gertrude Stein, for instance) spectators "have the chance not to be consumers of goods and beauty, but co-authors."[88] The role of the spectator as coauthor lies in the continuous feedback to the actor. The spectator's response stimulates the performer and accounts for the impulse to change and reshape the performance. Spectators should ideally return to the theatre night after night, to examine themselves, as do the actors on the stage who play Vladimir and Estragon: "as long as we turn up at an agreed-upon hour, night after night, we are saved; if not, we shall be punished. That is Christian dramaturgy: life waits, that life should begin after it has come to an end."[89]

Tabori readily admits that like most theatre professionals he knows frustratingly little about who the audience really is — "that ignorance which is veiled by subsidies."[90] He refrains from talking about the ideal spectator and considers the audience to be a cross section of society that suffers the maladies of modernity, primarily overrationalization and insensitivity. "The people whom we serve are more sick than vicious,"[91] he asserts, recommending warm-ups for them too, to alleviate their inner tension and to free them from the shackles of social constraints. The audience also must be sensitized, coached to tap inner resources and to respond perceptively. While Tabori, like Brecht, seeks to engage the spectator intellectually, his primary objective is to engage the spectator through the senses, "the skin, the guts, and the genitals as well,"[92] and emotionally. The quest for a lively and sensual response from the audience parallels the call upon the actor to experience through the senses rather than cultivating argumentative logic.

The therapeutic powers of the theatre naturally apply to the audience as well as to the actor. In his early piece "On the Goodness of Theatre," written in 1966 upon the inauguration of the experimental Berkshire Theater Festival in the United States, Tabori elucidates his belief in the shamanistic appeal of the theatre, a conviction he shares with other avant-garde theatre-makers. "A good audience is a brave one," he writes. "It is willing to look into the mirror we would hold up to it, a mirror which, by the rules of our art, does not flatter nor confirm the world's delusions, but magnifies and thus exposes them. It takes courage to look into such a mirror, and still hope. Since the Greeks, the theatre has been our great healer, our great teacher, and what may amount to the same thing, our great clown."[93]

Hamlet's way out of the infinite vexation that led to depression and paralysis is through acting. It is the play-within-the-play that finally prompts him to act. For Tabori, "the mystery of Hamlet's metamorphosis is also ours,"[94] and just like Shakespeare's protagonist, any spectator can be incited into action through performance. Recognizing psychological difficulties and social malaise is an imperative precondition for the release of tension that has accumulated in the spectator/patient. "We need a radical Aristotelian purge," Tabori maintains,[95] yet he does not interpret the purgatory appeal of performance in terms of the cardinal notions of pity and fear. Rather, his formula for catharsis is composed of heightened sensitivity and genuine concern. The accent is on the engagement of all the individual spectators, their awareness that what they perceive or feel concerns them no less than the actor. In this cathartic outlet, an amalgamation of "the celestial and the excremental,"[96] lies the redemptive power of the theatre, the hope for the betterment of the human condition.

It is not the product but the process of producing which matters most in the theatre. This maxim, which Tabori borrows from Strasberg, points to the quintessence of his theatrics. The never-ending, inventive pursuit that conflates theatrical experimentation with the keen exploration of the human psyche is fueled by hope on the one hand and the awareness of inevitable failure on the other hand. Drawing upon Jean-Paul Sartre's idea that failure is part of our existential condition, Tabori's alter-ego, assistant-director Goldberg in *The Goldberg Variations*, describes the essence of theatre-making as "failing, always failing, yet again failing, failing better."

A THEORY?

It would be both wrong and misleading to propose that Tabori's views on the theatre in the age of reproducibility, on theatre-making as work-in-progress, on the actor as the soul or "concept" of performance, or on the creative process as the dialectic of spontaneity and structure — that all these ideas amount to a theory or a method. Tabori himself has never claimed to have anything as formal or structured as that.[97] On the contrary, as a latecomer to the art of the stage who had no systematic training, he has always been cautious and unassuming when it comes to evaluating his own work. His respect and high esteem for the actor is doubtless linked to his sense that acting is "an autonomous profession."[98] And he readily admitted to Maria Sommer that he realized how complex and demanding acting was only when he "dilettantely" took upon himself the role of Lobkowitz at the premiere of his own *Mein Kampf* in 1987. "Now I know how difficult it is to do the simple, how easy the difficult can be if it is approached appropriately," he acknowledged.[99] Similarly, he played down his accomplishments as a director: "I am an apprentice, yes, without any coquetry . . . I am slow on the uptake, from a literary and artistic point of view, I'm actually thirty years younger than all the people my factual age."[100]

But there is a more substantial reason why a Tabori theory is untenable. A master of impressionistic and anecdotal writing, Tabori has always doubted the relevance and validity of dogmatic or abstract stipulations and has consciously eschewed anything that sounds too comfortable with itself, formulaic, or normative. Speaking of "Master Brecht," to whom he is closer in spirit as dramatist than as director, he insinuates that "like all great theoreticians, he did not always take his own theories seriously,"[101] thereby owning up to his own predilection for paradox. All prescriptive methods are short-lived;

modes and fashions are ephemeral; even "the avant-garde, well-digested by the Establishment, has become middle-aged." [102]

Theories and prescriptions go against the grain of the creative process and impede personal and individual development — on this point Tabori agrees with seminal innovators. [103] The best and only thing one can do is to deduce from practical experience, to revise and reshape the ideas triggered by rehearsal or performance, generate new ones, and try them out in practical situations. The result is then an empirically grounded self-critical aesthetic which, like theatre-making, is a work-in-progress. Fully aware of the fact that his writings espouse ideas disseminated by contemporary innovators, Tabori writes, "I'm not all that eclectic, but what I have to offer comes from experience, not dogma. I have no System or Recipes." [104]

Though eclecticism is a well-known topos of the avant-garde, the question of how much Tabori is indebted to seminal contemporaries is a large and complex issue, as may in fact be discerned from my occasional allusions to affinities above. Briefly: is it all a case of déjà lu *and* déjà vu?

The renunciation of dominant modes in mainstream theatre, such as the rejection of the institutional stage, underpins the work of all avant-gardists, from Artaud to Grotowski to Julian Beck or Richard Schechner. Tabori adopted Brook's notion of the Dead Theatre, took up Grotowski's metaphor of prostitution in the commercially oriented, spurious theatre, and rejected what he figuratively called the "cathedrals" in favor of the "catacombs." The alternative theatre he chose is close in spirit though not in practice to Brook's experimental theatre, which he considers "the best theatre model," both "admirable and practicable." [105] His "catacombs" offer an original variation of the Poor Theatre, which he explicitly cites in his programmatic essay "Unterammergau or the Good Germans." The "catacombs" not only attempt to shift the focus from the myriad of auxiliary components to the actor, but purport to furnish a "difficult theatre" which uncompromisingly challenges societal and theatrical conventions in its exploration of the human.

Like most avant-gardists, Tabori extols presentation rather than representation; that authentic performance which creates experience instead of imitating life. Aware of the pitfalls of realism, he pursues the reality of the performance, considering the process of experimentation more valuable than the final product. This was, of course, a cardinal point in the work of Grotowski, Brook, and others. For

Tabori, perfectionism is neither desirable nor attainable, and this is in fact one of the issues he criticizes in the approach of Brecht, whom he much admired in other respects.

Like the founder of the Berliner Ensemble and like Brook or Chaikin, Tabori too considers the group the only adequate framework for theatre-making in a technically advanced age, in which "the star is dead." At the same time, he emphasizes the actor's obligation to attend to individual needs. Like Brecht, he considers rehearsals a learning process, but unlike Brecht, that celebrated "apostle of anti-emotionalism,"[106] Tabori is interested in the psychological aspects and ramifications of theatre-making.

Tabori's description of acting as a process of self-exploration is of course far from original. The idea was commended in Strasberg's Studio, advanced by Brook, who defines theatre unambiguously as a terrain of self-discovery, and supported by Chaikin when he describes the actor as a detective, proceeding from the visible to the hidden, exploring uncharted territories.[107] Opposed to Brecht's rationalistic approach or what he defines as "the limitations of an anti-psychological aesthetic,"[108] Tabori advocates irrational spontaneity and the exploration of the subliminal. He is primarily interested in the actor as an individual human being; or in the words of Grotowski: "I am interested in the actor because he is a human being."[109] Therefore, it is not the fictitious role of Hamlet that concerns Tabori, but what the specific actor can make out of it. Grotowski too eliminated the notion of "an objective Hamlet." That role to him was a "catalystic effect" as it "sets in motion the machinery of our self-awareness."[110]

Tabori goes out of his way to stress that the actor must seek the role from within, referring to Strasberg's work as the exemplary organic conflation of self and role. It is from Strasberg that he borrows the image of the actor as both instrument (piano) and product (concerto), an idea propounded by many contemporary theatre-makers. Strasberg's concern with the further development of the actor and the permanent reexamination of the actor's "bag of tricks" characterizes Tabori's work at the Theaterlabor and elsewhere.[111] His intensive work with the actors is not intended to improve acting skills as much as to transform fear and inhibition into creative energy, to eradicate blocks. This is effected through improvisations and games, a variety of exercises which develop concentration and relaxation, and the training of affective memory, techniques which he borrowed from Lee Strasberg (though many of the exercises go back to Stanislavsky via Boleslavsky).

Along with productions based on straight drama, Tabori presented stage adaptations of prose works, explored in some of his own plays the narrative Brechtian technique, experimented with collage presentations in which he and the actors deconstructed and recontextualized texts, and ventured, especially in his early period, on presentations which grew out of improvisations or teamwork. When a text was the starting point, Tabori recommended that the actors take their time, read the text again and again so as to feel their way into it, a procedure also advocated by Brook. Like the English director, the "magician," whose work he has followed closely and reveres "without ifs and buts,"[112] Tabori seeks to enrich the context and kindle the actor's imagination by offering myriad stimuli, the fruits of "research," ranging from painting and film to slide-lectures and excursions. Essential to the gradual approximation of the text is the search for the subtext: "Behind every fable there is a personal howl or giggle, the 'secret play' as Brook calls it."[113] Tabori entrusts the actor with this task, demonstrating like Grotowski or Brook his deep respect for the actor.

Adamant in his resentment of the patronizing director, Tabori does not curb his criticism of the imperious director, railing against those "godfathers" who mitigate the freedom of the actor. He does not spare Brecht, whom he considers "not much of an actor's director," nor Grotowski, whose method of provoking the actor's resistance was carried to an extreme, demanding, according to Tabori, too high a price.[114] It is Peter Brook whom he considers "a great master," primarily because of the unmitigated freedom he offers his troupe: "He does very little stage-direction, offering assistance instead, improvisations, games. Matters are discussed intensively. And then he leaves the actor to himself and returns some time later to correct most cautiously. And this is how this incredible simplicity evolves."[115]

Avant-garde echoes may likewise be discerned when Tabori describes theatre-making as the dialectic of spontaneity and structure. Grotowski's conviction that "spontaneity and discipline, far from weakening each other, mutually reinforce themselves" comes readily to mind.[116] And like Grotowski, for whom he harbored ambivalent feelings (that "Super-Guru"),[117] Tabori too recognizes the therapeutic effect of performance. Adverse to the idea of a ritualistic performance, which culminates in the "self-sacrifice" of the "holy actor," Tabori is nonetheless close to Grotowski's followers, who believe in a shamanistic performance, "exorcising the 'disease' of the community in the form of taboos, hostilities, fears."[118]

The preceding analysis, though in no way comprehensive, may be taken as proof of an embarrassing degree of eclecticism, which at times may even verge on plagiarism. Tabori's indebtedness to theatre luminaries such as Artaud, Brecht, Stanislavsky, and Brook cannot be ignored; his way of raiding everyone else, finding what he wants and fitting it to his agenda, should not be overlooked. Yet I would argue that Tabori developed his own ideas about the theatre in a continuous discourse, a dialogue of consent and dissent, with each of them. Moreover, Tabori has never made a secret of the influence of these luminaries on him, while suggesting in his obituary to "Dear Lee" that one must beware their menacing influence. One incidentally recalls what Grotowski had to say about Brook — how well his comment could apply to Tabori — "When an eminent creator with an achieved style and personality, like Peter Brook, turns to Artaud, it's not to hide his own weaknesses, or to ape the man. It just happens that at a given point in his development he finds himself in agreement with Artaud, feels the need of a confrontation, *tests* Artaud, and retains whatever stands up to this test. He remains himself."[119]

In lieu of a comprehensive, methodologically coherent theory, Tabori developed his notions of the theatre on the basis of his experience as a keen observer of theatre practice, his work as a translator and adapter of plays (mainly Brecht),[120] his work as a creative dramatist, and, finally, his experimentations with actors in the United States and in Europe. His ideas on the theatre were assimilated with his remarkably prolific reading of world literature and a passionate interest in the arts; with his theoretical and intimate acquaintance with psychotherapeutic methods as well as with — to use Martin Esslin's statement about Brecht — firsthand experience archetypal of the predicament of the twentieth century, namely, persecution, exile, and forced peregrination.[121] If theatre is home (*Heimat*) as Tabori, a modern Ahasuerus, often maintains for himself, then it is a home which one shapes and molds individually, in a never-ending process of inventiveness.

TABORI'S THEATERLABOR

Our task in the theatre ought to be not the turning of people into actors, but the turning of actors into people. George Tabori, "Unterammergau"

THE MAKINGS OF A UNIQUE EXPERIMENT

When George Tabori founded his Theaterlabor in Bremen in 1976, he introduced to the Federal German Republic an experimental theatrical phenomenon of a kind already known in the international theatre world. Inspired by Grotowski's experimental laboratory in Wroclaw (earlier in Opole), theatre labs began emerging in the mid-1960s, in Scandinavia, Paris, Brussels, and Tokyo; meanwhile in the United States avant-garde groups such as the Living Theatre, Schechner's Performance Group, and Chaikin's Open Theatre explored new territories.[1] For Tabori, a Jewish vagabond aged sixty-two, who had no systematic training in the theatre and only a mixed track record in the United States, the opportunity to conduct a theatre lab was the fulfillment of an old dream.

The offer came from Peter Stoltzenberg, director of the Theater der Freien Hansestadt Bremen. He had seen Tabori's German debut as playwright and director, *The Cannibals*, in Berlin and was much impressed by the sweeping sincerity of the performance. Tabori, who had just been making his first steps in West Germany and its theatres — notably with alternative groups or small workshops in established provincial theatres — accepted Stoltzenberg's offer. His first production in Bremen was David Rudkin's *Afore Night Come* (premiere 25 March 1975), his last, exactly three years later, was *Hamlet* (premiere 19 March 1978). During these three years, the Bremen theatre gave him a "kind of *Heimat* [home],"[2] and he guided/directed seven productions, four of them officially within his Theaterlabor.[3] I have included three productions from the period immediately before the official establishment of the lab, since Tabori's principles and working method were consistent, though they could naturally be intensified in the lab. There is also a distinct continuity as far as the actors involved are concerned.

Even though he entreated, from the beginning of his negotiations in Bremen, to be granted a completely autonomous group, his wish was not fulfilled until later, when it became clear that his rehearsal method and lax treatment of texts were opposed to the creeds and practices fostered by the German theatre establishment. In 1976 Stoltzenberg created for Tabori the conditions necessary for the unbridled operation of an experimental theatre-lab. No German theatre-manager before or since ventured on a similar experiment. Tabori was granted his own ensemble as well as the stage-designer Marietta Eggmann, who participated in rehearsals and training exercises.[4] What had once been the Concordia Cinema was converted into a rehearsal studio and performance space under the new name "Studiobühne Concordia." Tabori's group was free to pursue its theatrical experiments, subsidized with public money. All the work contracts, including Tabori's contract as director, followed the customary arrangements. According to the initial plan, one or two members of the lab were to be replaced after two seasons by other members of the permanent ensemble, to ensure flexibility and foster the interchange of experiences and ideas. Even though they were liberated from the harassing pressure of deadlines and a tight timetable, there was a tacit agreement (partially fulfilled) that there would be 120 performances per season, including 3 new productions. Besides performances in Bremen, the group went on tours in Holland, Belgium, and Poland, recorded radio-plays, and gave performances in juvenile prisons.

The conditions allowing for this exceptional project were terminated in 1978. Stoltzenberg's successor, Arno Wüstenhöfer, refused to support the lab's experimental work. The senator in charge of cultural affairs, Hans-Werner Franke, expressed the view of many opponents and critics when he declared that he had had enough of that "soul vomiting" (*Seelenkotze*).[5] Tabori had been aware of the difficulties all along and had complained long before the official end about the "provincial malice" in Bremen, which forestalled and discouraged every experiment.[6] Stoltzenberg's attempts to find the lab a new home in Hamburg, Berlin, or Munich were fruitless, and the group was disbanded. Nevertheless, some of its members stubbornly followed Tabori on his various stops in Germany and Austria.

One of these staunch followers who followed Tabori through thick and thin was Detlef Jacobsen (b. 1936). He was the only member of the group who had worked with Tabori before the Bremen experiment, playing in Tabori's production of James Saunders's *Kohlhaas* in Bonn 1974, which he regards as "Tabori's first directorial success in Germany." Jacobsen recalls that the man he encountered there took him by surprise. "I saw *The Cannibals* at the Thalia Theater in Hamburg [1972] and imagined Tabori to be a short, perspiring, agitated, and paunchy fellow. I was surprised to find him tall, quiet, lanky, and perfectly slim."[7] After ten years of theatre work with various directors on divers stages, his first collaboration with Tabori was a key experience for Jacobsen. "All of a sudden, after ten years of theatre practice, somebody turns up with totally uncustomary views, somebody who implements and thus confirms my own ideas about theatre making."[8] Tabori's unconventional, original rehearsing method, his plea for the private subtext in a given role, and the chance to get to know oneself through theatre work were refreshingly different from anything Jacobsen had experienced. Pitied or scorned by colleagues for that "Tabori self-indulgence," Jacobsen nonetheless stuck with Tabori. When Tabori called him one day and said, "We're going to Bremen," Jacobsen unhesitantly followed.[9]

Similar expressions of serious appreciation for Tabori as an unorthodox director, as well as respect and deep affection for him as a sensitive and open person, have been voiced by other members of the lab. Though they were professionally trained, most of them were novices with only two or three years of actual experience in the theatre. The actors rarely expressed harsh criticism or resentment of George, as they called him, although they made no secret of the conflicts and arguments which accompanied their work. And Jacobsen discloses: "George has a wonderful quality, namely the capacity to recognize his own mistakes and correct them, the desire to constantly improve himself. He was intolerable during some rehearsals. But then, all of a sudden, at midnight, a call — George. He wanted to apologize, he hadn't been nice during the rehearsal. I hadn't come across anything similar with other directors. In Germany, people look upon such a gesture as a sign of weakness."

Actor Günter Einbrodt (b. 1939), who was to play Hitler in the Burgtheater premiere of Tabori's *Mein Kampf* (1987), recalls how suspicious he had been before viewing the production *Afore Night Come*. "After about ten minutes I was electrified. I saw my colleagues play so well, in a way I had never seen them play before. It was as if they were transformed." A few days later he ran across Tabori at a party. The elderly director was sitting on the floor in a corner of the noisy room, like a drunk hippie. Einbrodt approached him, saying, "*Herr* Tabori, I would like to, I must, I want to participate in your next play, unconditionally, doesn't matter what you do."[10] Inspired by Tabori's working method, Einbrodt later spent a year at Strasberg's Actors Studio and upon his return conducted his own workshop for professional actors in parallel with his acting career.

A group portrait with the master whom they vehemently refused to consider a guru shows fourteen actors. The core of the Theaterlabor consisted of four young actresses — Brigitte Kahn, Brigitte Röttgers, Veronika Nowag, and the dancer Ursula Höpfner — and the actors Detlef Jacobsen, Rainer Frieb, Günter Einbrodt, and Klaus Fischer. Actors Nico Grüneke and Manfred Meihöfer and the French dancer Jean-François Quinque participated in some of the projects, while Heiko Steinbrecher, Jörg Höpfner, and Murray Levy (a former member of the Bread and Puppet Theatre Group) participated as actors, assistant-directors, and/or stage-managers.

Unlike some of the avant-garde groups who made communal living an essential principle of their theatrical collaboration, the members of the Theaterlabor maintained a fair degree of privacy, even though they often shared everyday trivia as well as cultural experiences. Detlef Jacobsen recalls: "Some of us really wanted to lead this kind of communal living, others, like me, were against it. And George, he didn't have the energy for it. After 12 to 16 hours of rehearsing, one wanted to be left alone." Their accounts attest to a strong feeling of (familylike) responsibility for the collective enterprise, which did not impede the exploration of each actor's individual pursuits. Stage-designer Eggmann notes that the objective difficulties — offensive remarks, taunts, antagonistic public reactions, devastating reviews — only cemented and consolidated the group, invigorating the members' commitment and galvanizing their perseverance. No wonder, then, that when it became clear that the existence of the lab was at stake, all its members formulated and signed an appeal in a last-ditch attempt to save it.[11]

Few and far between were the voices lamenting the disbanding of the lab. Many felt a sense of relief that this dubious project — a nonconformist director obsessed with psychotherapeutic crap and his sheepishly devout sectarians — had come to an end. Among German theatre critics, the only ones to realize the uniqueness of this enterprise and deplore its loss were Erich Emigholz, who had followed the entire project from its inception while writing for the *Bremer Nachrichten*; Peter von Becker, editor of *Theater Heute*, who crowned Tabori "the most original theatre man in Germany";[12] and Georg Hensel, theatre critic of the *Frankfurter Allgemeine Zeitung*, who wrote, "Doubtless the end of this Theaterlabor means the loss of an experimental field not only for Bremen: a spark has been extinguished even before it could spread to other theatres."[13]

DISCIPLINE AND SPONTANEITY:
REHEARSING PRAXIS IN THE THEATERLABOR

"For me, work in the theatre is the lab for examining the dialectics of freedom and order, spontaneity and constraint."[14] For Tabori, every experience in the theatre, insofar as it is real and genuine, is an experiment; an autonomous theatre-lab offers optimal, almost utopian conditions for empirical experimentation. Actors, like other artists, possess an acquired technique — "a bag full of tricks, which applause has proven valuable"[15] — but very few of them realize that it is absolutely essential to continue exploring, to unremittingly re-examine and ameliorate their craft. The lab's primary objective was to enable its young professional members to "look into their drawers" and reconsider their contents. But Tabori hoped for more: to free the actors from the debilitating fetters, the noxious habits they had adopted in the mainstream theatre, the abject "cathedrals"; and to restore a kind of primordial innocence that would enable spontaneous and direct experience. Tabori encouraged introspection, initiating his actors into a process of self-discovery and sensitization. Borrowing Lee Strasberg's image of the actor as both the instrument and the music itself, the piano and the concerto, Tabori urged actors to tune and retune this instrument, that is, to expand and enrich their sensual and emotional storehouse, to create a personal "score" rather than to act as the fictitious Other. "Tabori said at that time something which I didn't really understand for a long time: 'The actor is the concept.' It is indeed so," recalls Günter Einbrodt.[16] And Jacobsen adds: "The great thing about George is that he gets a lot out of every actor, he makes the actor productive. Unlike other directors, he does not demand or tell the actor to do this or that, he encourages the actor to find something in himself."

Theories and methods propagated and practiced in the lab were considerably influenced by seminal figures in modern alternative theatre, particularly by Strasberg's Method, which Tabori closely observed for many years. Tabori never made a secret of his wish to carry on experimenting in the light of other alternative theatre models. The practical work conducted in the lab attests to his cunning ability to collect bits and pieces from various theatrical methods, adapt them to concrete needs, and even misread some ideas for his purpose. "Everything we knew about modern, experimental things in world theatre we learned from George," says Jacobsen, who, upon Tabori's initiative, traveled together with his colleagues to Bochum to attend a seminar conducted by the revered Strasberg.

Rehearsals, and sometimes productions too (for instance, *Hamlet*), began with warm-ups, which, like the tuning of an instrument, were intended to limber up body and soul. Relaxation and concentration exercises were carried out by each member individually and by the ensemble as a group. The participants in Tabori's staging of Rudkin's *Afore Night Come*, many of whom later participated in the official lab-project, report that they had spent two out of nine rehearsal weeks on "preliminary training" and various exercises.[17] These were meant to help actors concentrate or sensitize specific parts of their bodies (feet, hands, breath) and to free them of prejudices (e.g., "feet are bad"). This practice was matched by partner exercises designed to train actors to decipher each other's body-signals as communicative codes. In one, an actor tried to imagine and feel a partner's back while leaning against it; in another, actors learned to observe the Other closely through "mirror exercises." As part of the preliminary training, which in many aspects resembled Peter Stein's *Übungen für Schauspieler* (Exercises for Actors) at the Schaubühne, Tabori introduced exercises intended to release aggression and confront anxieties. He initiated a series of group games (e.g., the "hand game," the "we-desire-peace-and-quiet game," the "cuddling game"), which helped actors gain awareness of each other.

The actors tried out new sensations such as walking mechanically like a robot or, conversely, losing control, going berserk. Finally, Tabori introduced his actors to Strasberg's sensory and emotional memory training. Actors were urged to recall, relive, and reexperience a moment in their past, becoming aware of the subliminal and storing this information for future use.[18]

For Tabori, rehearsing means exploring the text (if any) and the subtext, which by necessity involves exploring the self. The German word *proben* (rehearsing) is linked to *ausprobieren* (trying out). Preparing each of the Bremen productions took an unusually long time, because for Tabori the working process was more important than the final product, which in any case was never sealed. "Perfection is blasphemy," and a so-called perfect theatre is but a dead theatre. The ideal production is consequently a work-in-progress, and the lab fully exploited the luxury of a flexible timetable. Press night had to be postponed more than once. Whereas work on *Afore Night Come* (in the prelab phase) lasted over nine weeks, work in the Theaterlabor on *Hamlet* took four and a half months and on *Talk Show*, the lab's official debut, stretched over half a year! Of the seven productions in Bremen, four were based on texts of plays: Rudkin's *Afore Night Come*, Euripides' *The Trojan Women*, Edward Bond's *The Swing*, and Shakespeare's *Hamlet*. One was based on Kafka's short story "A Fasting-Artist," and two — *Sigmunds Freude* and *Talk Show* — were to a large extent composed by the ensemble, with minimal use of a given text or script.

Under the guidance of Tabori, the actors spent hours and days reading the text. Casting came only after weeks of an intensive encounter with the script. Working on *Hamlet*, he referred his actors to Susan Sontag's essays in *Against Interpretation*, in which the American critic advocates an alert, unbiased, and thorough reading of the work itself rather than the study of secondary sources. A text is open to any number of interpretations, none more valid than another, claims Tabori. The actors report their playful approximation of Shakespeare's text, which they read in parts or as a whole: "When it didn't satisfy us, we tried the whole thing over again, individually and collectively, in a nonsense language."[19] This unusual experimentation with the text, its deconstruction, opened up new perspectives. "It was no longer important what one actually wanted to impart to the others," recalls Einbrodt. Semantic communication became subordinate to the given situation, just as Strasberg advocated when he maintained that it is not the word but the situation which is the core of the performance. It was through this intense experience of voicing the text that the actors realized the disadvantages of Erich Fried's lyrical translation of *Hamlet.* They decided in favor of Heiner Müller's new translation of the play, which enabled them — according to Tabori — to approach Shakespeare's text realistically and not rhetorically, to recite it naturally rather than formally.

Similarly, the group spent days reading, relating, and feeling their way into Kafka's "Fasting-Artist." The text was read solo or in choir, and even in the form of a canon. Brigitte Röttgers, who documented the exciting rehearsal process, reports that on one occasion passages were repeated impromptu, "as in jazz, organically, and freely."[20] The actors also conducted "variations with a sung text." This approach, reminiscent of jazz improvisations, likewise underlined Tabori's *Improvisations of Shylock* in Munich in 1978. It was halfway into the rehearsal phase that the casting was determined. As always in the Theaterlabor, this was done democratically, as a joint decision of Tabori and the actors. Similarly, it was a mutual decision to abandon a straight reading of Frederick S. Perls's *Gestalt*-therapy session protocols, "with which none of us could get along,"[21] in favor of an improvisational approach in *Sigmunds Freude.* Ultimately, the actors introduced their dreams, personal inhibitions, and problems, drawing on the session protocols for a structural model.

The explicit aim of this close, intensive reading of the text was to enable each actor to relate and react to it individually. Tabori urged the actors to feel their way into the text, to discover the secret embedded in the score, to unravel the "central element which lies in the subtext,"[22] that which Peter Brook calls "the secret play." The deliberate slow approximation of the text triggered a long journey inward, whose endpoint was unpredictable and of secondary importance; "The actor is more interesting than the role," quipped Tabori, "producing more productive than the ultimate product."[23]

Tabori hardly ever imposed his own concept or interpretation on the actors. Adamantly opposed to the figure of the authoritative director, a kind of animal-trainer who domesticates subjects to perform at his will, Tabori would either withdraw quietly, allowing actors the freedom to approach the text by themselves, or would sit in a circle with them, thinking aloud, telling stories, inspiring and encouraging them. Following Brecht's "inductive process,"[24] Tabori did not consider his role as director, or, in his words, playmaker, to be realizing an idea, but stimulating and organizing the productivity of the actors. The pronounced respect and confidence he had in his actors generated great freedom and a high degree of individual responsibility.

The *Hamlet* production illustrates this attitude beautifully: even though Tabori had very clear ideas about the play, which he had elaborated at length in his remarkable essay "Hamlet in Blue,"[25] he chose not to acquaint the group with this essay so as not to impose his approach or obstruct the actors' flow of creative associations. Another instance of this *laissez-faire* approach was *Sigmunds Freude*. Instead of the customary stage script, the actors received a stack of typed notes, a description of a collagelike production, and a list of some thirty-four case-episodes partly based on Perls's session-protocols (collected in the German edition *Gestalttherapie in Aktion*). It was important for Tabori to make it absolutely clear that the suggested episodes need not constitute the performance's structure or plot. "They are meant to give impulses and open a discussion. . . . The point is that even with these notes we will be starting at zero-point," Tabori wrote, echoing the dictum of the English director George Devine.[26] Subsequently, the group began reflecting on the nature of happiness, investigating through improvisation moments of felicity. Among these were the moment in which Leonardo da Vinci comes upon the smile of the Mona Lisa and Milena's letters to Kafka. In the course of this phase Tabori brought up Perls's protocols, which were then revised and modified by the group.

Far from being an ubiquitous, domineering, and dogmatic director, Tabori is best described as an animator, who awakens and revitalizes, suggests and inspires, stimulating the actors, stirring and invigorating their senses and emotions. Gundula Ohngemach deems Tabori's notion of *recherche* an activity intended to stimulate and prod the actor to explore the role.[27] Notably, this "research" could range from a lecture with slides on the routine and difficulties of running a plantation (in the case of Rudkin's play) to a group visit to a zoo — observing the animals' conduct in the cages as a way of learning about repression and aggression in captivity (for Kafka's "Fasting-Artist"). Particularly rich and manifold was the impetus Tabori gave the group at the outset of the *Hamlet* production. He initiated a group visit of the Taganka *Hamlet* production in Paris and the viewing of Francis Ford Coppola's film *The Godfather*. He briefed the actors on Dover Wilson's writing and introduced them to paintings by

Francis Bacon, his favorite painter,[28] to acquaint them with the way Bacon painted the dissolution and disintegration of bodies. Furthermore, rehearsals were accompanied by the reading of Freud's *Mourning and Melancholia*, the Mitscherlichs' *The Inability to Mourn*, and Niccolò Machiavelli's *The Prince*. These readings bear upon the ensuing production — for instance, Hamlet's inability to mourn his father's death or Claudius's opportunism and pursuit of power.[29] Even so, this extratheatrical research was never meant to impose on the actors any binding interpretation of a play, but was designed to widen their horizons and stimulate them to consider the text from varying perspectives.

Essentially, each production was shaped and reshaped by what the actors discovered collectively and individually as they went along. For instance, work on *Hamlet* began with the joint pursuit of the subtext, with visual associations based on the annual garden party given by the German chancellor. The emphasis during this preliminary rehearsal phase was on the sociopolitical aspects of the play; inspiration was drawn from actual events and the still-vivid memory of the dramatic autumn of 1977, when the industrialist Hanns-Martin Schleyer was abducted and killed. The group was concerned with questions of power and its abuse, the ramifications of political manipulations and intrigues. During the course of rehearsals the emphasis gradually shifted to Hamlet. He was to be present in all the scenes, observing the mechanisms of a corrupt court and experiencing reality as a nightmare. The group chose the setting, a snowy landscape, dotted by a lone telephone booth. The booth was an isolated retreat as well as a place of imprisonment: Hamlet could receive calls but not place them, and the door could be opened only from the outside. As the idea of Hamlet's nightmarish perception came to dominate the production (the typical Taborian *Grenzsituation*), stage-designer Eggmann and the actors decided to abandon the booth for a scholar's abode, which was signified — in line with Hamlet's ascetic frugality and the aesthetics of a "poor theatre" — through two suitcases, a chair, and a bed. Rather than shaping the production concept, the set emerged from and was altered during the rehearsal process, out of specific immanent needs. Ultimately, only an old iron bedstead remained, suggesting the play's two-pronged conflict, in line with the group's Freudian interpretation: the conflict between father and son with the bed as the locus of death and the mother-son Oedipus complex with the bed as the symbol of sexuality.

Improvisation was a key element in the group's work. Along with the improvisations mentioned, the actors performed animal improvisations intended to further their understanding of the aggressive streak in human nature.[30] Another improvisation game initiated by Tabori was designed to familiarize the actors with the impulse to kill. Each of the participants was to imagine how to kill the other actor, an exercise which was eventually incorporated into the *Hamlet* production itself. What mattered then was the actor's visceral experience and immediate involvement. Thus, actors in Rudkin's play, set on a plantation, were obliged to carry and load baskets of apples, while the two actors playing Hamlet and Laertes traveled to Hamburg to watch and participate in dueling matches organized by a students' society so they could understand, intimately, the fascination of fencing.[31]

This belief in firsthand experience as the only way of attaining optimal involvement found its most extreme expression in the rehearsal of Kafka's "Fasting-Artist." Brigitte Röttgers's rehearsal diary attests to an ever-growing preoccupation with eating, being deprived of or renouncing food.[32] The group began by forgoing alcohol for one evening, then abstained from smoking for a day, and finally decided to start the day without having breakfast. After comparing notes and relating their physical and psychic experiences, they decided to fast for twenty-four hours. It was Tabori who, a few days later, proposed fasting longer, like the artist in Kafka's story, and spoke of fourteen days. The group adopted the idea and pushed it to an extreme: "It was a spontaneous idea, as one of them, Murray [Levy] had already once fasted," Tabori recalls.[33] It was agreed to follow Kafka's model and fast for forty days. The actors abstained from eating from 9 May 1977 to 20 June 1977, forty-two days in all, during which they allowed themselves only tea, diluted fruit or vegetable juices, and occasionally a glass of wine or buttermilk. The fasting experience, officially authorized and medically supervised,[34] nonetheless raised a political storm in Bremen, partly because it coincided with the hunger strike of some of the Baader-Meinhof group members. (This, in fact, is why the actors spoke of fasting and not of hunger, and why the title "Fasting-Artist(s)" is more appropriate than the customary "Hunger Artist.") Evaluating the experience in retrospect Tabori summed up this deliberate overlapping of art and life in the following words: "The point was to consummate an experience, to experience difficulties. . . . The group that fasted — and this was my experience with it — really had sensed it; they had the right to be what they were, because they were authentic."[35]

It was during the course of this radical experience that the production received its "final" shape. Textual passages were assigned, and the group unanimously decided against using the group cage as a major stage prop. Reminiscing about those days, Klaus Fischer emphasizes that "I was interested in the way we worked, and in the ensemble; everything else was unimportant to me. What was important was the 'we.'"[36]

Rehearsals hardly ever concluded with opening night. The premiere was explicitly described as "an open rehearsal, changeable in form and substance,"[37] an echo of the lab's guiding values: "Freedom and spontaneity, the unpredictable and accidental, and thus the dangerous." "A few hours before the premiere, we still tried all kinds of things out," recalls Jacobsen; he adds: "We sometimes didn't even know when things 'really' began. George wanted to find out whether an actor could move from the general rehearsal directly to the premiere, without a pause. This resulted in fabulous performances, while on other occasions the performance would sag because the group didn't quite know how to hold together something which was born out of an improvisation. This holding together is of course linked to the waning of spontaneity." Far from being final and complete, productions were often altered after critiques had already appeared, taking into consideration spectators' responses and comments, the actors' own evaluation of their performance, and even ad hoc requirements (when the group went on tour, for instance).

It is important to note that Tabori was always available to his actors — before, during, and after the performance — assisting, inspiring, consoling, or encouraging. On one occasion, during a performance of Bond's *The Swing*, Tabori and some of the actors played a prank. Dressed as a stagehand, he sat at the corner of the stage like a mute drunk and surprised Detlef Jacobsen, who was thus confronted with one of those unpredictable factors which Tabori had taught the group to use and integrate into their performances. What followed was a "wild improvisation" which ended when Jacobsen, assisted by two colleagues, carried Tabori out in a basket.

A production as a work-in-progress, a collective and individual creative experience characterized by incessant, keen pursuit and total involvement, intensified by the conviction that acting and being, theatre and life, are inseparable — this is the quintessence of

Tabori's Theaterlabor. But above all — the prevalence of pleasure: the fun of trying things out, the joy of playing games or improvising, the excitement of discovering the secrets of the text or the self, the satisfaction of finding an accurate solution to a scenic problem, the hilarity of letting go and playing silly — the gaiety of the *Homo ludens*. "What mattered was the joy of acting. 'Have fun' was always the slogan."[38]

THE PRODUCTIONS

The productions which Tabori conducted in Bremen, seven in all, attest to his perspicacity in choosing material suitable to the given conditions or to the needs and objectives of an experimental group. In an unpublished protocol Tabori states: "Customarily, the ensemble is there to put into effect certain programs. The group, on the other hand, means to do just the opposite: certain programs are here, so that the group may realize itself against the society for which it performs. . . . If we really want to find new ways, we must find materials, themes, and plays which are right for the group, which contribute to its development." At the same time, the list is typical of Tabori: not only does it include works by two of his favorite writers — Kafka and Shakespeare — it also reveals many of the motifs and concerns underlying his own work, before and after the Bremen years. These motifs include the deliberately provocative examination of the complex relationship between the victim and the victimizer; the imaginative, nuanced probing of human conduct in extreme situations (*Grenzsituationen*), including the upsurge of hatred or violence; the obsessive preoccupation with sickness and death; and the passionate interest, influenced by psychotherapy, in the subliminal and the irrational.

Tabori chose to make his debut in Bremen with a contemporary British play, David Rudkin's *Afore Night Come* (premiere 25 March 1975). He was attracted less by the plot — the murder of a newly arrived plantation worker by his fellow workers — than by the wide spectrum of human passions, which he linked to "libido images."[39] The performance focused on the interpersonal relations between the plantation laborers, experienced and new workers, high and low in the hierarchy; it enacted the dynamics of violence, the gradual development from frustration to aggression, from hostility to the killing of the scapegoat.

Tabori mitigated Rudkin's extreme realism by freeing the play from the particularities of its setting in "a rural pocket on the crust of the Black Country." The German translation he chose omits the slang of the original. In addition, Tabori emphasized the symbolic dimension of the play through the repetition of images such as apples, a knife, the ever-present pitchfork. The production culminated in a terrifying and cruel ceremony — Roche's murder, which was presented as ritual murder with mythical and Christian connotations. Roche was the innocent sacrificed by a frustrated, unknowing lot; he was their illusion of hope for deliverance or redemption, on whose body a cross was painted.

This pivotal motif was also expressed physically, through the set and the mise en scène. In the small auditorium of the Concordia, the distinction between spectators and actors was annulled, and both were subjected to the principles of open space or confinement. Spectators sat in six groups and watched the play through wire mesh, like prisoners. The group's intensive rehearsal work was evident not only in the highly charged and tense atmosphere, but also in the "group dynamics in this orchard Eden,"[40] as well as in the nuanced characterization. Spens, the foreman, mediating between the plantation owner — in a wheelchair — and his workers, was a petty gray man, dressed in gray, an upstart, a bureaucrat with a tie, who expressed his recently acquired superiority through an arrogant, haughty tone. Indeed, Spens evoked the image of a Nazi administrator, an armchair culprit, "a bookkeeper of evil."[41] A touch of homoerotic affinity colored the encounter between Larry, the student, and the sensitive but retarded Johnny.[42] The central figure in Tabori's production was clearly Roche, the tramp. His appearance and behavior marked him as an outsider, a threat to the group and to the prevailing order, and therefore ultimately its victim. Roche (Uli Eichenberger), wearing a scarf on his head and dark glasses, a shabby coat and no socks, at times suggested a preliminary study of Beckett's tramps, which Tabori was to direct nine years later. Intelligent and sensitive, lazy and smug, he was redeemed by a childlike inquisitiveness, a sense of humor, and biting wit. He presented himself as a wandering bard telling anecdotes and reciting poems (one of which was written by the actor himself!). This born artist and prodigious raconteur, nicknamed by his mates Shakespeare, in whom art and life were inseparably intertwined, was a truly Taborian figure. Like Shlomo Herzl in Tabori's *Mein Kampf*, Roche speaks of a book he wants to write; a gifted storyteller, he ultimately becomes a victim with a smile on his lips.

In his first staging of *The Trojan Women* (premiere 14 April 1976) — the second followed in Munich in 1985 — Tabori likewise focused on a radical situation, an extreme instance of human cruelty and, conversely, on human suffering. While in *Afore Night Come* he freed the plot from its particular social context, in his production of Euripides he transferred the classical drama to the present. This he did by means of a modern minimalist set, contemporary costumes, and a flexible approach to the text (in Mattias Braun's modern translation), which enabled the cast to enrich Euripides' drama with their own associations.

The stage of the Theater am Goetheplatz [43] resembled a "clinically cold waiting room." [44] The walls were painted light green, the floor was covered with fabric varnished white. At the rear was a washbasin with a mirror, lamp, and towel. This anonymous space beneath a ceiling of frosted glass evoked the sense of confinement, "where people are stripped of their names and their individuality, degraded to numbers." The stage was strewn with garbage cans, black mourning clothes, and high-heeled shoes. Against this setting of turmoil, destruction, and heartlessness, the play opened with a twenty-minute mute prelude, an intensely powerful interlude which set the tone for the entire production and clearly bespoke Tabori's reading of Euripides' drama. The extended tableau presented a fearsome sight: the women of Troy being brutally handled by the soldiers (in modern uniform) — molested, injured, tormented, debased. Clad in torn and smeared clothes, blindfolded, with shorn hair and bound hands, the women were quite clearly the victims of male brutality, the real victims of a senseless war. Even though Tabori presented a universal image of victimization and suffering, the reverberations of recent German history could not be ignored, as, for instance, when the soldiers looked into the wide-open mouths of their victims, searching for gold tooth fillings. The entire production, which abridged the original text, centered on the psychic repercussions of war, posing questions of individual responsibility in times of collective barbarism. Unlike the original text, in Tabori's version the chorus was occasionally split into several distinct voices, as an allusion to individual agency. There are two other significant deviations from the original: the depiction of Helene as a victim of her own femininity, stressing her passivity and helplessness by transferring her text to the boy Astyanax, and the staging of the murder of the latter. Like Roche in *Afore Night Come*, Astyanax was sacrificed in a ritual murder. Tabori's production, intense and gruesome, was designed to generate pity and fear, awakening consternation through its shocking relevance to the times. Ironically, it was the production's bracing terror that drove some spectators out of the theatre long before the show was over.

This obvious provocation, the deliberate irritation and baffling of the audience, was an important element in Tabori's work in Bremen — so too in Edward Bond's *The Swing*. The production (premiere 25 March 1977) depicted the process of stigmatization and ostracism in a society which champions violence and brutalization as legitimate survival strategies. Even though Tabori joined rehearsals in midstream (he had been in Munich directing *Metamorphoses*), the production clearly bears his mark; it is excellent proof that, even without Tabori's physical presence, the group continued to work according to the principles he propagated. The historical case — the public execution of a black man accused of murder in Kentucky in 1911 — was related in the prologue by a stagehand. No sooner did he complete his irony-laced monologue than he was seized by other actors and his face was sprayed black. Henceforth *he* was the black man, the victim. The message was immediately transmitted: anyone, black or white, could become a scapegoat, the victim of mass hysteria or hatred. Truly, at the end of Tabori's production of Bond's play, it is ironically a white man, the well-meaning homosexual Fred, who is lynched.

With this ritualized murder, underscored by "parabolic and visual images,"[45] the group sought to provoke the spectators and engage them actively in the play. Fred (Rainer Frieb) was tied up naked to the swing and was executed by being bombarded with tomatoes. Reminiscent of active audience engagement championed by the Living Theatre, spectators in Bremen were invited to join in. The entire scene was accompanied by the singing of the American national anthem and the presence of an overeager photographer trying to document the occasion. As it turned out, only a few spectators joined in the "do-it-yourself" lynching. Occasionally, spectators accepted some of the tomatoes offered by the actors, but aimed them at the "perpetrators" or threw them, by way of protest, at the entire company. Some thought, as critics did, that this was ludicrous impertinence, a tasteless theatre gimmick.[46] Detlef Jacobsen recalls that during the spontaneous discussion which ensued, "it was mostly women, who went up on the stage in order to disenchain the actor on the swing. Occasionally a spectator would chase me — I played Mr. Skinner, who incited the crowd to throw tomatoes — pursuing me until we were out in the street." The production ended with a deflation of tension. The actors sneaked across the stage to the sound of blues and Dixieland music like marionettes in slow motion, "as if seeking to indicate that man, swayed by his emotions, may also become their victim."[47] The evening was rounded off with a scene somewhat parallel to the prelude, in which stagehands assembled the props, including Fred's corpse, with unruffled routine gestures.

The group's repertory included two productions uncommon in their attempt to explore how theatrical and therapuetic experiences conflate. Approximating a role, like an encounter with all the shadows of the self, profits from the deployment of therapeutic skills, Tabori suggested, and he maintained that the key to the success of a production or therapy lies with the actor and the patient, respectively. It depends on the actor's willingness to become involved, to fathom deep-seated passions, to reenact seminal experiences, impulses, or desires. Underlying *Sigmunds Freude* (premiere 28 November 1975; titled in English *James' Joys*, a witty homophone) was the wish to find out what happiness is all about and to share the feelings of joy, pleasure, and bliss which always "begin when pain ceases."[48] It was in the midst of the rehearsal process, when the actors were engaged in individual improvisations, that Tabori brought along Frederick S. Perls's protocols, the documentation of his *Gestalt*-therapy in action. Fully aware of the deprecatory German attitude toward psychotherapy — skeptical, condescending, disapproving — Tabori told the group about his encounter with Perls and recounted his own personal therapy in the United States, which culminated in a "satori," a sudden experience of enlightenment comparable to Joyce's epiphany.[49] Inspired by Tabori's notes/preliminary guidelines and Perls's accounts (which they found unpalatable at first) the actors developed their own concept of the show, as Tabori had hoped when he set out to work with the ensemble. The production was a collage fusing improvisation with case studies and personal experience — "dramatic material coming from the actors' exploration of their inner selves" as in productions of the Open Theatre or the Performance Group.[50] This extraordinary theatrical experience, which was to last three to four hours, and which was revised from performance to performance, highlighted the quintessence of Tabori's work with the group: acting and being were inextricably linked. The actor discovered the role by exploring an authentic self and was the concept, as Tabori advocated. And as in Perls's *Gestalt*-therapy, the self was discovered by deconstructing experience and reshaping it, acting out conflicts, resuscitating and re-experiencing buried emotions, similar to the procedure of sense memory. "Tabori reclaims Aristotle's notion of catharsis, but understands it as the attempt to liberate the inner world from the weight of unfiltered emotions," wrote Erich Emigholz.[51]

As in previous productions, the ensemble adopted the principle of "empty space" or the "poor theatre." The acting area designed by Marietta Eggmann, a swiveling circular stage covered with red velvet, evoked a "soul landscape."[52] In an armchair on the edge of the platform sat the therapist, Fritz (Perls's nickname), and opposite him were two chairs for the patient to choose from (representing the two sides of the conflict). The hundred spectators allowed into the theatre (in accordance with safety regulations) sat surrounding the stage, a "merry-go-round of neuroses."[53] Each performance consisted of eight to ten episodes, most of which began with the therapist prodding the patient to recount dreams and then to enact all the characters or objects in them. Actors made sharp transitions from playing human roles to inanimate objects and traded the roles of patient and therapist back and forth; this effectively prevented the audience from settling into simplistic identification. The collage included the case of a drug-addicted social worker who acts out the "top dog" and "underdog" in himself; the erotomaniac and exhibitionist who converses with the volcano in himself and experiences its eruption; a show-master plagued with gastric ulcer, who is haunted by a dream in which policemen beat up a child; an actor who imagines he is his own motorcycle; a chap who, having grown up with a domineering father, imagines he is a crushed beer-mat; a call girl, twice divorced, who cleanses her guilt feelings by cleaning her flat, etc. It is noteworthy that hardly any of the case-episodes or minidramas in *Sigmunds Freude* appeared in Tabori's original list of over thirty suggestions. It seems that while Tabori was interested in dramatizing the magic of "simple" happiness, the relief following anguish, thirst, or cold, or "the extra-ordinariness of . . . trivial moments,"[54] the group was drawn to the possibility of revealing nightmares, fears, anxieties, frustrations, and the relief that comes from seriously confronting them.

The closing scene, a subversive tableau, was a collective experience suggested by Tabori: the group hastily built an imaginary wooden machine, like a huge toy, in order to readily crush it with a wooden hammer on a cream-cake. The accompaniment of Bach's cantata BWV 50, *Nun ist das Heil und die Kraft*, and the showering of pillow feathers all over the stage deflated the dream-session, turning it into a "defamiliarizing apotheosis."[55]

The extraordinary quality of *Sigmunds Freude* was reflected in the reception it found among critics and theatregoers. Spectators, who were meant to be considered as "playmates in a great kindergarten . . . not as dodos, schoolboys, or *Scheißbürger*" or as participants in a "feast,"[56] were apparently extremely confused or disoriented; they did not quite know how to relate to the show and whether the actors were performing or not. Occasionally, spectators would join in and depict their dreams. Detlef Jacobsen in the role of Fritz, the therapist, was taken by surprise. "I was in no position to treat anybody," he said with a smile. "Luckily, the fellow's dream was not terribly complicated. When he finished relating it, I asked him how he felt. 'Somehow, I'm relieved,' the chap replied. So I said, 'You see, this is the first step,' whereupon Brigitte Kahn came upstage and took over. She had been sitting like all the other actors, wearing their costumes, in the audience." On several occasions spectators confessed that the show had helped them recognize and overcome some of their own problems. Devastating reviews came from some critics who spoke of psychological dilettantism on the stage, of construed spontaneity devoid of any artistic merit.[57]

Talking and acting out as a therapeutic and theatrical strategy was also the guiding principle of the lab's official debut, *Talk Show* (premiere 23 October 1976), which conceptually and substantively had a great deal in common with *Sigmunds Freude*. The textual point of departure was Tabori's play *The 25th Hour*. When Tabori presented the group with his play-script, he immediately noticed that they were dissatisfied and displeased. For the next rehearsal the following afternoon, he brought along a totally new version. "He wrote it down during the night, a completely new play which he photocopied, sorted out, filed, and handed out to us. The new play was wonderful, it was entitled 'Talk Show,'" reminisces Detlef Jacobsen. In the course of the excessively long rehearsal period (nearly six months) the group, guided by Tabori, developed a sequence of episodes, ten minidramas, variations on the theme of sickness and death. The play-text, which allowed the actors free space for improvisation, was modified to suit each actor, taking into consideration his/her idiosyncrasies and whims. In an interview entitled "The Marx Brothers in Zauberberg," printed in the show's program, Tabori defined *Talk Show* as a "comedy about dying and sickness" and related the German word for comedy (*Lustspiel*) to pleasure (*Lust*), maintaining, as he did in *Sigmunds Freude*, that pleasure and suffering are locked in a dialectical embrace, as pleasure begins when suffering ceases. Here too theatrical and therapeutic experiences are conflated. Only when we confront death, talk about it, act out our apprehensiveness or panic, does the absurdity of extinction become conspicuous. Tabori stated: "I can only deal with this theme [death] seriously, if I deal with it comically." Humor then is the major means of challenging death: therapeutically it relieves fear and anguish, theatrically it may offer a redeeming ironic distance or comic relief. "Death is the most notorious criminal," maintains Tabori, adding his own everlasting yea to life: "for me [the point is] to make death ridiculous in view of living." [58]

Characteristically, *Talk Show* reduced theatrical paraphernalia and fostered proximity with the audience. The entire Concordia studio became "a mattress vault" (alluding to Heine's biography), [59] a mattress-lined training space where the actors performed. Spectators were asked to take off their shoes, help themselves to plastic footwear, and recline or sit comfortably to watch the show. Wearing light blue or pink uniforms, the actors were the patients of the Lazarus hospital — an obvious reference to the New Testament miraculous healing episode — in Hollywood. While *The 25th Hour* focused on the fictitious fate of Arthur Prince, *Talk Show* brought together artists, celebrities, film stars, and intellectuals, all of whom suffered physically and/or mentally. The actors kept their own names or were addressed by the names of Hollywood stars, even though they did not imitate them. As in *Sigmunds Freude*, each member of the group had a theatrical high point: each related and acted out his or her pain to the doctor, improvising on elementary experiences such as birth, sex, or physical decrepitude. Here too roles were constantly interchanged and "patients" slipped into the role of the seemingly omnipotent healer. It soon became evident that the doctor was worse off than any of them; at the end of the show he was the one operated on. The nine patients circled his bed as in a ritual, praying for a sign of life.

Talk Show thus offered a sustained metaphor of a diseased society. "Life is an incurable sickness" for Tabori,[60] who had seen through the deceptive facade of Hollywood, a world of manufactured dreams where, to use John Webster's words, "a rotten and dead body [is hidden] in rich tissue."[61] In this sense Hollywood, "necropolis" as he renamed it, is the paradigm of transience and pathology; as such, it is the ideal background for testing human behavior in extreme situations.[62]

The scrutiny of extreme situations was the quintessence of the lab's production based on Kafka's "A Fasting-Artist" (premiere 10 June 1977).[63] The group had been working on *Hamlet* when one day Tabori introduced Kafka's story — a typical Tabori digression or enrichment — which resulted in a unanimous decision to postpone Shakespeare in favor of Kafka. "I had always hoped to find some material wherein the problems of the group would find direct expression, and it is clear that 'A Fasting-Artist' is particularly appropriate. On the one hand, it is a metaphor for artistry or the art of acting; on the other hand, . . . the group can only realize itself if the members can realize themselves individually."

Kafka's story offered a framework within which to reflect and act out the principles Tabori had been advocating all along, namely, that there is no discrepancy, no "hole" as he put it, between living / being and genuine acting. Here was a unique opportunity to examine and verify those premises, posing major questions relating to the essence and meaning of the art of theatre: Can an actor be the role performed? Should the actor be(come) the figure represented? How much, if at all, does an actor depend on spectators to practice his or her profession? (a question which led to radical decisions in the case of Grotowski's lab, for example). In what way, if at all, is the art of acting affected by extratheatrical considerations or objective conditions, by changing tastes and fashions, or by commercial considerations exerted by impresarios or any theatre management?

It was at an early stage of rehearsals that the group decided to change the original title from singular to plural, and the production was henceforth called *The Fasting-Artists*. This decision stemmed from the realization that only by processing the materials of the play — emotionally, intellectually, and physically — could each actor contribute to the shaping of the collective theatrical experience. A similar strategy was adopted a year later, when thirteen actors improvised the role of Shylock in Tabori's *Improvisations on Shylock* (see chapter 12).

For *The Fasting-Artists*, the acting area of the Concordia resembled a circus arena,[64] covered with earth and straw. From a big table in the center rose a tree, stripped of its bark and varnished white, symbolizing the territory of the leopard (the panther in Kafka's story); it was flanked on either side by the artists' cages, made of boxes, ladders, and chairs. Each cage had a plaque bearing the name of the actor inside it; there were also photographs of him/her before and after the forty-day fasting period and personal effects such as books, pictures, watches, etc. The eight fasting-artists,[65] with bulging Hasidic-looking top hats, wore shimmering black tricots which emphasized their emaciated bodies and suggested their affinity to the circus leopard as an object of amusement. The dialectical tension between life and art, nature and artifice, was underscored by the presence of two live peacocks moving about undisturbed — symbols of longevity, pride, and vanity.

The performance opened with the ladies (responsible in the story for taking the faster-actor out of the cage and bringing him to the fast-breaking meal), who handed each spectator a flower and introduced him/her to a seat. The impresario then took over; to the sounds of a barrel-organ, he presented the actors in the cages to the visitors, while three gamekeepers (Tabori being one of them) played chess and drank beer. Spectators were thus immediately drawn into the show, confronted concurrently with the fictitious and the real. They listened to the actors' complaints (solo or in choir) about the declining popularity of their art of fasting, and also to each actor's background and personal experience of fasting. This extended introduction was followed by a dialogue based on Kafka's text, in which the disagreement between the artist and the impresario was enacted. The artist complained of being used and abused by the commercially minded manager, of the titillation-thirsty audience, of never being allowed to fully live or experience art.

The production reached its climax (as the actors had planned during rehearsals) with the forced termination of the fast, which emphasized the misuse of authoritative power. The impresario appeared, using a whistle and a whip like a brutal animal-trainer, while a march played in the background, alluding to the vulgarization of ceremony. The artists tried in vain to refuse the food, reciting passages from Kafka's story, his diary, or their own notes written during their fasting period. "Violence can be a great liberating force, but there are times when the most practical, the most human, and, if you like, most violent act is simply the refusal to do something under duress, a gesture not without mystery, of saying No; of not eating though one is starved."[66] Refusal, or defiance, became, as it had been in *Cannibals*, a sign of free choice and self-assertion and, as far as the theatrical metaphor was concerned, the perfecting of the producer and the product.

When silence finally fell, only the ticking of the metronome, a reminder of the passage of time, could be heard. The artists began to eat, some in haste, others with hesitation; some were fed, others vomited. In his dramatized version of Kafka's story, Tabori had suggested reactions to the dramatic climax, deconstructing Kafka's text and opening it to various digressions. Each actor thus formulated a reaction on the basis of previous experience with forced feeding and authoritative coercion. They then broke bread with the spectators ("tasty bread," as one critic noted) and assembled to form a living image of the fasting-artist. A short Jewish tune was sung and a mute epilogue followed: the leopard crossed the stage and withdrew up his tree with a piece of raw meat thrown at him by the impresario.

The group continued to rehearse and reshape the production after opening night. In the following season, it came up with a second version in which resignation and repressed anger replaced resistance and defiance. In the revised version the leopard's role gained prominence. As previously, it was portrayed by Ursula Höpfner, whose naked golden body was covered every evening anew with thousands of black spots to appear sensuous, agile, and mysterious. The leopard not only tried to assault the artists, vying for spectators' attention, seeking to release the "animal within" — it also bit one of the actors to death. Noteworthy is Erich Emigholz's critique of this later version: he, like others, found the second version too finished and thus inferior to the first rough version, which was much more in keeping with the experimental nature of the lab.[67]

Postponed due to the group's enthusiasm over Kafka's story, *Hamlet* was the last official production of the Theaterlabor (premiere 19 March 1978). As usual, the text was deconstructed and abridged and was used by the group as a vehicle for an exploration, a voyage of discovery into irrational, subliminal regions. Once again Tabori encouraged the actors to go against the German mainstream: to beware of compulsive intellectualization, which is but a substitute for real experience, for emotions and passions. According to Tabori, Hamlet's problem lies in "his dread of the undiscovered country, not beyond Jordan but within himself";[68] his fear of looking inward, his failure to experience any emotion to its fullest, his habit of suppressing the unpleasant and undesired, his tendency to rationalize all in hope of (self-)control. For Tabori, these are, in fact, the German attributes of Hamlet: "I am struck by the Germanism of Hamlet as well as by the Hamletism of Germans," he pronounced in his original essay "Hamlet in Blue," written a few years before the Bremen production.

Hamlet in modern garb, as a psycho-protocol of tormented souls rather than as a tapestry of intrigues — this was the special flavor of the lab's production. Underlying the scrutiny of anguished souls was Tabori's Freudian-colored dictum, "Every son wants to do in his father."[69] Conversely, *Hamlet* is an accurate demonstration of how parents, living or dead, burden their children, tyrannize them emotionally, and render them perpetual victims.

In line with the lab's principle of a minimal and functional set, the stage, surrounded by spectators, was the scene of a "nightplay."[70] The floor was covered with tar, and spectators' chairs were fixed into it. Black drapes hung on the walls; there was a large dark canvas on the ceiling, from which icicles were suspended. Through a hole in the middle of this cold, nocturnal setting dropped a luminous construction of electric bulbs, clustered like grapes. The deliberately diffuse light emphasized the nightmarish atmosphere of that "soul landscape." Following the group's decision, the bed in the center of the stage was the focal point, symbolically and literally. The bed — "where all the momentous things in life take place,"[71] birth, sickness, death, and sexual activity; the platform of the unconscious where dreams and nightmares are enacted — underscored the psychotherapeutic trajectory of the production while pointing to Hamlet's self-centeredness.

The presentation was framed by improvisations and tableaux, and, in addition, the actors approached the audience directly, before and after the play as well as during intermission. The point was to draw spectators' attention to the essential freedom of the actor, who is forever shaped and reshaped, to kindle their imagination and elicit their response. To begin with, the actors offered an improvisation, the fruit of rehearsals, on the theme of killing oneself or the other: Hamlet and Laertes conducted a fencing duel; Ophelia "rehearsed" her drowning; the others were involved in wrestling or stabbing to death. This improvisation, which also served as a warm-up exercise, was followed by a direct address to the audience: they were welcomed, introduced to the plot and main characters, warned of the unhappy ending, and apprised of the focus of the production, namely, Hamlet's complex relationship with his father. During the course of this prelude, actions were matched to words, following Strasberg's dictum that not the word but the situation is the center of a play. The Ghost of Hamlet's father tossed and turned in bed, and when the others assisted him they found that he was covered with plasters and bandages, tokens of physical abuse.

It was only then that the actual play began, not at the beginning of the first act, but in the middle of the second act. The story of Hamlet, an intellectually inclined young man in modern clothes and sunglasses, was presented as a "case-history par excellence."[72] In keeping with Freudian analysis, Hamlet was shown to be suffering from a father complex and an Oedipus complex. The Ghost of his father, clinging to Hamlet's back like a child riding piggyback, beautifully conveyed the literal and figurative burden. Hamlet was urged to avenge his father's murder, but was paralyzed through an emotional blockage. The closer he came to it, the more he resisted it. According to Tabori's production this resistance — obviously a neurosis — was the result of his inability to feel genuine sorrow or to mourn deeply.

Here is Tabori's link with the German mentality, which he described in his essay "Hamlet in Blue." Like the Germans in post-Holocaust Germany who failed to engage in sincere and meaningful mourning-work — according to the Mitscherlichs in their seminal study *The Inability to Mourn* — Hamlet is rendered "duty-bound by grief" but fails to feel deep (and curative) sorrow. Instead, he struggles with a conscious obligation to the dead, which results in melancholia: "He suffers because he can't suffer and, by the terms of filial obligation, he ought to"; and while "the mourner laments his loss, the melancholic castigates himself."[73] It is only after the mousetrap episode (which is not dramatized but only recounted) that Hamlet is freed from his debilitating melancholia and starts acting: it is already too late.

Related to Hamlet's pathological relation to his father is, in Tabori's psychogram, his Oedipus complex. The rivalry between father and son over the mother/wife love reached its peak in an episode in which the queen enticed Hamlet to bed, seductively took off her own and Hamlet's clothes, and exchanged them. This intensely erotic scene, which reminded one of the critics of a Strindberg scenario,[74] was invented during rehearsals by Hamlet (Einbrodt) and Gertrude (Kahn) as a reaction to their own personal inhibitions.

Other significant alterations included Horatio's homoeroticism (an element featured in other lab productions); the Ghost's assault on the praying Claudius and their ensuing wrestling match (III.ii); Ophelia's strewing of trivial objects such as an electric lightbulb, a pen, and an old shoe instead of flowers over her dead father; the presentation of Claudius as an animal-trainer (an image taken over from the Kafka production), whose brutality and abuse of power were suggested by the piece of bloody meat clenched between his teeth; or the staging of the gravediggers' scene as a "Cologne-style carnival,"[75] with the two actor-fathers, Polonius and the Ghost, as gravediggers.

The performance concluded as so often in the lab with a direct appeal to spectators, echoing the prelude. The actors wished the audience an enjoyable time watching the forthcoming bloodbath. Red wine was served while the actors painted their faces blood-red and moved toward Hamlet with the stilted motions of marionettes (as at the end of *Afore Night Come*). Following Hamlet's famous line "The rest is silence," the actors repeated, as in the prelude, the main concerns of the performance. The Ghost reappeared, this time dressed in smoking jacket and top hat, and walked silently across the stage. While spectators applauded, the actors mingled with the crowd, thanking them personally for their attention. At times maddeningly crass, the performance was also, just as often, piercingly brilliant.

FINAL REMARKS

The Bremen Theaterlabor was Tabori's most intense, vigorous, and imposing attempt to give a concrete shape to his concept of a different, alternative theatre. Simultaneously, in the course of the actual work with the group — an intensive work-in-progress — he expanded or modified his initial concept of an alternative theatre in the light of empirical practice. The various theatrical experiments which followed, in Munich for instance, lacked the framework, the conditions, and the cohesive team that successfully developed a symbiotic working dynamics with Tabori. Years later, when he tried to repeat the experiment in Vienna, at his Kreis theatre and the adjacent workshop à la Strasberg's Actors Studio, the enterprise lacked the pristine quality, the unconditional spontaneity, of the Bremen lab. What is more, in his later undertakings Tabori worked with celebrated professional actors who brought with them a wealth of theatrical experience that they did not, and probably could not, efface.

Many critical comments were voiced against the Theaterlabor. In addition to receiving biting criticism of the uneven quality of productions, dilettantism, or psychotherapeutic dilly-dallyism, the group was chastised for willfully withdrawing into its own shell, indulging in private rituals. The actors were spoken of as a sect wallowing in private mythologies, cultivating a form of private mysticism, or submissively following the will of its guru. I have tried to provide concrete evidence for the team's democratic spirit as one of the lab's major principles. Nevertheless, there can be no doubt that the role played by Tabori, senior in age and more experienced, the charismatic director of the project, was greater than the actors were willing to admit. They adamantly opposed the impression that they were "crazy guru-dependents."[76] Many years later, examining the project in retrospect, theatre manager Stoltzenberg admitted that "every group needs a 'Guru': Peter Brook, Ariane Mnouchkine — we had George. Such people cannot be produced at will, they are a stroke of luck."[77]

THE *METAMORPHOSES* PERFORMANCE

Tonight he might turn into a bird.
Each night a rehearsal for death.
Practice makes the master.

George Tabori, "Breakfast"

KAFKA CONNECTIONS

"Esteemed gentlemen of the academy," Tabori addressed the eminent jury and the crowd of well-wishers that had gathered in his honor when he was awarded the prestigious Georg Büchner Prize in 1992. Those familiar with Tabori's work were not surprised, though evidently amused, to discover that he chose to launch his speech with the opening of Kafka's *A Report for an Academy*.[1] Tabori went on to describe his work in the German theatre and his relationship to German culture in terms of "that embarrassing word: love," though ironically that love was, as in the case of Kafka's ape-man, "a love story about a foreigner among the natives, for example, a Jew among Germans."[2]

Throughout his life Tabori felt attracted and inspired by Kafka, the man and the prose writer. "My first literary models were [Mann's] *The Magic Mountain* and Kafka's *The Metamorphosis*," he recalls.[3] His first film script, an adaptation of Mann's novel, was to remain unfilmed, but his periodic attempts to bring Kafka's prose to the stage proved more successful. His two major Kafka productions go back, not surprisingly, to Tabori's experimental phase. In the course of one year, 1977, he directed *Verwandlungen* (Metamorphoses) at the Kammerspiele in Munich (premiere 23 February 1977), and *Die Hungerkünstler* (Fasting-Artists) with his own troupe at the Theaterlabor in Bremen (premiere 10 June 1977). Fifteen years later, in 1992, Tabori presented a Kafka collage entitled *Unruhige Träume* (Uneasy Dreams) — a revised and reshaped version of the *Metamorphoses* at the experimental workshop of the Burgtheater in Vienna (premiere 29 April 1992). At the same time, he prepared a one-man show based on Kafka's *A Report for an Academy*, with the severely disabled Peter Radtke. The ape-man's report premiered under the auspices of the Burgtheater at the old conference hall of the Parliament in Vienna (12 July 1992). It then went on tour, was featured at international festivals, and was presented at the Zoological Gardens in Berlin against the background of lemurs in glass cages. During that same year, Tabori was appointed artistic director of the 1992 "Mittelfest" in Cividale de Friuli, and he decided to devote the entire summer festival to the world of Kafka, with some forty projects and productions.[4]

Tabori's oeuvre includes a short prose text entitled "Breakfast" (1983).[5] This is a painstakingly precise yet succinct account of the morning rituals of the fictitious menage of Kafka and Milena, with obvious allusions to the morning routine at the Taboris'. The text is a beautifully composed collage, moving and amusing, which combines quotes and metaphors from Kafka's prose with reflections on his physical suffering and mental agony with snapshot recollections of Tabori's own past. Toward the end of this mosaic homage to Franz with the "diabolical ears," Tabori introduces the biblical prophet Jonah — his favorite biblical figure[6] — in modern garb. A retired prophet, he tries to wriggle out of going on yet another mission, this time to Nineveh, by hiding under his mother's bed. When he finally gets to Nineveh, after the ordeal in the whale's belly, it turns out to be a Kafkaesque American Sodom, a place of hostility, violence, and cruelty. Disconcerted, he approaches God as the Almighty steps out of a Cadillac on his way to a pub. Embittered, he asks why God made a fool of him and what happened to the promised bang. To this God replies: "Sorry about that, but I had just invented mercy."[7]

For Tabori, Kafka is — along with Beckett — an unquestionable prophet of our times,[8] a seer tenaciously committed to truth, who, like Jonah, attempts to escape his innate vocation and his pitch-black view of humankind. Nothing has happened since Kafka's death which cannot be found in his works, Tabori maintains.[9] Kafka's somber vision of the human condition is marked by pathological sensitivity, an obsessive precision, and the uncompromising dedication to unraveling all the facets of existence. He is branded: his wounds are our wounds, and his vision, though thoroughly pessimistic and disconsolate, reassures us, makes us hope against hope: "If one encounters K., one is able to survive the worst, and one is free from the persecutors and 'the fear which makes human beings human.'" The close affinity Tabori feels toward Kafka is reinforced at the very end of "Breakfast," when the protagonist (Kafka or Tabori) is asked to write a commentary on the nature of happiness, like the prose piece "Vom Wesen des Glücks," which Tabori actually wrote.[10]

What is it that draws Tabori so forcefully to Kafka? Although Tabori was born almost thirty years after Kafka (and only ten years before his death), both belonged to the Jewish minority living in central Europe on the margins of the Austro-Hungarian monarchy. One lived in Prague, the other in Budapest, but both were nonetheless exposed to the German language and were steeped in German culture. Nonreligious, living in an assimilated Jewish environment, each discovered his Jewishness and harbored ambivalent feelings toward matters Jewish.[11] Kafka tried for a while to learn Hebrew, admitted he lacked any firm Jewish roots,[12] and was only superficially interested in the Zionist adventure in Palestine. Tabori's knowledge of Hebrew is minimal; although he did spend some time in Palestine, during the Second World War, he never made an effort to master the language. While keeping track of events with genuine concern, he has not made a secret of his ambivalent attitude to Israel, admitting on one occasion that the Jewish state "is to me absurd theatre, the last of the Jewish jokes."[13] Tellingly, both Kafka and Tabori were enchanted — in sharp contrast to the vast majority of assimilated European Jews — by the world of Hasidism, that religious-mystical folk culture which emerged among east European Jews in the mid eighteenth century. Whereas Kafka confessed to his close friend Max Brod that Hasidic tales were the only Jewish stuff with which he always felt at home,[14] Tabori seems particularly drawn to the melancholy and rudimentary wisdom of these tales, to their bittersweet humor.[15]

But there are more substantial affinities between the two. For Tabori, Kafka offers a rare example of the ideal fusion of art and life. It is the stubborn quest for the truth in his writing and in his life — pursued at any price — which accounts for the compelling and exemplary authenticity of Kafka's output. Kafka risked all and sacrificed all, like Tabori's ideal actor operating "without a net," totally absorbed in the "dangerous theatre." Like the genuine actor who shuns tricks and simulation, Kafka neither lies nor aggrandizes himself; Kafka "never writes for an effect or for the impression he will make. He writes out of the deepest echo of the head and the heart." [16]

Indeed, Kafka's total renunciation of hyperbolic and extravagant rhetoric, his economical, almost austere style, parallels Tabori's commitment to the poor and pure theatre: a performance on a bare stage with scant props, in which the presence of the actor is what really matters. [17] For Tabori, Kafka is a prophet, like Beckett, offering an ailing civilization "a diet, an enema, and a purgatory," while eschewing common tricks, ornaments, and hollow consolations — in short, fake and shoddy distractions.

Moreover, Tabori's writing and his theatre productions share divers motifs and metaphors with Kafka's prose. Prominent among these are the intricate and convoluted relationship between father and son; the insistent preoccupation — a form of hypochondria — with sickness, physical decrepitude, medical care and doctors, and dying; the theme of eating, feeding or fasting, resisting food, digesting or throwing up; the related images of meals (especially breakfast), specific foods such as milk (with its allusions of breast-feeding), milk-based porridge, and meat; and finally, the world of animals — wild beasts, caged, tame, and circus-trained animals, panthers, apes, insects, fowls, and birds of prey.

THE BEUYS CONNECTION

The production of *Verwandlungen* (*Metamorphoses* as opposed to the original *The Metamorphosis*), a collage subtitled "a free improvisation after Kafka," [18] is based to a large extent on Kafka's prose works *The Metamorphosis*, *The Judgment*, and *In the Penal Colony*, with occasional reference to Kafka's letters to his father or to Milena. [19] The three-hour performance underscores the reciprocity between Kafka's life and his art. At the same time, it is an impressive *mise-en-abyme*, a reflection on the nature of performance itself, in which the actors change roles from playing protagonists in a Kafka scenario to being quasifictitious actors rehearsing a Kafka production.

Most theatre critics who reviewed the production took no notice of Tabori's motto for the evening: "It is not too difficult to transform a man into an insect. The question is, how does one transform an insect into a man." Hardly anyone bothered to relate the presentation to Joseph Beuys's action-performance with a coyote entitled "I Like America and America Likes Me" (René Block Gallery, New York, 23–25 May 1974), the image that inspired Tabori's "Kafka-Overpaint."[20] These factors are essential to the understanding of the production and deserve close examination.

Tabori's motto points to his penchant for subversions and witticisms. He seems to propose that the shocking image with which Kafka's *The Metamorphosis* opens is not surprising at all. Tabori clearly objects to the denigration and condescending attitude people often display toward animals, insinuating that the transformation of a man into an insect may be perceived as an act of defiance and protest, as in Kafka's story. At the same time, the physical transformation of man to beast can be seen as a metaphor for the spiritual brutalization of humankind, a phenomenon of our age. In fact, the obvious associations with anti-Semitic Nazi propaganda, aligned with the German word *Ungeziefer* (which Kafka uses in his story), drive the point home. In the later production of *A Report for an Academy*, Peter Radtke, the disabled actor, presents Kafka's ape-man in his one-man show as a victim of rationalization and intolerance.

This is where Beuys's art Happening comes in. Beuys, who lived for a few days with a coyote in a fenced-in area which divided the "action"-space, proposed to draw attention to the way people project their inferiority feelings onto scapegoats.[21] The subversive image of the prairie wolf, once adored by the Indians and later hunted and denigrated as the mean coyote by the colonial white settlers, is intended to unsettle spectators, to provoke them to question and redefine accepted precepts and narratives. Indeed, this is also Tabori's intention in his Kafka collage. Is the insect, or the coyote, perhaps superior to modern humans?

And more: Tabori's presentation, specifically defined as an improvisation, resembles Beuys's *Aktion* in that it is a performance and not a re-presentation. It emphasizes the here and now, the authentic happening in time and space, which, for Tabori, is the gist of a genuine theatre experience. The performance consciously introduces and explores the element of chance or randomness. While the coyote is the unpredictable "author" in Beuys's emphatically unscripted performance,[22] the improvisations of the actors — the coauthors and coproducers of the Kafka collage[23] — suggest the same element of variability and risk. I say "suggest," because, although Tabori pursues a notion of creativity similar to that of Beuys (both extol the work of art which emerges from and flows back to life; both reject the dichotomy between life and art; and both recognize a basic potential for creativity in every human being),[24] Tabori's *Metamorphoses* is, in fact, a prestructured and well-rehearsed performance. The improvisational or arbitrary component, the fortuitous, which was essential during the rehearsals, loses some of its initial momentum in the planned and carefully rehearsed performance.

Furthermore, in Tabori's production the stage is clearly modeled on the ur-environment which Beuys had created.[25] The extended prelude which precedes the verbal exchange draws on images of the coyote performance. To elaborate: similar to Beuys's performance space, the acting area of the Kafka collage is divided into two sections — fore- and backstage acting areas — by a wire fence.[26] This separation deliberately baffles the spectators, for the inevitable question — where is the realm of freedom really? — remains an open one, calling for individual consideration. Spectators are encouraged to be active and reflective in both performances. They watch the *homo ludens* — Beuys with the coyote; the fasting-artist(s), the ape-man, or the insect in Tabori's approximation of Kafka. Significantly, the metatheatrical element is accentuated by means of a small illuminated model of a stage-design placed on the marginal line between the two areas. While the forefront of the divided stage presents the conscious, the back-area suggests the subconscious, the domain of dreams and anxieties. Like Beuys, Tabori uses scant props, the basics — a bed, a table, chairs, everyday objects — which recur in his stage iconography. Beuys's ubiquitous hat and walking stick appear in Tabori's collage (the hat and the walking stick are also significant images in Kafka's text *The Metamorphosis*).

THE PERFORMANCE

The prelude setting the tone of the entire production is a compelling tableau based on Kafka's story *The Vulture* and incorporates images from other Kafka texts as well as elements from Beuys's interaction with the coyote. Animal images abound in Kafka's prose, in Tabori's works, and in the works of Beuys — more often than not with positive connotations. A female in black and red gloves (Beuys wore brown ones) rushes to and fro across the back-area, ducks, claws her fingers, stares, and climbs up the fence. She is the vulture assaulting the sleeping protagonist, the Son, Gregor Samsa, against the background of the prerecorded narration. Nightmarish figures clad in black — the other characters in the collage — scurry across the stage while the Son rolls around restlessly, trying to defend himself and tousling with the brown blanket until he is finally smothered.

It is the brown blanket which turns out to be the central, polysemous signifier of Tabori's tableau. It echoes, of course, the grayish-brown felt with which Beuys covered himself at the outset of the interaction (one of the few elements used throughout), that felt which has become a hallmark of his autobiographically charged iconography. It suggests life-giving warmth, a sense of security. Emerging from under the brown cover signifies the ensuing metamorphosis — how easily, as Tabori's motto propounds, human turns into beast. It further denotes sleep and dreams, as well as awakening to a harsh reality. Subversively, the reality of the unreal, of dreams and hallucinations, turns out to be the more tangible and menacing reality. Finally, the blanket insinuates death: in the last scene it is used as a winding sheet to cover Kafka's dead body.

The presence of death looms over the entire performance and circumscribes it; from the squashing of an insect by the irritated actor/Father at the beginning to Kafka's slow and agonizing death at the end; from the harrowing spectacle of the "device" in operation (*In the Penal Colony*) to the improvisations on the last moments of Hamlet (offered by the Son) and of Goethe's Götz von Berlichingen (carried out by the Father).

Aware of the pitfalls of straight stage adaptations of Kafka's prose, Tabori typically went his own way in *Metamorphoses*. He deconstructed the original and recontextualized the selected excerpts as a stage script about a group of actors working with a director on Kafka's prose. Although his rendering of the Kafka extracts shows a deep loyalty to the original, Tabori quite clearly does not seek a linear enactment of Kafka's allegories. Rather, he is interested in the actual encounter between the actor, as an individual, and the text. How does a particular actor read and understand the text? Is a given situation approachable in more than one way, given to more than one interpretation? How does the confrontation with the text — or, in turn, with the subtext (i.e., Kafka's biography) — affect the performer physically, emotionally, and intellectually? These were some of the major issues that preoccupied Tabori and the actors during the three months of intensive rehearsals — an uncommonly long period in German theatre practice.

Tabori conceived the production as a group project, similar in concept and working method to the presentations of his own permanent troupe in Bremen, especially the highly enterprising *Sigmunds Freude* and *Talk Show*, which the Theaterlabor had just performed. The "Address to the Actors" attests to his unconventional approach to the production as well as to his intentions.[27] The emphasis lay with the inventive energy of each actor, in the hope of procuring a unique experience defying the prevailing norm of the perfectionistic and the reproducible — that which Tabori considers lifeless, "a totem." *Metamorphoses* was perceived as a presentation "without a net," an example of the "dangerous theatre" extolling the fortuitous, encouraging the improvisational. In stark contrast to the epic theatre and the Brechtian "there once was," the heart of the performance (like Beuys's interaction with the coyote) was the actual experience, immediate, visceral, real, genuine — Tabori's "there is."

The stage script was presented to the actors not as an authoritative and binding text, but as "an open scenario, a fable about improvising, which should be the basis for our improvisations." Although changes and modifications were introduced in the course of the intensive teamwork, and new elements emerged from the improvisations (like the vulture prologue or the squashing of the insect), the performance did not deviate from Tabori's stage script as radically as in productions such as *Talk Show*. This may be due to the fact that the group, having had no previous working experience with Tabori, was less familiar with his theatrics and personality than the members of the Theaterlabor, who had consciously chosen to engage in a radically different form of theatre-making. What did emerge prominently in the "final" version was the improvisational quality of the presentation. One critic surmised that "this was primarily not a Kafka evening, but an actors' happening."[28] Another colleague spoke of a "dramatized workshop well worth seeing."[29]

Structured as a (fictitious) rehearsal, the vulture prelude is followed by a simulated encounter with the text of Kafka's *The Metamorphosis*. The scenic arrangement can in hindsight be considered an étude for the opening scene of Tabori's highly acclaimed *Godot* production (1984).[30] The actors sit round the table, holding the text in their hands, trying to feel their way into it — an essential element in Tabori's process of working on a play. The stage instructions, namely, those sections of Kafka's narrative which have not been transposed into a dialogue, are read aloud by the Assistant-Director. In the course of the "Rehearsal," various other elements typifying the dynamics of theatre-making crop up and converge with the "acted" Kafka material: animosity and rivalry between actors, quirks and vanities, conflicting views or disputes over the mise-en-scène, squabbles and bickering.

The main plot element of the first scene, entitled "First Rehearsal" — Samsa's metamorphosis and the discovery of his new identity by his family and the visiting Chief Clerk — offered Tabori and the group the opportunity for professional self-reflection. How does one go about shaping a given role, in what way are stage directions helpful or harmful, and what part does, or should, a director play in the creative interaction? The Director in this performance is a prodigious personification of a theatre-maker à la Tabori, or perhaps of his mentor, Lee Strasberg. A remarkable, strong-willed stage veteran, he takes a dim view of theatricality, of passing modes and fashionable conventions. Instead he advocates the invigorating and stimulating reciprocity between life and art and quotes Kafka's view that the actor must be more intensive, more powerful, so theatre can have an influence on life. One should only perform plays which are incisive, argues the director: "A play must be the axe for the frozen sea in us." Tabori puts Kafka's words in the mouth of the Director with one alteration: while Kafka spoke of books, Tabori (or his Director) speaks of plays.[31]

Rather than demonstrating or setting an example for the actors to follow, the Director encourages them to tackle the role slowly, patiently, and ultimately to find the role in themselves. He supports the actor playing the Son in his painstaking efforts to find out how Samsa's "distressing squeak" was meant to sound.[32] Like Strasberg, he makes room for contingencies: "Don't play the joker, please, simply play the situation" (*Verwandlungen*, 14). The actors are advised to draw on their own reservoirs, tap their own resources — experiences, physical sensations, and neuroses, or what the actor/Director calls "psychosomatic sensibility" (22).

The complex relationship between father and son, the son's fear of becoming a mirror image of the father, or "the helplessness of the son as opposed to the superiority of the father," to quote critic Georg Hensel,[33] is further elaborated in the second scene, "The Second Rehearsal," which is largely based on Kafka's *The Judgment*. The

Son in blue jeans, outspoken and free in his gestures, unperturbed by the conventions of institutionalized acting, is almost an exemplary member of Strasberg's Actors Studio. The Father, on the other hand, is a theatre veteran, who is suspicious of the proposed new working method, abhors improvisations, and favors straight acting (impersonation) and pathos. He finds it difficult to conceive of the conflict between father and son in terms of an ancient, archetypal rivalry, let alone accept the Director's suggestion to foreground the comic element in it.

The relationship between father and son is a key element in the work of Tabori, as in Kafka's prose. "Each son wants to knock off his father at some point," Tabori wrote upon the premiere of *Cannibals*.[34] The tension of the love-hate relationship is poignantly displayed in the scene. "If only he'd [the Father] fall and smash to pieces!" is the Son's line, to which Tabori adds, "I hate this ass, I hate him!" This is one of the rare cases in the production where Tabori took the liberty to change the wording of Kafka's text or add to it. He likewise expands the scene to include the Son's physical assault on the Father, biting his neck and drawing blood, only to declare a few minutes later (a direct quote from Kafka's story), "I did love you, always."

The third scene, or "Third Rehearsal," adds a new dimension to the recontextualization of Kafka's narrative. The Director introduces the horrific device used to inscribe the offense on the body of the condemned, describing the way it functions with fanatic meticulousness. Notably, he is both the officer and the onlooker in Tabori's rendering of *In the Penal Colony*. The exchange of roles or perspectives is a frequent topos in Tabori's theatre, prompting a reconsideration of the inept classification into perpetrators, victims, or passive onlookers. It also adds a historio-political dimension to the collage. The "re-told" oscillates between the grotesque and the horrible, as Tabori introduces the Jewish comedian Levy, modeled on the Yiddish actor Yitzhak Löwy, whom Kafka befriended and admired.[35] Levy outlines a fictitious Kafka play entitled "Mordecai or the Revenge of the Prodigal Father" — a deliberate reversion of the legend of the prodigal son, conflated with the biblical story of Mordecai, Esther's uncle and surrogate father. No sooner does he delineate the plot than allusions are made to the Holocaust and to German-Jewish relations after it ("Where were you in 1944? . . . I knew straight away that we know each other," *Verwandlungen* 24).

Tabori juxtaposes the narrative of Jewish martyrology and redemption and memories of the Holocaust. Identities are blurred or deliberately confused. In the fictitious Mordecai play, the son is a Jew turned Christian ("Only a Jew knows what a Goy is, because a Goy is someone who doesn't know that he is a Goy, he only knows what a Jew is, and this makes him a Goy," 25), who joined the SS and participated in the atrocities. Thirty years later he feels drawn to the scene of the crime, like Fyodor Dostoyevsky's Raskolnikov,[36] and upon return discovers that his father is a watchman at the Bergen-Belsen memorial site.

This deviation into history, into a past made present, leads us back to *Penal Colony* and the precise delineation of the device, using a puppet (as in Tabori's *Improvisations on Shylock*, 1978) as a surrogate victim. The recontextualization of Kafka's story is enacted when the original "Honor your superiors!" — that sentence which the device inscribes on the victim's body — is changed into "Honor the Germans!" (*Verwandlungen*, 27).

Who then is the victimized, who is the one condemned to die? A puppet? An anonymous Jew? The father? The son? Kafka himself? This equivocation is evidently intentional. It converges with Tabori's conviction that the beauty of theatre-making lies in probing and experiencing a myriad of contradictory situations and scenarios.

The final scene, entitled "Main Rehearsal," rounds off the performance by reverting to *The Metamorphosis*. The conclusion joins together the preceding motifs and underscores the intermingling of fiction and reality, theatre and life, culminating in the presentation of Kafka's own death. Again, as in the prelude, it is an overpowering image which holds the spectator in suspense: Gregor Samsa as the insect, crawling and crouching all around, refusing the milk — "his favorite drink" — by way of defiance, like the fasting-artist, being deprived of his possessions, ignored, rejected, ostracized. Tabori, whose work abounds with images of eating and savoring, accentuates this motif in his Kafka collage: Gregor's rejection of the milk and the fresh food; his preference for the half-rotten vegetables and the disgusting leftovers; the breakfast scene with the lodgers; and the exact description of the father bombarding his son with apples — a scene which was enacted in Tabori's later version of the story, namely, in *Uneasy Dreams* (1992). Similarly, in the sustained finale enacting Kafka's death, his inability to eat or to drink is foregrounded. The Son/Kafka smells a fresh strawberry "lovingly" and spits it out after nearly choking on it. Fear and unbearable pain are commingled with zest for living, until he, the Son and Kafka, finally cries out to the Physician/Director to put an end to his agony: "Kill me, otherwise you're a murderer."

Tabori's *Metamorphoses*, a performance which signaled the onset of an innovative work phase under the auspices of the mainstream stage in Munich, enjoyed a most favorable reception. "Tabori's great power stems from the freedom which he exerts in the theatre, the unperturbed manner in which he ignores his own laws," wrote critic Thomas Petz.[37] Some explicitly praised the unusually high quality of acting, others "the merging of the horrifying with the comic, of unease with fun."[38]

Fifteen years later, Tabori's second Kakfa collage, *Uneasy Dreams*, drawing to a large extent on the same sources,[39] proved to be far less successful. The presentation was set in a boxing ring, which could also be taken to be a circus arena. The actors vacillated between the grotesque and the nightmarish, between slapstick and trepidation, with the severely disabled Peter Radtke playing the insect. The production seemed to lack the cohesiveness of the earlier collage. Kafka's texts became, as it were, the pre-text for a family melodrama tinged with "sour kitsch."[40] Ironically, Tabori proved his own conviction right: histrionic excess or an arsenal of affectations taints the performance and deprives it of the arresting power of authenticity.

Along with Shakespeare, Beckett, Brecht, and Dostoyevsky, Kafka has exercised a profound influence on Tabori's work. The four productions based on Kafka's prose, which Tabori directed during the course of fifteen years, are among his most enterprising theatre ventures. In his dramatic collage *Babylon Blues* (1991), Tabori creates a sort of epitaph for the much-admired Kafka, typically enough combining wit and melancholy. His alter-ego in this episode is Master Zvi, a "Talmid Chacham." He describes how Kakfa, writhing in pain, sighs with relief when the angel pierces his ailing body with a needle. Tabori concludes the anecdote on a softer, conciliatory note: "As the angel removed his hand, he seemed a small boy, dreaming a nice dream."[41]

*Hell becomes bearable through
the presence of a witness.*

George Tabori, "Berlin Connection"

Hans Magnus Enzensberger was both skeptical and apprehensive when George Tabori approached him in 1979 with the idea of creating a performance on the basis of his much-discussed epic poem *Der Untergang der Titanic* (The Sinking of the *Titanic*, 1978).[1] The poet, an experienced man of the theatre himself, tried to dissuade Tabori, but found that he was not easily deterred. "Meeting him for the first time, one gets the impression of a mild and accommodating man. But this impression is deceptive. Tabori is obstinate. He knows exactly what he wants."[2]

Tabori knew what he was after. Enzensberger's poetic pastiche about the dramatic sinking of RMS *Titanic* on its maiden voyage in 1912 proved to be an ideal text for an inventive and innovative performance in Tabori's experimental "dangerous theatre." In thirty-three cantos (*Gesänge*) and sixteen lyrical interim-texts (*Zwischentexte*), Enzensberger interlaces the cries of the passengers with reflections about the sinking of the legendary liner, presenting the ship as a metaphor for the collapse of capitalist society — indeed, a Ship of Fools. An image of human ingenuity frustrated by elemental forces (the iceberg), it is likewise a metaphor for the disillusionment with science and technological progress. Braided into Enzensberger's apocalyptic vision are autobiographical elements: the irrecoverable loss of his original manuscript, somewhere between Havana and Europe,[3] and the disenchantment with the euphoric hope to reform the world in the spirit of socialism as experienced by the politically engaged poet, a faithful representative of the so-called Generation of '68.

Tabori renders Enzensberger's poetic vision as a vivid

and compelling apocalypse of ice: an avalanche of stage images — sensuous, immediate, compelling — evoking the struggle for survival, the menacing helplessness, and ultimately resignation and demise. In Tabori's *Titanic*, the iceberg which crushes all hopes becomes the driving force for a voyage into the self. Tabori's rephrasing of Kafka's maxim that a genuine play is the axe for the frozen sea in us comes readily to mind.[4] The social and political aspects latent in Enzensberger's epic are overshadowed by the fervent Taborian exploration of the human psyche, the subliminal. In an interview he gave on the day of the premiere (8 May 1980), Tabori said: "The language, the metaphors, the images, are only the tip of the iceberg which sunk the *Titanic*. Underneath it are concrete fears, especially the fear of suffocating, of drowning."[5]

Indeed, Tabori consciously shifts the perspective: beyond the vivid images and verbal description, the drowning is in the mind, albeit as real, tangible, and harrowing. His interest lies quite clearly with the psychological dimensions of the catastrophe. Together with the seven actors he explores basic and authentic states of anxiety, horror, isolation, despair, and exhaustion as well as the unquenchable desire to live to the full, even to experience the titillating sensation of fashioning and practicing one's own demise. On the edge of existence, in a borderline state (*Grenzsituation*), the awareness of the irreversible, the inescapable doom — some critics spoke of an "end-of-all-times" metaphor[6] — turns out to be the centrifugal force for a dialectical performance characterized by its sensuality, directness, and immediacy. Images of vivacity and vigor combine with tableaux of mortality and demise; cries, clamor, shrill shouts, whispers, or melodious singing intermingle with a medley of prerecorded sounds of dripping water, shifting ice, and noisy machines; the black and the white (of the setting and the costumes)[7] interplay with the lights and darks produced by stage-lights; hasty and abrupt movements and expressive gesticulations are juxtaposed with the immutability of a dead-end situation; and last but not least, the (non)sense of morbidity and exasperation is tinged with redeeming humor or, as critic Thomas Thieringer put it, "music-hall-despair and slapstick-misfortune."[8]

In an impressionistic essay entitled "Berlin Connection" Tabori compares Enzensberger's *Titanic* with the combined paintings of the prominent American artist Robert Rauschenberg. As Joseph Beuys's interaction with a coyote inspired Tabori's original recontexualization of Kafka's *Metamorphosis*, Rauschenberg's assemblage principle sets a model for his *Titanic* presentation. Not only does Rauschenberg believe, like Tabori, that painting — or for that matter theatre — relates to both art and life, but his combined paintings integrate elements of art objects (brushwork, overpainting, collage) with "nonart" objects from daily life, ready-mades (watches, pillowcases, stuffed birds, traffic signs, etc.), creating a composition close to Tabori's theatre-collages in its dynamic inclusiveness. This is what Tabori says about the American artist, whose compositional principle admittedly influenced the tradition of performance known as a Happening: "Rauschenberg may be the most striking dramaturg of our age. . . . In his 'combined paintings' . . . , in this highly dialectical art-form, he allowed private and public mythologies to clash and merge into each other." [9]

Tabori presents Enzensberger's poetic apocalypse as a visual dystopia, which paradoxically expresses the cherished "principle of hope." The closing verse of the last canto, "howl and swim on," echoes Tabori's principle of hope, so close in spirit to Beckett's hope-suffused despair, which Tabori fondly quotes: "Fail. Fail again. Fail better." [10] No wonder, then, that the *Titanic* production was followed by experimentations with Beckett texts. In fact, on various occasions Tabori's troupe presented the *Titanic* along with Beckett's *Le dépeupleur*, as Tabori had initially planned. [11] And there is yet another similarity between Enzensberger and Beckett, according to Tabori: each one rehearses his own death in his oeuvre, returning from the nether regions to practice it again and again. In the case of Enzensberger, the experience of dying is related to the lost manuscript, while the principle of hope lies in the creative process itself — retrieving the lost work suggests the recollection of the past and an ever new involvement in it.

As the troupe soon came to realize, the poet who "rehearses" his own death may be considered the subtext for the *Titanic* performance, its secret play. This brings us back to Rauschenberg's "dramaturgical" principle, for Tabori designs the performance as an interplay between the mythical and the private, the collective and the individual. Although the actors figure as anonymous participants in a collective experience and the performance abounds in group tableaux (the actors assembled on the white sofa or joining to form a chorus line), major significance is attributed to each actor's personal experience of fear, despair, self-assurance, suffocation, etc. It is this personal approach to the text, the authentic encounter of each single actor with conflicting sensations, which parallels the poet's "rehearsal" of his own demise and is the core of the entire performance. The keyword in Tabori's account of Enzensberger's *Titanic* is "response," alluding to Rauschenberg's overpainting of Sandro Botticelli's response to Dante Alighieri's *Cantos*. Enzensberger's verse-epic, "a comedy" on the fate of the liner scudding through the ice field,[12] is the German poet's response to Dante's *Divine Comedy* — a text referring to a text, a discourse which effaces the breach between past and present. "We neither play Enzensberger nor Beckett," says Tabori, "but we respond to them, just as they respond to the previous hells."[13] Thus each of the seven actors responds to the text, the given situation, in a different way, tapping an individual reservoir of experiences; each voice is unique, and all these voices generate a polyphony of responses, a "plurality of readings," which as such resists the notion of a monolithic and binding interpretation.

In contrast to the multitemporality, the divisibility of time which characterizes Enzensberger's text, the *Titanic* performance is characteristically an experience of the "here and now." Enzensberger moves back and forth in time(s); memoried past overlaps with the amnesiac present; attempts to forget and forgo, to misremember and consign to oblivion, merge with a determination to retrieve and record, to recapitulate and reassess. In Tabori's production, recollection is inscribed in concrete experience; the present involvement circumscribes all time(s). And, as so often with Tabori, the final product is merely an open rehearsal of a work-in-progress, or, as Andrzej Wirth so accurately put it, "the public got to see only the tip of the iceberg."[14]

A year and a half after the Theaterlabor group disbanded, six of the original participants joined Tabori in Munich for his new project.[15] Despite the fact that the *Titanic* production was carried out under the auspices of the Kammerspiele, all the actors were paid through the special job-creation program (*Arbeitsschaffungsmaßnahmen*) introduced by the government to help bring the unemployed back into the labor force. In a letter to Hans-Reinhard Müller, artistic director of the Kammerspiele, Tabori made it clear that his alternative theatre work with the group sought to combine training *and* production. Further, he defended the group by dismissing as "senseless theatre paranoia" allegations that it constituted "a state within the state" in the Kammerspiele.[16]

The letter to Müller also documents the fact that Tabori planned the *Titanic* as one of three projects at his workshop, the other two being Beckett's *Le dépeupleur* and John Cassavetes's *Knife*. He intended the *Titanic* project to serve as a test-case for the audience and its reaction or, in his words, "a research programme about problems of communication."[17] Ideally, the presentation would be staged in various different locales (a jazz-club, church, bookstore, street, the Olympic stadium in Munich, etc.) in front of people from diverse social groups. "In each performance we could investigate the different social, political, metaphysical, philosophical, etc. aspects of Enzensberger's text and conduct a legitimate social experiment." Although the plan did not materialize the way Tabori had envisaged it, the *Titanic* production was performed often and in diverse settings after its premiere at the theatre workshop. Among the memorable presentations were those conducted at the Atlas Circus in Munich, in various factories, and at the entrance of the Freie Bühne in Berlin.[18] The most exciting of these presentations was undoubtedly the performance on board the steamer *Kurfürst* (Elector) sailing on the Wannsee in Berlin, with about one hundred passengers/spectators who — in stark contrast to the elitist company aboard the *Titanic* — were neither nouveau-riches nor part of high society.[19]

The period of rehearsals extended over three months. Enzensberger, who was present only twice, felt totally out of place, "a fifth wheel," as he put it. The atmosphere in the crowded, dimly lit smoke-filled room of a rented flat in Munich "resembled that of the steerage deck of an old-time steamer. . . . The rehearsal proceeded chaotically, as if each of those present were unleashing his obsessions."[20] Improvisations focused upon the exposure to physical danger and the confrontation with a treacherous situation. According to the rehearsal notes, the group agreed fairly soon that water, "the most dangerous, the most active of all elements," was to be the crux of the presentation.[21] "During the first rehearsals work was done with water sounds, on which the actors had to concentrate. . . . It concerned drowning. Cold, wet, the fear of drowning — this is the subtext of the poem. Ideally each would disclose his/her fear of suffocation and drowning. This play also concerns the question: how can we break away from our anxieties?"

In the course of rehearsals, the actors were sensitized to water: they smelled and tasted it, compared its qualities to those of oil, felt water on their bodies, and were exposed to a plethora of water sounds inviting their reactions. Stanley Walden, in charge of the music and sound effects, recalls producing a "vocabulary of real water sounds" and the "first sound of the production," which was, typically, another joint undertaking. "We produced the 'perfect wave' by pulling a piece of linen, as wide as the breadth of a swimming pool, over the water of an indoor pool. On either side, two assistants turned the microphones toward the 'wave,' while five of us ran all around the pool. The result was an acoustic image in stereo. I recorded it again on a four-track-tape, and the 'wave' roared, amplified electronically through the speakers distributed all over the space and directed to the audience. It was the first sound of the production. It generated a sense of unavoidable fear and terror. An appropriate preparation for the experience of going down." [22]

Water and ice were the central acoustic and visual elements of the show. Water in its various states — liquid or frozen, in diverse quantities and forms, standing still or flowing, dripping, trickling, leaking, splashing — evoked an arresting juxtaposition of the real and the fantastic, a contraposition of living and dying. The stage resembled both a vast ice field and a ship's interior. The rear, or the ship's hull seen from inside, was a wall of whitewashed wooden boards. The entire acting area had a springy slanting floor, which was covered with transparent plastic foil with fine cracks. Two set pieces demarcated a binary opposition: at the rear was a white sofa on which the actors assembled, rested, or waited for their cues, while at the front a big siluroid and some goldfish swam in an oversized aquarium lit with fluorescent green light. The aquarium, like the pails suspended from rods occasionally pouring out water and the bared theatre machinery and lighting system, marked the deliberate attempt to avoid an illusionistic presentation. At the same time, the aquarium with the fish and the remnants of a doll in it — a "combined painting" conflating the animate and inanimate, the living and the inert — was a powerful image of a macrocosm encapsulated. When, toward the end of the production, one by one the actors plunge into the 18-degrees Celsius cold water, in which the fish swim (almost) unaware,[23] water signifies the extinction of humanity. On the other hand, for the siluroid, water is the most basic precondition for survival, whereas being exposed to air — that good fresh air which the drowning passengers so frantically grasp for — means death. The water-filled aquarium is thus simultaneously a life-sustaining sphere and a coffin.

During the rehearsal period, the actors experimented with all kinds of ideas relating to the aquarium and the fish. As usual, Tabori welcomed every proposal with "Let's try it!" Stanley Walden recalls: "Nothing was rejected a priori. Naturally many of the ideas were ultimately discarded."[24] In fact, before settling on the aquarium, the group sought to evoke the sensation of deprivation and loss by means of a suitcase filled with personal belongings and water.[25] No sooner did they agree upon the aquarium than a suggestion was made to drain it during the performance to enact the extinction of the fish. A dead trout was introduced as a "magic object" to stimulate associations and reactions. Later the group toyed with the idea of cooking a carp and eating the fish soup in front of the audience. Cooking and eating, recurrent themes in Tabori's theatre, were meant to endow the spectacle of dying with an archetypal, quasi-mythical dimension. The intention was "to show something which most people do not wish to see . . . the fish, a Christian and a sexual symbol, . . . analogous to the meal of the gods. The ritual is the reenactment of the godly sacrifice."[26] The idea was eventually abandoned.

The performance, a sequence of visual, acoustic, and rhythmic permutations, opened with a tableau: the actors — women in white, men in black, all wearing black hats — reposed on the white sofa, smoking, stretching out, yawning, sighing. An image of a decadent, complacent, and satiated company, marked by indifference, chilled emotions, and boredom, this scene is an obvious allusion to the jaded company on board the *Titanic*. In this static black-and-white opening scenario, the company performs the sixth canto of Enzensberger's original poem, a text referring explicitly to Germany ("where Europe is darkest, in Berlin") and questioning the notion of the real and the fictitious. The actors then begin to move the plastic to the sounds of waves roaring and machines rattling. Little by little they slip under or get entangled in the foil, wriggle with it, and grope for fresh air, expressing in movement and mime the hopeless struggle against drowning. Only then is Enzensberger's first canto staged. While most of the cantos are voiced by the actors (who sometimes choose shrill cries, at other times whispers), Tabori also incorporates segments of Enzensberger's own recorded reading, thus fusing presentation with representation. In counterpoint to these recitations are light or humorous moments, such as the singing of the hit song "This can't possibly shake a seaman" (Canto 13). This kind of juxtaposition runs throughout the performance. The revuelike moments, slapstick numbers, and speech in various German dialects converge with the highly dramatic, pathos-suffused episodes; the light moments are designed as foils for the somber picture, providing an ironic innuendo and the necessary emotional distance. This two-sided strategy, straddling the traumatic and the jocose, also characterizes the numerous episodes in which the actors must confront water and ice. They dance, crawl, or bounce on water and ice; slide down the slanted stage covered with wet plastic foil; climb the backdrop, roll down, stagger on the wet cloth, slip and topple over. Indeed spectators were not sure whether they were watching some dangerously thrilling acrobatics or wonderful slapstick.

Parts of Enzensberger's *Titanic* were enacted: the painting entitled *Nomads in the Desert* by Salomon Pollock, which decorated the large drawing room of the liner (Canto 24), and the sumptuous dinner relished by the first-class passengers in view of the envious other travelers (Canto 7). On other occasions the group adopted an associative approach to the text, as in the episode (Canto 12) when — at the cry of "Emergency rocket!" — the actors threw their hats in the air, in the manner of a revue or circus number. Similarly, on the verge of drowning, they grabbed their last opportunity of living life to the brim, as it were, by frantically dancing a tango. The episode enacting the cruel struggle of survival, "everybody against everybody," was presented as a wild exchange of hats during which the actors took turns blowing a toy trumpet and was rounded off with moving embraces and farewell kisses. The performance concluded with another impressive collective tableau: all of the actors, lifeless "watercorpses," cast their own death masks out of plaster, smearing their faces in gypsum — seven mutilated white faces with mouths agape, shattering in their silent outcry. The actors then distributed the masks — a chilling *memento mori* — among the spectators.

The performance was received with mixed feelings. Some showered praise on Tabori and the group; others argued that the audience, far from being consternated, were piqued, even titillated, to see how far the actors would go. Still others condemned the show as a failed experiment and as a disservice to Enzensberger's text. The poet, who years later cooperated with Tabori on the production of *Delirium*,[27] said that the *Titanic* performance revealed aspects of his text he had not recognized before, haunting his memory with its black and white, arcane quality.

STAGING BECKETT

There is by now something called Beckettish, as there used to be Kafkaesque or Brechtian. These are labels, not the thing they label, logos for librarians, critics, hostesses, pubcrawlers, bullshitartists.

George Tabori, "First Rehearsal Day Talk"

In a short, moving obituary which he composed as a mosaic of verbal segments and images taken from Beckett's work, Tabori portrayed the late poet as a man of contradictions ("Sam was a prophet, that is, the great realist . . . a churchless Christian"), whose life and work coalesce into a compelling metaphor of the human condition.[1] We who survive Beckett, "the lost ones,"[2] are left with the legacy of a naysayer who suggested that "the greater the unhappiness, the greater the happiness once unhappiness finally comes to an end." Ever since he came upon Beckett's work at the beginning of his own career as a theatre-man, in the 1960s, Tabori has been fascinated by Beckett, whom he considers "the poet of our age."[3] Over the years Tabori directed a variety of Beckett's texts, wrote articles about him, quoted his lines in interviews, program-notes, and even in his own plays, corresponded with Beckett ("his small cards were like love-letters to me"),[4] and met him in Paris.[5] Tabori summed up his feelings toward Beckett in the following words: "I admire, love him. Love is probably the right word. He speaks to me more than anyone else living nowadays. Nobody since Kafka has given me so much. I love this man."[6]

What is it that has so appealed to Tabori? His own writings about "the grandmaster" and the various productions he directed especially in the 1980s disclose that the private Beckett (whom Beckett himself tried so vehemently to keep private) fueled Tabori's imagination no less than Beckett's poetic visions of humankind. Tabori doggedly sought what he defined as "the subtext, the subcontinent" of Beckett's hermetic texts. Beckett's writing is entirely autobiographical, personal, sincere, and therefore concrete, accessible, and intelligible, argues Tabori in the face of many a critic.

The severe structure of the text and Beckett's seeming inclination toward formalism are, in Tabori's view, the artist's ever fresh attempt to safeguard and ensconce himself, since the "subtexts in him are volcanoes," which, in turn, mirror infallibly the chaos of the modern psyche.[7]

Indeed, Tabori finds in Beckett's writing a sustained and succinct metaphor of the paradoxical nature which underlies human existence. He maintains that Beckett depicts in his plays borderline situations (*Grenzsituationen*) typical of modern existence and adds that, despite the intrinsic hopelessness of such situations, Beckett's characters — Winnie, for example — signify the unquenchable human desire to live. In Tabori's opinion Beckett is "the only 'positive' poet at the moment, advocating a principle of hope which can only be credible in utterly hopeless situations."[8]

Beckett's strong appeal for Tabori undoubtedly increased through their shared experience of a partly forced, partly self-imposed exile. Tabori, an exemplary nomad-Jew, a lifelong sojourner in seventeen countries, feels a strong affinity to the Irish poet who chose to live and create in exile. "The Jews and the Irish have a lot in common, the jokes, the palavering, the patricide. We slaughtered God and made a joke out of it. . . . Blasphemy is a particularly subtle form of belief. Godot is God, . . . a very Jewish-Irish God, terrible and funny," writes Tabori,[9] whose attitude to his Jewish identity is no less complex than Beckett's relationship to his Irish origin. The hope to be salvaged from an utterly hopeless situation, which Tabori considers to be the overriding metaphor in Beckett's works, is, to his mind, also the quintessence of Jewish fate. As he put it: "For the Irish and also for the Jews the situation is often hopeless, but not serious."[10]

DANGEROUS THEATRE IN THE CIRCUS:
BECKETT EVENING I

Beckett Evening I (premiered on 4 December 1980), the first of three evenings which Tabori called his Beckett-project,[11] took place in the tent of the Atlas-Circus in Munich, that performance site which is so closely associated with Tabori's concept of the "dangerous theatre." The cast of ten actors (most of whom had worked with Tabori in his Theaterlabor in Bremen), eighteen circus artists, and an assortment of tamed animals offered the audience seated in the round a Beckett-collage of twelve short plays, pantomime or television scenes, and prose texts.[12]

The motto underlying the production — "I am unhappy, but not unhappy enough. This is my unhappiness"[13] — alludes to the deliberately equivocal nature of the presentation. Exploring Beckett's vision of the human predicament, Tabori and his actors discovered and intimated to the spectators the principle of hope which seems to be embedded in hopeless situations. The sustaining energy of the production derived from the unresolved tension between antithetical qualities: the abstract or formalistic character of the Beckett oeuvre and Tabori's attempt to render it concrete; the pedantically conceived text as opposed to the spontaneous approach of the actors who augmented it by exploring the underlying authentic emotions, that is, the subtext; and, finally, the tension between horror and frivolity, Beckett's distinctively bleak vision of our terrestial condition and the entertaining spectacle.

The choice of the circus as the acting area for *Beckett Evening I* (Tabori would return to the circus years later, for his production of Mozart's *The Magic Flute* in August 1998) accorded beautifully with the willfully nurtured ambiguity which colored the entire production. The arena was both the circumscribed circle, that enclosure in which humans are trapped, as well as that world in which imagination, creativity, and joy predominate. The tame animals, indispensable members of any circus, suggested the state of being captured and trained, while at the same time they appeared as the incarnation of nature and freedom, an image of spontaneity and the unconscious. The circus is a world in which aggressive directness exists alongside amusement. Tabori included customary circus stunts such as the exchange of hats, the throwing of knives, and a game with fire in his production. The evening underscored his belief that the circus may offer a superior kind of theatre, his greatly desired "dangerous theatre," in which horror and delight, visceral risk and energy, are inseparably related, and in which both the expected and the unexpected may be anticipated.

The production opened with a horse and pony-ride show. The animals obediently made their rounds while a trainer in dark glasses and whistle, Tabori's allusion to the Holocaust,[14] directed them with whip lashes and shrill whistles. Summoned by an unseen voice, the actors slowly convened, either wearing typical circus costumes or dressed in sloppy rags, ready to enact their roles or, in Tabori's vernacular, to find the role in themselves. The prologue which followed was made up of references, mostly nonverbal, to various Beckett texts. The actors took off their hats and shoes (*Waiting for Godot*), peeled and greedily ate bananas (*Krapp's Last Tape*), folded and unfolded large white pieces of cloth (*Endgame*), and rehearsed Estragon's unsuccessful suicide. This prelude set the atmosphere for the scenes which followed. It likewise pointed to Tabori's staging principle: the exploration of Beckett's world demanded the unconditional, total engagement of each participant. The actors were to take Beckett literally, find their own personal subtext in the text, pursue the concrete experience behind the image, and transmute the word into action or sensation.

Three scenes in *Beckett Evening I* deserve closer attention, being artistically more accomplished and satisfying than the other episodes and illustrating Tabori's approach to Beckett. In the short scene entitled *Breath* the actors were hidden under large white sheets. Actor Thomas Kylau stood amidst the white "human" patches, reading out the entire Beckett text, made up of stage directions, counting the passing seconds, and stating the name of the edition and the publisher of the text he was using (a device which Tabori was to use again in his production of *Godot*). The scene seemed to exist relatedly on two levels. It was a model-image of theatre work and at the same time a sustained stage image of dying or the last gasps of living. In a commentary on this scene Tabori said: "Death is always present in Beckett's work, waiting, not for Godot, but for you and me, an inch, a gasp away, the only real thing for the living, if they'd be willing to look."[15]

Tabori's rendering of *Not I* was of unusual intensity and striking originality. The ecstatic monologue of the old woman who overcomes her muteness and bursts out in a compulsive tirade was a spellbinding celebration of life and hope. Actress Ursula Höpfner delivered the text very fast and excessively loud, oscillating between exaltation and hysteria. She was tied to a wooden board, enclosed by knives fixed all around her by a knife-thrower. Her enforced physical inaction and her animal-like subjugation were diametrically opposed to the extreme inner freedom expressed in her monologue. In an attempt to explain why he had not closely followed Beckett's stage directions for *Not I*, Tabori made clear that he considered the monologue to be a kind of screamed confession by a mute person rather than a moderately pitched rational discourse.[16]

The auditor in Tabori's version of *Not I* was not human, as Beckett's text suggests, but an elephant, an animal which in many iconographic traditions symbolizes sagacity and strength. The elephant, "a Mother archetype" as one critic suggested,[17] overheard the extraordinary confession and reacted occasionally by producing sounds of nervousness and pain. The woman and the animal were captive yet free. Their articulation in word or sound signified a deeper sense of liberty, the driving energy in an otherwise immutable, deathlike existence. The woman ("Mouth"), who was being born or set free through the elocutionary act in the light of two blazing torches, left the arena riding triumphantly on the elephant's back.

Consciously deviating from Beckett's meticulously formulated instructions, Tabori's version of *Play* was nonetheless one of the highlights of the evening. The triangular relationship between a man and two women was expanded into a stage image of human yearning for recognition, such as actors hope for and relish. Unlike Beckett's stage direction, which confines them to gray urns with only their heads protruding, Tabori's actors were in constant movement; they wandered all over the arena, restless and anxious. Each member of the peculiar triad was calling attention to himself/herself; correspondingly, each actor sought recognition and acknowledgment. The desire to stand in the limelight was taken literally: whoever was illuminated by the spotlight had the brief opportunity to shed light on his or her version of the relationship story. At the height of this frenzied chase the quality of lighting changed and with it the connotations of light. The three figures in the circus-arena were suddenly terrorized by a searchlight. They appeared like haunted animals, trapped by an unseen hunter, and tried to hide beneath the hospital beds on which they had been sitting. "Tabori stages the horror, the state of being exposed; training in the circus becomes a horrifying act of training. Man becomes animal, a wretched nothing; Beckett's emotionless resumé becomes Tabori's horror vision."[18]

The atmosphere prevailing in *Beckett Evening I* was one of contradictions, oscillating between bristling fear and a deep sense of hope, veering from unfathomable despair to immense joy. The production demonstrated clearly Tabori's conviction that happiness and unhappiness are inextricably related. "The *B. Abend I* is what may be called a success, people come in growing hordes. . . . The press is split," Tabori informs Beckett; he admits: "it's been Love Labor's Won, I can't get anything right, that's my method, before getting it wrong. So the pigeonholers may be acooing, but there are a few moments that shine like pearls in a rotten oyster."[19]

WORD INTO FLESH: *THE LOST ONES*

A brief note from Paris reached Tabori in Munich. "Wishing you the best of agonies," wrote Beckett in reaction to Tabori's letter announcing his plan to stage the prose text *Le dépeupleur* (The Lost Ones).[20] Tabori was well aware that his new enterprise, the "centre piece" of his Beckett project,[21] would involve tribulation and agony. He made no secret of the immense difficulties ahead when he addressed the actors at the outset of rehearsals, saying: "This piece isn't only difficult, it is impossible, so rejoice."[22] Tabori was familiar with the abundant secondary literature which offered to interpret and explain the text[23] — over two hundred bodies climbing, crouching, or posing motionless in a cylinder, that "report of an investigative committee on the situation in purgatory," as Alfred Alvarez described it.[24] In fact, Joachim Kaiser's interpretive comment, suggesting that Beckett's *The Lost Ones*, "thoroughly thought out and dry as a grammar of despair, . . . [is] like an immense, scenic instruction for a drama which must not take place,"[25] prodded Tabori to stage it: "We shall now try to play it all the more," he told the actors.[26] The original plan to stage the text subsequent to *Beckett Evening I* in the confines of a circus-ring ("we'll have no stage, only a circle as befits hell") fell through.[27] The production finally premiered in a factory hall in Bochum on 1 July 1981.

Once again Tabori discarded the convention advocating loyalty to the text (*Werktreue*) — "correct reading," in his translation — in favor of a personal associative grappling with it. The three different zones of the cylinder and the groups of bodies that seem to be related to it were, by way of example, absent from his production. Beckett's text, prerecorded, was read out quite some time after the actual presentation had started, and no attempt was made to generate an effect of synchronicity.

"Searching is what matters, as *Der Verwaiser* shows, rather than the finding which may anyhow be hopeless," Tabori commented on Beckett's text.[28] Truly, an unremitting, almost obsessive pursuit characterized the practical work on the text. Renouncing any binding, mandatory interpretation of *The Lost Ones*, Tabori and the actors were engaged in finding out together more and more possibilities of experiencing and consequently understanding the text. The production history of *The Lost Ones* is a striking illustration of Tabori's conviction that the process is more significant than the final product. During the rehearsals he and the actors came up with ever fresh ideas on the possible staging of the text, and one experiment followed another. The version which eventually premiered in Bochum was not the final production. It was revised and changed in Cologne and yet again altered in Berlin.[29]

This relentless collective search after a wide range of possible versions of Beckett's text rested on an exhaustive exploration of the subtext, which Tabori applauded: "My passion for B. is undoubtedly perverse. What draws me to him is a search for a subtext that may not be there, to find a Beckett that is not." The imaginative exploration of the subtext turned out to be a learning process which in turn generated alternative variants. These diverse variants were welcomed by Tabori, who considers such experiments to be "an antidote to the Deadly Theatre."[30]

Tabori's fascination with the "learning process" and his obsessive quest for a stimulating subtext are particularly interesting in light of his own lifelong experience as a permanent wanderer, a modern Ahasuerus who neither has nor wishes to have a geographical home. I believe it is his position as an outsider, a man who acquired a number of languages yet never really made any of them his linguistic home, which made him so sensitive to the subtleties of language as such and attracted him to Beckett, a self-exiled Irishman writing in two languages. Consequently, it is not surprising that on his explorative journey through the subtext, apart from looking for clues in Deirdre Bair's biography of Beckett ("Beware the Bair," warned the grandmaster after he had heard of *Beckett Evening I*),[31] Tabori paid special attention to the three different titles, in three different languages, of Beckett's text.[32]

The original title of the text, *Le dépeupleur*, evoked in Tabori the idea of mass murder, the image of a man who systematically depopulates a given place. His primary association was Auschwitz, yet other names followed: Hiroshima, Gulag, Uganda. The Jewish perspective set in again as Tabori compared the seemingly dispassionate style of narration to the way a Jew who had escaped Nazi Germany by the skin of his teeth would recount his life story or tell of the extermination of his parents.[33] Tabori promised Beckett to play the text as a game of chess between grand masters: the game — a hobby he shared with Beckett, who apparently sent him the computer chess program "Mephisto" — was a poignant image of human determination to defeat and destroy fellow humans.[34]

The English title *The Lost Ones* shifted, according to Tabori, the emphasis from the victimizer to the victim. "These bodies are lost, but only in the English text, each searching for its lost one," he asserted, suggesting the image of people who indulge in longings for a lost love, a lost soul, or even the lost self.

Finally, the German title *Der Verwaiser*, which Tabori adopted for his production, suggested an additional subtextual dimension, namely, "the futile search or pursuit of the lost beloved, the only creature who is absent." [35] The German title forefronts the "orphan" rather than "people," the one who had been left, forsaken. Tabori paraphrased the opening sentence of *The Lost Ones*: "An abode where lost bodies roam, each searching for the one he lost." The quest and the longing become the metaphor for the human condition. It is the quest that marks the cycle of nature, birth and death, childhood and parentage, and it is the longing which so closely relates Eros and Thanatos.

"This is a central theme with Beckett: not having been properly born . . . he tries . . . to return to the womb, which is also the grave," observes Tabori, who takes up this motif in his own writing.[36] And he elaborates further: "This is a general pathology. We are all condemned to search for the hole, which once was our abode, a lost paradise; we enter a hole, for a moment a light flickers, yet it is time and again the wrong hole; the right one must remain taboo." [37]

Tabori orchestrated these diverse subtextual perspectives in his production. His aim was to "make the audience see" the agonized yearning of the orphan or lost one. This for him epitomized the essence of all theatre, and he described it with an original, polysemic compound in German: *Sehen-Sucht* (*Sehen*: seeing; *Sucht*: yearning, also pathological addiction; *Sehnsucht*: longing). *Seh(e)nsucht* is probably the most adequate compact description of Tabori's production *The Lost Ones*. In it the word is animated with breath; it is transformed into putrid flesh.[38]

The production was launched with a perplexing tableau, which one critic aptly described as an "environmental triptych."[39] Tabori was clearly out to find "a grammar of bodies."[40] On the left side of the acting area in the factory hall were nine naked men, sitting or lying on hospital beds, motionless, their faces covered with plaster masks. Opposite them, on the right-hand side, were nine naked women on a sloppy rostrum sitting or squatting, equally motionless, their faces, too, covered with plaster masks. Behind the women one could see bits of Veronika Dorn's scenic elements for Tabori's earlier *Titanic* production: long black plastic pipes, an old shabby sofa, a large aquarium in which a fish was swimming to and fro. Tabori was quoting himself, as it were, alluding to the elements shared by the two productions. The scene suggested a still life, the only moving creature being the fish, that phallic symbol of life renewed and sustained, yet trapped. Between these two still human poles, in the center, was a metal tower, the scenic "equivalent" of Beckett's cylinder, in which a number of platforms, accessible by reposing ladders, were structured one above the other. The tower was bandaged with transparent plastic, revealing its entrails — the metal rods and joints — and the entire structure was bathed in the dull yellowish light emanating from above.

The ticking of a metronome was heard. Languidly, as if compelled by an unseen force, the actors began to move. The men took off their masks and made their way to the women, who likewise revealed their faces. Bodies were facing bodies, an extraordinary encounter of fair and foul flesh. Both male and female smeared each other with a white clammy substance which they scooped out of pails. Finally, when all were covered in white from hair to toe, they started moving toward the tower and assembled at its feet. The beat of the metronome ceased. The prerecorded reading of Beckett's *The Lost Ones* was heard through the amplifier.[41] Traugott Buhre read the text, accentuating the enormous difficulty which it presented: he repeated sentences, stumbled over phrases and reread them, raced through others like a man trying to rid himself of a cumbersome task. Against this auditory background, yet avoiding activity which would parallel or illustrate the verbal description, the bodies began to move into and onto the tower. They ascended the ladders, moved from one platform to another, crouched and climbed, yelled aggressively and threatened each other as they frantically looked for a place to shelter and rest — a live scene of human struggle for survival and security, the permanent quest for the "hole" or a protected niche. Typical of Tabori's approach was the fact that the actors preserved their individuality (in contrast with the prose text) throughout the collective experience, each offering an individual version, so to speak, of the struggle for security. As this intense and aggressive search subsided, energy was directed toward encounters of compassion and tenderness. In peace and quiet the bodies cowered like embryos or lay on the platforms, searching for one another: the actors touched, kissed, caressed, and felt each other, longing for human proximity, indeed for the absent one.

The production received mixed reviews. "Tabori's speculation of creating an indubitable, authentic expression out of asceticism . . . does not succeed. What is left? Bad metaphysics," writes Michael Erdmann, while critic Hedwig Rhode argues that the stark performance makes use of the original text in a radical fashion. Tabori's approach to the Beckett text was unmistakable: while proceeding from Beckett's bleak configuration of the human condition, his intention was to seek reassurance and hope rather than scenes of hell and despair. "In Beckett's abode love is absent, and that must be the worst of all hells. . . . It sometimes seems to me that for the first time in the history of civilization we must be prepared to live without affection and warmth, that we have to scratch our itching skin while we crawl into the grave where no one can be embraced. If we could turn our inside outwards, it would look like the scorched land of Hiroshima." [42]

HOMELESS IMMIGRANTS: *WAITING FOR GODOT*

The original Beckett project did not include the staging of *Waiting for Godot*. *Beckett Evening I* and *The Lost Ones* were to be followed according to Tabori's initial plan by a production of *Happy Days*. The offer to direct *Godot* reached Tabori at a time in which it was absolutely clear that his Beckett project could not be completed due to financial and technical hindrances. Tabori took up the offer. The play was premiered in the workshop-studio of the Kammerspiele in Munich on 4 January 1984. lt was to be one of his finest, most highly acclaimed productions: the leading actors, Peter Lühr and Thomas Holtzmann, were voted best actors of the year, Tabori's production was lauded as second best of the season, and the presentation was an unexpected box-office success.

As for Beckett, he was apparently horrified by reports he heard of the production. Although familiar by then with Tabori's idiosyncratic approach to his texts ("I hear you give your actors a lot of freedom" [43]), he authorized, perhaps surprisingly, the production. In a letter to Klaus Herm he wrote: "I heard about Tabori's *Godot* and squirmed. Since then there has been one für Kinder. A version for the mentally deficient no doubt in preparation." [44]

As opposed to the relatively clear starting point with which Tabori began rehearsals on the two previous Beckett productions, where he himself had chosen the texts, determined the course of the sequence, conducted staging experiments ignoring any existing models, and finally addressed his troupe with an introductory speech by way of offering them a frame of reference for the particular production, he seems to have had only a very vague concept when rehearsals on *Godot* commenced. In fact, the evidence available to us — his own statements and actors' reports [45] — indicates that the staging concept which appeared so clear on the first night and won the unanimous praise of the critics was discussed, molded, revised, and crystallized in the course of the rehearsal period itself.

Tabori, who has always rejected the idea of an omniscient, authoritarian director imposing his will on the actors, seems to have outdone himself. Thomas Holtzmann recounts how he and Peter Lühr sat week in, week out, at the director's desk, read, discussed, and memorized the text while "George was watching us"; "He always sat there with gaping eyes and did not intervene much." On a number of occasions the two actors were in fact skeptical about the entire undertaking. "Nothing would come of it," they thought. Yet Tabori, occasionally seized by "mortal fear," "always seemed soothing and comforting" and managed to create an atmosphere of "calm and relaxation." He recalls: "We constantly drank coffee and once or twice, no, I did not give instructions, I made suggestions, and these were, yes, accepted." [46]

Once again Tabori seems to have been stimulated by the "secret play," that subtext which Beckett himself staunchly deprecated. Fascinated by the autobiographical experience underlying the text, Tabori tried to find affinities to and clarifications of *Godot* in other Beckett texts, especially in *Mercier and Camier*. He went to Paris to speak to Beckett, knowing well that the great master would be the wrong source for any questions concerning *Godot*, and he immersed himself in Bair's biography of Beckett. It was within the pages of this biography that Tabori found the subtext which kindled his imagination and generated the central concept of his production. *Waiting for Godot* was a play about "recognizable human conflicts"; "Estragon and Vladimir are neither clowns nor tramps, but refugees, intellectuals," Tabori maintained; he drew attention to the fact that Beckett and his wife, who had been active in the French Resistance during the war, had to flee Paris in 1942 and look for a temporary shelter in the south of France.[47] Beckett's fate as an intellectual fugitive who had known the taste of danger and threat found an echo in Tabori's own fate as an intellectual immigrant who fled the Nazis and found only temporary shelter in various countries in the course of the war.

Despite Tabori's discreet and modest guidance the final production was clearly stamped with his theatre approach. The most striking feature about it was the attempt to keep the metaphorical quality of the play while simultaneously allowing for a realistic dimension to unfold. Waiting for the enigmatic Godot, Gogo and Didi were oscillating between despair and hope — an incarnation of human hope against hope. "Let's go," says Estragon; he and Vladimir do not move; theirs is a departure leading everywhere and nowhere. At the same time Tabori rejected the almost traditional staging of the two protagonists as tramp clowns in favor of a psychologically oriented presentation: here were two individuals, no longer agile young artists but "bourgeois-dressed people" whose relationship insinuated a "quasi-Strindberg partnership with bickering and squabbling."[48]

The unconventional quality of Tabori's *Godot* was apparent from the outset. The acting area was marked by a circle of sand with spectators seated on benches and pillows all around. In the middle of the circle was an elongated table — two tables which had been joined — surrounded by simple chairs. While spectators were taking their seats, waiting for the show to begin, nine people were sitting around the table, drinking coffee and chatting, waiting for yet another rehearsal to start. Among them were the prompter, the scenery designer, the dramatic assistant, and the director, Tabori.[49] No country road, no tree: instead of the latter ("The Giacometti tree," according to Tabori), a dangling plastic-cord was hanging down from the single plain lamp placed above the table. In act II, corresponding to Beckett's demand that the tree should have four or five leaves, a green branch resembling a willow replaced the bare branch. The sparse use of lighting, scenery, and properties in this strikingly intimate production was intended to underline Beckett's discernible will to reduction and simplification. The only prop Tabori added was an alarm clock which was placed on the rehearsal table. At the end of the production the clock was on the floor. Time was up, or, alternatively, time no longer mattered.

Against this nonillusionistic background the play evolved as an imaginary rehearsal. Holding the popular green Suhrkamp edition of *Godot* in his hand, Thomas Holtzmann read out the opening stage direction, a procedure which recurred a number of times in the course of the production and accentuated the play/rehearsal-within-the-play motif. He and Lühr were exploring the roles of Vladimir and Estragon, "becoming" Didi and Gogo, only to return time and again to their own selves and their encounter with the roles.

Mostly alone on the stage, the duo displayed a complex relationship marked by interdependence and tenderness, cruelty and homoerotic affection, while at the same time underlining the joy of acting, the felicity of discovering the text or of improvising. The rehearsal perspective suggested an open-ended experience: not only was waiting a never-ending occupation for Vladimir and Estragon, so was the acting — or rehearsing — of the play, for Holtzmann and Lühr created an ever-changing show, ever open to alterations and fresh improvisations. "Here is no allegorical vehicle, no offer to explain the world, but a ritual, a play according to its own rules," observed critic Rolf May.[50]

Tabori's willful resistance to interpretation — yet another reading of Beckett's famous play — should, to my mind, also be seen as his attempt to debunk the myth of Beckett as an unintelligible, abstract dramatist whose plays are meant for an erudite elite or for scholars eager to decode symbols. Tabori clearly sought to bring the play closer to the audience, relieve Beckett of the shackles of holiness, and make him more human and accessible. Behind this wish was an experience he had in the United States. In the early 1960s he was close to a theatre group made up of black and white actors. He suggested playing *Waiting for Godot*. "They played *Godot* and told me later that they had performed mostly for Blacks, in churches, in villages, in the fields, where no theatre had previously been seen. Children came, elderly people, and they all said: We know these types. They sit around, do nothing, talk and wait for something. No one had any problems understanding them."[51]

Focusing on "recognizable human conflicts" while rigorously following the original text, Tabori's *Godot* offered scenes of hatred, compassion, despair, and tenderness in a sequence which seemed to have no beginning and no end, neither a climax nor any real development. This plethora of human emotions was vividly manifest through the exceptional acting of the two leading actors, Thomas Holtzmann as Vladimir and Peter Lühr as Estragon. "Two old men, cantankerous, tender and inescapably allied together, a strange old couple, the one [Estragon] with sore feet, the other [Vladimir] with an invincible urge to pee, waiting for something which will not come."[52] Peter Lühr presented a frail yet vivacious, cynical and childlike Estragon, whose physical agility was supplemented by vocal virtuosity. He entered the acting area somewhat bent, in a winter coat, his white hair unkempt, carrying a file with papers under his right arm — an intellectual and poet, full of childlike eagerness. Thomas Holtzmann's Vladimir was his counterpart, a heavy, broad-shouldered, bespectacled, serious, and at times tragic partner.

The complementary relationship of Pozzo and Lucky seemed like an interlude in the ritual of waiting, "the penetration of the outer world."[53] Their first appearance was a show of sadism and brutality: Pozzo (Claus Ebert) dressed like an elegant Mafia boss, all in black with patent leather shoes and a whip in hand, was the archetypal despot who harassed and bullied the servile, dogged Lucky (Arnulf Schumacher) with the collar around his neck. Lucky crawled, danced, carried things mechanically, and delivered his long fragmentary meditation lying flat on the table like a man haunted by a senseless nightmare, trying to rid himself of it without understanding what it is all about. The second entry of Pozzo and Lucky offered a scene of unfathomable suffering. Pozzo, blind, was carried by the dumb Lucky. The messenger assumed to have been sent by Godot — a boy in Beckett's text, a grown man with a hat hiding his face in Tabori's production — let the sand which he had picked up from the scenic circle flow through his fingers, a personified hourglass reminiscent in gesture only of the passage of time.

Waiting as action and inaction, as the expression of hope against hope, was undoubtedly the central aspect of Tabori's production. *Waiting for Godot* is a play about waiting for Godot, nothing more but equally nothing less, argued Tabori; waiting is pure theatre, he explained, with its inherent tensions and anticipation. "As long as we appear at the appointed hour, night after night, we are saved," he maintained in his essay "Waiting for Beckett." [54] Hope, one may conclude, lies not in an encounter with Godot but in the actual waiting for him.

THE PRINCIPLE OF HOPE: *HAPPY DAYS*

Tabori's production of *Happy Days* originally planned to be "the coda" of his Beckett project,[55] premiered after a good many delays at the Kammerspiele workshop in Munich on 13 April 1986, as homage to the master's eightieth birthday. A dubious tribute it turned out to be, and one which would no doubt have upset Beckett enormously, as it deviated consciously from his meticuously formulated vision.

To begin with, Tabori dispensed with the unforgettable overriding stage image of the play, that image which, as in all of Beckett's plays, "encapsulates the essence of the meaning." [56] Winnie's mound was replaced by a bed, a key-prop in Tabori's theatre ("The first home [*Heimat*] of a human being as well as his last").[57] Thirty-two spotlights focused harshly on the steel-framed bed, with its four corners tied by cords to the ceiling. The wings at the back were covered with blood-red paper, and the stage itself was strewn with red sand as seen on tennis courts.

Tabori's Winnie, far from Beckett's idea of "a woman of about fifty," was played by the young and attractive Ursula Höpfner, wearing a nightdress with a low décolletage and ample necklaces. Though paralyzed in both legs, she proved to be a bundle of endless energy as she crept, leapt, wriggled, and gesticulated among the big eiderdowns. Höpfner's Winnie delivered the text in a rather uniform manner, disregarding Beckett's clearly specified instructions, while trying to convey her frustration, anger, or passion through gestures. Her lifelong mate, Willie, was Peter Radtke, a severely disabled dwarf who played the role of the child victim in Tabori's idiosyncratic production of *M* (for *Medea*) a year earlier. Contrary to Beckett's detailed stage directions, Tabori's Willie was visible throughout the entire performance and finally even managed to penetrate Winnie's kingdom as he crept from his wheelchair to the bed, dressed up ludicrously in white cutaway gloves and an elegant top hat. Physically close at last, the two panted in excitement, yet the bed turned out to be an image of matrimonial hell: Winnie and Willie were scuffling for love, continuously hurting each other, vying with one another for recognition.

As in his previous Beckett productions, Tabori sought to imbue the metaphysical with a concrete, human experience. "I have 'normalized' the play, have taken it away from the metaphysical," he told an interviewer. "I wanted to go back to the existential source, I wanted to fathom the couple and show it. In their hell both are still trying to hold on to life. Despite the impossibility of a relationship, Winnie seeks to keep the man. . . . Go on doing, go on talking. Here is the the principle of hope."[58]

Once again, then, Tabori's emphasis lay on the dynamic, pendular swing between revulsion and longing, frustration and hope. Instead of focusing his attention on the play as an abstract configuration of the visual and the rhythmic, he offered his audience a "love story."[59] The love-hate relationship of Winnie and Willie, colored by tenderness, animosity, and interdependence, was much closer to the relationship of Vladimir and Estragon in Tabori's *Godot* than people cared to think. In this production, much more than in *Godot*, Tabori's psychogenic approach to Beckett's text became apparent. His interest lay clearly in the labyrinth of human passions, in emotional invalidity or mental handicap, conveyed through the physical semiparalysis or disability of both protagonists. Instead of being buried in sand, Tabori's Winnie and Willie were victims of their own paralyzed bodies and their thwarted emotions. This approach found a compelling expression when Winnie, with her head imprisoned between the steel bars of the bed, spoke to Willie at the opening of act II or when she put the revolver, an emblem of sexual longing, between her legs instead of on the ground to her right, calling: "There, that's your home from this day out."

However, in the final judgment, Tabori's staging failed, primarily because it did not capture the quintessence of Beckett's original vision, indeed, because it rejected the stage image of the woman buried in the mound, of which the verbal discourse is only an extension. It also failed in terms of its own staging concept. Tabori undermined the psychological foundations and credibility of the two protagonists by fusing, for example, extraneous, incongruous musical excerpts into his production.

The performance began with a rehearsal segment of Richard Wagner's *Tristan and Isolde* (prelude to act III, the expression of yearning and inability to escape life). The voice of the Viennese conductor Karl Böhm was heard, commenting and instructing as the music was played, while Willie in his wheelchair circled the bed from which Winnie was glaring longingly, with her arms stretched out to him. Toward the end of the play, when the two were united in bed, Tabori deflated the moment of physical proximity and turned it into tasteless parody with the couple singing a duet from Franz Lehár's operetta *The Merry Widow*. In addition to these inappropriate musical comments, Tabori further travestied his own reading of Beckett's play by incorporating the groans and whistles of whales to accompany Winnie's agonized craving for Willie.

Equally questionable was the casting of the severely disabled Peter Radtke as Willie. Several critics felt that it was most unlikely for an attractive and lively Winnie as represented by Ursula Höpfner to be so passionately enthralled by such a man.[60] Some criticized Tabori for having whimsically augmented Willie's role; others accused him of having pursued a titillating sensationalism.[61] Clearly Tabori's failure to honor and respect Beckett's demands was in this case self-defeating. The farfetched and wayward reading, along with the miscasting of Willie, resulted in a highly problematic production.

END OF ALL GAMES: CONCLUDING REMARKS

Nearly fifteen years after his early experimentations with Beckett, Tabori, by now a revered "theater-guru," turned for the last time to the "grandmaster." At the age of eighty-three he finally made an old dream come true with the staging of *Endgame* at the Akademietheater in Vienna (premiered on 31 January 1998). Tabori outdid Beckett, as it were, radicalized him: he eliminated the characters of Nell and Nagg from the play (parts of their dialogue were delivered by Hamm and Clov) and dispensed with the minimal scenic elements which Beckett required. Tabori took Beckett's "bare interior" literally: no door, no windows, no bins. A circle was drawn with a piece of chalk on the stage; the position of the windows, the door, and the bins was likewise crayoned. "Let's imagine," says Hamm (Gert Voss) to Clov (Ignaz Kirchner): indeed, the game takes places in the mind, fueled by imaginativeness and theatrical ingenuity. A cardboard at the rear read: "Rehearsal. Entrance forbidden." Recalling his *Godot*, Tabori staged *Endgame* as a rehearsal. An extended prelude, so typical of Tabori's theater work, introduced Hamm as the director in a black T-shirt and a dingy dark suit with the text in hand and Clov, with a cigarette between his lips and a cup of coffee, as his assistant. Here were Mr. Jay/Voss and Goldberg/Kirchner, the tyrannical director and his servile assistant out of Tabori's own *Goldberg Variations*. Beckett's Hamm and Clov, resembling famed Tabori pairs such as Shlomo Herzl and Hitler (*Mein Kampf*) or Weisman and Copperface (*Weisman and Copperface*), were a pair bound in friendship that was essentially a power relationship,[62] master and slave/servant, a peevish, moody sick man and his long-suffering, submissive male nurse, father and son, a quarrelsome yet insepa-rable couple.

"Try again," director-Hamm/Voss urges his partner. "Play it again, Sam," he eggs on. This is the End-Game, nothing less than merely a game, as Beckett insinuated. Critic Gerhard Stadelmaier aptly observed: "Beckett's demand to play in a simple manner is taken jokingly in full earnestness."[63] For Tabori, life is tolerable as long as the game continues. Where there's theatre, there is hope.

Tabori's Beckett productions are all original and experimental stagings which neither adhere to the principle of correct reading (*Werktreue*) nor follow the model which Beckett himself set or of which he approved. Underlying these productions is Tabori's con-viction that Beckett, far from being the abstract, incomprehensible, or absurd writer he is reputed to be, registers in his writings elemen-tal human experiences which as such are recognizable by and intel-ligible to most spectators.

Tabori was eager to present a sensuous Beckett and thus encour-aged the actors to concentrate on the body and its expressiveness. In his attempt to present a simple and accessible Beckett ("Beckett is the simplest voice I know"),[64] Tabori based his practical work dur-ing the rehearsal process on an extensive investigation of the subtext in Beckett as well as on the actors' collective and individual attempts to discover the assigned roles in themselves.

Tabori clearly favored a nonillusionistic staging concept and sought to enrich his experimental mise-en-scène of Beckett's texts by bringing the world of theatre into the actual production, as a structural framework in his *Godot* and in *Endgame* or as a visual meditation on the "dangerous theatre" in *Beckett Evening I*. He was fully aware that his productions ran against the authoritative versions set by Beckett. In fact, he was hoping to liberate the text from the dogmatic model so as to open it to ever-fresh readings. Conscious of the enormous challenge of staging Beckett, he told his actors, "We're not going to make it, and that is good."[65] His resolve and grittiness are aligned with Beckett's desperate formula for the modern artist as driven by a "fidelity to failure" and the mind-binding imperative of *Worstward Ho*: "Fail. Fail again. Fail better."

The Tabori family. Cornelius Tabori stands in the middle; seated in front of him is his wife, Elsa. Aunt Martha is on Elsa's left; grandmother Fanny Kraus-Ziffer with grandson Paul is on her right. Courtesy of George Tabori.

Cornelius Tabori in Budapest shortly before his deportation to Auschwitz. Courtesy of George Tabori.

Lear's Shadow. *Theater der Kreis, 1989. Detlef Jacobsen and Ursula Höpfner.*
Courtesy of Detlef Jacobsen.

opposite top
Lear's Shadow. *Theater der Kreis, 1989.*
Left to right: Detlef Jacobsen, Ursula Höpfner, and Hildegard Schmahl.
Courtesy of Detlef Jacobsen.

opposite bottom
Lear's Shadow. *Theater der Kreis, 1989.*
Left to right: Renate Jett, Ursula Höpfner, Hildegard Schmahl, Detlef Jacobsen, and
Isabel Karajan. Courtesy of Detlef Jacobsen.

Samuel Beckett's The Lost Ones *(Tabori's* Beckett Evening II*). Bochum, 1981. Photo by Thomas Eichhorn, courtesy of Thomas Eichhorn.*

opposite
Tabori's adaptation of Franz Kafka, "A Fasting-Artist." Bremen, 1977. Photo by Jörg Höpfner, courtesy of Ursula Höpfner-Tabori.

Gert Voss as Alfons Morgenstern surrounded by the cooks in Tabori's The Ballad of the Wiener Schnitzel. *Vienna, 1996. Photo by R. Walz, courtesy of the Burgtheater, Vienna.*

Leslie Malton as Ruth and Michael Degen as Weisman in Tabori's Weisman and Copperface. *Vienna, 1990. Photo by Thomas Räse, courtesy of the Burgtheater, Vienna.*

Branko Samarovski (left) as Murdoch and Gert Voss as Zucker in Tabori's Requiem for a Spy. *Vienna, 1993. Photo by R. Walz, courtesy of the Burgtheater, Vienna.*

Ursula Höpfner and Erich Schleyer in Tabori's Don in Heaven, *part of the double-bill* The Mass-Murderess and Her Friends. *Vienna, 1995. Photo by Abisag Tüllmann, courtesy of the Burgtheater, Vienna.*

opposite
Gert Voss as Mr. Jay in Tabori's Goldberg Variations. *Vienna, 1991. Photo by Oliver Herrmann, courtesy of the Burgtheater, Vienna.*

Babylon Blues. *Vienna, 1991. Left to right: Ursula Höpfner, Günter Einbrodt, and Julia von Sell. Photo by Oliver Herrmann, courtesy of the Burgtheater, Vienna.*

opposite
Peter Wolfsberger as Constable Feinschreiber and Ute Springer as the prisoner in Tabori's The Last Night in September. *Vienna, 1997. Photo by Andreas Pohlmann, courtesy of the Burgtheater, Vienna.*

*George Tabori
and dog Gobbo
in Vienna, 1998.
Courtesy of
Ursula Höpfner-
Tabori.*

A SHAKESPEARE COLLAGE

He is the most un-English of poets, full of Greek insanities, Russian torments, German depths and all sorts of Continental lecheries.

George Tabori, "Reflections on the Figleaf"

Tabori's oeuvre teems with references to Shakespeare. No other author is conjured up as frequently in Tabori's prose and theatrical work, no other dramatist as extensively quoted, paraphrased, or associatively assimilated as the Bard. The long list of Tabori's stagings features only seven productions, besides innumerable plans for others based on Shakespearean texts — none of them, it should be noted, traditional, straightforward renderings.[1]

Shakespeare the man and his poetic world inspired some of Tabori's most brilliant and mercurial reflections in prose, among them "Lovers and Lunatics," "Reflections on the Figleaf," and the seminal essay "Hamlet in Blue." In Tabori's miscellaneous writings, I came upon some delightful *aperçus* on Shakespearean characters.[2] His semiautobiographical play *Peepshow* (1984), a farcical rendering of what might be considered a dramatized *Bildungsroman*, features in the main role the son Willie, a poet in the making, along with the Dark Lady, the Father's Ghost, and innumerable allusions to Shakespearean drama.

Shakespeare was an intimate spiritual companion throughout Tabori's life. As a child in Budapest, he listened spellbound to Grandma Fanny's renditions of Shakespeare stories. Years later, as a film scriptwriter and a novice playwright in the United States, he read and reread his Shakespeare, exchanging impressions and opinions with his brother, Paul, in London. "It may shock you, but I consider

Shakespeare one of the worst playwrights (technically) in the world," confesses Paul, in the same breath hailing him as "the greatest poet and almost the greatest philosopher."[3] George defends the Bard against Paul's unjust verdict, seeking untiringly to rescue him from scavanging academic scholars and from "bourgeois critics."[4] For him, Shakespearean drama is not the object of self-serving and all too often pedestrian research, but a pulsating corpus of imaginative creation to which he responded cognitively and emotionally.

Moreover, Shakespearean drama serves as a model against which other works are measured; it sets, as it were, unwritten rules for effective and proficient writing — Tabori calls it "technique" — allowing simultaneously for unmitigated freedom of experiment. "I've learnt more from Shakespeare and Brecht than [from] any other source," he confides in this revealing correspondence, which dates back in all likelihood to the early 1950s.[5] And he goes on to explain: "They were (or rather are) the greatest technicians, and the intensity and passion and freedom they could create was always in direct ratio to the precision of their structure."[6]

In later years, Tabori was to adopt a more detached, even critical, attitude to Brecht's theatrics; his esteem for Shakespeare remained unabated, however, and was indeed to increase, if anything. Shakespeare's plays, supremely exemplifying Tabori's ideal of the dialectics of structure and freedom, discipline and spontaneity, prompt playmaker Tabori and his actors to embark on a theatrical experience which is at the same time a process of self-exploration, an encounter with deep-seated passions. The bare platform — Shakespeare's "wooden O" — is Tabori's ideal stage, "our greatest model,"[7] since it refocuses attention on the actor, calls for the active imaginative participation of the audience, and "bridges the gap between life and art."

Apart from the two productions based on *The Merchant of Venice* (1966 and 1978; see chapter 12) and the Bremen *Hamlet* (1978; see chapter 3), all other stagings belong to the last station of Tabori's odyssey. It was in Vienna, in his own long-yearned-for theatre, Der Kreis, with his troupe of familiar actors, that the veteran theatreman, by then seventy-five years old, felt free of all restrictions and inhibitions and ready to venture on his "Shakespeare Cycle" project. What he defined as Shakespeare's secret — "the heart of silence, which throbs in his plays"[8] — had fascinated him through all those years: those questions which Shakespeare posed in his plays and left unanswered, the deliberately blurred motivation of his characters — Hamlet's secret, Lear's "dark purpose," or Iago's malignity — which could never be fully rationalized or fathomed.

It was indeed this riddle, the enigma at the core of each play, the openness of the text to ever-fresh readings, which kindled the imagination of Tabori and the actors and infallibly brought about a creative discourse with the text. Shakespeare is no public sacrum, no "frozen national monument decorated with a figleaf, discreetly."[9] His characters are neither demigods nor saints in a pantheon, but flesh-and-blood figures. The actor's business then is to feel a way into the character(s), to engage with the riddle, or, in Tabori's words, "to find the role in himself." The journey into the inner world of the Bard is also a journey into the self. It rejects out of hand the ubiquitous and standard concept of playacting and instead calls for genuine involvement, the willingness to expose oneself, feel a thought, think an emotion, experience with all the senses. For no other dramatist displays as broad a canvas of human passions as Shakespeare did, taking no heed of conventions or decorum, flying in the face of taboos, as great "artists and sorcerers" do:[10]

> His [Shakespeare's] blessed threat consists in the ever-present intrusion of his realities in our own. . . . If we are willing to start a love-affair with him — to listen with our third ear, think with our privates, feel with our bowels, smell with our hearts — we are bound to fall through a deep hole walled by mirrors into our own biographies. There we meet our secret selves — the lover Troilus who pimps for his beloved, the fanatic moralist Angelo ready to rape his nun, the impotent fighter Macbeth, who looks for his manhood in murder; all the poor puritans, like Hamlet, demanding chaste constancy from the women, meaning "Don't sit under the appletree with anyone else but me"; the machos who confuse seduction with rape, the dread daddies — Lear, Prospero, Shylock, Brabantio — with their ill-disguised longing to slip into their daughters' drawers; the incomparable realists like Iago and Edmund, who shatter our dearest illusions, without which we cannot live; and the fabulous women with their armory of withering wit, cockteasing charm, crossing their knees beneath the visiting moon, whenever their fools and knaves are panting with libido.[11]

The encounter with Shakespearean drama, first and foremost the Shakespeare collage *Lovers and Lunatics* (*Verliebte und Verrückte*, 1989), was no doubt Tabori's most adventurous undertaking in his own Kreis theatre, "the greatest adventure of my theatre-life," as he put it.[12] The collage was originally conceived as a preliminary approximation of Shakespearean drama, a kind of pilot project in preparation for the full production of the plays, which he ultimately did not fully realize. Thirteen years after Peter Stein's impressive marathon *Shakespeare's Memory* (1976), Tabori offered a six-hour-long encounter with Shakespearean drama.[13] Stein's monumental project, based as it was on extensive research, aimed at relating Shakespearean theatre to its historical context, resulting in "a kind of living museum of the Elizabethan age."[14] Tabori, on the other hand, confined himself to the text, sought to excavate the passions underlying it, pursued intertextuality, and tried to establish parallels or interconnections which would shed new light on the playwright and his poetic world. Here again he deployed his favorite strategy of deconstructing the text and recontextualizing it. His objective was the "fragmentization of particular plays . . . , a deconstruction which could lead to the dark heart of the poet and to ours; a learning process about the cross-connections between Lear's daughters and Macbeth's witches, for instance."[15] Truly, the project constitutes a fine example of Tabori's alternative style of theatre: it is a joint effort of the actors, who approach a well-known text collectively as well as personally in a direct and authentic manner; it is a democratic process of theatre-making, rejecting the star-oriented system, in which each member of the ensemble is, nonetheless, given a moment of individual glory.

The performance was shaped in the course of nearly six months of rehearsals. The attentive reading of texts was accompanied by improvisations on specific situations and experimentation with particular scenes. Tabori was assisted by his codirector Martin Fried and by Ursula Voss, who was in charge of the dramaturgy. The ensemble itself consisted of thirteen actors, seven males (Tabori included) and six females. Some were Tabori devotees, who had gone with him through thick and thin in Bremen and Munich; others, like Hildegard Schmahl, were distinguished professional veterans of the institutionalized stage.

The presentation was launched with a prologue, Theseus's key speech on the power of the imagination (*Midsummer Night's Dream*, V.i. 4–22), which indirectly argued the advantage of the bare stage or Tabori's preference for the "poor theatre," while at the same time establishing the principle of his idiosyncratic recontextualization —

the principle, namely, that Shakespeare's entire oeuvre, "seething" from the brain of "the lunatic, the lover and the poet," is "of imagination all compact." An ardent supporter of the unlocalized and convertible *platea*, Tabori opted for a nonrepresentational stage, void of ostentatious paraphernalia. The proscenium stage displayed "a scanty setting":[16] an acting space bounded at the rear by a firewall made of sooty bricks. At the center of the space was an elevated wooden rostrum which was used as a table, a gangway, or an imaginary arena. A throne draped with red and black cloth was the only stage-prop. The actors all wore simple long dresses in timeless black-and-white.

On this almost bare stage the actors carried the production, supported by a tacit agreement with an audience that was prepared to contribute its part and partake in the revel of the imagination, as in fact in Elizabethan theatre.

"Lovers and madmen have such seething brains, / Such shaping fantasies, that apprehend / More than cool reason ever comprehends": Theseus's observation is indeed the motto of Tabori's collage, its underlying principle. Deconstructing over a dozen of Shakespeare's plays,[17] Tabori dispensed with the plot; he consciously discarded the spatial and temporal données and studiously disregarded considerations of genre. Instead he focused on a selection of scenes and fragments and recontextualized them to show the power of love to restore and to destroy, to purvey joy, pleasure, happiness, or, conversely, to wreak havoc and inflict misery. Underlying Tabori's collage was his awareness that "cool reason cannot comprehend the lover or the lunatic"; that Shakespeare's "answers," far from pretending to provide any assurance, stimulate the actor to become intimately acquainted with a certain situation or to explore particular feelings or sensations.

The first scene in this Shakespeare mosaic brought together the Duke of Gloucester and Edward's widow, Lady Anne. Seated on the majestic throne which he was determined to get by hook or by crook, the would-be king bites his fingernails and plays with a doll — the ruthless Machiavellian tyrant as a frustrated, neurotic child, who never really outgrew his childhood traumata. Indeed, we seem to be given a peep into the children's room, for Anne, Gloucester's playmate, rages and cries while the humpbacked Richard tears apart the surrogate doll with savage malice. Cruelty and ruthlessness are the result of an infancy deprived of love and tenderness, as well as of inferiority feelings preying on the adult: "Deform'd, unfinish'd, sent before my time / Into this breathing world, scarce half made up" (*Richard III*, I.i.20–21). Ascending the throne is shown as a belated compensation, the pursuit of power as an act of self-assertion or vengeance.

The "battle of the sexes" or "the beautiful war between the thighs," of which Shakespeare was "the greatest expert and greatest victim,"[18] is the proclaimed leitmotif of the composition, whose provisional, fragmentary, and interchangeable structure is deliberately stressed. The vitiated relationship between Gloucester and Anne is juxtaposed with two scenes of wooing and lovesickness. The sweet folly of love declarations and dalliance between Silvius, Phebe, and Rosalind (*As You Like It*, III.v.) is succeeded by a quartet of enamored suitors from *Twelfth Night*. Ursula Höpfner switched from the virtuous Rosalind-Ganymede to the enchanting, impetuous Viola-Cesario. Tabori captures the lovers' anguish as well as their ludicrousness, blends romance with slapstick. While the love-smitten Orsino indulges in his melancholy, Viola-Cesario steals the show as a Chaplin-like clown with a top hat or as a love-stricken adolescent sucking on a lollipop. Sensuous and nimble, this delightful tomboy Cupid personified approaches the cold-hearted Olivia, like an "impudent incubus,"[19] makes advances to her, fondles and smooches with her, and tries to penetrate her through all her body orifices — nostrils, ears, mouth, and still further down.

The insouciant Olivia is soul mate to rigid Isabella in *Measure for Measure*. Tabori insinuates an incestuous affinity between the dispassionate Isabella, who would not succumb to Angelo's solicitations, and her brother, Claudio. This scene is followed by a gripping portrayal of Macbeth and his Lady. The usurper, a weakling unsure of his masculinity, "a feeble armchair culprit,"[20] who dictates a report on the apparition of the three witches, is totally under the thumb of his wife. Recounting their experimentations, Detlef Jacobsen (Macbeth) and Ursula Höpfner (Lady Macbeth) recall how they came upon the key to the relationship through a nonverbal game. "Try and find out an animal you'd like to play," Tabori suggested, whereupon Höpfner began to stretch her limbs, loll about, bend, and slink like a cat. A fighting-game between the cat and a dog ensued. The two vied and grappled with each other like tempestuous lovers in bed. Once it became clear that the cat was superior, Tabori instructed the two to start with the text. In the discussion which followed, the concept became clear: "Macbeth has potency problems. With the dagger in his hand, incited by his wife to murder Duncan in order to be the most powerful himself, he submits to this proof of his virility and gathers strength through the blood of his fellow man."[21] The dagger was ironically replaced by a knitting-needle which Lady Macbeth placed in the hands of her husband. She had been knitting and endlessly turning the red wool ball while coaxing him to murder Duncan.[22]

The striking image of Macbeth carrying his dead wife in his arms was set alongside the spectacle of Claudius carrying Gertrude in his arms in the *Hamlet* fragment. Tabori adopted a Freudian reading and related Hamlet's moodiness and inability to act to his oedipal relations with his mother. The dual role of the female as both victimizer and victim was underpinned by allotting the parts of Gertrude and of Ophelia to the selfsame actress (Leslie Malton), a strategy Tabori also deployed in casting Klaus Fischer as both Angelo and Claudio.

The second part of the collage, with an almost bare stage now resembling an arena, opens with a scene from *Troilus and Cressida*. Cressida (Isabel Karajan) emerges from under the red bedcover to be informed by Pandarus that political tactics require her instant return to the Greek camp. Cressida/Karajan contests the decision, protests, and resists it. She tears at her long hair, raves, gesticulates agitatedly, screams and howls her wild sorrow until she is hoarse. She is yet another manifestation of female vulnerability and abuse or, as Tabori puts it, "women as victims of male ambition or male hypersensitiveness."[23]

The selfsame actress, Isabel Karajan, notably, plays Katharina in an excerpt from *The Taming of the Shrew*. Petruchio tames his unruly, self-willed wife-to-be like a determined animal-trainer, chastens her, spanks and even canes her, assisted by his male companions. He deprives her of food and finally crams the wretched woman into a sack. This scene of cynical taming, bordering on rape, "a thrashing scene in punk manner,"[24] tilts over with an ironical twist: the self-possessed Kate sings the praises of womanly devotion, addressing herself not to her husband, but to individual spectators in the auditorium.

A reversal of roles marks the next episode in the collage: Cleopatra, enraged by the report of Antony's marriage to Octavia, vents her pain and frustration by hitting the messenger from Rome. Here is a moving psychogram of a woman past her prime, pampered and flattered by her attendants, who is yet painfully aware of the dwindling of her sex appeal and consequently her powers to determine matters.

Hildegard Schmahl, the aging queen, dominates the stage together with her acting-partner Tabori in the concluding two episodes of the collage. As Portia from *The Merchant of Venice* she neither is the young, charming bride nor appears disguised as the learned judge Bellario. In fact, this is the one and only pairing that is not warranted by Shakespeare's text, in a collage dedicated to the struggle between the sexes. For Portia and Shylock are two aging partners, worn out by endless disputes and unable to resolve the differences between them. While she still hopes he will for once reveal his feelings and display a touch of human warmth, he maintains a cool aloofness and, no less embittered than she is, feels that "she does not really listen to me."[25] Rehearsing the episode (IV.i), Tabori and Schmahl diverted from the text, tapped their own experiences, rephrased the exchange in their own words: "For God's sake, Hildegard, how often do I have to tell you, I insist on the contract," Tabori would retort to her concerned attempt to save his soul, whereupon she would only complain that he stubbornly demanded his revenge. For overshadowing this mésalliance, indeed this mixed marriage, is the history of friction and distrust between Jews and Christians, a rupture which left them both scarred. Not only is the trial scene recontextualized in a post-Holocaust milieu, but spectators were inevitably conscious of Tabori's biography and of current political controversies, including the growing impact of Jörg Haider and his far-right Freedom Party and the election of a Nazi collaborator, the ex–U.N. secretary general Kurt Waldheim, to the presidency in Austria.

Tabori/Shylock makes his way onto the stage while the Cleopatra episode is coming to its end: an old man in a long gray coat, with his forehead covered by a broad hat. He gropes his way, bumps against a table, stumbles over a stool, his hands trembling. It is only when he faces the audience that his wounded left eye, covered by a blood-drenched bandage, is visible. The one-eyed Jew, weary and scarred with experience, a man more sinned against than sinning, expounds his vision of justice, while Portia in a dark dress with a provocative décolletage advocates Christian mercy. The vulnerable old man takes a clasp-knife out of his coat pocket, but has no idea how to go about using it. Portia should help and instruct him. It jumps open in her hand, and she points it toward him; he takes it as well as her hand in gentlemanly gratitude. "I pray you, give me leave to go from hence; / I am not well," he mutters, a foreigner amidst "Venetians," also stigmatized on account of his foreign accent and intonation in German. On his way out he seems to lose his balance; he staggers, recovers, and sits at the feet of Schmahl/Juliet, transformed into her Romeo.

The end precedes the beginning, to quote T. S. Eliot's verse, for Romeo's and Juliet's is a virginal love, honest, undefiled. Tabori: "At the end [of the collage] we show the beginning, before everything went wrong. Here are only longings, hope, love."[26] This image of prelapsarian love is, however, marked by an ironic undercurrent. The actors, senescent and disillusioned, are only play-acting the juvenile lovers, rehearsing the passionate heroes they can never really *be*. The utopia of unblemished love is underscored by self-irony and "the absurd pathos of aging." "Call me but love, and I'll be new baptized" (*Romeo and Juliet*, II.ii.50) implores the 75-year-old Romeo with soft cadence, slowly, delivering the lines partly in English, partly in German, a pensive, consciously sentimental lover, who lends himself to temporary playfulness. Theatre-making then is an escapade of the imagination, and actors, like "The lunatic, the lover and the poet / Are of imagination all compact," as Theseus propounds in the prologue to the collage.

Those critics — by no means few and far between! — who wrote scathing reviews, accusing Tabori of offering his audience a potpourri or hotchpotch of Shakespeare evergreens that lacked any unifying interpretive concept, comparing the performance to "Czerny-etudes and no orchestral sounds," failed to understand what it was all about.[27] Not only did Tabori consider the performance a preliminary "project," an extended étude, a kind of tuning in, in preparation for the work on the full plays, but he also explicitly rejected from the outset the well-wrought conceptual structure. The collage as a formless, hybrid work offered the ideal modality for open-ended experimentation, a work-in-progress marked by its tendency toward the fragmentary, the fractured, the sketchy, seeking to free the performance from an outworn, coercive, and comprehensive interpretation. The stylistic medley was likewise deliberate: it grew out of the actors' personal ongoing experience with the texts. The collage was, from its inception, an iconoclastic assault on the formalistically structured staging of Shakespeare's texts. The highly rated coherence, whose lack many of the critics seem to have lamented, was in fact rejected from the outset by Tabori, who nonetheless related the patches of the mosaic through the overriding theme of "the battle of the sexes." Tabori subtly worked out parallel patterns or, obversely, contrasts in the various episodes and often used minimal props as linking signs or as intertextual cues. Thus the knife, for example, signifies vendetta in the hands of Richard, Hamlet, or Shylock. Likewise the purple-red cloth features as a significant emblem in many of the episodes: it is the red drape of a blood-dimmed throne; the kerchief of guilt with which Hamlet wipes off Ophelia's tears; an ecclesiastic token in the hands of Angelo; the fatal "ocular proof" in Othello's hand; the cloth with which the vindictive Shylock polishes his knife; and finally the handkerchief into which Romeo sobs.

VARIATIONS

A sick old tyrant and lecher, a Dirty Old Man, as the English call it, becomes what the Jews call a Mensch, *not just a human being but a good one.* George Tabori, "Cues"

Twice or, to be more precise, three times, Tabori grappled with *King Lear*. On neither occasion did he offer his audience a full-fledged and "straight" production of the Shakespearean tragedy, and at the sunset of his life he professed that there were only two plays he would still like to direct, one of them being *King Lear*.

Lear had agitated Tabori's imagination since the beginning of his professional interest in theatre: "A character I've always wondered about," he wrote to his brother, Paul. What struck him in the play was "the scale of emotions" accommodating radically contrasting feelings, ranging from one extreme to another, or "the arrogance to humility pattern," as he called it.[1]

It was no accident that Tabori was almost Lear's age, "fourscore and upward," when he chose to grapple with the story of the old king, who loses his royal authority and mental equilibrium on account of his ill judgment, in putting the love of his three daughters to the test. Aware of the fact that Shakespeare's tragedy was the "grandest and most demanding drama ever written,"[2] he needed —so it appears in retrospect— the assurance and self-confidence as well as the artistic freedom to experiment at ease, which his own Kreis theatre afforded him. Coming of age likewise played a significant role: "For this play the director should himself be old," Tabori maintained.[3] He admitted, moreover, that he felt a strong affinity to the "Dirty Old Man," who gradually "becomes what the Jews call a *Mensch*";[4] a man at the sunset of his life whose wisdom — that Shakespearean notion of "ripeness is all" — is gained at the cost of awesome suffering, decrepitude, and loss. The daring rendezvous with Lear was made possible not only by the rich accumulation of previous theatrical experience, as Charles Laughton surmised, but also, obviously, by the personal experience of a lifetime.[5]

Upon his seventieth birthday Tabori confessed he felt closer to Lear than to Hamlet, since, unlike Hamlet, the "old man relieves his pain by howling."[6] It was this readiness to lay bare body and soul, exposed and vulnerable, instead of indulging in a ritual of heroic dignity, which endeared to him Laurence Olivier's portrayal of Lear — "the only 'correct' one I ever saw."[7]

The three productions drawing on the *Lear* fable can best be described as variations on *Lear*, distinctively idiosyncratic, highly experimental. Tellingly, all three were done in a time span of eighteen months (1988–1989), the one variation and its feedback serving, as it were, as food for thought for the following performance. All three share, as we shall see, thematic, formalistic, and visual elements.

The initial encounter with *Lear* was an indirect one, through Gaston Salvatore's play *Stalin*, the first production which Tabori directed single-handed in his Kreis (premiere 8 March 1988). Between this and the second variation on *Lear* entitled *Lears Schatten* (Lear's Shadow), which premiered in Bregenz on 22 July 1989, Tabori directed his Shakespeare collage *Lovers and Lunatics*, conceived originally as an introduction. The third and last variation was a radically revised version of the Bregenz presentation, entirely different in concept and structure, and it premiered at the Kreis in Vienna on 12 September 1989.[8]

All three variations attest to Tabori's original — even, at times, eccentric — approach, manifested, for example, in his decision to cast an actress in the leading male role or to elide whole lines, leave out dramatic personae, or even cut out entire scenes. Tabori's main interest lies unmistakably in the divided self and the dialectics of the conscious and the unconscious. He shapes the interplay of the consciously rational with the subliminal in an anti-illusory spectacle which foils spectators' possible identification and celebrates the experience onstage as the superior reality, genuine, authentic, and liberating.

The first meeting with the old king "as full of grief as age," through the intermediacy of Salvatore's text, was a kind of preparatory étude. Salvatore, a self-exiled Chilean author writing in German, brings together in his chamber-play for two Joseph Stalin and the Jewish actor Itsik Sager, director of the Jewish theatre in Moscow and an acclaimed Lear performer, unmistakably modeled on the renowned Samuel Mikhoels. The Russian dictator, troubled by nightmares, invites Sager/Lear to his Datscha. His strategy is two-pronged: the Jew is summoned to ease his vexed mind and to entertain him through long and sleepless nights; he also serves as camouflage for a pogrom now under way against the Jews. This nocturnal tête-à-tête turns into a merciless discourse on politics, power, and art. Lines from *King Lear*, and fractured dialogue, flow into Salvatore's text. The mistrustful dictator fails to understand how Lear at the acme of power could possibly relinquish control of his own free will. What first appears as a mere intellectual dialogue gradually reveals itself as a "cat-and-mouse-game."[9] Sager/Lear must play for his life: whenever his joke pleases the listener or raises a smile, he can save one Jewish soul. This macabre game ends with the foreordained lethal checkmating of the Jew by Stalin. The full reach of Stalin's tactics and the futility of Sager's self-delusion become cruelly evident when the Jew learns that his own son, who had been taken hostage, is no longer among the living.

Whoever watched the three-and-a-half-hour-long production could not help feeling that there was more of Tabori in it than of Salvatore — as Klaus Reitz corroborated: "Gaston Salvatore's play becomes at the end almost a Tabori play."[10] Indeed, not only did Tabori prune and trim the original text, omitting much of the integrated historical information about Stalin or the Revolution, but his production — in striking contrast to the original staging of the premiere — was not a realistically styled, historically oriented staging. The historical truth was only of marginal significance. Shakespeare's *Lear* with its "dialectics of power, . . . its contradictions of illusion and reality," art and life, permeated Tabori's production, affording it an ahistorical, universal significance.[11]

It was unmistakably the perverse play, the subtly conducted game of power, which kindled his imagination. The psychodrama for two, which Tabori fashioned out of Salvatore's original, brings to mind the intricate relationship between Shlomo Herzl and Hitler in Tabori's own *Mein Kampf*, which opened only a year earlier, in 1987. Stalin craves the company of Sager, just as Hitler depends on Shlomo, and the Jew — an actor here, an inspired raconteur there — walks the tightrope, balancing between self-adaptation and resistance till he inescapably falls into the trap set for him. The inevitable catastrophe is tinged by subversive humor, wry witticisms, and pungent jokes told by the Jew. Tellingly, Tabori gives Sager/Lear the Hölderlin quotation, which was Shlomo Herzl's motto: "Must you forever be playing and jesting? You must, oh my friends, which sickens my soul. For only the desperate must."

In *Stalin*, as in *Mein Kampf* and in many of his other productions, Tabori calls in question the clear-cut categorization of perpetrators and victims. His Stalin, a sadist yet no monster of depravity, has, like his Hitler, something of the gruesome comic and the fatuity of Chaplin's Great Dictator. "An inhuman dictator becoming human,"[12] he — like his predecessor Hitler in Tabori's *Mein Kampf* — is a moody, cranky, at times childish, at times lonely and vulnerable figure, unremittingly complaining about back pain. The despot and his scapegoat, both of them white-haired, fully seasoned men, also bring to mind Vladimir and Estragon, the aging intellectuals in Tabori's staging of *Waiting for Godot* (1984), who cling together for better or for worse. Stalin's and Sager's interdependence, the inability to ascertain who is the real victim, who the victimizer, underlines the final episode. Sager leans back dumbfounded, amidst his son's belongings, against the notice-board on which he has pinned the snaps of those Jews he believes he has saved. Actress Angelica Domröse/Stalin enters, this time as Cordelia. "Howl, howl, howl! O! you are men of stones," Lear/Sager cries out (*Lear*, V.iii.257), whereupon Cordelia/Stalin takes his hand gently. As the lights fade, the two leave the stage and vanish in the dark.

Are the victimizer and his victim, the omnipotent dictator and his Fool, not two facets of the selfsame self? Tabori's mise-en-scène insinuates such a view. In fact, this implied duality of the Self and its Double, Man and his Shadow, is the marked common denominator underlying Tabori's three *Lear* variations.

The set, albeit scanty, promoted this schism.[13] Split into two groups, spectators were seated on both sides of a narrow gangway covered with a red carpet. A door was at one end of the gangway and close to it a tiled stove with a Russian samovar. At the other end was a dilapidated throne and a makeup table with a portrait of Karl Marx hanging over it. Halfway up the gangway was a wide table with a chandelier hanging above; chairs were placed on it upside down, symbolizing Stalin's executed victims. The dual perspective was further accentuated through the contrapuntal interplay between "life" — i.e., the performance of the two actors — and the re-presentation of events on video monitors installed all around. These monitors, an effective means of alienation, also insinuated the notorious system of close supervision common in totalitarian regimes. Spectators could watch historical accounts of the Stalin era as well as scenes from Bako Sadykow's documentary film *Adonis* (which was prohibited in the Soviet Union), an elegy for animals sent to the slaughtering block — a hackneyed metaphor for the deportation of the Jews.

The most radical and perplexing expression of this dualistic interpretation was Tabori's decision to cast the actress Angelica Domröse in the role of Stalin. Domröse was already onstage as spectators were taking their seats. She, like her husband, Hilmar Thate, in the role of Sager, was getting ready for the evening. In a provocative miniskirt and high-heeled shoes, with her hair tied up behind, she capered across the acting area as though she was doing her warm-ups, then made up her face, pasted black lines and a beard on it, and slipped into the uniform in full view of spectators. The feminine, feline figure gradually becomes a beast of prey with a silvery-white mane of hair, boots, and, toward the end of the evening, the mustache which was Stalin's hallmark. Casting Domröse in the titular male role — "an inspired alienating stroke," in the eyes of critic Heinz Sichrovsky [14] — Tabori urged Domröse to retain her feminine identity. "Play it as a woman," he advised her,[15] as he was to instruct Hildegard Schmahl playing Lear a few months later. The feminine erotic spell of Domröse/Stalin was intentionally underlined, and it gained still more from the fact that Domröse's husband played opposite her. The everyday interpersonal tension between the two and, conversely, their mutual history (both had left the German Democratic Republic before Germany was unified) echo Tabori's initial intention of examining Shakespeare's plays in the light of "the battle of the sexes."

The division of the self is taken a step further in the first, Bregenz version of *Lear's Shadow*. Drawing solely, if freely, on Shakespeare's text, Tabori splits — or duplicates — the titular role between two actors: the decrepit, senile, mostly mute Lear (Detlef Jacobsen), reclining in a wheelchair throughout almost the entire performance, and his articulate and vigorous counterpart, played by actress Hildegard Schmahl. One embodies broken-down majesty, regressing to infantile pastimes, playing with dolls, placing small branches in his white hair, falsly cuddled and ultimately grievously abused by his daughters; the other is his active counterpart, ironically his shadow, or his double, who goes through all the stages of the tragic decline.

The key to Tabori's extraordinary approach lies in Lear's question: "Who is it that can tell me who I am?" To which the Fool replies: "Lear's shadow" (*Lear*, I.iv.238–239).

We are back, as so often with Tabori, on psychoanalytical territory — or to be more precise, back to Freud's discussion of the Double as related to the Shadow. Freud mentions Otto Rank's analysis of the Double-Motif (*Doppelgänger*) as a shadow-image which functions as a tutelary spirit imparting instruction as well as the fear of death to the soul. And he elaborates further: "A special agency is slowly formed there [in the ego], which is able to stand over against the rest of the ego, which has the function of observing and criticizing the self and of exercising a censorship within the mind, and which we become aware of as our 'conscience.'"[16]

The first version of *Lear's Shadow*, performed at Bregenz, presents the *Lear* fable as a psychotherapeutic case-study. Lear's "shadow" has to experience all the consequences of his fatal error of judgment, his hamartia, and go through humiliation and suffering, aided this time by the cognitive, self-observing, and self-critical faculties. The (re)enactment of the decline is perceived as the indispensable prerequisite for healing. Edgar's aside, which referred originally to blind Gloucester, whom he accompanies to the cliffs of Dover, is directed in the Bregenz version to Lear: "Why I do trifle thus with his despair / Is done to cure it" (*Lear*, IV.vi.32–33). The divided self is ultimately reconciled: the circle closed. We are back at the beginning, only this time, in the closing scene, the senile king awakens from his lethargy and reenacts the division of his kingdom before he collapses, blind and full of grief, with the beloved Cordelia in his arms, under the map of the kingdom.

Indeed, the trouble with this *Lear* variation is that it is set unswervingly on the therapeutic trajectory.[17] Tabori subjugated the original to his purpose and reduced the rich texture to a contrived and affected composite of platitudes, at times indeed a travesty. Reducing the plot to suit his interpretive purpose, he left out entire scenes, including the Gloucester subplot. It was Lear, not Gloucester, who was brutally blinded by the evil daughters, wearing white nurses' uniforms under their black attire, like nurses in a psychiatric ward, sadistically feasting on those "eyes" afterward. Kent was reduced to a ludicrous loyalist, who delivered his abbreviated text with a Swiss-German intonation. The show, incongruous and eccentric, using baroque rock as occasional background music, degenerated all too often into a grotesque Punch-and-Judy show.

What made things worse was Tabori's determination to "isolate the erotic aspect of the play,"[18] which, in his opinion, happens to be the most violent expression of Shakespeare's sexuality. In other words, he decided to depict the relationship in the Lear family as a series of manifestations of perverse, obscene, indeed incestuous sexuality. The old king is shown as a "Dirty Old Man," a lecherous father, who misuses his patriarchal authority to indulge his narcissism and pays dearly for his deviant sexual fantasies. According to Tabori, *Lear* is "more of a love-story than, say, *Romeo and Juliet*, and a most extreme expression of the basic split in Shakespeare between the desperate demand for 'chaste constancy,' or gratitude in women, and the equally desperate recognition of the impossibility of such patriarchal demand; especially as it involves the most painful taboo that sickens the father-daughter relationship. My heart belongs to daddy, but not my belly [I believe he meant 'womb']. Three daughters, three witches, three caskets."[19]

We are back yet again with Freud. It is interesting that Freud hardly went as far as Tabori did in his discussion of Lear's motivations. Although he relates the three daughters to the three caskets — Tabori must have been familiar with this analogy — his main concern lies with Lear's ultimate reconciliation with Cordelia, the silent one, the lead casket, or the acceptance of demise.[20]

Little wonder, then, that many protested against this constricting view of Lear and spoke of a tasteless and excessive spectacle revolving around an erotomania.[21] Truly, the performance abounds with sexual innuendos, with fondlings, amorous gestures, caressing of thighs, and concupiscent advances. Lear appears in the opening scene with a whip in hand, signifying his political authority and — a parallel to Friedrich Nietzsche's famous whip — also sexual tyranny. His daughters wipe the bloodstains from the floor, as a token of servility as well as an allusion to the taboo relations between father and daughters. When he speaks of "our dark purpose," they lift up their skirts. Symbolically loaded, too, is the division of the kingdom: Lear bites into a red apple, that forbidden Fruit of Knowledge, emblematic here of the monarchy, and passes a piece each to Regan and Goneril from mouth to mouth. Cordelia disobeys, sets marital love above all else — "Sure I shall never marry like my sisters, / To love my father all" (*Lear*, I.i.103–104) — whereupon Lear is overcome by his tempestuous rage and confronts her as if about to rape her. Bearing in mind that Lear was performed simultaneously by male and female actors, one is indeed tempted to surmise that, with the redemption of the self at the end, the feminine and the masculine are equally reconciled.

Only two months after the devastating reviews of the Bregenz performance, Tabori premiered in his Kreis a radically revised, practically new *Lear* variation. Although he felt he had been misunderstood and wronged, putting the blame on the inappropriate theatre hall and the harassing timetable, he apparently believed that the experiment did not really come off the way he had envisaged.[22] His Vienna variation did away with both the therapeutic and the sexual undertones, but, to the surprise of many, stuck to the controversial casting of a woman in the titular part: Hildegard Schmahl played Lear, this time without a male double.

Why this insistence on giving the role of the king to a woman? Rumors had it that the designated actors, Michael Degen and Hilmar Thate, could not keep their appointment. Tabori himself endorsed all sorts of explanations by way of legitimizing his decision. After all, men played the parts of women on Shakespeare's stage, why not then try it once the other way round? In one of many interviews he suggested that "a woman may understand Lear better than a man"; in another he maintained that "Lear has a patriarchal problem, and this can best be worked out with a woman in the role."[23] Dissatisfied with these evasive replies, I turned to Detlef Jacobsen, who played the senile king in Bregenz but was left out in the Vienna version. "It was clear from the start that Lear would be a woman. We, the members of the Kreis, spent days reading the text over and over again, as is common practice with George. But the men, who had all been so keen to do *Lear*, felt that George concentrated on the women, on the daughters, and finally they said, well then, do it with them and with Detlef. This is how we came up with the Bregenz version. After it premiered, we continued to rehearse, and I felt more and more that George was uncomfortable with my role as male-double. I decided to make the decision for him." Jacobsen adds: "It was ever since he saw a Japanese production of Chekhov's *Three Sisters* that

George had been dreaming of doing *Lear* with women only." Incidentally, Robert Wilson directed *King Lear* in Frankfurt with actress Marianne Hoppe in the part of the old king in the following season (1990).

Another Tabori production of *Lear* followed — yet again not a full production, but a variation which, this time, focused upon the treacherous Goneril and Regan, on Lear's derangement as a form of liberation or "self-knowledge through loss of self."[24] Tabori decided to avoid a full-fledged production "not out of avantgarde vanity, not even in loyalty to our dedication to experiment, but in recognition of the difficulties that this grandest and most demanding drama ever written offers."[25] The Vienna variation was more concentrated, albeit studiedly fragmentary and fractured; less affected, quieter in tone and manner ("without wild outbursts"), sterner, more intimate, almost "ascetic."[26] The cast was reduced from seven to five (all female!) and the text abridged and tightened further (Kent, for instance, was left out); Cordelia appeared only in the opening and closing scene.

The visual aspect of the variation had a lot in common with the primary colors — white, red, and black — of the *Stalin* production or the Shakespeare collage.[27] Red elongated pieces of cloth, between flexible bars, covered the acting area vertically, suggesting an enclosure or a trap or, to some, "a labyrinth."[28] Schmahl/Lear entered, accompanied by her loyal Fool. She put on the heavy black cloak over a wide stola and clumsy buskins in view of spectators, slowly approached the big red throne, and placed the majestic crown on her head to become the aging king.

Lear, self-centered and somewhat melancholy, asks for declarations of love and shares the apple with Goneril and Regan, clad in black with gilded crowns. Yet the scene has hardly any smack of the sexual or the erotic. Schmahl's face was covered with pasty white makeup, her eyelids dyed white, her hair wild and snowy — a vexing and equally moving image of human frailty. Here indeed is no Dirty Old Man but a dejected monarch who realizes that, being old and powerless, he is only a burden on his daughters. The ensuing gradual loss of mental equilibrium is thus shown as a form of escapism and is counterpoised by the Fool, who impersonates Tabori's cherished "Principle of Hope." Stripped of all majestic robes, with trousers and a black undershirt which lays bare her bony limbs, Lear/Schmahl goes through the agony on the heath (a bare stage).

The final moving scene marks the epitome of this process of self-knowledge: Lear, blinded and chained, experiences inner liberation when he touches his dead Cordelia. Here too nothing is left of the erotic undertone which prevailed in the Bregenz version. Instead, Tabori's deep-rooted conviction comes through — namely, that sensual experience, that which touches the skin or goes under it, is superior to cognitive knowledge. The tale of Lear, stripped of regal pomp, disillusioned and vulnerable, "reduced to a naked Being," "offers not the triumph of evil but of reality," maintains Tabori.[29]

Though unquestionably superior to the previous version, acted with competence and intense commitment, the Vienna variation received mixed reviews.[30] Tabori's dogged decision to cast Lear as a woman remained, despite Schmahl's arresting performance, a matter of dispute, as did his free handling of Shakespeare's text. Tabori himself, though much more satisfied with this version, nonetheless rightly felt he had "not yet reached my destination": "When I am eighty, like Lear, I'll do it again," the 75-year-old said.[31]

ALL OVER AGAIN

One may think of Hamlet without Freud, though not profitably; it would be hard to think of Freud without Hamlet. George Tabori, "Hamlet in Blue"

Twelve years after his first *Hamlet* production (1978), Tabori came to grips a second time with the tragedy of the Prince of Denmark (premiere 22 May 1990). Both productions were put on with actors close to Tabori and well-acquainted with his theatrics and rehearsing method — the first with actors of the Theaterlabor in Bremen (see chapter 3), the second with members of his Kreis, a good many of whom had participated in the theatre lab. Both productions were experimental by definition, taking dramaturgical liberty with the original text, eliding lines and rearranging episodes; in both cases a modern translation was preferred to the classical Schlegel-Tieck text. Ironically, both productions marked the end of an experimental phase.[1] The Theaterlabor disbanded after the first *Hamlet*; Tabori gave up his dream of running his own theatre, the Kreis, after the second and moved to the limelight of the institutionalized stage, the "cathedrals."

The Hamlet of the Bremen version, played by Günter Einbrodt, was an intellectual young man caught between filial duty to avenge his father's murder and his inability to feel genuine sorrow, to mourn deeply ("the Germanism of Hamlet"),[2] and consequently to act. The Kreis Hamlet is a "dear, clever, decent, sensitive young man," who nevertheless finds himself at the end of the play "between seven corpses, a killer with a dirty waistcoat and blood-smeared hands"[3] —the living evidence of Tabori's conviction that it is impossible to be both a good man and a good politician.

The controversial aspect of the production was Tabori's decision to allot the titular male role once again to a woman, this time to his wife, Ursula Höpfner (who played Ophelia in the Bremen production). The history of *Hamlet* productions has, of course, chronicled Sarah Bernhardt's meditative Hamlet and Adele Sandrock's prince in the 1898 *Hamlet* parody, yet the choice of Höpfner for the main part was in line with Tabori's conscious experimentation with women in male roles — Domröse in *Stalin* and Schmahl in both *Lear* versions. Asked why he allotted the role to a woman, Tabori justified his choice linking, as it were, his interpretive concept with certain characteristics intrinsic to female acting: a woman in the role of Hamlet because "a woman impersonates much better the dear, clever, sensitive Hamlet, who in my eyes has so little of the typical masculine." A feminist interpretation then? Hardly. Höpfner's was a rather androgynous Hamlet. Wearing black jeans and a black leather jacket —Hamlet in modern garb, like his Bremen predecessor — with her hair trimmed square but not too short, her physical build slender, almost frail but agile and expressive, she looked like a page boy or an adolescent who has not quite outgrown his puberty.

As so often with Tabori, indeed, as in the Bremen version, the performance was launched with an extended tableau. On the defiantly empty, triangular stage, suggesting the triangular love conflict and contained by high screen-walls,[4] veiled women in black bewail the dead king, undress him, and, lamenting, perform the ritual washing. "A Jewish ritual," maintains critic Paul Kruntorad.[5] Perhaps, but if so, not a kosher one: according to Jewish *Halakha* men, never women, would be entrusted with the washing of the male corpse. One of the mourners whets a large sword, a central image in the production, symbolizing power, unnatural death, vengeance, and sexuality. Hamlet draws hesitantly near, kneels over the body, and delivers the famous soliloquy "To be or not to be" (III.i), addressing a father from whom he refuses to part. Hardly has he brought "the question" to an end when in bursts the whole merrymaking court. Claudius and Gertrude celebrate their wedding with a festive banquet, with pheasants, whisky, and vodka — "The funeral bak'd meats / Did coldly furnish the marriage tables" (I.ii.180) — to the sound of Johann Strauss waltz-music. It is a decadent, hedonistic society: ladies and courtiers in modern evening dresses and smart dinner-suits, their faces hidden behind animal masks. Detlef Jacobsen, who assisted Tabori and trained the actors, recalls that animal improvisations and game-exercises were a decisive factor during the first weeks of rehearsal, as in fact they were in the earlier *Hamlet* version. Claudius masked as a bull was an unscrupulous upstart, avid for pleasure and luxury, a tyrant with heavy fur coat, reminiscent of the Rumanian dictator Nicolae Ceausescu as he tries to save his skin accompanied by his Securitatae bodyguards. Gertrude as a black pussycat, elegant and sly, was his companion for mischief and orgies, an avatar of Imelda Marcos fleeing for her life with packed aluminium suitcases. Laertes and Ophelia are "rollicking teenage partners at a dancing lesson," inclined to incestuous love, while Polonius is a pale and not too crafty old courtling.

Hamlet, the only one wearing no mask, is the vulnerable, good boy in a society sick to its core and hollow. When his father in a fashionable dotted dressing gown and slippers, a smug and rather ludicrous ghost, helps himself to a glass of wine once the buffet has been abandoned, the son wavers. The ghost puts an authoritative hand on the boy's shoulder, presses the sword in his hand. Hamlet hardly knows how to hold it (recall Tabori's/Shylock's incompetence with the knife in the Shakespeare collage!) — a son condemned to avenge his father's murder; "the burden of the dead fathers," as critic Georg Hensel entitled his review of the first *Hamlet* version.

The decent and sensitive adolescent is drawn against his will and better conviction into the vicious circle. "I must be cruel only to be kind" is Hamlet's conclusion (III.iv. 179); once again, to the sweet-schmalzy Strauss music, a vendetta is exacted with minimal bloodshed, no duels, only elegant stabbing — "a society liquidating itself."[6] Dying in Horatio's arms,[7] Hamlet accentuates the "I could tell you — " as if the real story, or perhaps his own story, has yet to be told. Reminiscing on Höpfner's Hamlet a few years later, Tabori said: "Her Hamlet was absolutely unforgettable. She was the first — Laurence Olivier included — who endowed the phrase 'The rest is silence' with meaning — it is not a general, sentimental farewell, but a smiling Shakespearean riddle."[8]

Crossing the stage strewn with corpses, the seasoned politician Fortinbras, whose victories have been noted on a television monitor, remains untouched by the bloody sight. He merely closes his nose to spare himself the repulsive stench, nods his head at the futility of it all, and passes by, while the gravedigger concludes with a good old Jewish sigh, "Oy. . . ."

The second *Hamlet* version, like the first, was, artistically speaking, a deliberate blending of styles and moods designed to defamiliarize the audience, prompt them to reconsider anew the well-known tragedy while underpinning its topicality (the Schleyer abduction in the first version, the crumbling of the thoroughly corrupt dictatorships in Eastern Europe in the second). Both productions were of uneven quality. Both contained coups de théâtre — the opening scene in both, for example — as well as extended, dull scenes made worse by poor articulation; imaginative staging (the final scenes in both) together with affectation and gags, such as the presentation of the wandering actors as Actors Studio members who engage ritualistically in warm-ups before they are instructed by Hamlet, a somewhat arrogant "enthusiastic amateur," according to Tabori.[9] In contrast to the early *Hamlet*, which keenly sought to promote ensemble work, the second version stood — or fell flat —with Höpfner's portrayal of the prince: "Solo for Hamlet," Wolfgang Reiter accurately titled his review.[10]

THE TRIUMPH OF A DEFEATED MAN

Killing may be a substitute for kissing or, more frighteningly, the other side of the coin.

George Tabori, "Reflections on the Figleaf"

There seems to be a good deal of irony in the fact that Tabori's finest Shakespeare production marked his move back to the previously rejected "cathedrals." His *Othello*, bringing to an end the ambitious Shakespeare project which he had envisaged for his own company at the Kreis, premiered at the Akademietheater, the smaller house adjacent to the Burgtheater on 10 January 1990 and received standing ovations and enthusiastic write-ups. The compliments bestowed on Tabori almost unanimously were, ironically, of the kind which ran against his theatre convictions. Some commended the neatly composed mise-en-scène, which in comparison to previous productions seemed less arbitrary and less wayward; others came to the conclusion that Tabori's directorial power depended largely on the theatrical cunning of his actors, ultimately first-rate professional stars of the "cathedrals" like Gert Voss in the role of Othello.

If Shakespeare was the greatest expert in matters of love, the "healer of loss and a destroyer of illusion,"[1] his *Othello* was yet another exemplary drama shedding light on the destructive powers of consuming passions. Moments of intense tenderness converge with images of highly charged sexuality and acts of gruesome violence. "Hatred, murder, violence and the longing to destroy, all belong to this word with delightful sigh and the preposterous form which it describes," Tabori maintains in "This Embarrassing Word: Love."[2] Not surprisingly, he chose as motto for the production Othello's "I will kill thee, / And love thee after"

(*Othello*, V.ii.18–19) and presented the murder scene as an extended coitus, culminating in a stifling kiss, death as the sweetest orgasm, Eros and Thanatos conjoined.

In fact, Tabori's *Othello* has much in common conceptually and visually with his previous, less accomplished Shakespeare productions. Once again he compressed the broad canvas of the original to an intimate chamber play (this is why he preferred the smaller Akademietheater to the big house), omitted whole lines, and reduced the cast to what he thought was the bare necessity. Again he opted for an ahistorical performance with occasional allusions to contemporary times. Aided by Erich Fried's modern translation, he cast all the Venetians, apart from the Duke, as navy officers in uniform, with air-raid sirens signaling the Turkish offensive. Iago provides Othello not only with the "ocular proof," that famous handkerchief, but also with an auditory proof, a cassette with a recording of Cassio's and Desdemona's illicit liaison. Furthermore, the celebration of the victory (II.iii) is staged as a booze party in a bar, with the pianist at the grand piano (yes, the association with *Casablanca* was inevitable!) accompanying the merry singing of the wine song and Iago commenting on the Austrians (not the English as in Shakespeare's text), who are "potent in potting."

Stage and setting, too, took after the previous Shakespeare presentations, with black, white, and red once again being the dominant hues.[3] The whitewashed stage, slightly raised at the rear where a metal door was visible in the last scene, was an elevated square platform, whose forefront angle jutted out into the auditorium. An iron railing, hip-high, demarcated the two frontal sides of the square shape, while two walls covered with red-pinkish satin were visible on the other two sides. This largely bare, enclosed acting area was a military headquarters in the beginning, later, alternately, a ship deck (with the ship's prow pointing, as it were, to the audience), a casino bar (a single black palm branch suggested Cyprus) with a piano in the middle and dartboard on one wall, or an arena in which Othello and Iago were grappling "catch-as-catch-can" with each other. In the final bedroom scene a bed was placed in the middle, under a naked, clearly antiromantic incandescent bulb. The bed, a simple futon, was enclosed by transparent white curtains, a mosquito net perhaps, which could likewise easily be associated with a bride's wedding veil and, conversely, a veil of shame or with winding sheets covering the dead Desdemona.

The key to Tabori's *Othello* lay in a mute Arabic-looking woman, in black attire, with her face covered at first by a black veil to reveal only an eye — just like the Moor's white eyeballs shining in his pitch-dark face — who was intermittently present on the stage.[4] Ignored by all other characters, she was what remained of the original Bianca, Cassio's courtesan, in the course of rehearsals. She walks across the stage at the beginning, jingling a tin money-box, accompanied by ominous, quasi-Oriental sounds emanating from loudspeakers. She eavesdrops slyly, moves like a shadow along the walls, lurks everywhere, with an equivocal half-smile hovering on her lips. During the feast, she is the woman who comes and goes, carrying a dish of fruit or attending to the drinks. Later she is the ill-foreboding dark figure, a harbinger of death, who places a candle in front of Desdemona's bed, which Othello will "put out." And when the play is over and the actors reap their due, she is the only one to stand apart from the others, a dark figure lingering on the white bed of love and death, an ill-omen come true. The transmuted Bianca imbues the performance with an unmistakably mythic as well as mystical aura.[5] The clue to her part lies, however, in a brief moment at the heat of the feud episode between the drunk officers and Othello. Emerging from his bedroom, the Moor chides the rivals, "Are we turn'd Turks, and to ourselves do that / Which heaven forbid the Ottomites?" (*Othello*, II.iii. 161–162). The veiled woman comes to the forefront of the stage and, turning her back to the audience, reveals her other face — thick-lipped and chocolate brown.

The Janus-faced figure is the emblematic key to Tabori's *Othello*: Othello and Iago are Man and his Double, the self and its alter-ego, or, in line with the *Lear* production, Othello and his Shadow. The two are inextricably drawn to each other by magnetic attraction, indissolubly dependent on one another, as Tabori subtly insinuates in his mise-en-scène. He structures the production as a three-part performance, with the long middle part, the heart of the play, concentrating on the interplay between Othello and Iago with only minimal interference by the other characters. Iago cunningly administers the venom of suspicion drop by drop while Othello sits facing him, so close that at one point he stretches out his legs onto Iago's shoulders, as if he were about to strangle him. No sooner does he smash, in a temper, the mirror in which he discovered his pain-distorted face — "'Tis destiny, unshunnable, like death" (*Othello*, III.iii.279) — than he encounters his other self, Iago. In a paroxysm he tears away the collar of Iago's white shirt (as is the Jewish custom in mourning the dead) and, shortly afterward, his own creme-white uniform jacket, symbol of his acquired status, right along the middle seam.

The final scene shows Iago in white, chained to the arm of Othello in black uniform. Awaiting their verdict, they are victims as well as perpetrators of evil. And when the dying Othello, stabbed by his own hand, crawls toward the nuptial bed to be united with his chaste wife, he drags along his alter-ego, his accomplice in crime, like a shadow.

Yet the great superiority of this production over some of the other Shakespeare renditions (the Bregenz *Lear* or the early *Hamlet* version) lies precisely in the fact that Tabori eschews a straightforward psychoanalytical reading, in fact, avoids inscribing "meaning." Instead of the reasoning, all-binding, and regulating approach, associated with modern hermeneutics, he opens up the text, as it were, releases control, entrusts it to the actors, who, likewise, avoid flat rationalization in favor of a puzzling ambivalence — which in turn entrusts the interpretation ultimately to the spectator. "Iago's viciousness is presented pretty much in cold blood, as a riddle," maintains Tabori, writing about the "secret," the "heart of silence," which throbs in every one of Shakespeare's plays.[6]

Ignaz Kirchner's Iago is neither a Machiavellian schemer nor a demon, but a kind of malcontent, moody, frustrated, and cynical, who ploddingly stages the downfall of Othello and, concurrently, his own destruction. He haunts the scene, pulls the strings, often stands apart, a loner observing others or carefully watching his victim, at times amazed at his own accomplishment, at times perplexed by the intensity of Othello's reaction. He reminded me more than once of Bosola in John Webster's *The Duchess of Malfi*, a spectator of the tragedy, who plays a pivotal part in the infliction of suffering. A keen voyeur, lasciviously observing the lovers (like Bosola!), he is a self-hating, sexually perverse intriguer, incapable of genuine love, emotionally deformed. Kirchner delivered the key soliloquy (II.i. 281–307) in an equivocating manner, which left spectators uncertain about Iago's real motivation. It could hardly have been his own love for Desdemona, hardly a vindictive impulse: Kirchner accentuated the "thought," namely, the vexation of the mind, rather than his certitude that the "lustful Moor / Hath leap'd into my seat." The absence of explicit motivation was the hallmark of Tabori's and Kirchner's Iago, reminiscent of Samuel Taylor Coleridge's "motiveless malignity." Stimulated only by others' sexuality, he consummates his sexual craving by masturbating to the orgiastic moaning and groaning of the lovers next door, uses Desdemona's handkerchief as a sexual fetish, sniffs at it, wipes his perspiring chest and armpits with it, or acts out his erotic fantasies as a transvestite in a tight leather corset. The only person he holds in his reassuring arms is his victim, Othello.

And this vulnerable, passionate Othello was brilliantly played by Gert Voss. Tabori describes the Moor as an outsider: "As a black man in a white society he has actually accomplished a good deal: he is a general, accepted in spite of being an outsider. Racism is naturally implied in the play. . . . He [Othello] knows that he lives in a fundamentally unfriendly world, in which he always has to prove himself. That's his problem as an outsider — similar to Shylock's. He must be better, on the battlefield as in bed. This is, so to speak, his unconscious pressure to prove worthy. And of course he is also older than Desdemona . . . and this relationship between an aging man and a young woman is something concrete and very special."[7]

The Moor is an outsider, tolerated and respected as long as Venice needs him to fight its campaigns — "not dark, but gold" is Fried's German rendering of "far more fair than black" (I.iii. 290) — lonely and forlorn in his agony. Gert Voss insisted on covering his upper body, neck, face, and hands with black-brown cream at an *early* stage of the rehearsals. "I need it," he told an interviewer; he admitted he needed the long rehearsing period, "the many detours before one makes up one's mind; one plays afterwards all these blind alleys and side streets one has been to," adding: "One has to get into it, totally, without any protection, and risk all."[8]

Surprising as it may at first seem, this is where the veteran professional star Voss and the experimenting antiauthoritarian playmaker Tabori met. Both committed themselves to a "dangerous theatre" involving total risk, both believed in trying everything out by way of feeling one's way into the text. What happened to Voss exploring and contemplating the Moor can best be described in Tabori's favourite dictum: he found the role in himself. Voss played the outsider, the Moor, with all the associated ubiquitous clichés, only to transcend them and show Othello as an individual human being. His Moor has raven-black frizzy hair, huge white eyeballs which sparkle with innocence and vulnerability in an otherwise pitch-dark face. Othello/Voss speaks with a husky voice, rolls his *r*s in a "foreign," guttural way, adopts the gestures and bearing of a black man, moving with agility, like a swift-moving panther or a nimble dancer. When he first emerges, a highly respected commander among Venetians, he appears "half noble wild, half cosy bear,"[9] as befits the occasion and his new stature. After striking his wife, he rushes offstage like a wild monkey ("goats and monkeys"!), beating his chest with his hands. Tantrums, the tearing of clothes, and the smashing of glass and china alternate with many moments of harrowing suffering. Gerhard Stadelmaier rightly observed that Voss/Othello implodes rather than explodes.[10] Tantalizing is the sight of Othello crouching on the floor, grunting like a stricken animal or whimpering, and more powerful than words are the sounds (the *uhhuu*s and *eehh*s) which he produces, like one thunderstruck and dumbfounded. The man who won Desdemona's heart as a wonderful raconteur (I.iii.) — like Tabori himself — is deprived of language. Othello remains to the end the gullible, susceptible, tender, lovelorn "nature boy,"[11] victim of his naïveté or, alternatively, victim of his other self.

His Desdemona, inexperienced and schoolgirlish at first, gradually discovers her femininity, exchanges the high-collared clothing for a décolleté dress, asserts her independence by smoking her first cigarette and tasting some champagne in the company of the seasoned Emilia. The last scene shows her totally naked, exposed, vulnerable, and innocent in her nuptial/death bed. Her slender arms flutter like a turtledove, captured, beating its wings; the Moor, with his knees straddling her lower body, stifles her as he consummates the marriage and seals off her life with a kiss. Transfixed, as in a trance, he remains kneeling and holds his naked bride in his arms like a precious sacrifice — a gripping, subverted Pietà image.

Tabori's Othello is the paradigmatic lover, whose love is "the art of the impossible."[12] The irrelevance of his race is beautifully insinuated when Voss wipes off the black makeup that has besmirched Desdemona: color alone does not stigmatize — as the Indian Copperface, in vain rubbing his skin, believes in Tabori's *Weisman and Copperface*. Everyone who comes in contact with the Moor gets something of his makeup, his Otherness, and, besides, all is merely theatre.

"Anything wrong?" asks Shakespeare, the Author, when he is forced to give up his beer at the actors' canteen and hurry onstage at the urgent request of Othello. Everything has gone astray, he discovers, and the audience of his *Othello* premiere has disappeared.

Much to Othello's surprise, Shakespeare is not in the least embarrassed, nor is he perturbed by the obvious flop. "I'm going home to Stratford, to write my autobiography," he informs his Burbage/Othello, who takes this opportunity to give vent to discontent and resentment he has harbored for years against the Bard ("I refuse to go on playing with a black face").

This brief scene is the last of three one-act playlets entitled *The Last Night in September* (premiere 10 January 1997), Tabori's last stage play. "We are such stuff / As dreams are made on; and our little life / Is rounded with a sleep" (*Tempest*, IV.i. 156–158), says Tabori's Othello/Burbage at the end of the short, snappy episode which, far from being a dramatic performance, is a private joke. Tabori's Author mistrusts accomplishment and frowns at success. The time has come to retire, and this homage to Shakespeare, the greatest of them all, is the most appropriate way of bidding the stage farewell — as usual, without a grain of sentimentality or self-pity, but with an affectionate and pungent joke.

EMBODIED MEMORY THE HOLOCAUST PLAYS

THE CANNIBALS

I once had a funny nightmare: Two cannibalistic critics wanted to eat me up as a roulade of beef. They sit in front of the pot, one of them looks inside and says: "Frankly, I don't really like Tabori." The other retorts: "Oh well, eat only the noodles." George Tabori

"It is ironic, isn't it, to have one's first real success in Berlin of all places?" Tabori wrote to his brother, Paul, in London after the unexpected "fantastic success" of his German debut,[1] *The Cannibals*, at the workshop of the Schillertheater in December 1969.[2] The play — about the inmates of a concentration camp who must choose among eating bits of flesh of their dead mate Puffi, starving to death, or perishing in the gas chamber — received lukewarm reviews upon its world premiere with the American Place Company at St. Clemens Church in New York a year earlier.[3] It is indeed ironic that this Holocaust play — "so single-minded, so relentless, so hysterically eager to hurt," in the words of *New York Times* critic Walter Kerr[4] — should have opened the doors of the German theatre to George Tabori. According to his American wife, Viveca Lindfors, he "never wanted to put his foot on German soil nor buy a German product." "Those he had hated now loved him," she remarks, describing in her memoirs the inordinate success of *Cannibals* in Berlin.[5]

Actually, the Germans did not quite "love" him. The

grim and haunting performance of a passionately engaged all-male cast left spectators and critics consternated, uneasy, unsure of how to react or what was expected of them. Tabori's stage vision of the concentration-camp universe was breaking new ground, avoiding the sentimental imprecision of German Holocaust plays of the 1950s as well as the impartial scrutiny of the causes, manifestations, and moral implications of fascism that marked German documentary theatre in the 1960s. For the first time, German theatregoers were challenged by a play that focused on the meticulously implemented genocide, and signally these victims were depicted neither as saints nor as faultless martyrs. As if this were not complicated enough, the taboo-breaker was a Jew, a newcomer to the local scene, whose incidental remarks around the time of the premiere were outlandish and puzzling.

Furthermore, Viveca Lindfors surely exaggerated matters by claiming that Tabori hated the Germans. There is no trace of hatred or vindictive feelings in anything he wrote during or after the war. On the contrary, the protagonist of his first novel, *Beneath the Stone* (written during the war and published in 1945), the German officer von Borst, is no unscrupulous, cold-blooded prototype of the master race, but rather "a Kafkaesque bel esprit."[6] It was not hatred but mainly guilt that preyed on Tabori's mind, the typical guilt of the survivor. Like so many of them, he could not bring himself to talk to anyone about the war or about the dear ones who had perished.[7] Years passed before he was able to articulate his pain. In an interview he gave on his eightieth birthday, he spoke explicitly of his immense luck during the war, of which he had been unaware, and of his guilt feelings as a survivor vis-à-vis the dead. He reproached himself in particular for not having saved his father. "It would have been possible [to save him]. I was a British press officer and I knew how dangerous things were for the Jews in Hungary. I called him up from Istanbul in 1941 and said, casually only, that he should visit me with Mother. I didn't press him either. I have never forgiven myself this."[8]

The Cannibals was born out of this pain and gnawing guilt. Tabori wrote the first draft in the mid 1960s in New York, "instead of having a nervous breakdown."[9] Many drafts were to follow. In fact, in the Tabori archive there are sundry handwritten and typed versions of the play in English.[10] The final English version is far from identical to the German stage script used for the German premiere, which underwent further revisions prior to its publication in the collected edition *Theaterstücke*.

The genesis of *The Cannibals* is itself a singular story. It affords us insight into the mind of a survivor ploddingly transposing his pain into a work of art and likewise sheds light on the reception of what has become known as Holocaust literature.

It was shortly after the war, as the dimensions of the catastrophe gradually emerged, soon after receiving the official notice of his father's demise in Auschwitz, that Tabori embarked upon a prose work that sought to depict the horrors of life in a concentration camp. "I am brushing up a new novel called *Pogrom*," he wrote from Hollywood to his brother, Paul, in October 1947.[11] Four months later the manuscript was turned down by Tabori's publisher, Boardman & Co in London. Boardman maintained that the novel was neither good nor original, as the basic situation was too similar to that of *Original Sin* (1947): "an adult is shown to be dominated by an unresolved Oedipus complex."[12] Tabori never mentioned this rejection when he talked about the novel years later. Instead he reported having burned the manuscript; he had no right, as somebody who had not been "there," to write about the subject. It took him years to realize that this was a lame excuse, "self-censorship," as he put it.[13] Some twenty years after this disheartening experience, he renewed the attempt to combat his own pain and confront the horror, using some of the original material in his play *The Cannibals*. Flying in the face of Theodor Adorno's famous maxim, he pronounced that to write about Auschwitz "is an imperative. One must overcome it somehow."

As so often with Tabori, however, matters are more complex than they seem at first and contain no small dose of contradictions. In a CBS interview he gave in September 1947, Tabori described *Pogrom* not as a novel but as an "anthology of stories . . . dealing with various aspects of the Jewish predicament."[14] The first of five stories describes "the social nightmare of deportation," while the third, possibly the origin of the later *Cannibals*, depicts a day in a concentration camp. But it is the fourth story in the collection entitled *Pogrom* which deserves special mention. It is "a kind of duel between an elderly refugee woman and a Fascist exile who had shot her husband." There appears to be a strong affinity between the elderly refugee widow and Tabori's mother, Elsa. When we met in Vienna in winter 1997, Tabori recalled that during an extended visit she paid him in New York soon after the war, his mother urged him to get hold of his father's murderer, who, she had apparently ascertained, was living in the metropolis. "His name was Uschinsky or something like that, and my mother told me, go kill him. How could I?" He made inquiries and soon realized that "nothing could be done about it, so I sat down and started writing."

There is yet another story connected with the creation of *Cannibals*, which was entitled "The Eating Play" in some of the earlier drafts. At the same interview, Tabori recounted what he heard from two Hungarian survivors he met shortly after the war was over: "One of them was a member of the Auschwitz-Kapelle [the Jewish musician prisoners whose Nazi-enforced performances accompanied the victims on their way to the gas chambers] and he told me that my father had said *'Nach Ihnen* [After you], *Herr* Mandelbaum.'" Naturally I was familiar with this episode recorded in Tabori's autobiographical essays, often recounted in interviews, and also incorporated in *Cannibals*.[15] What struck me was Tabori's final remark: "I don't know if he really said it, my father, but that is unimportant anyway."

Likewise, it is irrelevant whether or not there were actual cases of anthropophagy among the inmates of Auschwitz, as Tabori suggests he had heard. His unconventional elegy to his father depicts people trapped in a human-made hell, where some of the victims manage to retain their human image while others submit to Nazi commander Schrekinger by consuming morsels of Puffi's flesh. The question he poses is in fact similar to the one brought up by Primo Levi: is it possible to maintain human dignity in the suburbs of hell, in a liminal situation (*Grenzsituation*)? "What matters . . . is the manner of their dying," writes Tabori. "Their resistance, the affirmation of their own humanity, was, I believe, wholly efficacious. One would read St. Augustine, another insisted on shaving even on the day of his murder, and my father was seen entering the shower room with a gesture of extreme courtesy as though saying, After you, Alphonse."[16]

Cannibals inaugurates Tabori's experimentations with theatre as a locus of remembrance (*Gedächtnisort*). Far from a devotional commemoration of the dead, the performance is in fact an absorbing visceral experience for both actors and spectators, in which the past is evoked, retrieved, relived, reflected upon. The emphasis is on the actual, immediate experience, on the presentness of the past. Tabori generates an effect of synchronicity or temporal overlap by casting the same actors as the victims and as the victims' sons; the sons confront their fathers and question their choices, even as they enact their stories. The personages who participate in the mnemonic ceremony are individualized examples of the camps' victims: a gypsy, a Greek, the homosexual Haas, the dispassionate medical student Klaub, the juvenile Ramaseder-Kid, the Jewish survivors Heltai and Hirschler, who, notably, are the only ones who comply with the Nazi ultimatum and partake of Puffi's flesh.

Yet Tabori is hardly interested in traditional characterization; nor does he care much for creating coherent, comprehensive biographies. Together with the actors he ventures to explore the eruptions of memory, the inconsistencies of character, the dynamics of an extreme situation, and the interchangeability — "dialectics" he calls it — of victim and victimizer. The episodic structure of the play (the English version consists of a series of episodes which Tabori rearranged and yoked together for the German performance) leaves scope for random improvisations. In lieu of the naturalistic reconstruction of the concentration-camp universe, he opts for a stylized evocative ritual, in which the dreamlike and the real coalesce; playacting, miming, and psychologizing blend into each other. It is impossible and inappropriate to try to reconstruct Auschwitz on the stage. Most attempts slide into kitsch, says Tabori, just as the site itself has been turned into a tourist museum, void of spirit, and incapable of kindling any emotions.[17] Consequently, *The Cannibals* was performed on a nearly bare stage, with only a rack of bunks, a winding metal staircase, and an oven with its coarse-looking pipe jutting out.[18] Apart from the two survivors in striped camp uniform, all the other actors wore shabby everyday clothes. The actors grapple, embrace, crawl, freeze in fear or expectation, or bend over in exhaustion, frailty, and vulnerability. They gesticulate eating noisily, chew, munch, lick their lips, belch, grab imaginary bits of liverwurst (thus engaging in "sense memory"), or stare hungrily at the meat cooking in the cauldron. They growl and bark like dogs, sibilate, moan, sing, tell jokes, imitate the burbling of water, or produce the hissing sound of gas oozing from the showers.

This ritualistic enactment is interspersed with sequences deploying Brechtian techniques to counteract any cheap emotionalism, to alienate the audience and to shock them into a serious and genuine (re-)consideration of the past. This is a ritual of remembrance in which, as Jörg Gronius observes, "the actors repeatedly abandon role and situation in order to concentrate on the process of remembering."[19]

The imperative to remember is cardinal to Judaism. The Hebrew Bible commands memory: the people of Israel are "enjoined to remember" and "adjured not to forget," as Yosef Hayim Yerushalmi asserts in his seminal study *Zakhor*.[20] Tabori speaks about the "void and the memory" which Jews would leave behind should they be wiped out entirely.[21] Remembering is an act of choice, of commitment. It shapes the present, molds one's identity. "If you forget the past, you are condemned to relive it," Tabori rephrases Santayana, warning against nostalgic sentiments or a cerebral, intellectualized approach to the past.[22] The past recalled and confronted cannot be "overcome," as so many in post-Holocaust Germany speaking of *Vergangenheitsbewältigung* were all too ready to believe. There are no shortcuts to atonement.

For generations of Jews in the Diaspora, memory flowed primarily through two channels, the liturgical and the ritual. The best instances, perhaps, are the Passover Seder and the Purim festivity. In the first, the culinary elements (such as the Seder plate or the Mazzah) accompanying the liturgical reading of the Haggadah signify not only a recollection of Egyptian slavery and the Exodus, but also its reactualization.[23] The Purim holiday commemorating the deliverance of the Jews from Haman's genocidal plot comprises similar ritualistic elements: the reading of the Megillah, the Scroll of Esther, its theatrical rendering as *Purimshpil*, carnivalesque masquerading and buffooneries. The festive meal includes triangular pastries called *Hamantaschen* (Haman-ears), which are relished as a culinary metonymy for the villain's downfall.

Tabori's theatre of remembering echoes this tradition. The language and stage imagery of *Cannibals*, not least the culinary images, accentuate the simultaneity of past and present. That which is recollected is reenacted as in a ritual, repeatedly, obsessively relived. Ironically, Tabori describes *Cannibals* as a "black mass,"[24] a subversive ritual which calls to mind Jean Genet's theatre. It involves the deliberate breaking of taboos ("There are taboos that must be broken or they will continue to choke us").[25] It eschews mythologized saints and grandiose figures, while striving for demystification: "Heroes have bowels," writes Tabori; he introduces into his black mass episodes of vomiting, defecation, and urination (the cooking pot also serves explicitly as a piss pot!). Little wonder that the two Jewish actors in the cast had such severe problems with the play that they at one point wanted to quit;[26] and that the head of the Jewish community in Berlin, Heinz Galinski, himself a survivor, objected to the play ("I was myself in Auschwitz and I never said piss")[27] and even tried to prevent the performance. Blasphemous as it may seem, Tabori insists on "mixing the celestial and the excremental"[28] — to shock, to provoke, and ultimately to purge and to cleanse. This is a ritual profaned, an intrinsically revolutionary, willed assault on the ubiquitous (even canonical by now) Holocaust lacrymatory and on "good taste"; an iconoclastic sacrum not alien to the gargantuan, the genital, and the excremental elements of Mikhail Bakhtin's carnivalesque spirit. "Sacer after all means not only sacred but unclean as well," Tabori points out.

Eating, like its adjunct cooking, is a recurring theme of the black mass; the other is the bond between sons and fathers. "I wanted initially to write about eating," Tabori recalls. "Eating is not only nourishment, it is also a ritual. . . . The other theme was Auschwitz, not as document, but as it was conceived in the minds of the sons or those born later."[29] Hence the dedication of the play, entwining the two themes: "In memory of Cornelius Tabori, perished in Auschwitz, a small eater."

Tabori was well acquainted with Freud's seminal study *Totem and Taboo* (1913), fascinated by the bearings of anthropology on psychoanalysis and the relevance of both of these to his theatre of remembrance. Freud describes extensively the ancient communal ritual of the totemic meal in which the totem animal serves as substitute for the father. He writes about the ambivalent feelings, ranging from admiration and love to rivalry or hatred, which sons harbor for their fathers, and about the subliminal impulse to kill and "devour" the father.[30] In his introduction to *Cannibals*, Tabori echoes Freud's observations: "Parricide is our oldest fable, still haunting this fatherless world where we, the sons, have not yet learned to live without the old man. . . . Each son wants to knock off his father at some point; but what happens when others do it for him, as in my case, and he hovers paralysed between relief and revenge?"[31] The answer for Tabori seems to lie in a belated and iterative theatrical enactment, a radical taunting ritual of mourning concocted by a son who almost desperately tries to break out of the trauma. As time went by, Tabori realized the dominance of the paternal Hamlet-ghost, discovered for himself the Freudian truism that the dead father may be much more powerful than the living one had ever been. "Some of our oldest myths, from the first father-murder to the Last Supper, have been enacted around a dinner table," writes Tabori, describing his play as "the extraordinary tale of a dinner party."[32]

Just as in ancient times the totemic meal was celebrated by the entire clan, and just as the sacrificial ceremony or the commemorative meal (Passover, Communion) is a communal occasion, so too the meal in *Cannibals*, the eating of Puffi's cooked flesh, serves as a collective ritual. Twelve internees partake in it, eat or choose to resist, and Puffi, the sacrificial dish, is one of them! He grumbles like a famished dog when the cook announces that dinner is ready.

The number of diners, twelve, is hardly accidental: the Last Supper was attended by the twelve apostles, and in Jewish tradition the number is associated with the twelve sons of the biblical forefather Jacob, the twelve tribes of Israel. Truly, this bizarre banquet, as in Shakespeare's *Titus Andronicus* or in Heiner Müller's *The Battle* (1975),[33] is a ritual perverted. Leah Hadomi rightly points out that it is "an inversion of the anamnestic Eucharist."[34]

The allusion to the Holy Communion, to the notion of transubstantation, is made immediately, in the opening scene. A cock crows (as in the opening scene of Tabori's *Mein Kampf*) to insinuate the betrayal, and Puffi, the offender turned sacrifice and savior of two Jewish eaters, Heltai and Hirschler, "takes a piece of bread from under his armpit" (*Cannibals*, 203). While the cook Weiss (white, in German) stirs the Puffi stew in the cauldron, the inmates describe in Beckett-like apocalyptic terms the inferno they inhabit, a world deprived of light even as the sun is shining, a planet of shadows (219, 235). Sharing fantasies of relishing a liverwurst leads to a brawl which culminates in a mock-Passion. Lang poses as crucified, his arms stretched aside, his head hanging down, while the gypsy raises him "as if he were the Host" (223), announcing the resurrection of Christ. This is followed by the "resurrection" of Puffi, who eagerly looks into the boiling cauldron. But as one of the inmates observes, "There is no Baaaah!" — no lamb to be a surrogate burnt offering — "There is only Puffi!" (224). There is no salvation, no redemption, and no Kingdom of Heaven. All there is, as the sagacious Uncle proclaims, is "The Kingdom of Children," whose mourning-work (*Trauerarbeit*) entails the totemic meal, the killing and devouring of the father, or, in Uncle's words, "cut him down and cut him up and eat him" (240) — a harrowing ritual of exorcism.

Tabori's black mass reverberates with allusions not only to the Christian sacrament, but also to Jewish liturgy. A ram's horn (Shofar in Hebrew) is heard (only in the English version!) as the play opens and again later, when Uncle is put on trial by the inmates. The blowing of the Shofar is associated with the giving of the Law at Mount Sinai (Exodus 19:16) and with the tradition of atonement at the turn of the Jewish year, particularly with the Day of Judgment, Yom Kippur. So too the custom of the surrogate rooster, which is echoed (this time only in the German version! [*Kannibalen*, 42]) when in the course of "a mad Hasidic dance" the cook swings the jacket of the Ramaseder-Kid above his head as if he were "offering a sacrifice."

Indeed, the sacrifice of the Ramaseder-Kid alludes to Abraham's near-sacrifice of his son, Isaac, a counterpoint to the images of Christ's sacrifice on the cross. Kaddish, the Jewish prayer for the dead, is chanted (in both versions!) over Puffi's body, and the biblical mourning custom of throwing sand or ashes is echoed as Uncle re-enters, a prophet outraged, with mud in his hands (sand, in the German version), which he slings at the others.[35]

Most striking perhaps are the myriad quotations from the Books of Moses, Exodus, Numbers, and Deuteronomy incorporated into the text and the idiosyncratic rendering of the Ten Commandments. Uncle, Tabori's homage to his father, is modeled on the figure of the biblical Moses, leader and archfather to his people, the Children of Israel. A wise old man of integrity, lisping and stammering through his beard like Moses,[36] he must serve as an intermediary between his protégés and a God who has, it seems, abandoned them.[37] To him they cry out their anguish and complain of excruciating hunger, like the Children of Israel, who, pining for the food they enjoyed in Egyptian captivity, challenged the prophet and his putative omnipotent God, demanding flesh to eat (Numbers 11:4). "You shall eat . . . until it comes out of your nostrils and be loathsome to you," Uncle rebukes the disbelievers (*Cannibals*, 210), and, like Moses, turns to the Almighty to cry out his own pain and despair, to protest against the burdensome vocation he never asked for.

With the stereotypical white gloves on his hands,[38] Uncle is the champion of moral principles, the lonely voice of conscience in the wilderness. "The only way to resist geese is to stay as ungooselike as possible," he preaches to his fickle disciples (*Cannibals*, 236). A forerunner of Shlomo Herzl in Tabori's *Mein Kampf*, who says, "Better be choked, than a choker," or "Better be hunted than a hunter," Uncle hides the knife meant to kill the German officer, the knife that could have liberated the victims. But it is undoubtedly his unrelenting objection to the cannibalistic ordeal that singles him out as the advocate of nonviolence and humanness. "There are times when the most practical, the most human, and, if you like, the most violent act is simply the refusal to do something under duress . . . not eating though one is starved."[39]

"Eat or die" is Tabori's central metaphor for the survival strategy. In his early play *The 25th Hour*, Arthur Prince partakes in a sumptuous meal so as to survive and have a chance in the decadent society surrounding him. Choking with tears, Shlomo Herzl takes Lobkowitz's advice in *Mein Kampf* and swallows bits of his dear chicken Mitzi, so as to be armed to face future calamities. Alfred Morgenstern of *The Ballad of a Wiener Schnitzel*, a gourmet, is forced to eat: the diners (cooks in Tabori's own staging!) in Herrmann's restaurant (*nomen est omen*) follow the chef's order and stuff the schnitzel down his throat. The meaty dish releases long-suppressed memories: Morgenstern realizes he betrayed memory and failed to mourn the dead. Conversely, the refusal of food is Tabori's metaphor for resistance and human dignity. Cassandra throws up the noodles offered to her by Menelaus in his version of *The Trojan Women* (1976), while the fasting-artist(s) defy the authority of the impresario and assert their sovereignty in his memorable rendering of Kafka's *A Fasting-Artist* (1977).

"Only be steadfast in not eating the blood; For the blood is the life; and thou shalt not eat the life with the flesh" (Deuteronomy 12:23–24). Tabori's Uncle enunciates (in the English version, *Cannibals*, 216) the cardinal rule of Jewish dietary law (which was delivered by Moses): the prohibition on the consumption of animal blood.[40] The blood is the biblical soul (*Nefesh* in Hebrew), the sacred value, and thus Jews must not eat raw meat. Tabori develops the culinary metaphor further: he inverts the pervasive notion among anthropologists, underscored by Claude Lévi-Strauss, whereby cooking is seen as the fundamental articulation of the distinction between nature and culture — cooking as a topos of civilization.[41] Furthermore, Puffi Pinkus exemplifies in person the perversions of human civilization: excessively obese ("the second fattest man in Europe") and hedonistic, he prospers by raising geese, fattening their livers artificially and exporting them "all over the civilized world" (*Cannibals*, 206).[42] This sarcastic attack on acculturation alludes, in turn, to the title of the play. The moral concluding it — tellingly enough transmitted over the loudspeaker by a faceless voice — mentions commonly cited and contested instances of cannibalism, and yet Tabori is hardly concerned with the carnivorous "Others" outside the realm of civilized culture.[43] His interest lies in human conduct in extreme conditions, in liminal situations. Aggression is mainly a function of the hunger instinct, he must have read in *Ego, Hunger and Aggression* (1947) by Frederick S. Perls, father of *Gestalt*-therapy. "Hunger is the best cook," Tabori writes in one of his many essays revolving around the metaphors of food and cooking.[44] The ever-present cauldron and the grisly image of the cook Weiss relentlessly stirring it are permanent reminders of human fallibility, of the cannibal atrocities within and not outside the realm of civilized culture. "After the 'kill,' the food itself has to be attacked," stipulates Perls.[45] With Tabori it is the ghost of the murdered that has to be confronted, as it refuses to rest in peace. It is the biblical *Nefesh*, the blood, that is unwilling to forget and be forgotten. The black mass, the reenactment of the totemic meal, is therefore a compelling work of mourning.

"Only few of us have succeeded in remembering what we wish to forget, and we can only forget what we have truly remembered," writes Tabori in his typically tortuous manner.[46] Jews and Germans alike, albeit for different reasons, try to disremember, to suppress, only to be overtaken by memory at one point or another. This is what Tabori's father, Cornelius, did, believing he could shake off his Jewish heritage and slip into a new identity as a cosmopolite. "No, you don't become a Jew. You are merely reminded that you are one," realizes Uncle in *Cannibals*.[47]

Tabori came to Berlin to codirect *Cannibals* out of curiosity: "I was curious to find out how a German audience would respond to a black mass whose texture was humor, not piety."[48] To be on the safe side, he ordered a getaway car for the opening night. He did not need it. A few boos were heard at the interval; there was a minor misunderstanding, and then twenty minutes of standing ovations at the end of the performance. The noted critic Rolf Michaelis, taken aback by the thunderous applause, suspected that "only a guilty conscience can go on like this."[49] "*Cannibals* struck the heart here, in

Germany," contends Maria Sommer,[50] Tabori's future publisher, who, piqued by the American reviews, had arranged for the play's Berlin production. Timing no doubt played a significant role in the inordinate success. The spectacular trials of Nazi officials — Adolf Eichmann in Jerusalem (1961), the "Auschwitz Trial" in Frankfurt (1963–1965) — and the continuous debate about the *Verjährung* (the statute of limitations of Nazi war crimes) in the German Bundestag and consequently in the media highlighted interest in the fate of the Jews during and after the Holocaust. This was further enhanced by the publication of the polemical study by the Mitscherlichs about the Germans' inability to mourn (*Die Unfähigkeit zu trauern*, 1967) as well as by the cultural-political controversies over Rolf Hochhuth's *The Deputy* (1963) and Peter Weiss's *The Investigation* (1965). Last but not least was the change in the sociopolitical climate in the Federal Republic in the wake of the tempestuous student revolt of 1968. The younger generation contested the past, posed questions to their parents, demanded to be told the plain truth instead of hackneyed phrases, and in so doing they put into question the seemingly solid foundations of German democracy.

Cannibals was premiered against this background, neither castigating the audience nor harping for sympathy, tears, or pious self-condemnation. Critics applauded the "brave, relentless play," "the most complex, most courageous, and most problematic play that has been staged in Germany after the war."[51] And yet there were others who questioned Tabori's taboo-breaking, taunting stage vision of Auschwitz. "Darf man denn das?" — Is this at all permissible? — was the leading question voiced by opponents and supporters alike.[52] Interestingly, an unrelated film entitled *Cannibal Holocaust*, "an infamous 'video nasty,'" was outlawed by the British censors in early 1980.[53]

Far away from the East Coast, where *Cannibals* was premiered, Tabori was to continue in the following years his relentless experimentations with the theatre of remembrance.[54] It was Germany, where history was palpable, where Jewish life began to reemerge but only hesitantly, that proved to be the best backdrop for the mnemonic performance.

VARIATIONS ON SHYLOCK

*We are prepared to deny Shylock.
Yet we know that he is putting
forward in our name such a justified
and fundamental historic grievance
and complaint that it must not be
left unsaid.*

Shlomo Bickel, *Great Yiddish Writers of the Twentieth Century*

Three times Tabori grappled with *The Merchant of Venice*, yet none of his stagings are faithful renderings of the Shakespearean text. Inspired by the arcane figure of Shylock, whose "secret" remains perennially unresolved,[1] Tabori downplayed the main plot in favor of inordinate focus on the Jew. Among modern-dress adapters of the play after 1945,[2] Tabori was one of the first to place Shylock's story in the context of the Holocaust, claiming that it is impossible to "do Shylock totally ignoring what has happened."[3]

Tabori's first staging of the play was tellingly entitled *The Merchant of Venice as Performed in Theresiensadt*. Presented at the Berkshire Theatre Festival in Stockbridge, Massachusetts, in 1966, the play is set in a concentration camp — that *univers concentrationnaire* which led to an irrevocable breach in modern consciousness — with Jewish prisoners performing for a Nazi audience. Twelve years later, in 1978, Tabori dispensed with the Belmont plot altogether, offering his German audience *Improvisations on Shylock*: a provocative and deeply disturbing performance highlighting Diasporic histories of anti-Semitism, conflating the past(s) and the present through temporal overlap and a poignant sense of immediacy. Finally, in 1989, Tabori included an adapted episode of *The Merchant of Venice* in his Shakespeare collage *Lovers and Lunatics*. Playing the part of the long-suffering Jew, scarred by experience, his Shylock was the ahistorical embodiment of the age-old narrative of friction and distrust between Jews and Christians. "The wound always understands the knife," maintains Tabori,[4] whose frail and broken Shylock becomes a living image of "negative symbiosis."[5]

Indeed, in all Tabori's interpretations, Shylock is unmistakably the victim, a man more sinned against than sinning. His story calls up collective memories of victimhood and deep-rooted anxiety, and the play evolves into a dramatic meditation on collective Diasporic experience. In Tabori's words, "It isn't an anti-Semitic play. It is a play about anti-Semitism."[6]

For Tabori there is no such thing as abstract memory. Genuine memory is necessarily sensual; remembering is an act of somatic recall.[7] Likewise "in the theatre the truth is always concrete, you cannot play collective nouns or 3rd degree abstractions."[8] Shylock's experience — concrete, paradigmatic — is rooted in a timeless tradition of hatred, discrimination, and persecution, which Tabori seeks to present in a way that would unsettle the spectator and demand conscious, active engagement. His Shylock is a Jew because the others unceasingly and painfully remind him of it.[9] Whenever not alone on the stage, he is the prototype Jew as non-Jews conceive of him, steeped as they are in preconceptions and prejudices. According to Tabori, Shylock — a singularly "ambivalent character" in the Shakespearean canon — is "neither the vicious capitalist, nor the noble victim of persecution; he is both, and the double-image is more than the sum of its constituent halves . . . Shakespeare shows the stereotype in order to unmask it."[10]

It was in his *Improvisations* that Tabori was particularly subversive, playing up anti-Semitic clichés and stereotypes to invert spectators' expectations and shock them into reconsidering these images of hatred. This controversial strategy, flying in the face of taboos, was likewise adopted by Peter Zadek (like Tabori, a director of Jewish origin working in Germany) in his 1972 production of *The Merchant of Venice*.[11]

Of the four productions inaugurating the first season of the Berkshire Festival in 1966, *The Merchant of Venice as Performed in Theresienstadt* was the only one directed by its official artistic director, Tabori.[12] Viveca Lindfors, Tabori's wife at that time and Portia in his production (which she mistakenly calls "The Merchant of Venice as Performed in Auschwitz" — a slip of the tongue which possibly relates to the fact that Tabori's father perished in that extermination camp and not in the "model" KZ-Theresienstadt), considers the performance "the most astonishing production as far as artistic statement is concerned."[13] Critic R. E. Krieger found the performance "most remarkable, compelling and harrowing" and wondered "what must have been running through his [Tabori's] mind as he directed it."[14] William Gibson, president of the festival, reported that "some people found it very exciting. Others were baffled. And others wanted to know what had happened to Shakespeare."[15] An anonymous reporter speaks of "violent reactions in the audience," ranging from loud protest to deep empathy.[16]

No wonder. Tabori, intent on a genuine and uncompromising grappling with the Holocaust, interested neither in a sentimental response nor in tearful sympathy, defied sociocultural proprieties and ran against taboos in his productions, first in America and later in Germany. Geographically remote from the scene of the Nazi crimes, preoccupied with the political tensions surrounding the Cold War, and absorbed in domestic affairs, America was slow to confront the Holocaust and scrutinize its own involvement in it with appropriate concern and earnestness.[17] Tabori's *Merchant* brought the menacing horror of the *univers concentrationnaire* to the American audience with pressing immediacy. Moreover, this was the first production in an American theatre which (re)contextualized Shakespeare's drama in recent history. Much like their European colleagues, American directors were reluctant to stage Shakespeare's play "after all that has happened," as the hackneyed phrase went. The few noteworthy productions preceding Tabori's include the 1957 staging with Morris Carnovsky as a "heavy, though an incisive and serious" Shylock and Joseph Papp's slightly modernized adaptation performed in Central Park (1962), with George C. Scott as a "guttural-voiced Shylock, . . . a man bitterly conscious of his wrongs, and implacable in his hatreds."[18]

A detailed account of the production sheds light on the rehearsal period and the gradual evolution of the mise-en-scène concept.[19] The festival company, including Alan Epstein (Shylock), Viveca Lindfors (Portia), Estelle Parsons (Nerissa), and Andre Voutsinas (Antonio), explored the play in workshops held in New York beginning in February 1966.[20] Realizing the substantial similarities between the fictitious scene and contemporary society, the actors decided in favor of a modern-dress adaptation, "a sort of Shakespearean *La Dolce Vita*." A few weeks later "the mise-en-scène metamorphosed into that of a concentration camp." The guiding question was revised and reformulated as "What would be the logical extension of the play's events in the twentieth century?" Though the account suggests close teamwork and collective decision-making, I propose that it was Tabori who brought the play into the concentration camp setting.[21] Theresienstadt was the appropriate site, since that "model" camp was the setting of diverse cultural activities, including theatre performances.[22] Once the framework of a play-within-the-play was chosen, the company discussed the reactions of both the prisoners and the Nazi officers to the "show." How daring could the inmates be during the performance? How would they shift from one fictitious role (in Shakespeare's play) to their role as Jewish prisoners? How would they provide the Nazi officers with a satisfactory spectacle and yet assert their dignity or posit theatre as a form of defiance?[23] The notion of the actor as "victim" or the performance as a form of defiance was to fuel later Tabori productions, particularly his memorable *Fasting-Artists*.

It was soon agreed that the entire audience would be "treated as Nazis." The actors prepared for all sorts of audience reactions — from protest to derision — and contemplated how these diverse reactions would ultimately affect their own acting, requiring them to improvise. After five months,[24] the production opened in Stockbridge on 19 July 1966.

Working within the limits of a proscenium stage, Tabori nevertheless opted for a "poor theatre," what he called "the aesthetics of poverty and horror."[25] The curtains strung on a wire across the slanted bare stage were filthy stained blankets with swastikas drawn along their lower edge. The few props used — prominent among them a large portrait of Hitler in the background — were illuminated by pitiless incandescent bulbs. The actors, some with shaved heads, wore striped prisoners' uniforms, "burlap sacks with armholes for coats . . . , sheets for dresses," cut-up newspapers for lace.[26] A folk singer and a guitar player accompanied the performance.

A sustained tableau — a hallmark of many later Tabori productions — launches the performance. It is a haunting opening scene. A trapdoor opens and an emaciated being crawls out, then collapses. Men and women prisoners gather obediently, silently, onstage as the war hit "Lili Marleen" is heard. Nazi officers storm in and take their seats in the front row of the auditorium as prisoners carry the sagging body away. "The stage is set. The play can begin."[27] It begins, but not with the Shakespearean text. Instead, inmates enter with pails of water and scrub the floor, slowly approaching the audience/the officers. The silent presence of these shadows envelops the entire play-within-the-play, the fable of the three caskets and Shylock's story. The performance of the adapted *Merchant* ends abruptly, at the climax of the trial scene (IV.i): Portia's eulogy for mercy becomes an aching plea. Enraged, one of the Nazi officers climbs onstage to take over the part of the Judge. Script in hand, he takes control of the show, ordering the Jew to kneel and beg forgiveness. "The tension is unbearable," recounts Viveca Lindfors (Portia). "The rest of the inmates, sensing their life and death is at stake, have entered the stage. Will he or will he not submit? The Jew playing the Merchant looks around, then slowly goes down on his knees. But he is not alone for long. Portia, played by me, is the first to join him. One by one, the other inmates follow."

The underlings "rehearse" the uprising; on the metatheatrical level, the actors defy the director's authority. They slowly crawl toward the front, like the inmates in the opening scene. "As we reach the edge of the stage there is a sudden black-out. When the lights slowly come up again, left on the stage are only piles of our clothes."[28]

Instances of history breaking into fiction and disrupting it, of the present reshaping our perception of the past, are doubtless the decisive moments in the production: for instance, Shylock's famous outcry "Hath not a Jew eyes?" delivered by a frenzied prisoner (Alan Epstein). He tears off his orange yarn wig (recalling the traditional red wig that instantly identified the Jew as a kinsman of Judas) to disclose a shaved head and flings away the false protruding crooked nose, that stereotype of savage anti-Jewish propaganda.

Tabori followed similar lines in his second variation on Shylock. The 1966 "Theresienstadt" *Merchant* contains the seeds of the 1978 *Improvisations*, with one crucial difference: the performance was conceived for a German audience.

For Tabori, Shylock's "secret," that silence throbbing at the heart of Shakespeare's play, is related to the pound of flesh. "If one takes the cutting away of the flesh seriously, one cannot avoid thinking of murder, and it is murder that links Jews and Germans."[29] Because of this cutting, "a secret lies over the relationship between Jews and Germans."[30] Ever since his return to Germany in 1969, Tabori sought to approximate this enigma, acutely aware that he was doomed to "Fail. Fail again. Fail better," in Beckett's sense. Perceived as a genuine effort by "the wound to understand the knife," *Improvisations on Shylock* evolved into a theatrical meditation on anti-Semitism or "6,000 years of injuries."[31]

Tabori did not intend the performance to be an indictment against his German audience. Nor did he delude himself that the theatrical experience would resolve the past. The performance was conceived as a private endeavor for Tabori, a quest he undertook with twelve young actors, most of whom were children during the war. Viewed from the other side of the ocean, American treatment of the Holocaust in theatre and film appeared shallow and one-sided, and Tabori realized that the particular German context called for a new and different staging. In Germany, in the immediate proximity of recent events, perpetrators, and crowds of silent onlookers, people "see matter in a more differentiated way, even if they do not see them the way I do." Henryk Broder, a prominent voice among Jewish writers in post-Holocaust Germany who rarely curbs his tongue, claims that the small Jewish minority in Germany today is a perpetually irritating reminder to the Germans of their crimes. "The Germans will never forgive us, Jews, for Auschwitz," he observes cynically.

Perplexingly free of hatred or vindictive feelings, Tabori refrains from pointing an accusing finger. His interest lies with the Diaspora Jewish condition and the wrongs of Jew-hatred, which he himself experienced and witnessed before, during, and after the Holocaust.[32] "The profound cause of anti-Semitism is neither economic nor xenophobic, but this unmastered [*unbewältigte*] feeling of failure," he maintains. "The presence of a single Jew suffices to remind us that *our* [emphasis added] history is a criminal one, and so we project our crimes on the one who, so we think, branded us as criminals."[33] What is striking about Tabori's statement is not so much the pronouncement that even a single Jew is a persistent reminder of the wrongs of anti-Semitism — a position shared by Broder — but the fact that Tabori summarily includes himself in the culpable, ignoble collective. This attitude is typical of Tabori and is related to his recurrent strategy of interchanging victim and perpetrator. "Every one of you should find in himself the Jew and the anti-Semite," he instructed the actors.[34]

Improvisations focused on the Jewish trope of the maltreated, downtrodden, and persecuted victim in an unequivocal manner and with no trace of the bittersweet or black humor permeating so many of Tabori's so-called Holocaust plays. The play opened after forty-five days of intensive rehearsals — of teamwork and collective decision-making in line with Tabori's notion of democratic theatre-making. The rehearsal protocol records ongoing modifications, some in response to changing circumstances, others purposely chosen. Indeed, as so often with Tabori, the "concept" of the performance developed during the course of rehearsals. The performance that emerged on opening night (and which was even further amended) was marked by a dualistic quality, the confluence of incongruous, antithetical elements.

Formally, for example, the performance followed the principle of "a structured freedom."[35] The texts used — excerpts from Shakespeare's play, an anti-Jewish ballad attributed to Samuel Pepys,[36] a Holocaust testimony — were synchronically combined to produce intertextual allusions. Shylock's story (the Belmont plot was discarded) was not performed in linear order, but was disrupted by and interlaced with improvisations, songs, and musical impromptus, commenting or reflecting on the plot in the tradition of the epic theatre. Improvisations are a decisive component of Tabori's theatre work, an integral part of his "training" and warm-up, but it was here that he studiedly sought to shape the entire performance according to aleatory principles, emphasizing individual inventiveness, contingency, and randomness. Like a jam session, the performance offered itself as experience — raw, sensual, unpredictable — and not as argument.

The grand piano in the middle of the rehearsing/acting area was indeed the key to the performance. The American Jewish musician Stanley Walden, a former member of the Open Theater, set the tone, gave the cues, provoked and animated the actors, took over when an actor stumbled. Following theatre avant-gardists experimenting with jazz, like Joe Chaikin, Tabori looked upon this fallback option as a salubrious measure to free the actor from the rigid, authority-oriented German theatre-making. A kindred spirit to Tabori in his critical view of German theatre practice, Walden diagnoses the German "drive towards supervision and clarity, the discomfort with ambiguity, the distrust of freedom and randomness in art and politics."[37] The notion of "a structured freedom" which underlined the entire performance was encoded by him.

What Tabori termed his "dialectic" strategy was also manifest in the depiction of Shylock. Focusing attention on the Jew and his lot, Tabori collectivized the victim experience and explicity referred to Shylock as "a rock [whose] injuries are 6,000 years old."[38] At the same time he multiplied the figure: there were thirteen Shylocks in the performance, the twelve actors and Stanley Walden.[39] Tabori created a disjointed narrative, eschewing cohesiveness in favor of rupture. Each actor responded to the fictitious Jew in a personal manner. This plethora of voices, suggesting a fractured identity, cumulatively conveyed Tabori's conviction that the truth, irreducible and divergent, lies in the plurality or profusion of voices. Related to the multivalent depiction of Shylock is the temporal overlap, the conflation of past(s) and present. The "rock of injuries" is an ahistorical metaphor of Jewish suffering in a performance historicized by references to the Holocaust.

The development of the performance "concept" can be beautifully traced with the help of the detailed rehearsal notes and is an exemplary "work-in-progress."[40] It was the first markedly experimental production which Tabori conducted in agreement with the management of the Kammerspiele in Munich, after his own Theaterlabor in Bremen was forced to disband. The initial point of departure was similar to the 1966 *Merchant*: "Shylock '44" was to be performed on the site of the concentration camp in Dachau, with the actors as prisoners. Spectators and actors would be bused from the theatre to the railway station in Munich, escorted to the Venice-bound train by a Bavarian band. The journey — overtly paralleling the journey that ended in the gas chamber — would be disrupted when SS storm troopers took the passengers (actors included) by surprise, shoved them into groups, and stitched a yellow star on their coats. On the way to Dachau, scenes from the *Merchant* would be performed, in juxtaposition to the prisoners' expressions of fear, hope, or grief. In Dachau trucks would transport the audience from the railway station to the camp site. The actors were to perform the play in the barracks under the permanently menacing presence of the guards. The audience would be taken back to Munich by buses, leaving behind the dim site and the lonely Shylock, only just baptized.

Tabori realized the tremendous momentum, the unique potential latent in Dachau as an acting site. At the same time, he was acutely aware of the sterile appeal of the site, which had been turned into an official museum, and of the danger of becoming kitsch. Following a visit to Dachau with his son Kristoffer, Tabori describes it sarcastically as "really nice in its false piety and so designerly that remembering anything other than the remembering of remembrance is impossible. Walking through there is like going through an illustrated magazine in the dentist's waiting-room."[41]

Even before rehearsals began, in September, Tabori had already made the first drastic change to the script. Acts I–III were to be performed in the theatre, the trial scene (IV.i) in Dachau. The journey to the site was to be interrupted five times, with incidents of physical abuse and savage brutality, in which the victims — not only Jews but also a transvestite, two opera guests, etc. — turn out to be the actors.

As in the American production, Tabori chose to consider the audience anti-Semitic. This enabled him to confront the audience through a strategy of heightened tension, seeking direct confrontation and ultimately shocking the audience into awareness of the fatal consequences of discrimination. The actors, Germans who benefited from what Chancellor Helmut Kohl called "the grace of belated birth" (*Gnade der späten Geburt*), spent hours discussing anti-Semitism, reflecting individually and collectively on "how to play a Jew, how to play an anti-Semite." Photos of Auschwitz, paper cuttings and documents, books by Elie Wiesel, novels by Bernard Malamud, studies of Fascism and the Nazi extermination machinery (e.g., Eugen Kogon's *Der NS-Staat*), and Salcia Landmann's bestselling collection of Jewish jokes were all brought in as part of Tabori's cherished "research," intended to make the subtext tangible.

About three weeks into the rehearsals, Tabori brought along a pound of raw meat.[42] The actors touched, smelled, and examined this exemplary "magic object," which was meant to awaken their senses and deepen their intimacy with Shylock.[43] "The meat [the German *Fleisch* means both flesh and meat] is a central symbol, a subtext that has something to do with the Christian fear of circumcision," Tabori maintained,[44] in line with Theodor Reik's interpretation of Shylock as castrator.[45] Here indeed two major Tabori motifs are intertwined: cannibalism and sexual phobia.[46] Shylock's insistence on the pound of flesh is a call for vendetta as well as an act of self-assertion; in Tabori's words, "an archaic male-madness to penetrate the enemy so deep, until he feels the passion of exclusiveness, the bloody need to be the only one."[47]

In mid-October, some ten days after rehearsals had been moved to an abandoned cellar occupied by a white grand piano, an official letter arrived, refusing the group permission to perform in Dachau. "This subtext is dropped," we read in the rehearsal notes. Forced to reconsider his entire concept, Tabori chose a radical change. The performance was to be an exhaustive investigation of Shylock, of "Shylockism."[48] Tabori favored the idea of multiplying the role, allowing some *or* all actors to experience Shylock. The group preferred the latter. At this stage it was also decided to conduct the performance in an almost equally appropriate bare acting area, with the piano as a permanent point of reference and with minimal props (puppets, bags of clothes).

Tabori suggested that each actor present an improvisation based on the elopement of Jessica with the ducats — a potentially melodramatic moment which Shakespeare prefers to report (II.viii. 12–22) rather than to present. Each actor offered an improvisation, one crying out in pain, one hopelessly forlorn, another imitating Fritz Kortner in the role of Shylock, and yet another delivering the lines in dialect. This episode, Tabori's favorite (nicknamed *Tannhäuserszene*), became the pivotal point of the performance. "I would my daughter were dead at my foot, and the jewels in her ear": Shylock's notorious exclamation became the official title of the production. The line used by anti-Semites to prove the Jew's greed and bestiality becomes in Tabori's treatment a tool for provoking, subverting, and inducing a radical reinterpretation.

It is quite difficult to differentiate retrospectively between Tabori's directorial influence and the contributions of the group. Yet based on the above, it is safe to say that Tabori's personal imprint was substantial. It was Tabori who proposed to interpret the trial scene as "an old nightmare" for which Shylock "had been preparing over 6,000 years, culminating in his Christening. The forced conversion is the climax of the historical abuse, the most outrageous injury he suffered." This is quite a surprising reading, coming from a man whose understanding of Jewishness, tortuous and equivocal, has hardly anything to do with Judaism as belief. The Christening episode was to be accompanied by the *Kol Nidre* melody (the traditional expiatory prayer sung on the Day of Atonement) played on the whining clarinet. In Tabori's opinion this was to be "the central musical statement of the play."

Work on the performance did not end with the official premiere. A letter addressed to "My dear Shylocks" insinuates that the Achilles' heel lay in fact with the underlying notion of "structured freedom,"[49] which was the backbone of the performance. Tabori, who was always present backstage, tried to maintain the balance between discipline ("do not fuzz the focus") and genuine spontaneity ("there's nothing worse than studied spontaneity").[50] For him the gist of the production lay not in divulging the "secret" at the heart of the text, but in the endeavor to approximate it, to viscerally experience "Shylockism." It was, as actor Klaus Fischer recollects, "a trip. The journey to Dachau . . . not only to the site Dachau, which was 'sightseeing,' though terrible and moving, but to Dachau in me. . . . The journey was paved with obstacles and resistance. Again and again the fear . . . of falling into this or that 'abyss.' George and Stanley provoked me to go further whenever I stopped, George with new proposals for scenes and games, Stanley with music."[51]

The three-hour performance took place in the rehearsing site, a cellar on Knöbelstrasse 4, the boiler room of an abandoned plant. The one hundred spectators entered through the backyard of a lighting factory, surrounded by run-down flats inhabited by foreign workers, with motley washing hanging out the windows. Reality attuned the audience for the ensuing spectacle, a sequence of "shocking images of bestial cruelty."[52] On the heating pipes along the yellowish walls hung puppets, shabbily clad, with yellow stars stitched to their clothing, suitcases in hand. Ironically, the spectators themselves intensified this allusion to the Holocaust as they hung their coats, scarves, and hats on hooks all around the acting area: a spooky reminder of the undressing area leading to the gas chambers. Neon lights shed a cold light, and a big incandescent bulb glared unrelentingly over the grand piano in the center. Anyone familiar with Else Lasker-Schüller's poetry would instantly associate the piano with her "blue piano" (*Mein blaues Klavier*, 1943), that metaphoric broken piano of her poetry which bewails the "blue dead."

As spectators took their seats on randomly scattered chairs on four sides of the piano, the actors wandered around telling perfidious Jewish jokes.[53] Those Shylocks who were not onstage at any given moment sat with the audience — yet another way of blurring the division between spectators and actors, reality and illusion.

A scenic prelude, so characteristic of Tabori's style, sets off the *Improvisations*. It is a provoking tableau based on anti-Semitic propaganda; the stereotypical Jew as seen through hostile Gentile eyes — multiplied: dark frock-coat, black velvet hat, crooked nose. One of these Shylocks suddenly jumps on the piano and delivers the anti-Semitic Shylock ballad attributed to Pepys, while the others, courting the grotesque and gruesome, gesticulate and grimace — "many monsters, Fagins, Süss-Jews," according to Peter von Becker.[54]

A silent puppet show follows, a shattering theatre of cruelty. Each actor, each one of those loathsome stereotype Jews, takes a surrogate "Jew-puppet" and tears off its clothes and yellow star. They torture the puppets (one uses a butcher's knife, another an electric drill, and a third dumps the doll in a plastic tub with nitric acid), mutilate them and entrust a hand or a leg to a random spectator.[55] Although many in the audience, embarrassed or shocked, decoded the gesture as a direct accusation, Tabori was primarily interested in leading spectators to reflect on "Shylockism" in terms of individual responsibility.

Blackout. Mesmerizing silence. Shylock emerges with a lantern, calling faintly "Jessica" (the first word spoken in the performance), seeks his daughter in the audience, then rummages in the plastic bags under the piano. Among the heaps of clothes — another prop evoking very specific memories — he finds a ring with a piece of bloody meat. The pool of blood under the piano spreads during the performance, notably toward the audience.

Only after this extended nonverbal spectacle concludes and the context is unmistakably defined do the actors begin performing the Shakespearean text. Tabori adopted the Schlegel-Tieck translation this time, possibly because this classical rendition emphasized, by its stark contrast to the setting, the utter rupture with the past caused by the Holocaust. Accompanied by Walden's rendering of Orlando di Lasso's "Madonna mia cara," Bassanio asks his melancholy friend Antonio to help him win the "fair lady . . . of wondrous virtues" in Belmont. Entitled "Shylock makes a bid, or the meat-market scene," the following episode (based on I.iii) resembles a doomed investigation of the "love-hate relationship" between Christians and Jews. Starting off as a civilized, matter-of-fact commercial exchange, the encounter soon unleashes suppressed animosity and pent-up aggression, culminating in a shrill feud, with Jews and Christians abusing each other on either side of the piano.

Lancelot's encounter with old Gobbo (II.ii) introduces Tabori's recurring motif of the father-son relationship. Not only does Tabori change the sequence of the original dialogue, but the misleading news of Lancelot's demise initiates a moving scene of mourning: the bereaved father mourns his son with a Yiddish folksong which was apparently chanted in concentration camps: "Zehn Brider waren wir gewesen . . . Sing mir mal a Lied'l, missen wir ins Gas." [56]

The following "Four fathers scene" presents another father taking leave of his child. Four Shylocks/fathers (Jewish folk tradition refers to three biblical patriarchs and four matriarchs) bid Jessica farewell before going out to supper: "one Jewish patriarch, one benevolent, one mythical and one lyrical. Jessica's fathers exist in her fantasy," explains Tabori. Significantly, Shylock has the last word: Tabori chooses to omit Jessica's concluding couplet in II.v, and Shylock rounds off this improvisation with another Yiddish song, mourning loss and ravage.

The Holocaust subtext is forefronted. In "Concentration camp story" actor Siemen Rühaak, playing the part of Jessica (the only woman in the group, Ursula Höpfner, played the part of Lancelot), enacts the excruciating torment and humiliation inflicted by a sadistic officer. Walden, as Klezmer, disrupts the torture and asks the audience: "Do you believe all this?" Provokingly and teasingly he reminds them that "it's only theatre." Michael Krüger has rightly observed: Tabori is out to stage "men-games" (*Menschen-Spiele*) instead of "theatre-games" (*Theaterspiele*).[57]

Jessica/Rühaak remains curled up like a vulnerable fetus on the piano. Two masquers emerge from the audience to abduct her. Lorenzo applauds the "sweet harmony" of the night, preempting some of the famous lyrical lines from V.i. The entire scene is sarcastically entitled "Kristallnacht," after the first mass pogrom organized by the Nazis on the night of 9 November 1938. Lorenzo scrambles up to his sleeping beauty and awakens her, literally and sexually, with wooing and intimacies. "The Christian 'takes' the Jewess, half-raping, half-liberating her."[58] Jessica, the bride, has been dressed in a white robe of Christening, like her father at the end of the evening.

With the episode "Shylock returns home" attention reverts to the Jew, the father, the victim. He frantically looks for Jessica everywhere, a grief-stricken man, lonely and broken. Shylock is made to wipe the blood on the floor, like the Jews who were forced by the Nazis to scrub the pavements. Shakespeare circumvents the pathos of Shylock's loss by having Solanio report his hysterical reaction (II.viii). Tabori, on the other hand, consciously indulges in it: he uses this pivotal moment to subvert stereotypes and reverse traditional expectations. Each actor/Shylock offers an individual reaction to the loss; notably, the emphasis is on Jessica's abduction rather than the loss of the ducats. One actor whines to the public, another questions the event itself, one delivers his text in a Rhenish dialect, another as slapstick, and still another, in operatic style, poses the question melodramatically, "Am I to blame for being a Jew?" These associative improvisations (*Tannhäuser*-Scene) best exemplify the jazz-like quality of the performance. It should be noted, however, that these "spontaneous" variations were carefully rehearsed; all in all, the aleatory principle, so crucial during rehearsals, had waned as opening night drew closer.

"I'll have my bond," Shylock doggedly insists in "Shylock freaks out," an episode combining lines from II. v, III.i, and III.iii, a studied improvisation. Unbearable pain at the loss of his daughter motivates the Jew, not the missing ducats. The daughter Shylock finds is a prostitute, "a Schickse." [59] Overcome by grief, incensed, and embittered, Shylock embraces her; then he storms, "Hath not a Jew eyes?" and assaults her, knife in hand, hindered by the onlooking actors. It is Tubal, his fellow Jew, who ultimately mollifies Shylock's anguish and encourages the vindictive trajectory in a "Vaudeville scene" which seeks to alienate spectators through exaggerated histrionic gesticulations.

A brief intermezzo, "Bassanio calms the audience," eases the tension prior to the dramatic climax, the concluding trial scene. Shylock of the previous two episodes (Rüdiger Hacker) is now the Duke of Venice; another Shylock, the protagonist of the "meat market scene" (Edwin Noel), is the judge Balthazar (rather than Portia). Shylock/Arnulf Schumacher appears with a pair of scales, law books, and a whetted knife. The suit he submits is not entirely personal, for on his back are three other Jews, who weigh heavily on him and slow him down. Tabori's Shylock goes beyond the Holocaust subtext toward the metaphoric, becoming the archetypal Diaspora Jew, burdened by history. [60] The man who whets his knife, bent and haggard, perspiring profusely, is a wreck both physically and mentally, a shadow of a man, like those Shylock-ghosts who crawl around, wailing and sighing, underneath the piano.

Spurned by the Christians, Shylock indulges in his grievance, sliding his knife all the way down Antonio's body, almost ritualistically. "Tarry a little," lest a jot of blood be shed, the judge admonishes Shylock, whose knife touches Antonio's genitals. Tabori alludes to the Christian suspiciousness and abhorrence of Jewish circumcision; the Jewish male body is conceived as deformed, hideous.[61] Panic-stricken, Shylock tries to flee the courtroom, but the doors are closed and he is trapped. His adversaries are busy preparing his Christening.

Indeed, Tabori takes Antonio's suggestion that "Shylock presently become a Christian" literally. The ceremony marks the epitome of injustice, intolerance, and humiliation. The Jew is transformed into a "Bavarian Gentile":[62] his hair is powdered blond, his cheeks painted rosy, and he is dressed in white stockings and a white dress. A cross is hung round his neck. The sacred Jewish prayer *Kol Nidre* is played on the clarinet. Abused and silenced, Shylock stands motionless in the center, a lifeless creature, a marionette in the hands of others, calling to mind the tormented and mutilated puppets at the beginning of the evening.

"It's possible in the afternoon / To play both books of preludes and fugues / And spend the evening gassing Jews." Gathered around the piano, amidst bric-a-brac of clothes, shoes, bags, the actors send their audience home with a Brecht-like song: "It's our world — welcome to it."

"We managed in our best moments to consternate and to hurt. The audience. Ourselves. In so doing, aesthetic and artistic boundaries were defied up to the point of bad taste," writes actor Rüdiger Hacker about the performance.[63] His observations point to the gist of Tabori's "theatre of embarrassment" (*Theater der Peinlichkeit*).[64] The performance sought to taunt and disconcert, to shock, to offend and to injure, to get under the skin. And this it definitely did. Spectators wept (and had to be consoled),[65] expressed anguish and consternation to the troupe.[66] The house was sold out weeks in advance; the production received wide coverage and was on the whole positively reviewed. "An extraordinarily moving theatre-evening. To marvel and to think about," wrote Peter von Becker.[67]

Among the critical voices were those who accused Tabori of pursuing sensationalism or fomenting "Jewish-Christian hatred."[68] Another voice, the self-righteous one, argued that "the only honest way of playing *The Merchant of Venice* today, is not to play it at all." [69] It was precisely against this attitude, a type of "false piety," [70] that Tabori resolved to conduct himself in his *Improvisations*, more consciously than in his earlier American production of *The Merchant*. Not to perform this play after Auschwitz is much the same as to turn one's back on the past, to encourage amnesia, to add offense to sin. For Tabori theatre-making is by definition an act of disclosure and demystification, an assault against taboos; in the case of the *Merchant* it is also the studied stripping off of the false masks of self-exoneration and self-righteousness. "A special-Shylock, extra dry, for Germans only." [71]

Tabori's various interpretations of Shakespeare's play break away from the depiction of Shylock common on the post-Holocaust German stage: Ernst Deutsch's noble, quasi-biblical Shylock (1963), advocating reconciliation, or Fritz Kortner's portrayal (1969) of an angry old man caught between misery and cruelty, dignity and grief. [72] Tabori's "naked Shylock" returns from the ashes neither to accuse nor to reconcile. A mnemonic figure, he is "an embarrassment to the author, the spectator, the actors. One doesn't want to see it and yet must look, and says: 'Not again!' or 'what's this supposed to be?' or 'spare me this!'" *Improvisations on Shylock* is Tabori's unequivocal reply to these voices, an exemplary product of his "theater of embarrassment." "One way to avoid embarrassment," he says, "is to wipe out the cause for it." [73]

MY MOTHER'S COURAGE

. . . Remember the heart of Jewish wisdom which suggests that while the goyim might flip a coin and choose either head or tails, the Jew might consider the possibility of the coin remaining suspended in midair.

George Tabori

My Mother's Courage is Tabori's subversive reply to Brecht's much-acclaimed *Mutter Courage*: it is the story of Elsa Tabori's miraculous escape from Auschwitz.[1] Basing his narrative on his mother's account,[2] Tabori relates how 55-year-old Elsa, arrested in Budapest in the summer of 1944 and deported together with 4,000 other Jews, saved herself by maintaining that her arrest was unlawful. She told the German commander that she had a protective pass issued by the Swedish Red Cross, which she had forgotten at home —to her own amazement, this saved her: Elsa found herself on a train heading back to Budapest. The story is too good to be true: "a heart-breaking scandal of the exception to the rule" and "a true legend" indeed.[3]

After this close call, Elsa Tabori survived the war by hiding in her stepbrother's apartment in the Hungarian capital, while her sons were in London. Her eldest, Paul, found her there in the winter of 1945, soon after receiving the official notice of his father's demise in Auschwitz. A year later Elsa left Hungary for good, settling in London.

The woman George met was strikingly different from the mother he remembered. "She had been very warm-hearted and loving. A soft woman, a real mother in the old-fashioned sense of the word. After the war, I sensed that at her core something had turned into steel. She appeared to be offended, deeply offended."[4] Like so many other survivors, Elsa Tabori, who had lost almost her entire family, refused to speak about the recent past. Tabori attributes this silence, this repression, to the fact that "what the survivors had to do and to witness was so humiliating, unbelievable, and absurd that there is no language for it."[5]

A letter he wrote to Paul in London after his mother's extended stay with him in New York in 1949 reveals Tabori's immense love and concern for her. "It's very difficult for either of us to appreciate her loss, it's far beyond the usual sense of grief. She must have a function; . . . the only function left to her is that of the 'mother.' In this respect she must never be left 'unemployed.' . . . I think I understand her now much more than I ever had in my life, and I'm very very proud of her; she has the element of true greatness in her."[6]

My Mother's Courage is Tabori's love song to his mother, who died in 1958, suffused with tenderness and lyricism; homage to a woman and a mother "neither angel nor wildcat,"[7] but a "weak and stupid woman . . . afraid of slight aches" (*My Mother's Courage*, 312), who plucked up courage almost unawares and pulled herself out of hell. Tabori has no intention of illustrating a point through the story. He does not seek to deduce a moral from the individual case; nor does he use the tale to reproach the Germans. As critic Klaus Colberg succinctly put it, "He wants to recount: this is how it was, or this is how it could have been."[8] The narration and in particular the stage production are evolving exercises in retrieving memories.

"It couldn't have been this way, it isn't true," protested Hanna Schygulla, in the role of Elsa, during a rehearsal.[9] As it happened, the particular episode in question was actually true, yet Tabori made no secret of taking poetic license in other instances, joining fact and fiction (*Dichtung und Wahrheit*). In *My Mother's Courage*, memory is verbalized and enacted, yet each telling is *sui generis*, rendering irrelevant the question of whose version is the "correct" one.[10] Insisting that his mother never lied, Tabori nevertheless admits that he somewhat amended her version, adding "some lies" "because I am a big liar, like any writer, and the dialectics of lies and truth are at the core of matters."[11]

That which Tabori loosely calls his dialectic approach, a theatrics promoting subversion, interpolation and the inversion of expectations, temporal conflation and fragmentation, is evident in *My Mother's Courage*, both the text and the production. Tabori presents us with what may be called a mock fairy tale of modern times — a tale of petrifying danger, miraculous deliverance, and a happy ending — which is overturned by ironic twists.

The opening scene describes Elsa Tabori's arrest in the summer of 1944. Tabori deploys a hybrid technique, interweaving the epic with the dramatic. The "Son" narrates his mother's adventures, diverts from the main story, oscillates by free association back and forth in time to recall and expand the family (hi)story. The narrative is punctuated with enacted episodes and is disrupted by Elsa Tabori's comments and remarks, which clearly produce an effect of alienation.[12] She resolutely counters her Son's version, corrects the minutest detail, comments on his lively imagination, protests against indiscretion, and disapproves of any sign of melodramatization.

Mother, Son, German Officer, Lover — the central characters have as in a parable no individual proper names. Moreover, Tabori deliberately had each actor playing multiple roles, alternately representing the "good" and "bad" characters. Helmut Pick as Hungarian policeman Iglódi had other roles, including that of George's incarcerated father, while Ute Kannenberg played the nasty, anti-Semitic janitor's wife as well as Elsa's sister, Martha. The original staging (like the film version) was introduced and concluded with Tabori's own prerecorded narration.[13] Klaus Fischer played the role of the Son, occasionally as "a circus conferencier."[14] Hanna Schygulla, the young star of Rainer Werner Fassbinder's films, had to put on thirty years to play the title role of Elsa Tabori, although "George did not want an imitation of an old lady," as she told an interviewer.[15] Clearly, Tabori proposed to tell a story, not to offer a mimetic representation.

There is no idyllic dreamland in Tabori's mock fairy tale. The opening sentence robs the spectator of all illusion, describing the sunny, warm summer of 1944 as "a vintage year for dying" (*My Mother's Courage*, 287). Tabori repeatedly juxtaposes the blissful and the horrible, speaks of "no terror in that landscape" (301) and of a benevolent sun, with a sense of impending cataclysm at the "gates of hell" (303). "Now?" asks the befuddled Elsa Tabori, when the two Hungarian detectives announce her arrest and deportation. Ingenious, almost childlike, she accepts the verdict, merely questioning the policemen's timing, since she was on her way to her sister's for a game of gin rummy. What she takes with her is notable too: not an apple, with its heavy biblical symbolism, as her Son suggests, but a prosaic plum. Tabori refuses to magnify the hardship or to ennoble suffering, persistently deflating and subverting any insinuation of larger-than-life heroism.

The stage and the setting he chose demonstrate unmistakably his defiance of a gratifying atmosphere.[16] The play was performed at the workshop studio of the Kammerspiele, in a hall which previously served as a youth theatre. One hundred spectators faced a plain, unadorned stage, where scaffolds and ladders surrounded the rectangular acting area. The stage was strewn with red sand, scattered bags, boxes, and a mortar mixer, juxtaposed with the furnishings of the Taboris' bourgeois home. Characteristically, the performance began with an extended prelude in which the actors recalled and mimed children's behavior. Music was a prominent factor during the entire evening, evoking memories, bringing back childhood, and connoting the humdrum of daily life. "George wanted to preserve as much creativity and spontaneity as possible in the performance," explains Stanley Walden, who was in charge of the music.[17] Schygulla, the Mother, recollected the experience of giving birth while other actors indulged in babyish rituals, pranced around, sucked their thumbs, scuffled with each other, crying or singing nursery rhymes. This was both a prelude of natural innocence and at the same time an exemplary theatrical warm-up exercise. The interpretation of the text emerged unforced out of this prelude, blurring the line demarcating illusion and reality: for instance, at the start of the play the actors debated what kind of hat Elsa would have worn on the day of her arrest. Klaus Fischer then slipped into the Son's role, while Tabori took his seat in the audience almost unawares.

The motif of innocence runs throughout the play. An almost childlike naïveté marks Elsa's manner when she is arrested by the police. Later, when she is asked to show her protective pass, she apologizes for not having it with her, "her voice girlishly high-pitched, like a girl of twelve" (*My Mother's Courage*, 309). Prudish and coy, she views sex as "a chore that had been put away with other childish things" (300). Once the ordeal is over, she is transformed from "a good little girl" to "a bad little girl" (312). Though she is a mother, Elsa has never lost that redeeming quality of childlikeness, ingenuousness, and candor; a fan of the film star Douglas Fairbanks, she is an elegant and cultured woman who had the makings of motherhood "even as a child" (294).

Something of this innocence colors the portrayal of Tabori's father as well. Doubly stigmatized as a "Jew and a Marxist of the reformist school" (*My Mother's Courage*, 288), he is arrested twice during the course of the original production: once in a comic vein, the second time transfigured.[18] More surprising is the ingenuousness of the two Hungarian cops who spy on Elsa Tabori and finally arrest her. Klapka and Iglódi, the executive envoys of the fascist regime in Hungary — "theirs," maintains Tabori first and later changes it to "ours" — are a couple of buffoons; far from being the emissaries of evil, they are the kind of pair one expects to find in a Laurel and Hardy or a Marx Brothers film. One suffers from asthma, the other from gout; both have retired from the police force, leaving behind careers of singular ineptitude, long lists of failed missions, and a reputation as dupes among their colleagues. The arrest episode thus resembles a boulevard fiasco, grotesque, funny, almost absurd at times. Having no police car at their disposal — they "were too unimportant to be provided with such luxury" — the two escort Elsa to the tram but fail to jump on it with her. Elsa Tabori stretches out a helping hand to her rather awkward captors. As the streetcar begins to move, Klapka's hat flies off while Iglódi absurdly rattles the handcuffs and stumbles against a lamppost. "Wait for me at the next stop!" Klapka calls after her, and one cannot help feeling that had it not been dead serious this would have been an exquisite comedy of errors.

In the vein of the well-documented tradition of Jewish humor, which wryly deprecates the persecutors and makes comedy out of dire circumstances, Elsa's pursuers are depicted as dim-witted adversaries. Tabori heaps surprise upon surprise, inverts expectations, and conflates the tragic with the comic. Elsa Tabori is given a ticket to freedom as it were, but she chooses to get off obediently at the designated destination — "how does one go into hiding at the age of sixty when you're a lady . . . and where to?" (*My Mother's Courage*, 293). At the next station, ironically known as the favorite meeting place for lovers, the two stunted emissaries of evil are astonished to see their *détenu* descend from the tram. "Where are you taking me?" she inquires; they reply: to "Auschwitz" and add sarcastically, "a Jewish bakery" (294).

Tasteless? Tactless? Embarrassing and offensive? Critic Armin Eichholz speaks of spectators being challenged by "Tabori's non-chalance," "his incredible courage to make jokes about Ausch-Witz" (*Witz* means joke in German).[19] This mercilessly acidulous, biting gallows-humor is a crucial element in Tabori's Holocaust plays. He has repeatedly shocked his audience by saying that "Auschwitz is the shortest German joke."[20] Tabori defends his profane humor against good taste. "Our best jokes are grounded in disasters," he argues,[21] very much like Jewish humorists, who time and again subverted the miseries of everyday reality and pogroms — what Freud called "oppressive restraint"—by drawing on irony and wry humor as a source of much-needed inner strength. "Every good joke is a catastrophe and every true humor is black. . . . Through the conflation of banter and pain, the tragic avoids becoming soppy."[22]

"A fairy tale, but no one would be saved from getting baked in the oven, except for one," says the narrator-Son (*My Mother's Courage*, 298). *My Mother's Courage* is no fairy tale, although Elsa Tabori's death sentence is miraculously reversed. In the prose version that preceded the stage-text, Elsa tries to console one of the deportees, a Gentile girl mistaken for a Jew, with various stories and fairy tales; however, when she recounts "Hansel and Gretel" she deliberately omits the part about baking in the oven,[23] thus taking the sting out of the entire tale. No bread was baked in the oven of Auschwitz, Arnold, Tabori's alter-ego in *Jubilee*, is forced to acknowledge. There are no fairy tales in a civilization that made Auschwitz possible.

The second scene depicts the train ride, including the "Primordial Scene" or *Urszene* (another allusion to the Garden of Eden), namely, the anonymous sexual intercourse in the dark train car — an event Elsa Tabori would have much preferred to omit from the story and erase from memory. In the original production this was enacted as a feverish orgasm between Elsa and the faceless man. Should we consider this yet another instance of Tabori's perverted imagination and coarse taste, as some have felt? Not in the least. This episode, an outcry of longing and humanity, is Tabori's retort to the mass extermination gas-chamber style, which he deems "a conscious method of desexualizing murder."[24] Intercourse in a dark cattle-car heading toward death, with a nameless and faceless man — no fairy-tale prince but a dank male itching for intimacy "one last time" — is a fine example of Tabori's persistent attempt to transform that "heap of naked humanity" into "a pyramid of lovers."[25] The hand that clasps Elsa's breast and struggles against her buttocks expressing yearning and tenderness "belongs to a body" which leans against her backside meekly, "apologetically." This erotic encounter restores the humanity to a lover, who is otherwise but a number in the huge crowd, a nonbeing. Like the other victims, he has "already been dismembered" and is just a mass of limbs, hats, hair, eyes, "adding up to a mutilated giant" (*My Mother's Courage*, 298).

An odd crowd of passengers squeezed into a train car; on one side a hand groping in the dark, sliding on a female body, while a little rabbi is praying nearby — a grotesque situation indeed, which could have been the fuel for a hilarious comedy. Tabori beautifully merges the tragic, the trivial, the bizarre, and the comic. The deportees, assembled for what he ironically calls "an exodus," are a motley bunch: a butcher holding a cleaver still dripping blood, a young man in pajamas with lips laced with toothpaste, some wide-eyed patients in asylum uniforms, etc. There are no sanctified heroes here, no idolized martyrs. Tabori seeks to demystify the victims and demythologize the Holocaust through strokes of realism and humor. Their questions — "Where could I fill this thermos bottle with tea?" or "Is there a dining car on this train?" (*My Mother's Courage*, 295) — sound like good jokes, but trailing behind them is a bitter afterthought, emphasizing the gullibility, vulnerability, and pettiness of the victims. "Do me a favor, and choose some other people next time!" (299), the rabbi protests to the Almighty in the vein of the classical Jewish joke about the miseries of God's Chosen People, also reminiscent of sundry Jewish characters from Sholom Aleichem to Philip Roth.

Arriving at the Hungarian border, at "the last stop to death," the deportees wait for their inspection before changing into a German cattle-train that is in fact much cleaner than their own Hungarian train. This third scene draws extensively on the theatre as metaphor. The deportees who at first pass by "like characters who had wandered into the wrong play" (*My Mother's Courage*, 301) soon become onlookers held in suspense by the principal actor, the commanding German officer, surrounded by Hungarian Greenshirts as his supportive supernumeraries. The stage is the courtyard where he makes his entrance. His audience, huddled in an abandoned, run-down brick factory, watches the goings-on mesmerized, peering down through the broken windows, aware that they will ultimately have to make their own entrance. "There is nothing like stretching a metaphor until it snaps," the narrator remarks (303). Tabori is aware of the pitfalls of the narrative art and the limits of representing the Holocaust, and his reference to it is in fact one of his strategies of countering clichés and eschewing melodramatization.

The man who gives Elsa the idea of protesting against her deportation ("the whole thing's a mistake!"), the good angel of fairy tales, is in fact a good-for-nothing, funny albeit moving mixture of a Schlemiel and a "nebbish" (*My Mother's Courage*, 305). The odd suggestion he makes is the only trump card of his life, and yet it does him no personal service whatsoever. Tabori's narrator indulges in the deliberately distorted image of this fallen angel and harps on his flaws. Alfredo Kelemen is said to be a prominent member of Cornelius (father) "Tábori's Pity Club," the most pathetic, "the worst" of the deplorable lot: a short "fat little zombie, googoo-eyed" (304–305), an eccentric who has tried his hand in all sorts of *Luftgeschäften* — as hypnotist or karate-master — failing every time. This Kelemen shoves Elsa Tabori toward the door, pushes her out, and makes sure she does not reenter. Even though "she had never felt lonelier," Elsa emerges out of the anonymity of numbers to become the protagonist of an incredible spectacle.

Here again Tabori debunks our dramatic expectations, inverting the notion of the heroic. There is no show of prowess, no act of audacity in the traditional sense. Incongruously elegant, the nearly 60-year-old woman makes an entrance that could be called ludicrous: she traipses duck-footed across the yard, with goat-shit sticking to her shoes. Neither valor nor confidence prods her on; on the contrary, she feels like a "traitor" for having abandoned the others. Strangely enough, the feeling of belonging to a big family of helpless victims reassured her; the proximity of anonymous bodies radiated warmth. "Among them she had felt safe; to them she could hang on in ultimate solidarity even as they were led into the fire," says the narrator, her Son (*My Mother's Courage*, 307). Slowly approaching the German officer, the arbitrator over life and death, she is not a woman of mettle but a vulnerable, pitiable wretch who feels "as if she were naked," talks with a "girlishly-high voice," and becomes the laughingstock of the officers surrounding the German commander. Later, when she finds herself safely on the train back to Budapest, her legs shake, she wets her panties, and she cries.

It is precisely this unheroic, timorous walk across the yard which defines Elsa Tabori's courage: "This nakedness becomes the measure of her courage," states her Son (*My Mother's Courage*, 307). It is the courage of the common person, born out of the banality of life, the courage of despair.

Why does the German officer believe Elsa's lie about the protective pass which she admittedly forgot at home? The question is left partly unresolved. "I didn't find it strange that a German saved her life. After all, this was an exceptional case," Tabori replied when pressed for his opinion.[26] Was it that the German officer had enough of his henchmen, those Hungarian fascists who laughed at Elsa's lame excuse? Did he let her go to show them that he alone was in charge? The fact remains that, as in Tabori's first novel, *Beneath the Stone*, the German officer serving the Nazi regime displays "human" traits. This may be taken as another instance of Tabori's defiance of sweeping generalizations ("There is no such thing as The Germans," he argues), his dismissal of the prevalent idea of collective guilt.

It seems to me that, like the coitus scene, this episode emphasizes the exposure of the intimate in a reality that is overwhelmed by "scientific impartiality."[27] The encounter between Elsa and the German, as reconstructed by Tabori, is indeed colored with the erotic. The German peers into Elsa's blue eyes, "as if through a keyhole"; she peers into his eyes "as if through the same keyhole; now the entire situation was reduced to these two pairs of eyes" (*My Mother's Courage*, 310). This is Tabori's retort to human-made hell, to the scientific method of killing which sought to desexualize murder in the site "of nakedness" (311).

But the eyes peering into the officer's eyes do not just plead innocence and mercy. Elsa's eyes see through the facade of authority and, much to her unease, discover not an enemy or a demon, but a fellow human being. Elsa realizes that she hates her savior for having to love him. The lesson she passes on to her son runs counter to the biblical dictum "an eye for an eye, a tooth for a tooth": "Beware of looking at the enemy in the eyes, my darling, or you might stop hating him and thus betray the dead" (*My Mother's Courage*, 312).

The concluding scene is devoted mainly to elucidating the character of the German officer, who accompanies Elsa in a first-class compartment of the train heading back to Budapest. Her savior is a blue-eyed man with "unusually white hands," but he is no fairy-tale hero. Seated opposite to him, Elsa notices that he is "smaller somehow, more normal" than he had seemed and that he has a balding pate. The gentleman, who had gone out of his way to address her politely in the courtyard, apparently looked into her purse while she dozed off and stealthily helped himself to one of her plums. The plum turns out to be instrumental in the "act of rescue" because of the very simple and mundane fact that it causes the officer to rush to the toilet just as the train approaches Budapest. "Jesus resides in my bowels," her savior tells her as he leaves her alone in the compartment, hinting that she should take this opportunity to "make herself scarce" (*My Mother's Courage*, 316).

Indeed, this conflation of the sublime and the trivial marks the characterization of the German officer. This little cog in the huge apparatus of extermination is a typical example of Hannah Arendt's theory of the banality of evil. Tabori deflates any sense of pathos by highlighting the officer's pretentiousness and his moral pose. An ardent vegetarian ("How could anybody stoop so low as to butcher a calf?" 314), he is sensitive enough to imagine the outcries of a lily being plucked or the pain of a plum being consumed. The altruistic spirit of one who loveth best all things both great and small is of course ludicrous in this context.

Pushing the point further, Tabori has the officer tell Elsa the story of his village priest, a rather hopeless flop, with "very white hands" — notably like the officer's own hands — who surreptitiously dug out the corpse of a brutally murdered Jew. That "same night the priest's chimney was belching smoke," and on the following Sunday, Maria's Ascension, he used the flesh and blood of this Jesus-surrogate as communion wafers for some dozen girls receiving their Confirmation. Here is a reversal of the myth of Jewish ritual slaughter — best known perhaps is that of Mendel Beilis in Kiev in 1911 — which purports that Jews slaughter Christian children each year to use their blood in baking Mazzah for Passover. The idea of the sacred Eucharist is turned topsy-turvy, and piety is shown to be the reverse side of manslaughter and cannibalism — a motif which runs through Tabori's theatre work.

Elsa Tabori arrives at her sister Martha's for a game of cards late in the evening. A fairy tale with a happy ending? Not quite. Martha and her husband, Julius, were exterminated that year, together with 80 percent of the Tabori family and hundreds of thousands of Hungarian Jews. Tabori prefers to end the play upon a distinctly minor victory. "By midnight, when they paused for a cold supper with tea, my mother had won two-thirty-five, so she had every reason to be pleased" (*My Mother's Courage*, 317).

Tabori's production concluded with a choral-like hymn in praise of his mother, Elsa. The son's homage to his mother insinuates the triumph of life over death. Fiction or truth? Tabori's mock fairy tale oscillates between the fictitious, the forged, the lie, and the truth which "is always pain." This is precisely why he chose to stage the play in a hybrid style, combining defamiliarization with realism, "mystery with pure scraps of gewgaws," [28] the tragic with the funny and the ludicrous.

"My Answer to Holocaust" — this was the title of the original production in its early phase, and Tabori meant it in two ways. Rehearsed in the spring of 1979, [29] this was his reply to the American television melodrama *Holocaust* (the story of the Weiss family), which was screened on German television in January, raising an unprecedented interest in the Shoah. [30] Beyond that, it was his private confrontation with a theme that had haunted him for years, as well as a studied reaction to the mystification and mythologization of the Holocaust.

Only five months after the premiere of his production, which was on the whole very well received, Tabori got a letter of rejection from Daniel Menaker, fiction editor of the *New Yorker*: "It's both horrifying and funny, and there's a great sadness underneath the energetic writing, but stories about the Holocaust are nearly out of the question for us, I'm afraid." [31]

JUBILEE

Sites. Sites without people.
These are the dry bones of memory.
Europe's fields are full of them.

Shlomo Breznitz, *Memory Fields*

"There are taboos that must be broken or they will continue to choke us," maintained Tabori upon the premiere of *Cannibals*, his momentous debut in Germany. The same assumption guided him in writing and staging *Jubilee* [*Jubiläum*],[1] created to mark the fiftieth anniversary of the National Socialists' rise to power in Germany. The city of Bochum in the industrial region of the Ruhr, 30 January 1983: the man invited by the established, subsidized municipal theatre to offer a theatrical vision commemorating the decisive turning point in the history of Germany and of the world was an outsider, nearly seventy years old; a theatre-man with an unusual, controversial record; a Jew who survived the war in the Middle East but lost so many members of his family, including his father, in Auschwitz.

It was not meant to be a solemn occasion or an institutionalized commemoration, of which there were so many in the German Republic before and especially in the years to follow. This form of collective remembering, these prescribed and organized ceremonies, like the diverse monuments for the victims of the Third Reich and the various memorial sites reconstructed as museums of synthetic horror, engender at most a conditioned consternation, the main symptoms of which are melancholy and piousness, hardly genuine, deep sorrow.[2]

Jubilee does not attempt to depict historical, political, or social aspects of the Third Reich, let alone to scrutinize them. Tabori's interest does not lie in presenting an accurate historical reality or in being faithful to factual truth. His theatre confronts the malaise of National Socialism and the systematic murder of European Jewry in a way that is highly original and daring, one might say revolutionary. Tabori's pursuit of the past does not seek, as so many Germans have, to overcome the past (*die Vergangenheit zu bewältigen*), to have done with it, since this approach is fundamentally erroneous. His interest lies neither in presenting an indictment nor in providing an outlet for feelings of revenge; neither in awakening spectators' pity nor in revering the perished and exalting them as martyrs; certainly not in evoking a sentimental response as did the dramatization of *Anne Frank's Diary* in the 1950s or the American television soap-opera hit *Holocaust*, shown in Germany in the late 1970s.

"It would be an insult to the dead, to beg for sympathy or to lament their crushed nakedness. The event is beyond tears,"[3] contends Tabori, who nevertheless focuses attention on the victims. Only ten days prior to Tabori's premiere, Heinar Kipphardt's *Brother Eichmann* was premiered in Munich, followed by exhilarating applause that was, embarrassingly, in some measure as much for the administrative murderer (*Schreibtischmörder*) turned victim as for Hans-Michael Rehberg in the titular role.[4] Tabori, who had earlier encouraged Kipphardt to carry on with his "Eichmann project," maintaining that "it makes fascism normal and present instead of leaving it in the demonic past,"[5] was most critical of the final result.

For his own part, Tabori tries to free the experience of confronting the past, to free the actors and the spectators from those conventions and taboos which burden and strain, distort, and falsify it; from sentimental pity, sanctimonious judgment, and that hypocritical philo-Semitism which, to many, is the reverse side of anti-Semitism.[6]

The systematic murder of millions binds together Jews and Germans forever, claims Tabori; he offers both sides a theatrical experience whose core I would term memory-work (*Erinnerungsarbeit*), paraphrasing the notion of mourning-work (*Trauerarbeit*) coined by the Mitscherlichs.[7] Indeed, Tabori's understanding of the theatrical experience as a form of activating memory is closely related to Freud's therapeutic approach — his *Erinnerungsarbeit* — which is a threefold experience involving "erinnern, wiederholen und durcharbeiten"[8] — remembering, repeating, and working through.

Tabori's theatre thus becomes a locus of remembrance (*Gedächtnisort*).[9] While it is aimed against the collective amnesia, this experience is far from being a ritual, which might insinuate a practice by rote and convention, with no need for individual initiative. Tabori's approach is marked by its concrete and sensual quality, in its totality. "True remembrance is possible only through sensual remembrance: it is impossible to confront the past without sensing it again in one's skin, nose, tongue, buttocks, legs, and stomach," he argues; he underscores the supposition that "what is remembered in the body is well remembered."[10]

The theatrical experience of remembrance, the exposure of the wounds and the reawakening of the pain, involves actors and spectators physically, intellectually, and emotionally. Tabori's *Erinnerungsarbeit* calls for a total immersion in memory, in the traumatic pain, and it deliberately blurs the demarcations between theatre and life, reality and nightmare, past and present — expanding, as it were, the volume of time. This is a highly intensive, visceral theatrical experience, taking apart and rebuilding, chaining and liberating. For "we can only forget what we remember."[11]

The setting of *Jubilee* is a cemetery on the banks of the Rhine. The ghosts of the dead, victims of the National Socialist terror regime, find no peace. They are disturbed by the hostile writings and the acts of desecration of Neo-Nazis such as Jürgen, acts which suggest the continuation of past hostility and hatred. "Thirty-four years of democracy and again the same old story," notes Otto, and Lotte adds, "There we go again" (*Jubilee*, 59, 73). Jürgen's anti-Semitism is not motivated by ideology. The blond youth in a black leather jacket hates the Other, the stranger whoever he or she may be; he bullies the weak and the stigmatized out of frustration and pleasure. This is his way of boosting his ego and of protesting against a detested bourgeois society. Offended and aggrieved, the dead rise from their graves. This is no *Techiyat ha-metim*, the Jewish resurrection of the righteous and the pious on the Day of Judgment. According to Jewish belief the body of the dead deserves the same care given a living person. The corpse must rest unscathed, undisturbed: "for thou shalt rest, and stand in thy lot at the end of the days" (Daniel 12:13). Thus, disturbing the dead is an unforgivable offense, and the resurrection of the dead in *Jubilee* is, in Jewish terms, a perverted, apocalyptic vision. The rising of the dead does not signal the forthcoming redemption but rather the reexperiencing of a painful past.

Taking part in Tabori's eerie *danse macabre*, in this "scenic oratorium,"[12] are Arnold the musician, his wife, Lotte, her spastic niece Mitzi, Helmut the homosexual, and his lover, Otto the barber. Tabori deliberately presents non-Jewish as well as Jewish victims: Jews have no monopoly on suffering, though he does not deny that they were the main targets of mass annihilation. Each of these victims recalls a private jubilee or cutoff date. Dying becomes the pivotal experience in each victim's private "Passion." None dies a natural death. Lotte dies when the Nazis rise to power, drowning in a telephone booth while calling her friends and acquaintances. Three others commit suicide — Helmut by hanging, Otto by drowning in the bath, having taken an overdose of sleeping tablets, and Mitzi by shoving her head into the oven — three victims who are forced to relive the horror, signifying the continuation of evil well after that legendary *Stunde Null* (Point Zero).

Jubilee is not structured as a logical and orderly development of scenes conveying a conventional plot, but as a collage — a sequence of scenes and acting-situations which are essentially fragments of remembrance. The theatrical experience draws its force from the cumulative effect of one intense episode following the other, while the episodes themselves have that anecdotal quality which is so typical of Tabori's writing.[13] There is no message or truth which Tabori intends to transmit to his audience. The truth, or what we normally call the truth, is a stranger to Tabori. Instead there are specific, private instances or anecdotes. "The true, the original is only within us, if we dare to discover it," he once said, speaking instead of "several truths."[14] Following Adorno, in a way, Tabori offers a theatrical experience which is liberated from the lie of being the truth,[15] an experience which is by definition fragmentary, like variations on a theme.

Tabori was not interested in directing his actors to play a fictitious Other, but, as always, in stimulating and encouraging the actors to try everything out and to give themselves room for a personal experience of the material at hand. Lively discussions of the past were complemented by a visit to the Jewish cemetery in Gelsenkirchen. In the course of rehearsals, which lasted five weeks, each actor tried to approximate the role, to feel a way into the role, or, in Tabori's words, to discover the role from within. Improvisations constituted an important factor not only during rehearsals, but also in the actual performance. Music was a crucial factor on this journey inward. Musician Stanley Walden accompanied rehearsals on the piano, stimulating the actors to offer improvisations on a given situation or to experience "sense-memory." Songs (such as Jürgen's rock song, the old hit "Wochenend und Sonnenschein" [Weekend and Sunshine], a song from the musical *Kiss Me, Kate,* or the melody of *Kol Nidre* [the prayer sung on Yom Kippur]) and instrumental music (the clarinet playing the leitmotif, the so-called *Erlösermotiv* of Wagner's *Parsifal*) constituted an organic part of the performance.[16]

"Each life has a beginning, a middle and an end, though not necessarily in that order," says Tabori in his introductory remarks to *Jubilee* (52). Indeed, all levels of time are interwoven in the play, the past freed of its "historicity" and made contemporary. On the thin boundary between chimera and reality, the spatial and the temporal dissolve to create a heterogeneous fabric, fragments of consciousness.

Tabori's Postmodernism is apparent not only in the questioning of truth or the collage strategy, but also in the echoes of other works resonating in his text and staging. It is clear that the episode of "The Jewish Woman" from Brecht's *The Private Life of the Master Race* (1935–1938) underlies Lotte's moving farewell scene,[17] although it stems also from a personal recollection: Tabori's aunt Piroschka committed suicide in a telephone booth.[18] The spirit of *Hamlet*'s gravediggers' scene lingers in the episode with Wumpf the gravedigger, a clever clown with a red rubber nose, and the spirit of Hamlet's dead father is evoked by the figure of Arnold's father, albeit the latter does not seek revenge. Kafka's world is echoed in the play's despair and dread, in Tabori's obsession with extreme conditions and liminal situations (*Grenzsituationen*). The grating bond between the murderer and the murdered — Tabori's stipulation that "criminals are wont to return to the scene of the crime; so are, occasionally, the victims" (*Jubilee,* 52) brings to mind Raskolnikov from Dostoyevsky's *Crime and Punishment,* an author whose work Tabori tried to bring to the stage.[19] Having mentioned Shakespeare, Kafka, and Dostoyevsky, dear to Tabori's heart, we should also mention Beckett, an author with whom he corresponded and whose works he staged, particularly during the period preceding and following *Jubilee.* The vivid image of Lotte sitting up in her grave (scene 2) or being submerged in the floods of water in a telephone booth which cannot be opened recalls the hopelessness that characterizes Beckett's world. Beckett is also recalled in the arrested motion, the stagnation, the time of waiting — real time, Godot's time — of which Arnold speaks when he tells of the little boy in the sailor suit, eternally await-ing his father (scene 7).

No less original than the text was Tabori's staging of *Jubilee*. Seek-ing to expand memory space (*Erinnerungsraum*), coalescing past and present, Tabori shifted the production from the auditorium, that conventional staging area, to the foyer. Fiction and fact, theatre and life, exterior and interior merged into each other. The foyer was covered with mounds of earth, tombstones, and foliage, and looking through the big glass windows spectators could see the traffic flow-ing in the Königsallee as well as a grave mound that was raised out-side as an extension of the inner space. This kaleidoscopic, multi-dimensional staging (spectators who watch the performance, who observe themselves or the other viewers, or those who are being observed by other spectators or the passersby outside, etc.) is a to-pos of Postmodern theatre, as manifest in the work of the New York group "Squat."[20] The neo-Nazi Jürgen emerged out of a taxi in front of the theatre and wrote the anti-Semitic slogan "Juda verreke" (with a spelling mistake!) on the glass window between a Star of David (a hexagram) and a swastika. On the opening night Tabori, in the role of the ghost of Arnold's father, left the foyer and walked along the pavement outside the theatre building. Under his woolen coat he wore the outfit of a concentration camp detainee, with number and yellow star. Snow was falling. Tabori knocked on the glass and later gave Stanley Walden — his "son," Arnold — a *chalah*, the Sabbath bread, covered with white cloth.

Eating is an important motif in Tabori's theatre, from *Cannibals* (1968) to *The Ballad of the Wiener Schnitzel* (1996). In the latter the schnitzel stuffed down Morgenstern's throat unleashes nightmares of a new Holocaust. Memory and fear are triggered through the senses. The forced ingestion is a catalyst prompting the Viennese professional diner Morgenstern to recognize his Jewishness. At the end of his self-afflicted and yet very real harassment, he sits with his wife amid the graves of his murdered relatives — a scene which is reminiscent of *Jubilee*, both imagistically and thematically. For years Morgenstern tried, like the dead in *Jubilee*, to flee the past, to shake off memories, "not to think of them [the dead]."[21] Only now does he understand that he had been unwilling and unable to mourn their death and grieve over the loss. One is reminded of Freud's obser-vations in *Totem and Taboo* concerning the taboo of the dead. The fear of the presence or the return of the dead person's ghost engendered in ancient tribes a great number of ceremonies performed to keep the ghost at a distance or drive it off.[22] The anguish Morgenstern experiences when he is personally harassed and humiliated as a Jew prompts him to acknowledge his own family and its history of suffering. Refusing to abandon the dead and leave them to their solitude, he lingers over the graves and, for the first time ever, can even shed "a genuine tear." His tears run down his face and moisten the schnitzel, which his wife offers him like a doting mother. "These strange people [the Jews] believe that as long as one talks about the dead . . . , they aren't dead," writes Tabori.[23] Remembering thus is the maintaining of continuity in consciousness.

In *Mein Kampf* Shlomo Herzl's dear chicken, Mitzi, is slaughtered, dissected, and fried by Himmlisch (alias Himmler). Shlomo picks up the remains; as he prays Kaddish over the dead chicken, tears trickle down his cheeks and mix with the morsels he is swallowing. In *Jubilee* Arnold shares the bread his father gives him — the Sabbath-*chalah* sanctified by the head of the table and passed on to the participants in the ritualized meal. This transcends the purely ritualistic-religious act or the symbolic reconciliation of father and son. It also suggests the principle of hope (*Prinzip Hoffnung*) which is crucial to Tabori's theatre. For a moment Arnold is made to believe that the Auschwitz ovens were used to bake bread, not to gas human beings, a grotesque variation on the "Auschwitzlüge." The lie turns into a moment-of-truth or a momentary truth. A similar connotation arises from *Mein Kampf*: Lobkowitz, the godly cook, serves Shlomo the chicken, saying, "Eat, my son, not in hunger, but in the hope to ingest the martyr's strength you will need in all the years to come."[24]

Jubilee is set in a cemetery on the banks of the Rhine, one of the largest rivers in central Europe, defining national boundaries. The river is overloaded with historical and literary associations, and Tabori, an exceptionally erudite European, knows them all. He is well acquainted with the repertory of legends and myths connected with the Rhine, one of the major arteries in German culture and folklore; from the Rhine-daughters who watch over the gold in the *Ring of the Nibelung* and Heinrich Heine's "Lorelei" (quoted in the play) to the romantic aura of the ruined castles along the river. Indeed, the symbolism of the Rhine often verges on the banal, and it is partly this quality which provoked the protest of post-1945 German artists such as Anselm Kiefer, painter of the cycle *Der Rhein*.

This wide range of Rhine associations — a manifold metaphor of Germanism — is deeply embedded in *Jubilee*. The riverbank, with its cemetery, is the domain of death. Tabori's preoccupation with death is almost obsessive; there is hardly a production or a play of his in which death has no dominion. In *Mein Kampf* he introduces death in the tradition of medieval allegories and the German Romantics, personifying it as Frau Death, whose emissary "exterminating angel" is Hitler. In *Jubilee* death is the realm of the Baroque *Vanitas* and putrefaction ("putrid flesh, an empty eye, a missing nose"; *Jubilee*, 51). At the same time the gravedigger's words ring in spectators' ears: only the dead have it good, since they enjoy eternal tranquillity. For Tabori, "life is an incurable sickness and death perhaps the only end to misfortune."[25]

But is it really so? The dead in *Jubilee* know no peace and quiet. The burden of private memories accompanies them in their state of nonbeing and quiescence, haunts them, and becomes a nightmarish presence. Tabori's wise "Shakespearean" gravedigger argues, moreover, that no two graves are alike. But the Holocaust has taught us the lesson of anonymous death, laid bare a pit which is no grave, a pit meant to obliterate and blot out memory rather than commemorate as graves or tombstones do. Naming the dead endows them with the dignity reserved for human beings, while the systematic mass extermination was an unprecedented humiliation, an indignity which only memory, or genuine *Erinnerungsarbeit*, can redeem.

Tabori has chosen the cemetery on the banks of the Rhine also because death is a "quiet return to the moist beginning; the wheel has come full circle" (*Jubilee*, 63). Tabori has often spoken of death as a form of birth. In his poem "Was mich ärgert, am meisten ärgert," he says: "Dying [is] like being born, only the other way round."[26] Wumpf the gravedigger describes the grave as "deep and moist as a mother" (63). Dying is the return to the maternal womb, the uterus full of amniotic fluid, the source of life, *prima materia*. In *Jubilee* Lotte and Otto die in water,[27] but there are those who die in the opposite element, fire: Mitzi, who sticks her head in the oven, and the millions sent to the Nazi crematoria. The symbolical significance of water is emphasized by a key sentence of Tabori's alter-ego, Arnold. Arnold asks: what happens when a song is sung to its end? He answers himself: "It remains." Whatever has taken place exists, lives on in memory. Helmut's reply to this sophisticated, philosophical argument is that *he* himself hears nothing, to which Arnold the musician (in the original production Stanley Walden with the clarinet) retorts: "I am a white whale in a sea of music" (*Jubilee*, 71).

Water is the source of infinite potential, the origin and endpoint of all things in the universe. The whale's belly is a place of death and darkness as well as rebirth and resurrection, and Jonah, "a retired prophet," is Tabori's favorite biblical figure. This tension between death and regeneration is part and parcel of Tabori's experience of remembering. In the European tradition of symbolism water is also associated with unconsciousness and forgetfulness; the mythological Lethe, or the German Rhine in *Jubilee*, is the river of the underworld, the river of forgetfulness. Tabori's *Erinnerungsarbeit* is based on the dialectics of forgetfulness and remembrance, suppression and recall, since "we can only forget what we really remember."[28]

The hidden tensions latent in Tabori's *Erinnerungsarbeit* also include the complex relationship between victim and perpetrator. Notably Tabori emphasizes the fact that the victims — not only the perpetrators — try to forget or suppress the gruesome past. As we learn from the Jew Morgenstern in *The Ballad of the Wiener Schnitzel*, it is not only the perpetrators who fail to mourn. Furthermore, it is not only the murderer who returns to the scene of the crime, as in Dostoyevsky's model, but also the victim, as Arnold testifies in *Jubilee*. In the locus of historical events, images are vivid, memories surface with sharp poignancy. In all his Holocaust plays, *Jubilee* included, Tabori contests the mythologization of Auschwitz: Auschwitz is not a remote and alien planet; the victims are not saints but flesh-and-blood men, women, and children, with their virtues and their faults, their dreams, and their passions. Like all human beings they are flawed by envy, rage, and baseness. Tabori makes his point theatrically: the interchange of roles is of major significance in his collage. At one point, the dead, the victims, slip into the role of the vicious victimizers (significantly, the actual perpetrators are not depicted in the play), while the neo-Nazi Jürgen, for instance, plays the prosecutor at a trial. Authentic material and documentary research (i.e., the report about the execution of the Jewish children in Neuengamme or the shooting of Jewish prisoners in the quarry at Buchenwald) are mingled with fiction. The victims are required to try to understand the motivations and state of mind of the Nazis they are made to play. This is typical of Tabori. The key sentence to the understanding of the tension between victim and perpetrator is to be found in Jürgen's monologue (scene 7). The "Nazi" — or, in the wider sense of the word, evil — is latent in all human beings. The difference between Jürgen, with the pistol as his signature, and others is that he has unleashed the evil spirit: "You do not have the courage to let out the little Nazi in you loose," he contends (*Jubilee*, 65).

Belonging to one side or to the other is a matter of choice. It is always possible to choose between alternatives, even in extreme situations (*Grenzsituationen*), and it is indeed this possibility of choice which makes humans human. This belief, shared by Primo Levi, is already expressed in *Cannibals* and underlies *Jubilee* too. In *Jubilee*, Arnold recounts the fate of his father, Cornelius (named after Tabori's own father). An inveterate humanist, Cornelius had refused to go into hiding even when the Nazis were about to arrest him. He would not give up his faith in human justice. So he turned himself into the Gestapo, dressed in the costume he had worn as an opera singer in Richard Wagner's *Parsifal* — his German identity.

The clear differentiation between victims and perpetrators is thus misconceived, based on an illusion or self-deception. It is the choice which determines what one will be, in any given situation. The complexity of being a victim is manifest in the fate of Helmut the homosexual and of Mitzi the spastic woman. Helmut, the archetypical sufferer, voluntarily hospitalizes himself and undergoes circumcision. This is less a sign of trying to overcome his guilt feelings than the wish to become the victim per se or, metaphorically, the Jew.[29] The figure of the physically disabled, the invalid, has preoccupied Tabori time and again in his own plays and in productions of plays by other authors. The best instances are his choice of Peter Radtke, in a wheelchair, for the leading male part in *M.* (1985), in *Happy Days* (1986), or in Kafka's *A Report for an Academy* (1992),[30] and the moving figure of Ruth, the "mongoloid" in his own play *Weisman and Copperface* (1990). Mitzi is *the* victim in *Jubilee*. Physical impairment — humanity in an extreme state — is in Tabori's vision the best symbol of resourceful inner energy, the fruitful dialectics of "extreme physical handicap and an inner freedom no less extreme."[31]

Last but not least: Tabori's theatre of mourning is so effective in its *Erinnerungsarbeit* because it is empowered by his very special humor, which is grotesque, biting, terrifying, macabre. The sources of Tabori's humor are a long Jewish tradition of bittersweet jokes and witty anecdotes and Hollywood slapstick (for example, Arnold throwing a cream-cake at Jürgen in scene 7). While dissociating himself from the vulgar and repulsive humor of virulent anti-Semites, he nonetheless incorporates in his play the awful joke about the Jews squeezed in a Volkswagen.

Tabori's humor is mercilessly funny. It can be bitter as poison, as in the beautifully rhymed, mesmerizing song about the extermination, which is based on a widespread German nursery rhyme, "Die Vogelhochzeit." Often a joke and tears come together, "Scherz und Schmerz," as for Tabori "humor is no laughing matter."[32] The Taborian joke, which gets stuck in the throat and at the same time liberates suppressed feelings, is a conscious attempt to break a taboo and yet another manifestation of his *Prinzip Hoffnung*. Directed against affected piousness and mawkish sympathy, his humor liberates the spectator from the conditioned consternation or *Betroffenheit*. It is this perspective of humor which affords us a more profound insight into the heart of darkness. It enables us to recognize the true dimensions of the tragedy and stimulates a sincere and valuable *Erinnerungsarbeit*.

MEIN KAMPF

A man is known by his laughter. Talmud, Eruvin

"It's a banal story, in the Hollywood sense of the word. A Great Love Story — Hitler and His Jew. A horrible case," Tabori said about his play *Mein Kampf*,[1] which premiered at the Akademietheater in Vienna on 6 May 1987. This instant hit, Tabori's most performed play,[2] brings together the Jewish *Überlebenskünstler* (survival-artist) Shlomo Herzl and the young Adolf Hitler in a dismal flophouse in Vienna sometime between 1907 and 1910.[3] Shlomo, a spirited storyteller and master of caustic wit, lovingly mothers the newly arrived Hitler and teaches him how to behave, much to the amazement and remonstrance of inmate Lobkowitz "the Loon," a former kosher cook who plays at being God. Shlomo painstakingly grooms the aspiring candidate for his fateful interview at the Academy of Art and consoles him when he fails, all the while advising his frustrated highfalutin roommate to go into politics. When Frau Death visits the home of the destitute looking for a certain Adolf Hitler, Shlomo chats her up while his chum hides in the toilet; later he finds out that the lady in black was not interested in Hitler "as a corpse," but rather meant to recruit him "as a criminal, as a mass murderer, as an exterminating angel" (*Mein Kampf*, 77).

It is a "Great Love Story" but with no happy ending. Accompanied by his ardent supporters, "the Tyrolean Leather Freaks" and his "bosom-buddy" Himmlisch (clearly, Heinrich Himmler), Hitler prances in during the last scene demanding to see Shlomo's long-expected masterpiece *Mein Kampf*. Exposed, Shlomo is forced to admit that the book exists only in his imagination. A gruesome punishment follows: Himmlisch, as master of ceremonies, offers a mock-religious sacrifice, and Shlomo is forced to witness his beloved chicken, Mitzi, being dismembered, disemboweled, and finally flopped into a frying pan. "I was too dumb to know that some people can't take love," he realizes and says Kaddish, the Jewish prayer for the dead, over her remains. The ever-present would-be God Lobkowitz emerges from a dark corner with a macabre piece of advice for his friend Shlomo: "Eat, my son, not in hunger, but in the hope to ingest the martyr's strength you will need in all the years to come" (*Mein Kampf*, 83). Shlomo follows his advice, choking with tears as he swallows.

Adapted from one of his short stories published in 1986,[4] the German version of the play is defined as a farce;[5] Tabori also referred to it as a "theological farce" in interviews he gave before and after the premiere.[6] However, "farce" is an elusive term, and critic Gregory Dobrov rightly observes that "well-intentioned studies of the subject have made little progress towards defining 'farce.'"[7] In fact, the collection of critical essays in which his statement appears evinces the lack of consensus on the precise specifications of this dramatic genre. At any rate, Tabori's *Mein Kampf* hardly features the familiar characteristics of traditional farces by Aristophanes, Plautus, or the ingenious master of the genre, Georges Feydeau: mistaken identities, hastily assumed disguises, hectic action often arising from amatory or lecherous entanglements, frantic tempo. Unlike classical farces, Tabori's play does not seem to focus upon situations and actions at the expense of character development, nor are its characters stereotypes. Indeed, *Mein Kampf* is best understood in the context of avant-garde experimentations with the farce mode, which seek to invert generic expectations. Drawing together "notions of black humor, elements of the grotesque and absurd situations,"[8] these experiments produce a bleak spectacle of the human predicament, oscillating between horror and the ridiculous: *farce en noir*, as Jessica M. Davis calls them in her study *Farce*.[9]

"Shlomo and Hitler are parts of a dream, a kind of directed dream," says Tabori.[10] Truly, the play may be seen as a dramatic phantasmagoria, a wild, carnivalesque flight of fancy in which the imaginary and the chimerical are real, substantial, and veritable. A perplexing interplay between frivolity and horror, levity and gravity, characterizes Tabori's stage vision, which by taking up characters and events from history, distorting and fictionalizing them, exposes as it were the fictionality of history itself. Tabori made it quite clear that he was not concerned with historical accuracy; nor did it make any difference to him that Hitler never encountered a certain Shlomo Herzl. Tabori's "acted dream" is his own personal encounter with Hitler, the man who "changed my life, poisoned my dreams,"[11] admittedly a fabricated narrative with a cathartic function. "It's my Hitler. Hitler in me. It's an exorcism, like everything else I write."[12]

The dramatic irony permeating Tabori's variation on "history" stems from spectators' awareness of the denouement. As critic Michael Merschmeier states, Tabori's *Mein Kampf* is "a German fairy tale," which "begins pretty innocuously but ends with nastiness and bitterness."[13] Structurally a traditional five-act play with a clear spatial and temporal order, the drama begins with a conventional exposition and develops linearly over the course of four consecutive days at a single locality, the asylum. Nevertheless, there is something fundamentally perplexing about the play: a sense of wild phantasmagoria, or what Tabori once described as an "apocalyptic" quality.[14] The drama displays a remarkable medley of styles, ranging from Lazzi spoofs of the *commedia dell'arte* to Chaplinesque moments, punctuated with the quasi-Baroque allegorical impersonation of Frau Death, intimations of Goethe's *Faust* in the figure of the innocent beloved Gretchen, and a sense of "Beckettian ambiguity."[15] Like so many of Tabori's productions, *Mein Kampf* is a collage, which works by hybridization, juxtaposition, or disjunction, by entwining fantasy with drab reality. Quoting, misquoting, or merely echoing innumerable literary, dramatic, and cinematographic texts — from Buster Keaton, the Marx Brothers, and Charles Chaplin to Michael Curtiz's *Casablanca*[16] — the play merges high-brow repartee with "low" farcical knockabout and the sinister, mesmerizing tragic shading of the grotesque.

Spectators are constantly made conscious of the experience of viewing: they recognize the patterns and mechanisms of the drama and appreciate the visceral gratification of enacting a wayward "dream." At the same time, viewers are also aware of the play's historical context and of the repercussions of the Holocaust on German-Jewish relations.

"When I think about the German-Jewish love-hate relationship, I sometimes see Laurel and Hardy, or Cain and Abel. Cain loved Abel, that's why he murdered him. Man, say the sages, wants to kill what he loves most," maintains Tabori.[17] As in all of his works, the oppressor and the oppressed, the victimizer and the victim, are inextricably bound in a symbiotic relationship. The story of the "Great

Love" that has gone awry corroborates Tabori's belief — the Eleventh Commandment of his alter-ego Shlomo Herzl — "Better be choked than a choker," "Better be hunted than a hunter" (*Mein Kampf*, 57, 60).

Onomastics plays a significant role throughout Tabori's writing; so too in *Mein Kampf*. Hitler planned the Final Solution to the Jewish problem, as he euphemistically termed it; Herzl, the founder of the Zionist movement, envisioned an end to the anomaly and misery of Jewish existence as a Diasporic minority by advocating the national solution. Recounting his family history to the newly arrived tramp, Shlomo Herzl mentions a distant cousin, Löw Pinsker from Odessa (*Mein Kampf*, 49). This, of course, is no mere coincidence, for Yehuda Leib Pinsker, leader of the Hibbat Zion movement, similarly argued that the only way of eliminating what he named Judophobia was by following a national-territorial trajectory.

But the name Herzl, as Shlomo himself points out, is also the diminutive of *Herz*, heart in Yiddish as well as in Viennese dialect. *Herz*, he continues, "rhymes with Schmerz, or jest" (*Mein Kampf*, 49), which epitomizes the gist of Shlomo's philosophy of survival. It is the heart which time and again blunders. Shlomo, a hapless gull with "a broken heart . . . , a bleeding heart" (43), convinces himself that he can teach his disciple love and compassion. At the end of their tempestuous relationship, he realizes that Hitler, callous and unable to shed a genuine tear, is a man who "can't take love" (82). This is but another instance in a lifelong series of miscalculations. Shlomo is a self-confessed loser whose vulnerability and misfortune earn our sympathy. Bearing the name of the biblical King Solomon, "wiser than all men" (1 Kings 4:31) — and also Freud's middle name — Shlomo is ironically enough an exemplary *Schlemazel* whose never-ending misfortunes illustrate Tabori's contention that "to the Jew disaster is a way of life." [18]

A homeless, poor, and incompetent bookseller — a clear antithesis of the avaricious usurer — Shlomo had worked for a while in a morgue, washing corpses. In line with the essential trope of anti-Semitism, Tabori's Jew is old, weak, and ugly, resembling "an animal" that needs to be "deloused." [19] In his 1987 premiere Tabori emphasized the Jew's ugly features, calling to mind savage anti-Jewish depictions. Played by Ignaz Kirchner, Shlomo was a stooped-over man with red ears, a protruding false nose (which Hitler mistakenly pulls), and scummy rags, who shuffled along nervously. Too old for Romeo-like fiery lovemaking ("I am too weak to mount your balcony"; *Mein Kampf*, 63), he can offer his blonde, fair-skinned Madonna-Shikse Gretchen — modeled on the innocent maid who falls prey to Faust's lascivious dreams [20] — only stories and anecdotes. Shlomo eulogizes his beloved in biblical style, quoting and paraphrasing from the Song of Songs, which is attributed to King Solomon (a renowned womanizer who is said to have kept seven hundred wives and three hundred concubines). While Jewish tradition takes a dim view of needless talk, Tabori's Jew is a spellbinding word-spinner, whose only weapon is as insubstantial as words. For Tabori, words are powerful tools, and he associates them with the Jewish way of surviving. Tellingly, he once rejected the use of arms for prevention against anti-Semitic attacks, saying: "The Jews have been long armed, with word and writing. I still find these more powerful than the sword." [21]

In Tabori's play, Shlomo is the would-be author of *Mein Kampf* and it is "his struggle" (46) and his defeat. Hitler, a megalomaniac blatherer, pours out diatribes of ambition, frustration, and hate which can be seen as foreshadowings of the infamous book he was to write in the Landsberg prison in 1924 and of his anti-Jewish political platform. Phrases from the historical document are woven into the speech of Tabori's Hitler. For instance, he describes the ugly Jews in Vienna — "these Shylocks" (58) — with caftan and sidelocks, those sex maniacs, who reek of "steamy lust" and who are out to pervert the youth and contaminate the Aryan race. [22] While Tabori is inspired by the historical figure of Hitler, he is not concerned with the factual truth. He examines Hitler's development in the light of his fictive formative experiences in Vienna, that "multiracial Sodom, . . . unmelting pot of scum" (53), which fueled the ambitious Jew-hater. Significantly, Tabori's play premiered in Vienna at a time when Austria was racked over the controversial election to the presidency of the Nazi-collaborator and ex–U.N. secretary general Kurt Waldheim. [23]

In Tabori's production Hitler is an egocentric, self-pitying braggart, a pig-headed spoiled brat who has never matured, a constipated hypochondriac who spins impossible daydreams adrift in the big metropolis. He is sometimes pathetic, mostly ludicrous. When he comes in from the cold, the first impression is that of a forlorn hobo, with snowflakes covering his Tyrolean jacket, a green rucksack on his back. It is Shlomo who gives him the mustachioed Führer look ("That mustache is typical Austrian lower-middle class. It sets a tone," says Tabori),[24] brushes his hair, buttons him up, lends him a winter coat.[25] Unaware of any threat, the Jew tames him and prepares him for his political role. The danger latent in such a portraiture is, obviously, that Hitler drops too easily and safely into a harmless caricature.[26]

Hitler has, of course, been the butt of biting parody and caricatures. Best known among these are Chaplin's *Great Dictator* (1940), Ernst Lubitsch's *To Be or Not to Be* (1942), and *The Resistible Rise of Arturo Ui* (1941), a parable play that Tabori rendered in English, in which Brecht transforms Hitler and his cronies into Al Capone and his henchmen in the world of Chicago's gangland. More recently Hitler's rhetoric of megalomania has been the subject of George Steiner's *The Portage to San Cristobal of A. H.* (1982),[27] whereas German playwright Arnold Bernfeld presented in his play *Little Hitler or the Conjunctive of the Pluperfect* (Stuttgart, 1994) a fictitious encounter between Freud and Hitler. In the United States, Lenny Bruce's satirical fantasy about Hitler's "discovery" by a quasi-Jewish agent, who advised changing the name Schicklgruber for the more appealing Hitler, was criticized for being tasteless, while Mel Brooks included the parody "Springtime for Hitler" in his film *The Producers* (1968).

Less known is the fact that Hitler, who had no sense of humor ("I can't stand jokes," *Mein Kampf*, 52) or self-irony whatsoever,[28] was the butt of jokes, parodic sketches, and caricatures before and during World War II.[29] Austrian refugee actor Martin Miller delivered a brilliant parody of Hitler in the London cabaret Das Laterndl in 1940,[30] while British poet R. F. Patterson attacked the Führer in *Mein Rant: A Summary in Light Verse of "Mein Kampf"* (1940).[31] It is striking that Hitler's infamous book was nicknamed *Mein Krampf* (My Cramp) among inmates of the Warsaw ghetto, where a Yiddish song sardonically expounded: "Lomir zayn freylach un zogn sich vitsen / Mir veln noch hitlern shive noch sitsn" (Let's be merry and tell each other jokes / we will live to sit *shiva* over Hitler).[32] In the Dachau concentration camp, Rudolf Kalmer's Hitler-satire *Die Blutnacht auf dem Schreckenstein oder Ritter Adolars Brautfahrt und ihr grausiges Ende oder die wahre Liebe ist das nicht* [The Night of Blood on the Rock of Horrors or Knight Adolar's Maiden Voyage and the Gruesome End or That Is Not the True Love] raised the inmates' spirits, ending with the moralizing song, "Everything is hell / Soon it will yet get well / Through this magic word: humor, humor."[33]

Tabori's Hitler is neither a simpleton nor a monster,[34] as taboo-breaker Tabori sets out to debunk the mythologized archvillain and depict the banality of evil. "It is my Hitler. Hitler in me," he said, shocking a complacent, self-righteous public by suggesting that one can only overcome Hitler after recognizing his traits in oneself — an idea that Jewish viewers in particular found morally repulsive. There is in Tabori's *Weltanschauung* no dichotomy of "good" and "bad" people. Shlomo and Hitler, victim and victimizer, "inseparable partners in an unholy symbiosis,"[35] are like two poles drawn to one another, two antipodes of the self — the one a born artist, master of tears and love, the other an "anti-artist," incapable of weeping and loving.[36]

Notably, Tabori diverges from the farcical mode with its unlikely pairs of characters, introducing an odd triad. Lobkowitz — whose name holds the suffix *Witz* or joke[37] — is "a kookie kosher cook, defrocked some years ago by his boss Moskowitz for mixing cream cheese with boiled beef" (*Mein Kampf*, 44),[38] a Jewish heretic who breaks Mosaic law and still plays at being God. The play opens with Lobkowitz addressing his soul mate, Shlomo: "So there you are . . . trying to sneak past me?" — which recalls God's discovery of Adam in Eden after he had tasted the forbidden fruit (Genesis 3:9). For three years, we learn, the two homeless tramps have been engaged in a game of make-believe comprised of quips and witty exchanges, slapstick and physical knockabout. Like the Greek chorus — or like Providence — Lobkowitz is continuously present on the stage, intermittently involved in the action or quietly observing it. He is there to warn the gullible Shlomo against looking after Hitler, an impulse that "borders on masochism"; and he is also present at the terrifying mock-religious sacrifice of the chicken, sharing Shlomo's anguish, consoling him, foretelling more calamities. The 73-year-old Tabori played the part of Lobkowitz when the designated actor suddenly became ill, presenting a soft-spoken, genteel, and somewhat melancholy cook/God, with a tall chef's hat towering over his graying hair and a triple eye painted on his forehead — the all-seeing eye of Providence or perhaps Shakespeare's inward eye, the eye of magic.[39]

The Lord, namely Lobkowitz, whose conversation with Shlomo in the opening scene evokes an exchange between two aging Jewish immigrants or *Klejne Menschalach* in one of those seedy coffee shops in the Lower East Side of Manhattan, is a *Schlemiel* and a loser, not unlike Shlomo. He gets beaten up and is forced, like the Jews of

Vienna after the *Anschluß*, to scrub the floor at the end of the play (which he does, subversively, with a toothbrush).

Tabori appears as the heretic farceur — to use Eric Bentley's coinage — who "does not believe that man was made in God's image." [40] Like his alter-ego Shlomo, who revels in "pagan giggle" (*Mein Kampf*, 45), Tabori prefers to think that God was made in our image, rather than the other way around, and the motif of God as a human projection, a capricious and at times clownish deity, whose Creation is a fiasco, who "tries again, fails again, fails better," runs through Tabori's entire work. We are in Beckett territory ("Godot is a very Jewish-Irish God, terrible and comic"),[41] and, not surprisingly, Tabori's text resonates with allusions to *Waiting for Godot*.

In fact, these intertextual allusions begin with the opening scene and constitute a crucial component of Tabori's collage. "So there you are," says Lobkowitz to Shlomo, whereupon the latter retorts: "Am I?": this is an almost exact parallel to the opening dialogue between Vladimir and Estragon in *Waiting for Godot*, and an exchange that is repeated in both texts.[42] There are further analogies between the Beckett pair hovering between pitiful anguish and desperate buffoonery and the Taborian couple: fear of abandonment, overanxiety about physical well-being, the beating up of Estragon or Lobkowitz — Beckett's enigmatic God(ot) made visceral.[43] Moreover, the peculiar relationship between Shlomo and Hitler is tinged with echoes of the symbiotic relation of Didi and Gogo. Both oscillate between their need for demonstrative affection (Hitler even asks Shlomo to kiss him, which the latter refuses, a deliberate subversion of the Judas kiss) and their flinching away from physical contact. Estragon recalls his attempt to commit suicide by throwing himself into the Rhône; Hitler threatens to drown himself in the Danube. Shlomo offers Hitler his coat; Didi lays his coat across the shoulders of the sleeping Gogo. Tabori's figures show the same penchant for wordplay of the Beckett duo; Pozzo's "twilight" reverberates in the title of Hitler's paintings;[44] and even the chicken is there: Pozzo eats it voraciously, Himmlisch cooks it, and Shlomo tastes and weeps.[45]

Tabori explicitly refers to Beckett's notion of time, the "Godotian" time, when Shlomo prays on the Sabbath while waiting for the weekly visit of the maiden Gretchen. "Waiting is the true time," claims Shlomo. "Waiting for the Messiah is what matters, not the coming" (*Mein Kampf*, 61).

Like Beckett's play, which Tabori directed impressively in 1984,

Mein Kampf teems with references to the New Testament. In fact, he chose to conclude the original English version of the play with a joke about the two thieves hanging on the cross.[46] Still, the plethora of Christian images and innuendos is ingeniously interlaced with innumerable undertones, quotations, or deliberate misquotations from the Old Testament and Midrash literature. It is this unusual conflation of the Jewish and the Christian, this extraordinary imagistic tumult marked by repetition, inversion, and simultaneity, that decisively determines the fabric of the text.

The fabula begins on (Holy) Thursday with the cock's crowing signaling the betrayal;[47] Shlomo rescues the "exterminating angel," Hitler, during the visit of Frau Death on (Resurrection) Sunday. The drama reaches its climax in act V on the Day of Repentance (the Jewish Yom Kippur) with the sacrifice of Mitzi the chicken, which alludes to the traditional expiatory sacrifice of the rooster (*Tarnegol kaparot*); the major difference is that here the chicken is no surrogate for the repenting believer, but the herald of future calamities; "If you start burning birds, you'll end up burning people," warns Shlomo (*Mein Kampf*, 81). The unholy triad of Shlomo, Hitler, and Lobkowitz is a subversive representation of the Holy Trinity, and the Trinity topos figures prominently in the text: Hitler makes a triple entrance: once unnoticed, then acknowledged, and finally a studied entrance. He displays and comments on three of his watercolors to Shlomo and Lobkowitz, who have been playing their game for three years, while Gretchen demands from Shlomo "three hints" as to his enigmatic book, before the Jew is forced to witness the gruesome sacrifice of Mitzi and concludes that "you proceed by crucifying me" (81). In vain does Shlomo try to educate his protégé in the light of Leviticus 19:18: *veahavta lereacha kamocha* (Thou shalt love thy neighbor as thyself). The subaltern Jew, who in the course of the play becomes more and more a Christ-like figure, instructs Hitler, the Anti-Christ ("You will be a king, who walks over a blanket of bones"),[48] in the vein of the New Testament's "Love thy enemy as thyself."

Echoes of the Old Testament, Midrash literature, and Jewish liturgy are no less prominent: there are allusions to Genesis, Exodus, the Song of Songs, Ecclesiastes, and the Book of Daniel, to name only some of the sources.[49] Tabori rarely assimilates source material verbatim; instead he inverts and corrupts it to engender verbal or situational humor. Examples include Shlomo's quasiromantic eulogy to the maid Gretchen, which draws extensively on the Song of Songs; Hitler's reversal of the eschatological vision of peace by envisioning the turning of "ploughs into swords" (*Mein Kampf*, 49); and Frau Death's twisting the famous Ecclesiastes passage into the mundane "a time for walking, and there is a time for sitting down" (74). It is from the Aggadah that Tabori adopts the story of Rabbi Eliezer and his enamored niece, who humbly offers to wash his feet and those of his disciples.[50] Furthermore, mention is made in Shlomo's story about his father's arrest and the taunting interrogation of the Angel Michael, lord and protector of his people. The story itself—"The organ-grinder's truth" (65)—a characteristic Tabori anecdotal digression full of twists and turns, relates how Shlomo, "the master liar of Pest," embroils his father in trouble, by reporting his ties with anarchists such as Georges Danton and Mikhail Bakunin and his plan to storm the tsar's palace. A miserable synagogue cantor with barely a notion of Jewish liturgy, an assimilated Jew who felt happier as an organ-grinder playing a popular song in praise of Vienna,[51] Shlomo's father did not accuse his son of lying; "And so it came to pass that, for a change, the father died for the son," concludes Tabori's alter-ego (67). Watching his father being cruelly interrogated, Shlomo beholds the angel Michael (Hebrew for "who is like God?") as he appeared to the prophet Daniel (Daniel 12); this is ironic, since according to the Aggadah, the angel Michael appeared before the father (Abraham), appealing to him to spare his son (Isaac).

In the final scene, enacting the sacrifice of the chicken, Tabori likewise courts subversiveness. In his rendering, white is worn not by the Jew (as is the Jewish tradition on the Day of Atonement), but by the culprits, Himmlisch and the seven cronies, who wear white smocks that will soon be stained with blood. Strikingly, Shlomo says Kaddish, the prayer of mourning, not over a beloved relative but over the carcass of a chicken that he will soon consume.

Food and eating is a perennial motif in the theatre of Tabori. The macabre concluding scene of *Mein Kampf*—with Himmlisch describing the dismemberment and cooking of Mitzi like the complacent narrator of a TV cooking lesson and with its undeniable allusions to the Last Supper—recalls, of course, the cooking and consuming of Puffi in *Cannibals* and the figure of the Nazi Schrekinger, an "expert on chickens." It will recur in a modified manner in

The Ballad of the Wiener Schnitzel, where the eight "Herrmann-Cooks," all in white smocks, stuff the schnitzel down the throat of the Jew Morgenstern, a professional gourmet.

This perplexing conflation of the Jewish and the Christian, the overlapping of the contemporary with the past, and the blending together of images and dramatic topoi associated with different historical traditions — this studied stylistic inconsistency lends the text of *Mein Kampf* its special quality.

Tabori used the same techniques of conflation and juxtaposition in the staging of the play. The set[52] — a staircase at the rear of the rotting wood floor, a table, an oven, a bench, a shabby armchair, and a bed resembling an unearthed grave — rapidly veers between the ahistorical and the near past of Nazi Germany. Similarly, costumes ranged from the abstract to the folkloric, from the iconographic (Frau Death's black cape) to the stereotypical (Shlomo in dark clothes and a protruding false nose). The musical accompaniment was a polyphony of styles. Stanley Walden had originally arranged a musical medley for violin, cello, clarinet, and horn, with citations from Gustav Mahler and Arnold Schönberg (both Austrian Jews who converted to Christianity), folklore melodies of Bavarian *Schuhplattler,* and a tango for Frau Death.[53] Due to technical problems the musical accompaniment had to be reduced, however, and Walden offered in lieu a mélange of Wagner tunes, Klezmer melodies, songs, and the Kaddish melody.

In truth, what distinguishes *Mein Kampf* is Tabori's defiance of uniformity, stylistic or dramatic, and his pursuit of indeterminacy and ambiguity. This was the hallmark of his own production in Vienna, and critic Michael Merschmeier defines it succinctly in his description of Kirchner as Shlomo Herzl: "Between Kaddish and jest, sentimentality and sarcasm, tragedy and triviality, Kirchner sounds every tone — and immediately lets the sound dissolve — trespassing the border lines, jumping back and forth between the diametrically opposed fixed points."[54]

There is hardly a review of *Mein Kampf* which does not celebrate its humor. Critics have made sweeping statements about Tabori's "Jewish humor," applauding it without bothering to explain what makes it particularly "Jewish." In post-Holocaust Germany, to be Jewish has come to seem honorific, and Jewish humor, associated with writers as different as Philip Roth, Ephraim Kishon, and Tabori, is extolled *grosso modo*. A discussion of *Mein Kampf* is incomplete without a serious consideration of Tabori's humor in general and its expression in *Mein Kampf*, as one of its finest instances, in particular.

Tabori names two sources for his humor. "On the one hand Hasidism — 'dust unto dust and a jest in between,' and on the other hand the Anglo-Saxon tradition, which joins together the tragic and the comic in the same play, as in Shakespearean drama, without being regarded as stylistically incongruous." [55]

In both the Hasidic and the English traditions, the joke, being the finest and most accomplished expression of humor, originates in catastrophe: "The content of every joke is catastrophe," says Tabori, and elsewhere he maintains that "the nub of every joke is tragedy." [56] Tabori belies the artificial barriers between the tragic and the comic, and many of his scenes are played for a laugh; yet the gaiety springs out of despair,[57] or, conversely, is a way of warding off despondency. Tabori repeatedly uses the image of the lifebelt (*Rettungsring*) to describe the function of the joke, though he insists that the jest is never a means of escaping reality, but "reality itself." He chooses Friedrich Hölderlin's epigram "Must you forever be playing and jesting? You must, oh my friends, which sickens my soul. For only the desperate must" as the motto for *Mein Kampf*, suggesting that it "conveys precisely the awareness that playing and jesting originate in despair." And he adds: "I think, however, that with me it's also the other way round: somewhere the fun and the joke cease and things go on again." [58]

I very much doubt whether this approach to humor and jest can be associated with Hasidic notions of *simhah* (joy) and optimism, as Tabori insinuates. For one thing, joy and optimism are closely joined with other Hasidic principles, such as *hitlahavut* (burning enthusiasm) and *dvekut* (attachment), which define the relationship between humans and their Maker and regulate the Hasidic way of worshiping God. In reply to my query, Tabori confessed that he never delved deeply into Hasidism, and it seems more appropriate to relate his sense of the gaiety of despair, the correlative of horror and humor, to the East European Jewish ethos. Maurice Samuel speaks of Diasporic humor as a mode of survival,[59] and much has been written about Jewish humor seeking to deflate dire circumstances and bitter times, to demystify the inflated importance ascribed to suffering.[60] Theodor Reik, who fled his native Austria in 1938, speaks in his study *Jewish Wit* of life's pathos reflecting itself most distinctly in jokes; like Tabori he contends: "There is behind the comic facade not only something serious . . . but sheer horror." [61] When Shlomo Herzl speaks caustically of God who "loves His Jews so much that He won't let them out of sight" (*Mein Kampf*, 44), the classical Jewish joke about the miserable Chosen People, told and retold over generations, reverberates: "Dear God, for five thousand years we have been Your chosen people, Enough! Choose another people now." [62]

Indeed, like Sigmund Freud, Tabori maintains that "the best jokes come from Jews," for whom, one may add, humor's topsy-turviness is a mode of survival, [63] or, to use Tabori's dictum, "the principle of hope." Following Freud, who recognized the cathartic function of the joke as a release from the strictures of social-cultural proprieties, Tabori points to the therapeutic effect of humor. For him laughter is a purgative experience; he speaks of "a good laxative, namely a good laugh," which is as liberating as a good cry. [64] In this sense, too, "humor is no laughing matter." [65]

Mein Kampf displays a sophisticated intelligence reveling in slapstick, verbal acrobatics, comic squirmings, and makeshifts. But it is the so-called Jewish humor I would like to look at first. As a born loser and a *Luftmensch*, Shlomo's métier is language. A master of quick-fire questions and answers, of epigrammatic wit, pithy aphorisms, and one-liners, he relies on rationality and realism, as Jewish humor habitually does. [66] In the vein of Diasporic Jewish humor, his joke often expands into an anecdote. But perhaps most striking is his Talmudic disquisitional style, his hair-splitting mode of logical argumentation known as *pilpul*, the best example of which is the quibbling about the twins who fall through a chimney, with which he confronts Hitler (*Mein Kampf*, 50). [67]

Freud maintains that humor serves an aggressive purpose and speaks of the tendentious joke as a means of exposing and countering obstacles. "By making our enemy small, inferior, despicable or comic, we achieve in a roundabout way the enjoyment of overcoming him — to which the third person, who has made no efforts, bears witness by his laughter." [68] This is precisely what Jewish humor has done for generations, scoffing at Haman, deprecating the oppressive *goy* in the *Shtetl*, bantering during the Holocaust against the archfiend Hitler. As an heir to this tradition, Tabori imagines Hitler derided by the subaltern Jew (particularly in act II, with Shlomo helping him prepare for the fatal interview at the academy). Hitler is the butt of Tabori's mordant, bitter humor, exposing the monster as a pathetic bloke who hides in the toilet, "groaning inside, taking, apparently, the hardest shit since Luther saw the devil in the privy" (74).

But Jewish gallows humor does more than wryly deprecate the oppressor by way of celebrating a temporary and often moral victory. Martin Grotjahn sees aggression against the self as the main dynamics of Jewish wit,[69] and in truth, there is no shortage of self-critical quips and self-mockery in *Mein Kampf*. Moreover, this self-deprecating humor is entwined with the deliberate stereotyping of the Self and the Other, not unlike the tradition of anti-Semitic distortions: examples include Shlomo's remark that Hitler doesn't "look Jewish" (49), the joke about the ugly, cross-eyed Jew with the goiter,[70] Shlomo's ironic distinction between the individual "good" Jew and the abhorred Jewish collective (68), and Hitler's pulling at Herzl's protruding false nose (57).

Indeed, Tabori's humor is characterized by the fusion of elements of Jewish humor described above with a variety of other comic essentials: farcical cinematic topoi (particularly from the silent film); traditional comic patterns of merrymaking and travesty; the coalescing of mundane and sophisticated humor. There are numerous instances of wordplay, malapropism, and equivocations (e.g., the search for the title of Shlomo's book — "Shlomo in Wonderland," "Shlomo and Juliet," "Ecce Shlomo," etc.; *Mein Kampf*, 45), delicious puns (the corruption of Hitler's name), and no shortage of repetitions that produce, as Henri Bergson suggested, comic fun and laughter.[71] There is the humor of misunderstanding (Herzl: "It's Talmud"; Hitler's reply: "Another cousin?" 50) and the fun of ridicule. And there is the slapstick and knockabout humor of Buster Keaton or Laurel and Hardy (Lobkowitz hitting Herzl, Hitler kicking Herzl, Herzl fighting back as Mitzi the chicken shits into Hitler's hand) as well as Chaplinesque sequences (Shlomo offering his beloved Gretchen gumdrops, having her cut his toenails, or pouring water into Hitler's ear to wake him up).

Last but not least, there is Tabori's iconoclastic and subversive humor, the sense of the macabre when all comic mayhem is seen in hindsight — "When my time has come I shall reward you suitably. I'll buy you an oven, . . . I'll find you a solution," Hitler promises the Jew (*Mein Kampf*, 55); elsewhere he vows to have Shlomo "burnt like a breakfast roll" (59). Tabori's fabricated narrative of the "Great Love Story — Hitler and His Jew," which plays off our knowledge of history, opens up the possibility of terrifying irony and hideous grotesquerie. "If the ending cannot be happy, let it at least be laughable," argues Shlomo (81).

This ultimately brings us to consider the reception of the play in Germany and Austria. I have often been asked by perplexed and uneasy spectators of *Mein Kampf*: "Is one allowed to laugh?" Others posited their dilemma somewhat differently: "Is it legitimate to laugh at a ludicrous Hitler in full knowledge of what really happened?"[72]

Tabori never made a secret of his wish to shatter taboos, to defy mystification, to shock spectators out of their lethargy, their consternation (*Betroffenheit*), or affected piousness. "If we cannot see beyond the taboos and the clichés, and look at each other as *Menschen* rather than as abstractions, you might as well light the ovens again," he wrote long before he embarked on *Mein Kampf*.[73] In his subversive style, in an off-the-cuff quip, he once remarked: "What would Hitler have done without the Jews, Iago without his Othello?"[74]

Ever since the German premiere of *Cannibals*, criticism has been leveled at Tabori's callous bad taste, his disgusting *chutzpah*. Tabori was time and again attacked for being unscrupulously outrageous, for being fascinated with horror, for his dangerous playing down of the Nazi malaise. Still, the nearly thirty years that have elapsed since the storm over *Cannibals* in 1969 and Tabori's respectable status in German-speaking theatre as well as his by-now established reputation as a taboo-buster have done their share. Thus the answer to the question raised in so many critiques of the play — "Is one allowed to do that?" ("Darf man das?") — is an almost unanimous yes. "Tabori, as an emigrated Jew, is in this respect privileged," writes Paul Kruntorad;[75] Thomas Rothschild elaborates the point: "One is allowed — if one is called George Tabori, a theatre-man with a faultless biography, who masters like no one else the grotesque overdrawing as a theatrical stylistic device."[76]

But what about spectators' reactions? It was Freud who pointed out that it takes three to make a joke — the jokester, the butt of the joke, and the listener — and Eric Bentley observes that the need for an audience is no less vital than the need for the joke.[77] We have already noted that Tabori's subversive humor is intended to administer an ugly jolt, to have a purgative effect; yet I am doubtful whether the majority of spectators of *Mein Kampf* experienced this catharsis. I have met spectators perplexed, hesitant, shocked, or unsure of how they are expected to react. I have encountered others who, as Peter Kemp so aptly formulated his own feeling upon viewing the play in England, left the theatre "feeling slightly uncomfortable, because it hasn't made you feel at all uncomfortable about its appalling subject."[78] I have spoken to some who were relieved to discover that a Jewish playwright absolved the majority of the Germans of the collective guilt, fellow-travelers and bystanders included, while putting the blame — like the so-called Intentionalists among historians of the Third Reich — on Hitler, who, on top of it all, is depicted as a laughable neurotic.

"Tabori's joke stands on knife-edge in the literal sense," contends Konrad Paul Liessmann in his discussion of the play.[79] The question then remains open: how many in the audience, in Germany or anywhere else, perceive *Mein Kampf* as Tabori intended it, and is a response such as he envisioned at all possible?

Hard of hearing, as blind as a mole, Tabori's alter-ego Dirty Don dictates his own obituary to his beloved, the young belle Amanda, nicknamed Lollypop, for fear lest others, well-wishers and enemies alike, would get everything wrong. "As you probably know, I am / a legend, that is to say, a lie," he declares,[1] debunking right at the outset the nimbus of awe that has shrouded him. In truth, Tabori, who embarked on his theatre career in Germany when he was in his mid-fifties, has become a cult figure. "Theatre-guru," "magician," and "a living theatre legend" are among the epithets that crop up time and again in critiques and articles about him. His close friend and admirer the late Erwin Leiser, an author and film-producer and a Jewish Holocaust survivor like Tabori, applauded the recipient of the Mülheim Prize for Dramatists (1990, for the second time) as "an institution in the German-speaking theatre."[2] And in an article tellingly entitled "From Provocateur to Media-Star," veteran theatre critic Werner Schulze-Reimpell describes Tabori as "a rare bird of paradise" in the local cultural scene,[3] indisputably enjoying a "fan-club."

Revered and celebrated, Tabori's career, first in the USA, later in Germany, was fraught with disappointments, crises, and even scandals. Disenchanted with the commercially driven film industry and deeply frustrated, he gave up his job as scriptwriter and left Hollywood, his first station in the United States, for the East Coast, where he tried his luck as playwright and later as director. His early plays and productions conceded little to conventional expectations and earned him more scathing remarks than compliments. Nearly twenty years in America did not bring about the breakthrough he so keenly longed for, that turning point in his creative career which he was bound to experience as a watershed with his debut, *The Cannibals*, in Germany in 1969. Naturally the quesion arises: what would Tabori's career have looked like had he stayed in the United States? This is, admittedly, a hypothetical question lending itself to tedious speculations, yet it is hard to imagine that Tabori would have enjoyed the success and the fame he found in Germany. Ironically, it is Germany of all places that offered him a second chance and proved to be the ideal matrix for his unconventional theatrical vision and his prodigious gift as dramatist.

Even so, approval and acclamation did not come readily to Tabori even in Germany; as Schulze-Reimpell maintains, "Tabori was not instantly everybody's darling." The controversial reception of *Cannibals* raised curiosity and interest in the work of the unorthodox theatre-man, a self-confessed taboo-buster; yet the projects that followed often met with skepticism and dissenting critique. Some of the productions he directed in his own alternative Theaterlabor in Bremen elicited a storm of indignation among critics and spectators; others were greeted with cheers and boos at curtain call. Few and far between were the voices lamenting the closure of the theatre-lab, and many felt relieved that this wayward and provocative troupe, inebriately bewitched by a subversive theatre-man, had at last disbanded. And yet, the enigmatic outsider, inadvertently dedicated to alternative theatre work, had made a name for himself, in Bremen and later in Munich, gradually winning acknowledgment, respect, and eventually, with his own *Jubilee* (1983) and Beckett's *Waiting for Godot* (1984), also due praise. Veritably, with Tabori, fame and notoriety went hand in hand.

What is it that singles out Tabori among German directors, and what is his contribution to German theatre as play-maker, as he prefers to describe himself? After all, there was no shortage of innovative directors and artistic purveyors in postwar Germany: Peter Stein with his exquisitely stylized productions at the Schaubühne, Peter Zadek and his flamboyant, often excessive renderings of Shakespeare and contemporary drama, Pina Bausch's explosive creativity in the newly fashioned *Tanztheater*, not to mention Brecht's followers and champions of the political theatre such as Harry Buckwitz, Peter Palitzsch, or Heiner Müller (in his capacity as director) and the theatre of images of guest director Robert Wilson.

Tabori offered a fresh, invigorating approach to theatre-making, marked by a genuine, unmitigated involvement, provoking originality and vigor. Propelled by an insatiable curiosity and the desire to try everything out, even at the price of failure, his alternative theatre-making was a healthy antidote to the rigid, prostrate German theatre system. Speaking with disdain and undisguised contempt of the lugubrious, mind-numbing routine of the heavily subsidized institutional stages, Tabori set out to salvage the uniqueness of performance through nonformalistic, antiauthoritative ensemble work. The aim was not to meet deadlines, bowl over the audience with extravagant paraphernalia and star acting, or prove commercially successful, but to show that a low-budget, "poor" theatre with the actor as the soul of the performance is the only authentic and viable form of theatre-making. Redefining the relationship between the actor and the role, and seeking to enrich the performance through extratheatrical stimuli ("research"), psychotherapeutic techniques, and the actors' reservoir of private experience, Tabori went against the German grain. In a theatre system distinguished by the paramount position of the director, indeed in the so-called *Regie-Theater*, Tabori pressed for an actors' theatre (*Schauspieler-Theater*). No other director entrusted actors with such immense freedom, initiative, and responsibility. No one in the German scene before him championed so adamantly the conviction that an arresting, authentic performance by necessity conflates life and theatre. Sensual immediacy, randomness and contingency, reflexivity and viewers' coproduction — some of the hallmarks of Postmodern theatre, which, incidentally, he would dismiss with a cynical smile — mark his theatre, along with the conflation of utmost seriousness and deep jouissance.

Defiant and outspoken, the outsider Tabori resolved to tear off the mask, the figleaf, as he called it, hampering the vitality of theatre-making in Germany. That which was routinely kept separate — the mind and the body, thought and feeling, the sacred and the profane ("celestial and excremental," in his words) — was to be integrated. And more: Tabori's disregard for sacrosanct norms, his defiance of taboos, threatened likewise to undermine and subvert the established codes regulating the collective or individual response of the Germans to the Holocaust and to matters Jewish. "There are taboos that must be broken or they will continue to choke us," he declared on the eve of his German premiere of *Cannibals*.[4] This shocking, deliberately provocative debut marked the direction his work was to take in the following years. In his so-called Holocaust plays and in his productions foregrounding Jewish fate, he confronts the history of Jewish suffering and the systematic murder of European Jewry during World War II in a way that is both daring and highly original. His interest lies neither in presenting an indictment to German society nor in providing an outlet for feelings of revenge. In his plays and productions he seeks to free our confrontation with the past from the conventions and taboos which burden and strain, distort, and falsify it, from sentimental pity, sanctimonious judgment, and the hypocritical philo-Semitism which is in many cases the reverse side of anti-Semitism. There is no place for a mystical reverence for the victims, for tears or solemn self-incrimination, such as have pervaded officially staged commemorations and many stage-plays or productions.[5]

Tabori's theatre becomes a locus of remembrance (*Gedächtnisort*), offering both actors and spectators a unique, engaging memory-work (*Erinnerungsarbeit*). Contradicting the indulgent mystification of the past on the one hand and those voices advocating to have done with the past on the other hand, Tabori proposes a mnemonic experience marked by sensuous immediacy and deeply unsettling. Rather than commemorate, he ventures to retrieve, recall, reexperience. The recollection of a welter of pasts, with a variegated fusion of the historical and the personal, overlaps with the present and is charged with relevance. Flying in the face of spectators' expectations, Tabori does not recoil from injecting humor into moments of horror or pain, shaking up the audience through shocking jokes and offputting quips. "I am regularly berated for making people laugh about such holy subjects as Hitler or Auschwitz or sex," concedes Tabori,[6] who considers laughter a legitimate, healing cathartic reaction and argues that the content of a good joke is always catastrophe. For many spectators, critics, and laypersons, opponents and admirers alike, this tastelessness, this crudeness, is the hallmark of Tabori's theatre, which Jörg Gronius termed "Theatre of Embarrassment" (*Theater der Peinlichkeit*).[7]

It is a pained laughter that Tabori evokes. And it requires the reorientation of the spectator (and the actor, of course); a willingness to face collective or personal repression (not least, on the part of the bereaved!), open-mindedness and genuine involvement. No wonder that the history of Tabori's reception in Germany and Austria is so ambiguous, colored by enthusiastic reactions as much as by scathing criticism.

It took quite some time, so it seems in retrospect, for theatregoers, media people, and other multipliers of culture and public opinion to become attuned to Tabori's original voice — to digest, as it were, his unpalatable, indeed *geschmacklos*,[8] oeuvre. *My Mother's Courage, Jubilee*, and ultimately the inordinate success of *Mein Kampf* are some of the important milestones on Tabori's road to fame. Ironically, once he reached eminence, it became fashionable to applaud his work. Honors poured in and prizes were showered on the nonconformist. Tabori, doyen of the German theatre, the "mild Nestor among German theatre directors,"[9] was now almost unanimously admired and celebrated. Leading theatres such as the Burgtheater were keen to engage him, and the critics turned magnanimous, ready to forgive or turn a blind eye on flaws and whims. In short, the gray-haired iconoclast was "in."

Has Tabori's theatre made German-Jewish relations less strained? Did his demythologization of the traumatic past make it more accessible? Did he, unknowingly perhaps, belittle the Holocaust and dilute the uniqueness of the Nazi genocide? Could it be that by breaking the taboo which secured Jews the status of flawless martyrs, or by calling into question the Jewish monopoly on suffering and victimhood, Tabori played into the hands of those Germans who were hoping to counter whatever guilt they felt (or did not feel) through the impeachment of the victims? Moreover, was Tabori in the final judgment so genially received because his theatre helped, as some felt, to absolve the Germans of their frustrating guilt? Is Tabori in fact the "good Jew" ("der gute Jude"),[10] who, though unwilling to forget, provocative, and hurtful, nevertheless seeks dialogue with any German willing to engage in it? Does he as a Jew exploit a kind of *Narrenfreiheit* or jester's license, that he enjoys in Germany and Austria, which inhibits criticism and guarantees success? Is he then the alibi-Jew or, as Konrad Paul Liessmann suggests, the conciliatory artist (*der Versöhnungskünstler*) the Germans are naturally so ready to embrace?[11]

Tabori himself has rigorously resisted being considered a conciliatory Jewish artist. The theatre he conceived of, that Theatre of Embarrassment, intends to debunk, unveil, shock, vex, and hurt, certainly not to suppress, exculpate, propitiate, or mollify. Thomas Rothschild argues rightly that catharsis as Tabori envisioned it rarely took place in his theatre.[12] Furthermore: from the very beginning of his artistic career in Germany and Austria, people failed to discriminate between the man and the work. Voices were often heard seeking to legitimate Tabori's provocative work, especially his treatment of the Holocaust, by recalling his private and familial biography. The personal magnetism of Tabori, bewilderingly well-read, generous, gentle, witty, and humorous, captured the public. "Everybody knows him, and nobody knows much about him," contends critic Elisabeth Loibl,[13] alluding to the fascination Tabori exerts on people. With his traveled and travailed life, he is seen by many as the honorific Jew, a witness of our century (*Zeuge unseres Jahrhunderts*),[14] a vestige of the renowned tradition of European-Jewish culture that was brutally severed with the Holocaust. An autodidact and globetrotter, rejecting a geographical *Heimat* and defying the social constraint of belonging somewhere, Tabori is undoubtedly one of the most conspicuous exponents of the nomadic Jew, the intellectual cosmopolitan for whom homelessness is an existential human condition and a source of inspiration.

For others, like theatre critic Peter von Becker, who played no small part in shaping public opinion to accommodate Tabori's work, Tabori is the only person since Brecht to embody the "ideal union" of playwright, director, theatre-manager, and actor. Beyond all controversy, one thing is absolutely clear to my mind: if the image of the Holocaust is being shaped not on the historian's anvil but in the writer's crucible, as Yosef Hayim Yerushalmi maintains,[15] then Tabori's contribution to the creation of this image in contemporary theatre is decisive.

NOTES

1. A BIOGRAPHICAL INTRODUCTION

1. M. Bardischewski and K. Martens, "George Tabori — Weltwanderer," Süddeutscher Rundfunk, 18 October 1987.
2. Sibylle Fritsch, "It's Not My Cup of Tea," *Die deutsche Bühne* 9 (1977): 12. See also Peter von Becker, "Zeuge des Jahrhunderts," in *George Tabori*, ed. Andrea Welker, p. 248.
3. George Tabori, letter to Viveca Lindfors, 10 April 1979, Stiftung Archiv der Akademie der Künste (SAdK), George-Tabori-Collection, Box 74.
4. So Tabori told me when I interviewed him on 10 February 1997. In his autobiographical essay "Budapest-Hollywood-Berlin" in *Tabori*, ed. Jörg W. Gronius and Wend Kässens, p. 105, he mentions three brothers and four sisters.
5. Personal interview with George Tabori, 10 February 1997.
6. Cornelius Tabori, *My Occult Diary*, pp. 93–95.
7. Paul Tabori found his father's library almost intact in Budapest after the war and brought it to London.
8. Emmanuel Bohn, "Zwischen Identitäten — Liga und Erfahrungsraum," in *Theater des Zorns und der Zärtlichkeit*, ed. Emmanuel Bohn and Siegmar Schröder, p. 58.
9. Andrea Welker, "Das Wort ist eine heilige Waffe und kein Ephebenfurz," in *Tabori*, ed. Welker, p. 301.
10. George Tabori, "Unterammergau oder Die guten Deutschen," in *Unterammergau oder Die guten Deutschen*, p. 34.
11. Paul Tabori, editorial preface to *My Occult Diary*, by Cornelius Tabori, p. vii.
12. George Tabori, letter to Viveca Lindfors, 10 April 1979, SAdK, Box 74.
13. Paul Tabori, *Restless Summer: A Personal Record*, p. 117.
14. André Müller, "Ich habe mein Lachen verloren," *Die Zeit*, 6 May 1994.
15. Georg Hensel, "Aus Katastrophen etwas Hilfreiches machen," *Frankfurter Allgemeine Zeitung*, 19 May 1984.
16. Paul Tabori, *The Anatomy of Exile*, p. 13.
17. Paul Tabori is the editor of *The Pen in Exile: An Anthology* (London, 1954) and a second anthology published in London 1956. Noteworthy also are his biographical sketches of refugees in *They Came to London* (London, 1943) and his semantic and historic study *The Anatomy of Exile* (London, 1972).
18. George Tabori, letter to Paul Tabori, 21 January 1949, SAdK, Box 35.
19. Paul Tabori, letter to George Tabori, 29 January 1953, SAdK, Box 35.
20. Paul Tabori's immense correspondence and his letters as BBC broadcaster are kept at the University of Reading, MS 1089, 1640, and at the BBC Archives Centre.
21. Fritsch, "It's Not My Cup of Tea," p. 12.
22. Paul Tabori, introduction, *Restless Summer*.

23. It is quite impossible to determine the title and date of these works. Characteristically, Tabori has given contradictory information. According to an interview (Müller, "Ich habe") the first novel was "Greta," the story of the miserable experiences of a woman who ultimately commits suicide. In his autobiographical account "Unterammergau" (1981) he suggests that the first novel was "about a German female impersonator who, unsuspected by everyone, was in fact a woman" and that this novel was turned down for being "too dirty." According to an interview he gave on CBS on 21 September 1947, he wrote his first play, "The Goat and the Cabbage," when he was twenty. The plot revolved around a couple and a detective who turned out to be the wife's lover. Tabori says the play was finally turned down only because of the pre-*Anschluß* nervousness. Cf. Reinhard Palm and Ursula Voss, ". . . So viele Ichs, so viele Figuren," in program for *Mein Kampf,* p. 120.

24. George Tabori in a radio interview with Bob Dworkin in the series *Meet the Author,* CBS, 21 September 1947, SAdK, Box 57.

25. Tabori, *Unterammergau,* p. 12.

26. Von Becker, "Zeuge des Jahrhunderts," p. 249.

27. Cf. his account of leaving home in Ursula Höpfner, "Der Begriff der Authentizität aus der Sicht eines Theatermachers: Ein Intensiv-Interview und seine Auswirkung," SAdK, Box 91b.

28. Tabori, "Budapest," p. 108.

29. Dworkin interview, CBS, SAdK, Box 57.

30. See, for example, *Unterammergau,* p. 27; or Dietmar N. Schmidt, "Aus Betroffenheit Kunst: Nathan, Shylock," in *Tabori,* ed. Welker, p. 105.

31. Personal interview, 10 February 1997.

32. George Tabori, "Der alte Mann und was mehr," in *Betrachtungen über das Feigenblatt,* p. 217.

33. George Tabori, letter to Paul Tabori, 21 January 1949, SAdK, Box 35.

34. Tabori, *Restless Summer,* p. 41.

35. Cf. George Tabori's account in his unpublished ms. entitled "For B. H.," written on the occasion of his production of *The Merchant of Venice* in Stockbridge, 1966, SAdK, Box 62.

36. Dworkin interview, CBS, SAdK, Box 57.

37. All three have written about their friendship with Tabori. István Eörsi (born 1931) in *Tage mit Gombrowicz,* pp. 156–159; Péter Nádas (born 1942) in "Eine Liebeserklärung," in *Tabori,* ed. Welker, p. 307; and Péter Esterházy (born 1950) in "Hymne auf den Mann," in *Tabori,* ed. Welker, p. 308.

38. Palm and Voss, ". . . so viele Ichs," p. 119.

39. Thomas Trenkler, "Ich bereite mich auf den Tod vor," *Musik und Theater* 10 (1997): 14–15.

40. Hannah Freund (born 4 May 1919) was the youngest daughter of the businessman Karl Freund and his second wife, Erna, née Levi. Her cousin Karl Freund was an art historian and the curator of the Hesse Landesmuseum. Karl Freund was deported to Auschwitz and murdered there. An account of his life is available in Gisela Bergsträßer, "Karl Freund (1882–1943)," in *Juden als Darmstädter Bürger,* ed. Eckhart G. Franz (Darmstadt: Roether,

1984), pp. 275–278. I am greatly indebted to Professor Eckhart Franz and Professor Friedrich Battenberg of the State Archives of Hesse for their assistance.

41. Tabori, *Unterammergau*, p. 13.

42. Ibid. Tabori writes *eierjeckes*, but it should be *Eierjecke* for the singular.

43. Their real names would have had to appear on the official bulletin board. See Tabori's account "Budapest," p. 114.

44. George Tabori, letter to Paul Tabori, 1 February 1943, SAdK, Box 35.

45. George and Hannah Tabori, letter to Paul and Kate Tabori, 12 November 1942, SAdK, Box 35.

46. Upon the news of the divorce, Paul Tabori wrote the following lines to his brother: "If I say that I am glad, I can only hope that you won't construct it as a criticism of Hannah; for even if I didn't see eye-to-eye with her in many things, I respected the fact that she was your wife and made allowances for many traits in her complex character. So I'll say, frankly and openly, that I *am* glad; that I hope we'll meet you and Viveca when you come to London" (Paul Tabori, letter to George Tabori, 29 January 1953, SAdK, Box 35).

47. George Tabori, letter to Paul Tabori, 8 April 1942, SAdK, Box 35.

48. Tabori, *Unterammergau*, p. 13.

49. George Tabori, letters to Paul Tabori, 1 October 1942, 20 December 1942, 1 February 1943, SAdK, Box 35.

50. See Tabori on this role in "Wiener Blut," in *Betrachtungen*, p. 77, or "Ein Goi bleibt immer ein Goi," in *Unterammergau*, p. 33.

51. George Tabori, letter to Viveca Lindfors, 10 April 1979, SAdK, Box 74.

52. Tabori, *Restless Summer*, p. 46.

53. I commented on the Yiddishisms in his texts and productions, and he said: "I am not aware of it." When I inquired whether he ever read any Hasidic writings, as some people assume, he looked at me wonderingly and mumbled, "No."

54. Herlinde Koelbl, *Jüdische Portraits*, p. 234.

55. The notes he made in Israel, including names of prominent Hebrew writers like Moshe Shamir and Shmuel Yosef Agnon, are in SAdK, Box 81/19. The unpublished ms. is in SAdK, Box 66. See also Tabori's letter to his brother, 30 March 1960, SAdK, Box 35. I also found an untitled ms. (Box 57), a 104-page play which takes place in a kibbutz.

56. George Tabori, letter to Paul Tabori, 12 May 1949, SAdK, Box 35.

57. George Tabori, letter to his children, 11 June 1967, SAdK, Box 72.

58. George Tabori, letter to Mr. Handman, 4 July 1967, SAdK, Box 67.

59. Koelbl, *Portraits*, p. 237.

60. Tabori, *Unterammergau*, p. 26. "I have been thinking a lot about it [Israel] — recently," he told me when we met. It was shortly after the assassination of Yitzhak Rabin, which he mentioned, pointing out that a Jew murdered a Jew. "The Jewish state suffers from all the conflicts of any modern state," he said. "The old hopes one had in the forties are gone."

61. Müller, "Ich habe."

62. See his reply to the letter sent him by the Israelitische Kultusgemeinde in

Vienna on 13 May 1988, SAdK, Box 76/6. He donated 3,000 Austrian Schillings (1 September 1988, SAdK, Box 76/9), but declined membership.

63. George Tabori, letter to Paul Tabori, 30 March 1960, SAdK, Box 35, and letter to Lena, 26 March 1967, SAdK, Box 72.

64. Tabori, "Budapest," p. 114.

65. There are handwritten notes for the play "The Hush Hush," SAdK, Box 56, in which the European idealist Kalman joins British Intelligence during the war.

66. *Beneath the Stone the Scorpion* was published by T. V. Boardman & Co. in 1945. Tabori mentions it, under an earlier title, "Suede Shoes," in a letter to Paul, 1 February 1943. For a discussion of this novel and the others, see Peter Münder, "Die Dummheit aller Dämonologien," in *Tabori*, ed. Gronius and Kässens, pp. 67–77; Jan Strümpel, "Flucht vor der Erinnerungen: George Taboris Romane," in *Text + Kritik* 133 (January 1997): 28–36. Among the English and American reviews of this novel are Harold Brighouse, *Manchester Guardian*, 16 March 1945; N. L. Rothman, *Saturday Review of Literature*, 18 August 1945; anon., *New Yorker*, 18 August 1945; Iris Barry, *Weekly Book Review*, 26 August 1945; R. J. Bender, *Book Week*, 26 August 1945; Kenneth Fearing, *New York Times*, 26 August 1945; and Orville Prescott, *Yale Review*, Autumn 1945. On the German translation entitled *Das Opfer* (1996), Peter Demetz wrote an illuminating review, "Boulevard Balkan," *Frankfurter Allgemeine Zeitung*, 24 May 1997.

67. George Tabori, letter to Paul Tabori, 1 February 1943, SAdK, Box 35.

68. See, for instance, "Budapest," in *Tabori*, ed. Gronius and Kässens, p. 116; and the cover to the 1996 German edition.

69. *Companions of the Left Hand* was published by T. V. Boardman & Co. in 1946. It appeared as volume 1210 in the series Armed Services Editions, designed to provide American soldiers overseas with interesting reading material. Among the English and American reviews are H. L. Faussett, *Manchester Guardian*, 29 March 1946; anon., *Kirkus*, 15 April 1946; G. D. McDonald, *Library Journal*, 15 June 1946; Sterling North, *New York Post*, 27 June 1946; Iris Barry, *Weekly Book Review*, 30 June 1946; R. G. Davis, *New York Times*, 30 June 1946; Merle Miller, *Saturday Review of Literature*, 27 July 1946; and John Farrelly, *New Republic*, 29 July 1946.

70. George Tabori, letter to Paul Tabori, 21 January 1949, SAdK, Box 35.

71. *Original Sin* was published by T. V. Boardman & Co. in 1947. For the English and American reception, see the following reviews: H. W. Hart, *Library Journal*, 1 June 1947; Charles Marriott, *Manchester Guardian*, 13 June 1947; anon., *New Yorker*, 14 June 1947; Donald Barr, *New York Times*, 15 June 1947; and Virgilia Peterson, *New York Herald Tribune Book Review*, 13 July 1947. Among the German reviews upon the publication of *Ein guter Mord* (1992), see Roland H. Wiegenstein, "Die Bekenntnisse des Tristan Manasse, keiner schönen Seele," *Süddeutsche Zeitung*, 16/17 May 1992; Reinhold Renger, "Stille Tage in Kairo," *Deutsches Allgemeines Sonntagsblatt*, 12 June 1992; Michael Merschmeier, "Wie wirklich ist die Wirklichkeit?" *Frankfurter Rundschau*,

4 July 1992; and Claus-Ulrich Bielefeld, "Sein Engel, sein Dummerchen," *Frankfurter Allgemeine Zeitung*, 31 July 1992.

72. Peter Zadek, "Herr Manasse findet eine Leiche," *Die Welt*, 9 April 1992.

73. George Tabori, *Original Sin*, p. 117. Again, Tabori was critical of the final product: "'Original Sin' was written with a vacuumcleaner, a wooden clinical case," he wrote to Paul on 21 January 1949.

74. George Tabori, letter to Paul Tabori, 1 February 1943, SAdK, Box 35.

75. Ibid. George reports in another letter to Paul (9 June 1949) that the novel was sold to Appleton Century for $1,500 advance payment. Peter Höyng quotes the American journal *Variety*, reporting that "Metro" paid Tabori $75,000 "for a short story, 'Basra,' which he is to develop into a novel." See Peter Höyng, "Car, radio, blonde wife, good address, job with big business: Taboris Jahre in den Vereinigten Staaten," in *Text + Kritik* 133 (January 1997): 20.

76. The handwritten ms. of "Eye for Eye," "an adventure" written in 1956, is in SAdK, Box 53. Among the manuscripts and handwritten prose pieces in this box are a novel entitled "Quarantine" and the prose works "Fuga" and "Bravado."

77. *The Caravan Passes*, dedicated to his first wife, Hannah, was published by T. V. Boardman & Co. in 1951. It appeared in German under the title *Tod in Port Aarif* in 1994. For the English and American reception, see anon., *Kirkus*, 1 January 1951; Hugh McGovern, *New York Times*, 11 March 1951; Virgilia Peterson, *New York Herald Tribune Book Review*, 11 March 1951; Vance Bour-jaily, *Saturday Review of Literature*, 17 March 1951; and anon., *San Francisco Chronicle*, 13 May 1951. Among German reviews of the 1994 German trans-lation, see Martin Krumbholz, "Prekäre Operationen," *Süddeutsche Zeitung*, 21–23 May 1994; Robert Weichinger, "Soso, die ganze Welt?," *Die Presse*, 21 May 1994; and Ulrich Weinzierl, "Die Karawane zieht weiter," *Frankfurter Allgemeine Zeitung*, 10 August 1994.

78. Tabori, "Budapest," pp. 116 and 118. For Tabori's years in the United States, see also Peter Höyng's above-mentioned article.

79. Peter von Becker, "Zeuge," in *Tabori*, ed. Welker, p. 250.

80. Michael Töteberg, "Auf dem Markt der schönen Lügen: Eine verleugnete Karriere: der Drehbuchautor Tabori," in *Text + Kritik* 133 (January 1997): 37–50.

81. George Tabori, letter to Paul Tabori, 9 June 1949, SAdK, Box 35.

82. Thomas Trenkler, "Ich bereite," p. 14; and von Becker, "Zeuge," in *Tabori*, ed. Welker, p. 252.

83. Franz Wille, "Jeder wirkliche Humor," in *Tabori*, ed. Gronius and Kässens, p. 55.

84. George Tabori's *The Journey* was published in 1958 by Bantam (New York) and by Transworld (London).

85. Tabori directed Strindberg's *The Stronger* and *Miss Julie* as a double bill at the Phoenix Theatre, New York, in 1958.

86. See David Caute, *Joseph Losey: A Revenge on Life*, p. 216. The filmscript of

"Black Comedy" and a number of letters relating to it are in SAdK, Box 48. There are innumerable letters from and to Losey among the Tabori papers (Boxes 65, 67, and 74).

87. See Bohn, *Theater des Zorns*, p. 57. *Insomnia* was first produced as a radio-play (RIAS Berlin and Bayerischer Rundfunk) in 1986. It was shown on German television (produced by Sender Freies Berlin) in 1974.

88. The film was awarded the prize of the City of Mannheim at the International Filmweek in 1981. For a review, see Wetzel Kraft, "Ein Indianer auf dem deutschen Christkindl Markt," *Frankfurter Allgemeine Zeitung*, 15 October 1981. See also Wille, "Jeder wirkliche Humor," p. 64.

89. Von Becker, "Zeuge," p. 251. Tabori wrote of his encounter with Marlene Dietrich in "Where Have All the Flowers Gone?" *Theater Heute* 6 (1992): 12.

90. Höyng, "Cars," in *Text + Kritik*, 133 (January 1997): 22.

91. Thomas Mann, *Tagebücher 1946–1948*, ed. Inge Jens, entries of 24 February 1948, 6 April 1948, 5 May 1948, 31 May 1948, and 27 August 1948.

92. Tabori, *Unterammergau*, pp. 15–16.

93. Von Becker, "Zeuge," p. 251.

94. George Tabori, letter to Paul Tabori, 12 May 1949, SAdK, Box 35.

95. Martin Kagel, "Brecht Files: Conversation with George Tabori," in *The Brecht Yearbook, Theater der Zeit* 23 (1997): 71.

96. According to an interview with Jörn Rowehr, "Nach der Illusion der Unsterblichkeit," *Berliner Zeitung*, 15/16 August 1998.

97. Tabori, *Unterammergau*, p. 13.

98. Ibid., p. 14. See also Tabori's account of his acquaintance with Brecht in *Frankfurter Allgemeine Zeitung* (Bilder und Zeiten), 7 February 1998.

99. Kagel, "Brecht Files," p. 71.

100. Kässens and Gronius, "George Tabori," in *Theatermacher*, p. 165.

101. A letter from Elisabeth Hauptmann, who assisted Brecht (14 March 1955, SAdK, Box 65), testifies to Brecht's respect for Tabori: "Dear Mr. Losey, please would you tell your friend, George Tabori, that Brecht likes the idea of him translating *Puntila*, and that he may go ahead. We know what a gifted writer he is."

102. Viveca Lindfors, *Viveka . . . Viveca*, pp. 23 and 237–238.

103. Kässens and Gronius, *Theatermacher*, p. 163.

104. Lindfors, *Viveka*, pp. 238–239.

105. George Tabori, "Die letzte der großen alten Huren," in *Betrachtungen*, pp. 181–184.

106. Lindfors, *Viveka*, p. 237.

107. Kagel, "Brecht Files," p. 70. Also P. Höyng, "George Tabori's *Brecht on Brecht* Production: A Success Story," in *The Brecht Yearbook* (1999): 97–107.

108. Kagel, "Brecht Files," p. 70.

109. The earliest version dates back to June 1985 (SAdK, Box 23). A second version bears the date July 1988 (Box 20), and there are two more versions of 1987 and 1990 (Box 27). See also "The Brecht File: A Film Treatment," in Box 79.

110. Maria Sommer, "Der kleine Klick," in *Tabori*, ed. Welker, p. 226.

111. Lindfors, *Viveka*, pp. 173–174.

112. Ibid., p. 202.

113. George Tabori, letter to Paul Tabori, 21 August, no year, SAdK, Box 35.

114. Lindfors, *Viveka*, p. 28.

115. The book came out in the United States in 1981, following its publication in Sweden (1978). Tabori read a draft and commented in a letter, 10 April 1979, SAdK, Box 74.

116. His invitation is dated 2 March 1988, SAdK, Box 76/8; her reply bears no precise date, same box.

117. George Tabori, letter to Viveca Lindfors, 10 April 1974.

118. Tabori, *Betrachtungen*, p. 101.

119. George Tabori, "Don im Himmel," in *Betrachtungen*, pp. 260–272.

120. Eörsi, *Tage mit Gombrowicz*, p. 158.

121. Ursula Grützmacher-Tabori, letter to George Tabori, 14 April 1985, SAdK, Box 73.

122. See the letter from Grützmacher's lawyer about translation rights and divorce dated 2 May 1986, SAdK, Box 73. See also the letter from Hanser Verlag, 11 March 1986, SAdK, Box 73, in which she insists that only her translation of *Mein Kampf* should be used. Otherwise, she would prevent the publication of the text.

123. George Tabori, "Lächelndes Rätsel," *Theater Heute* (1995): 123. Also Tabori's fictionalized autobiographical account "Berliner Betten," in *Betrachtungen*, p. 259. In an interview with *Der Spiegel* (23 [1992]: 271) he speaks of his German wives: "The first [Hannah], a Jewess, was the most German, the second [Uschi I] the cleverest, the third [Uschi II] the most loving." Jörg Höpfner, Uschi II's brother, was one of the members of the Theaterlabor who accompanied Tabori to Munich when it disbanded. He was the photographer of the group and also acted as director-assistant and stage-manager. He was killed in a road accident in June 1980. Tabori wrote "Tod am Nachmittag" (Death in the Afternoon), in *Betrachtungen*, pp. 179–198, in his memory.

124. Anon., "New Play in Manhattan," *Time*, 31 March 1952; Walter F. Kerr, "Flight into Egypt," *New York Herald Tribune*, 19 March 1952; Other write-ups include Wolcott Gibbs, "Flight into Nowhere," *New Yorker*, 29 March 1952; Manfred George, "Flucht nach Ägypten als europäisches Schicksal," *Aufbau*, 28 March 1952; and H. B. Kranz, "Flucht in die neue Welt," *Die Welt*, 4 April 1952.

125. Lindfors, *Viveka*, p. 189.

126. George Tabori, letter to Paul Tabori, 21 August, no year, SAdK, Box 35. Cf. also Palm and Voss, ". . . So viele Ichs," p. 122.

127. Tabori, *Unterammergau*, p. 14.

128. Von Becker, "Zeuge," p. 252.

129. Cf. *New York Herald Tribune*, 1 May 1952.

130. Anon., "New Play in Manhattan," *Time*, February 1953. See also Wolcott Gibbs, "The Emperor's Clothes," *New Yorker*, 21 February 1953.

131. Ursula Höpfner, "Der Begriff der Authentizität aus der Sicht eines Theatermachers," p. 39.

132. George Tabori, letter to Paul Tabori, 21 January 1949. For more about Paul's love for and idealization of his father, see *Restless Summer*. Paul suffered from gnawing guilt feelings. "I tried to put him into my books and stories, hoping to preserve his image in a dozen of different ways, under a dozen of different names" (pp. 34–35). That was even before the news of Cornelius Tabori's demise in Auschwitz.

133. Lindfors, *Viveka*, p. 214.

134. Personal interview, 10 February 1997. Tabori has often mentioned his acquaintance with Monroe. He first met her through a friend with whom he shared a flat in Brentwood in Los Angeles. He and Monroe spoke about *The Brothers Karamazov*; she said she would like to play Gruschenka's part. Tabori did not realize who the blonde beauty was until she had gone. The next time they met, in New York, she was Arthur Miller's wife. "It was a festive dinner, and she didn't quite fit in." "I'd like to thank you," she said to Tabori. "What for?" "For Gruschenka," she said. See Thomas Trenkler, "Ich bereite mich," *Musik und Theater* 10 (1997): 14. Also von Becker, "Zeuge," p. 253.

135. Lindfors, *Viveka*, p. 217.

136. George Tabori, "Lieber Lee," in *Betrachtungen*, pp. 185–191.

137. Tabori wrote the foreword to the German translation, *Traum der Leidenschaft* (Munich, 1988). It is included in *Betrachtungen*, pp. 192–199. There are letters to and from Strasberg in SAdK, Box 65. One of the letters is from Paula Strasberg to Tabori (no date): "Dear George, after years of talking about this, Lee finally said 'Yes' to four talks on 'Director and Direction in the World Theatre.' The talks start on Thursday, January 9, 1964 . . . at the Actors Studio."

138. George Tabori, letter to Paul Tabori, 21 August, no year.

139. They performed Brecht's *Señora Carrar's Rifles* and Beckett's *Waiting for Godot*. Tabori recounts this cultural-ethnic experience in his conversation with Rolf Michaelis entitled "Ein begeisterungsfähiger Skeptiker," *Theater Heute* 6 (1976): 29–33.

140. They performed *Señora Carrar's Rifles*, Terence McNally's *Cuba Sí*, and the dramatic collage *Three Boards and a Passion*. Lindfors, *Viveka*, p. 247.

141. George Tabori, "Warten auf Beckett," in *Betrachtungen*, p. 59.

142. See, for example, "George Tabori's Brouhaha," in the *Times* (London), 29 August 1958. Various versions of this postcolonialist play and Tabori's correspondence with Peter Hall are in SAdK, Boxes 6, 58, 59.

143. George Tabori, letter to Helene Weigel, 22 September 1967, SAdK, Box 67.

144. James Davis, "Conflict Theme of Niggerlovers," no place, no date, SAdK, Box 81/24. Jonathan Randal maintains that the double bill is "an illiberal play about liberals" and concludes that "both plays, imitative and pompous, suggest that the more liberal a man sounds, the more likely he is to be a fraud" (*New York Times*, 15 October 1967). Likewise harsh is Alfred Watts Jr. in the *New York Post*, 2 October 1967: "Since Mr. Tabori's concoction lacks wit, humor, taste, satirical force or effective pertinence, it seemed to me an evening of steady and complete disaster." Following a production in Paris

(24 January 1973) there was a review by Louis Dandrel, "Une réalité en blanc et noir," *Le Monde,* 25 January 1973.

145. Lindfors, *Viveka,* pp. 255 and 28.

146. George Tabori, "Protest einer ewig jungen Sau," *Die Zeit,* 10 January 1992. See also Tabori's unpublished ms. "Who Killed Niki?" SAdK, Box 56.

147. Lindfors, *Viveka,* p. 27.

148. Welker, "Das Wort ist eine heilige Waffe," in *Tabori,* p. 304.

149. Gundula Ohngemach, "Gespräch mit Stanley Walden," in *George Tabori,* p. 38. For American reviews of *Pinkville,* see Clive Barnes, "Pinkville Rages at War's Brutality," *New York Times,* 18 March 1971; Arthur Sainer, "'It Was No Big Deal' Revisited," *Village Voice,* 18 March 1971. For the German production (premiered on 19 August 1971), see Karena Niehoff, "Berlin: Eine Stadt, die rosa ist?" *Süddeutsche Zeitung,* 18 August 1971; Hans Fröhlich, "My Lai und die Ästhetik," *Stuttgarter Nachrichten,* 26 August 1971; Kurt Lothar Tank, "Massaker-Messe für My Lai," *Deutsches Allgemeines Sonntagsblatt,* 5 September 1971; Ernst Wendt, "Kriegs-Theater," *Theater Heute* 10 (1971): 14.

150. Lindfors, *Viveka,* p. 260.

151. Tabori was in charge of "staging" their wedding ceremony (ms., SAdK, Box 69) and some twenty-five years later was the guest of honor at the wedding of their daughter, his grandchild. He wrote about it in "Rauchverbot im Paradies," *Die Woche,* 20 September 1996.

152. Lindfors, *Viveka,* p. 260. See also Tabori's letter to Paul, 9 June 1949, SAdK, Box 35.

153. Welker, *Tabori,* pp. 301–302.

154. George Tabori, letter to Lindfors, 10 April 1979.

155. Gundula Ohngemach, *George Tabori,* pp. 134–135. See also George Tabori, "Vom Wesen des Glücks," in *Tabori,* ed. Welker, pp. 79–80; and Sibylle Fritsch, "Nur im Gefühl liegt die Wahrheit," *Psychologie Heute* 2 (1994): 40–42.

156. Bardischewsky and Martens, "Weltwanderer."

157. Tabori, "Budapest," p. 122. See also George Tabori, "Dieses peinliche Wort: Liebe," in *Tabori,* ed. Welker, p. 319; and Tabori, "Berliner Betten," in *Betrachtungen,* pp. 242 and 244.

158. For reviews of the production, see, among others, Christoph Müller, "Hoppla, wir leben," *Der Tagesspiegel,* 10 May 1972; anon., "Neurosen auf dem Trampolin," *Der Spiegel,* 15 May 1972; Felix Fiat, "Clowns gegen Tabus," *Osnabrücker Zeitung,* 15 May 1972; Hermann Dannecker, "Clowns probten den Zerfall," *Trierische Landeszeitung,* 16 May 1972; Wolfgang A. Peters, "Artisten auf dem Bettcouch," *Frankfurter Allgemeine Zeitung,* 26 May 1972; Karena Niehoff, "Vaterland und Freud," *Süddeutsche Zeitung,* 30 May 1972; Christoph Müller, "Eklektische Mixtur," *Theater Heute* 7 (1972): 13–14.

159. Program for *Kohlhaas,* Schauspiel Bonn, 1972. See also "Wie ein Stadttheater-Ensemble mit der Regel bricht," *Theater Heute* (1974): 70–71.

160. For reviews of Eörsi's *Das Verhör,* see Günther Grack, "Trübe Geschichte," *Der Tagesspiegel,* 7 October 1984; Friedrich Luft, "Spielfeld der absoluten

Macht und Menschenqual," *Berliner Morgenpost*, 7 October 1984; Wend Kässens, "Im Brennglas Schärfe und Hitze," *Basler Zeitung*, 9 October 1984; Benjamin Henrichs, "Weihnachten in der Hölle," *Die Zeit*, 12 October 1984; Roland H. Wiegenstein, "Szenen aus dem Gefängnis," *Frankfurter Rundschau*, 23 October 1984; and Henning Rischbieter, "Eörsis Verhör," *Theater Heute* 11 (1984): 34.

161. For reviews of Achternbusch's *Mein Herbert*, see Beate Kayser, "Mein Körper ist ein tapferer Bursche," *Die Tageszeitung*, 22 April 1985; Charlotte Nennecke, "Mutter und Sohn — heillos verstrickt," *Süddeutsche Zeitung*, 25 April 1985; Rolf May, "Iphigenie in Gauting," *Die Tageszeitung*, 27 April 1985; Michael Skasa, "Mein lieber Herbert," *Süddeutsche Zeitung*, 27 April 1985; Renate Schostak, "Altötting triumphiert über Athen," *Frankfurter Allgemeine Zeitung*, 4 May 1985; and Peter von Becker, "Mein Herbert," *Theater Heute* 7 (1985): 26–27.

162. For reviews of *Der Voyeur* (premiered at the Berliner Theatertreffen in Berlin, 15 May 1982), see among others Wilhelm Roth, "Theatralisch faszinierend ein depremierendes Bild gezeichnet," *Volksblatt Berlin*, 18 May 1982; Ingvelde Geleng, "Jüdischer Ödipus unter Schwarzen," *Husumer Nachrichten*, 19 May 1982; Karena Niehoff, "Ungeliebter Menschenfreund," *Der Tagesspiegel*, 20 May 1982; Andreas Roßmann, "Ein Schluß ohne Wirkung," *Hannoversche Allgemeine*, 21 May 1982; Gerhard Stadelmaier, "Wer liebt schon Neger?" *Stuttgarter Zeitung*, 21 May 1982; S. W., "Wollust mit moralischem Anspruch," *Frankfurter Allgemeine Zeitung*, 26 May 1982; Roland H. Wiegenstein, "Der Voyeur," *Frankfurter Rundschau*, 27 May 1982; Eva-Elisabeth Fischer, "Tabori-Glibber," *Süddeutsche Zeitung*, 2 June 1982; and Michael Stone, "Furcht und Elend in New York," *Frankfurter Neue Presse*, 7 June 1982.

Director John Boorman made a film of it, entitled *The Last Leo*, with Marcello Mastroianni, but Tabori distanced himself from the production and withdrew his name. Jan Strümpel discusses the play in "Einstein, Auschwitz, gefüllte Fisch: Jüdische Identität in George Taboris *Voyeur* und *Weisman und Rotgesicht*," in *Verkörperte Geschichtsentwürfe*, ed. Höyng, pp. 15–30.

163. Tabori's *Peepshow* premiered at the Schauspielhaus Bochum on 6 April 1984. For reviews, see Ingrid Seidenfaden, "Frivole Bilder vom Leben und Lieben," *Abendzeitung*, 9 April 1984; C. Bernd Sucher, "Besser spät als nie," *Süddeutsche Zeitung*, 9 April 1984; Rainer Nolden, "Willie oder: Nicht geboren zu sein ist das Beste," *Die Welt*, 9 April 1984; Werner Schulze-Reimpell, "Willies Zögern vor der Welt," *Hannoversche Allgemeine*, 10 April 1984; anon., "Sterbe wohl, Willie," *Der Spiegel*, 16 April 1984; Ulrich Schreiber, "Schwarzgrimmen als Existenzialproblem," *Frankfurter Rundschau*, 17 April 1984; Michael Stone, "Rückblick eines 70 Jährigen," *Der Spiegel*, 26 May 1984; Peter von Becker, "George Taboris Peepshow," *Theater Heute* 5 (1984): 2–3; and Gabriela Pagener, "Peepshow grotesk verfremdet," *Allgemeine jüdische Wochenzeitung*, 15 June 1984. See the interview with Tabori, "Wo liegen auf der Bühne die Grenzen des unbürgerlichen Erotischen?" *Guckloch* (May 1984).

164. George Tabori, "Wir sind keine Götter: Brief an die Schauspieler des *Totenfloß*," in *Betrachtungen*, pp. 203–206.

165. Responsible for the impressive set was Andreas Szalla, who often worked with Tabori (*Das Buch mit sieben Siegeln*, 1987; *Schuldig geboren*, 1987; *Der Tod dankt ab*, 1987; *Verliebte und Verrückte*, 1989, and others). See Szalla's letter to Tabori in *Tabori*, ed. Welker, p. 176.

166. Armin Eichholz, "Männer mit Charakter," *Die Welt*, 2 December 1986. For other reviews, see Joachim Kaiser, "Schrecklich dynamisches Totenfloß," *Frankfurter Rundschau*, 1 December 1986; Rolf May, "Katastrophe, ein Kinderspiel," *Abendzeitung*, 1 December 1986; Gerhard Stadelmaier, "Kinds- und Clownsköpfe," *Stuttgarter Zeitung*, 2 December 1986; Barbara Schmitz-Burckhardt, "Ein Clownspiel," *Frankfurter Rundschau*, 5 December 1986; Wolfgang Müller-Funk, "Meisterstück oder taube Nuß?" *Die Presse*, 6 December 1986; Renate Schostak, "Leben beim Sterben," *Frankfurter Allgemeine Zeitung*, 6 December 1986; Sigrid Löffler, "Von Zombies und Affen," *Profil*, 9 December 1986, pp. 72–74; and Michael Merschmeier, "Todesreigen auf dem großen Fluß," *Theater Heute* 1 (1987): 26.

167. Günther Hoffmann, "Baader-Meinhof, das ist schon Legende," *Die Zeit*, 7 February 1986.

168. Hoffmann, "Baader." See, among others, Thomas Wolgast, "Erst fehlten die Filmrollen, dann kamen die Schläger," *Stuttgarter Nachrichten*, 1 February 1986; Werner Burkhardt, "Alles kreiste," *Süddeutsche Zeitung*, 20 February 1986; Klaus Wagner, "Die Umstände waren tödlich," *Frankfurter Rundschau*, 24 February 1986; and Harald Mueller, "Westdeutscher Abend," *Theater Heute* 3 (1986): 3–5.

169. Ulrich Schreiber, "Das Land, in dem da da ist," *Stuttgarter Nachrichten*, 9 June 1983. The play was premiered at the workshop studio of the Schauspielhaus in Cologne. Interestingly, it was one of the early productions of the Living Theatre in the early 1960s.

170. Stanley Walden, "Die Musik für Doktor Faustus Lichterloh," in *Tabori*, ed. Welker, p. 162.

171. George Tabori, "Die Stein," in *Tabori*, ed. Welker, pp. 160–161. Tabori often mentions Stein, as in "Staats-Theater," in *Betrachtungen*, p. 118; "Warten auf Beckett," in *Betrachtungen*, pp. 51 and 58; "Traum der Leidenschaft," in *Betrachtungen*, p. 192.

172. Tabori, "Stein." For reviews, see Rainer Hauptmann, *Kölner Stadt Anzeiger*, 6 June 1983; Jochen Schmidt, *Frankfurter Allgemeine Zeitung*, 6 June 1983; Andreas Roßmann, *Nürnberger Nachrichten*, 8 June 1983; and Andrzej Wirth, "Faustus — Lichtgestalt?" *Theater Heute* 8 (1983): 30–31.

173. George Tabori in an interview with Matthias Weidemann, *Bild*, 24 November 1994. See also his interview with *Die Bühne* (May 1986): 26.

174. Markus Deggerich, "Triumph auf der Bühne," *Stuttgarter Nachrichten*, 28 November 1994; and Hartmut Regitz, "Dicke Frauen, nackt," *Stuttgarter Nachrichten*, 2 February 1995.

175. Among Tabori's recent productions are also an evening including Béla Bar-

tok's *Bluebeard's Castle* and Arnold Schönberg's monodrama *Erwartung* (Holland, 1997), and *The Naked Michelangelo*, based on a late work of Dmitry Shostakovich, which Tabori directed with dancer Ismael Ivo at the Schaubühne in Berlin (premiere 19 June 1998). For reviews, see Joachim Kronsbein, "An der Frisur gefummelt," *Der Spiegel* 26 (1998), p. 172; Stephan Mösch, "Feixen mit den letzten Dingen," *Frankfurter Allgemeine Zeitung*, 20 June 1998; and Hartmut Regitz, "Ein Übervater im schwarzen Rock," *Stuttgarter Nachrichten*, 22 June 1998. In August 1998 Tabori directed a production of Wolfgang Amadeus Mozart's *The Magic Flute* in a circus tent in Berlin.

176. For reviews, see among others Walter Gürtelschmied, "Theater mit blutigem Ernst zum Ausprobieren," *Unhabhängige Tageszeitung* (Vienna), 8 May 1986; Ulrich Weinzierl, "Leben als Generalprobe," *Frankfurter Allgemeine Zeitung*, 9 May 1986; Paul Kruntorad, "Eine Opernprobe," *Frankfurter Rundschau*, 15 May 1986; Otto F. Beer, "Bajazzo, zum Quadrat," *Süddeutsche Zeitung*, 31 May 1986; Imre Fabian, "Es wird ernst mit dem Ernst," *Opern Welt*, July 1986; and John Higgins, "Festival Time in Austria," *Times* (London), 9 July 1986.

177. Kurt Honolka, "Der Sieg des Auges über das Ohr," *Stuttgarter Nachrichten*, 30 July 1987.

178. Cf. Sigrid Löffler, "Tabori — eine Erledigung," *Profil*, 10 August 1987, p. 8.

179. Anon., "Zerstörung siegt über Lebenstrieb," *Abendzeitung*, 25/26 July 1987.

180. For reviews of the production and accounts of the scandal, see Marianne Reißinger, "Sex, Puppen und das Jesuskind," *Abendzeitung*, 30 July 1987; Lothar Sträter, "Musikalische Vision von Grauen und Hoffnung," *Mannheimer Morgen*, 31 July 1987; Elisabeth Sparrer, "Die Kirche wettert gegen George-Tabori-Regie," *Abendzeitung*, 31 July 1987; Peter Cosse, "Gewinsel," *Frankfurter Rundschau*, 1 August 1987; Sigrid Löffler, "Auf den Knigge gekommen," *Profil*, 3 August 1987, pp. 8–9; Löffler, "Tabori — eine Erledigung," pp. 8–9; Peter von Becker, "Skandal in Salzburg," *Theater Heute* 9 (1987): 8–12. See also the documentation in Welker, *Tabori*, pp. 174–184.

181. Bruno Maderna's *Satyricon*, after Gaius Petronius, was a joint production of the International Summer Academy of the Mozarteum, the Opera House Leipzig, and the Salzburg Festival. It premiered on 16 August 1991. For reviews, see, among others, Winfried Wild, "Sitten wie im alten Rom," *Schwäbische Zeitung*, n.d.; Pierre Petit, "Musique sans feuille de vigne," *Le Figaro*, 19 August 1991; and T. G., "Tödliche Antike," *Die Furche*, 22 August 1991.

182. "Dicke Frauen, nackt," *Stuttgarter Nachrichten*, 2 February 1995. The premiere took place on 26 November 1994 in Leipzig. For reviews, see among others Wolfgang Schreiber, *Süddeutsche Zeitung*, 28 November 1994; Georg-Friedrich Kühn, *Frankfurter Rundschau*, 28 November 1994; Karl-Heinz Löbner, *Freie Presse*, 28 November 1994; and Wolfgang Sander, *Frankfurter Allgemeine Zeitung*, 28 November 1994.

183. For reviews, see among others Ingvelde Geleng, "Der Pierrot ist jetzt sehr

müde," *Nürnberger Zeitung,* 3 October 1987; Hellmut Koischenreuther, "Kaiser, Tod und Pest," *Tagesspiegel,* 3 October 1987; Stefan Koch, "Der Tod steigt aus," *Mannheimer Morgen,* 5 October 1987; Gerhard Kramer, "Poetische Todes-Parabel," *Die Presse,* 9 October 1987; Gerhard R. Koch, "Im Angesicht des Todes," *Frankfurter Allgemeine Zeitung,* 10 October 1987; Georg-Friedrich Kühn, "Die Oper aus Theresienstadt," *Rheinische Post,* 14 October 1987; and Rudolph Ganz, "Die Wohlwelt des Sterbens," *Frankfurter Rundschau,* 15 October 1987. The production was shown in the framework of the Bloomsbury Festival at the Bloomsbury Theatre in London, 10–12 May 1988. It received excellent reviews. See Richard Fairman, "Der Kaiser von Atlantis," *Financial Times,* 11 May 1988; Stephen Pettitt, "Chilling Score," *Times,* 11 May 1988; Geoffrey Norris, "Dark Music of the Death Camps," *Daily Telegraph,* 13 May 1988; Michael John White, "Art Out of Hell," *Independent,* 13 May 1988; David Cairns, "Why Opera Must Give Music the Last Word," *Sunday Times,* 15 May 1988; and Rodney Milnes, "Der Kaiser von Atlantis," *Opera* (July 1988).

184. George Tabori, "Verliebte und Verrückte," in *Betrachtungen,* p. 84. For Tabori and his Kreis, see Gotthard Böhm, "Rattenfänger von Alsergrund," *Bühne* 4 (1987): 6–10; Thomas Thieringer, "Ein Theaterlabor in der Porzellangasse," *Süddeutsche Zeitung,* 28 April 1987; Sibylle Fritsch, "George für Alle," *Profil,* 11 May 1987, pp. 79–80; and Sibylle Fritsch, "Konzept Katharsis," *Profil,* 18 May 1987, pp. 76–77.

185. Tabori's production of Thomas Brasch's *Frauen, Krieg, Lustspiel* premiered at the Kreis on 10 May 1988. For reviews, see among others Karin Kathrein, "Blutige Gefechte um Hredlickas Pferd," *Die Welt,* 13 May 1988; C. Bernd Sucher, "Chaos mit Variationen," *Süddeutsche Zeitung,* 13 May 1988; Ingrid Seidenfaden, "Die Wut in weißen Wäsche," *Abendzeitung,* 14 May 1988; Sibylle Fritsch, "Theater, Troja, Tod," *Profil,* 16 May 1988, pp. 99–100; René Odenthal, "Krieg und Spiele," *Die Tageszeitung,* 17 May 1988; Rolf Michaelis, "Hilfe, ich lebe!" *Die Zeit,* 20 May 1988; Sigrid Löffler, "Klaras Kopfkriegskunst," *Theater Heute* 7 (1988): 12–14; "Kopflastige Fingerübungen," *Neue Zürcher Zeitung,* 18 August 1988; and Peter Kümmel, "Ein Bär rüttelt am Gerüst," *Stuttgarter Nachrichten,* 22 August 1988. Tabori participated in Brasch's film entitled *Der Passagier* (The Passenger) in 1988.

186. The play, which he wrote together with Ursula Voss, premiered in Graz on 25 October 1988, before it was shown at the Kreis. Tabori incorporated a brief episode about Masada in his "Samspeak," in *Betrachtungen,* p. 65. For reviews, see among others Paul Kruntorad, "Freitod der Verlorenen," *Nürnberger Nachrichten,* 27 October 1988; Hansjörg Spies, "Sterben oder Überleben," *Wiener Zeitung,* 28 October 1988; cbg. "Jüdisches Schicksal," *Neue Zürcher Zeitung,* 1 November 1988; Hilde Haider-Pregler, "Überzeitliches Bedenktheater," *Wiener Zeitung,* 9 November 1988; Wolfgang Freitag, "Josephus Flavius' Masada im Theater Der Kreis," *Die Presse,* 9 November 1988; Otto F. Beer, "Selbstmord als Waffe," *Süddeutsche Zeitung,* 14 November 1988; Wolfgang Reiter, "Masada — Auschwitz," *Theater* 43 (18 November

1988); and Werner Krause, "Offene Leidensskala," *Bühne* 12 (1988): 38–39. See also Hans-Peter Bayerdörfer, "Celan auf der Bühne," in *Celan Jahrbuch* 3 (1989): 151–166.

187. Cf. Yael Zerubavel, *Recovered Roots: Collective Memory and the Making of Israeli National Tradition* (Chicago: University of Chicago Press, 1993). Also Barry Schwartz, Yael Zerubavel, and Bernice Barnett, "The Recovery of Masada: A Study in Collective Memory," *Sociological Quarterly* 27 (1986): 147–164.

188. The adjacent Actors Studio ceased operating earlier.

189. George Tabori, "Trennungsträume," in *Betrachtungen*, pp. 112–116.

190. "Keine Zeit zu trauern," *Profil*, 23 July 1990, pp. 76–77.

191. A letter Tabori wrote to S. L. (probably theatre critic Sigrid Löffler), 9 October 1988, documents the difficulties he encountered all along. Tabori speaks of the discrepancy between the "local standards" and his own. "As I am not willing to adjust mine, I have to think of my Grandmother, bless her, who always said: 'you shouldn't piss against the whirlwind.'"

192. Gerhard Stadelmaier, "Satan der Weise," *Frankfurter Allgemeine Zeitung*, 16 November 1991. See also Sven Siedenberg, "Lessing hätte nicht applaudiert," *Süddeutsche Zeitung*, 23/24 November 1991; and Tabori's earlier intimations on Lessing's play upon Claus Peymann's production in Bochum (1981), "Ein Goi bleibt immer ein Goi," in *Unterammergau*, pp. 29–35. For reviews of Tabori's *Nathans Tod*, see among others Sibylle Wirsing, "Fegefeuer in Jerusalem," *Der Tagesspiegel*, 16 November 1991; "Die Macht des Bösen," *Neue Zürcher Zeitung*, 19 November 1991; Benjamin Henrichs, "Das Märchen wird verbrannt," *Die Zeit*, 22 November 1991; Armin Eichholz, "Aufklärung auf Whisky-Niveau," *Die Welt*, 26 November 1991; C. Bernd Sucher, "Nun komm', was kommen soll?" *Süddeutsche Zeitung*, 28 November 1991; Marcel Marin, "Bittere Abrechnung mit einer Versöhnungsutopie," *Esslinger Zeitung*, 7/8 December 1991; and Franz Wille, "Nathans Not," *Theater Heute* 12 (1991): 2–3. Barbara Fischer offers an analysis of the production in her article "Bilanz am Sterbebett der Toleranz: George Taboris *Nathans Tod*," in *Verkörperte Geschichtsentwürfe*, ed. Höyng, pp. 197–213. See also Klaus Buhlert, "Keine Prinzipien — Nur Nerven," in *Tabori*, ed. Welker, pp. 288–289; and Gert Heidenreich's poem "Asche und Rampe: Tabori's Nathan," in *Tabori*, ed. Welker, p. 287.

193. George Tabori, "Wiener Blut," in *Betrachtungen*, p. 77; and Sigrid Löffler, "Der Claus ist kein Gentleman," *Profil*, 6 June 1988.

194. Elfriede Jelinek agreed to have her play about the murder of four gypsies in a small Austrian town produced by an Austrian theatre company only with Tabori as director. The play premiered in the Kasino am Schwarzenbergplatz (the smallest stage of the Burg) on 12 April 1997. See "Österreich im Herbst" (interview with Tabori), *News* 37 (1997). For reviews, see Ulrich Weinzierl, "Österreichs Todsünden," *Frankfurter Allgemeine Zeitung*, 22 September 1997; Paul Kruntorad, "Talk Show," 24 September 1997; and Sibylle Fritsch, "Spiel mir das Lied vom Tod," *Illustrierte Neue Welt* 10 (1997): 17.

195. Tabori's *The 25th Hour* was premiered in Holland (Toneelschuur Haarlem, Toneelgroep Centrum-Bellevue) in 1997 under the direction of Eddy Hab-

bema. Earlier, in June 1982, a staged reading of the play in English took place at the L.A. Theatre Works, Los Angeles. It took many more years, however, until the play had its German premiere under the direction of Karin Beier at the Schauspielhaus in Düsseldorf, 20 September 1992. Tabori revised the text and directed it at the Akademietheater in Vienna on 13 February 1994. For reviews, see among others Werner Schulze-Reimpell, "Die Tragödie, der Tod und sein Engel," *Theater Heute* 12 (1992): 34–35; Sigrid Löffler, "Hyänegelächter im Altersheim," *Süddeutsche Zeitung*, 15 February 1994; Wolfgang Reiter, "Schwamm drüber," *Neue Zürcher Zeitung*, 16 February 1994; and Wolfgang Kralicek, "Tumor & Humor," *Theater Heute* 5 (1994): 45–46.

196. *Rosa Luxemburg — Rote Rose für Dich* was premiered at the Volksbühne in Berlin on 29 October 1993. The title is based on Sean O'Casey's *Red Roses for Me*. See SAdK, Box 36.

197. The play was premiered at the Akademietheater on 11 June 1995. Among the reviews, see Sigrid Löffler, "Gevatter Tod," *Süddeutsche Zeitung*, 13 June 1995; Ulrich Weinzierl, "Alle Lust will Aufschub," *Frankfurter Allgemeine Zeitung*, 13 June 1995; Paul Kruntorad, "Monologische Monotonie," *Frankfurter Rundschau*, 14 June 1995; and Franz Wille, "Der Tod in Wien," *Theater Heute* 8 (1995): 16–18.

198. Cf. Tabori, "Don im Himmel," in *Betrachtungen*, pp. 260–272.

199. The play was premiered at the Akademietheater on 10 January 1997. As for its title, Hungarian-born Joel Berger surmises that it is related to the farewell poem "Szeptember végén" by the renowned Hungarian poet Sándor Petőfi (1823–1849). For reviews, see among others Karin Kathrein, "Abschiedselegie beim Bühnentürl," *Kurier*, 12 January 1997; Paul Kruntorad, "Beifall für Taboris makabre Endspiel-Gags," *Welt am Sonntag*, 12 January 1997; Robin Detje, "Alles schon verkraftet," *Berliner Zeitung*, 13 January 1997; Hans Haider, "Ein Adieu mit Prospero auf der Zunge," *Die Presse*, 13 January 1997; Richard Reich, "Drei kurze Stücke zum langen Abschied," *Neue Zürcher Zeitung*, 13 January 1997; C. Bernd Sucher, "Happy Days und vorletzte Abende," *Süddeutsche Zeitung*, 13 January 1997; Ulrich Weinzierl, "Stets von neuem sein letztes Stück," *Frankfurter Allgemeine Zeitung*, 13 January 1997; Wolfgang Kralicek, "Bonjour Petitesse," *Falter*, 15 January 1997; Sibylle Fritsch, "Tabori oder die Kunst des Abschieds," *Illustrierte Neue Welt* 2 (1997); and Franz Wille, "Good-bye, William," *Theater Heute* 3 (1997): 59.

200. The play premiered at the Akademietheater under Tabori's direction on 17 June 1993. For reviews, see among others Richard Reich, "Das Leben ein Trauma," *Neue Zürcher Zeitung*, 19 June 1993; C. Bernd Sucher, "Nimm nichts, reise leicht," *Süddeutsche Zeitung*, 19 June 1993; Gerhard Stadelmaier, "Der Zungenkuß des Judas," *Frankfurter Allgemeine Zeitung*, 19 June 1993; Paul Kruntorad, "Divertimento, versickernd," *Frankfurter Rundschau*, 22 June 1993; Rolf Michaelis, "Schwarze Scherze," *Die Zeit*, 25 June 1993; and Sigrid Löffler, "Die Stunde der Komödianten und Agenten," *Theater Heute* 7 (1993): 35–36.

201. The play is a stage version of an earlier story bearing the same title, which

was published in the collection *Son of a Bitch* (Munich, 1981). Three years earlier, in 1978, the story was produced as a radio-play with the Norddeutscher Rundfunk. Wend Kässens discusses the story in "Die Scherze der Verzweiflung," in *Tabori*, ed. Gronius and Kässens, p. 83. Erwin Leiser writes extensively on *Weisman and Copperface* in "George Tabori und der Baum der Bekenntnis," in *Tabori*, ed. Welker, pp. 214–215. An outstanding and comprehensive discussion of the play is offered by Seth L. Wolitz, "From Parody to Redemption: George Tabori's Weisman und Rotgesicht," in *Verkörperte Geschichtsentwürfe*, ed. Höyng, pp. 151–176. For reviews of the production which premiered at the Akademietheater on 23 March 1990, see among others Paul Kruntorad, "Indianer, Jude, Spastikerin," *Frankfurter Rundschau*, 26 March 1990; Andreas Razumovsky, "Asche auf Vaters Haupt," *Frankfurter Allgemeine Zeitung*, 27 March 1990; Otto F. Best, "George Taboris jüdischer Western," *Süddeutsche Zeitung*, 30 March 1990; Rolf Michaelis, "Rohrkrepierer aus der Wortpistole," *Die Zeit*, 30 March 1990; and Peter von Becker, "Der wüste Western," *Theater Heute* 5 (1990): 9–13.

202. Cf. George Tabori, "Vom Wesen des Glücks," in *Tabori*, ed. Welker, pp. 79–80.

203. For the various drafts, see SAdK, Box 11. The play premiered under Tabori's direction at the Burgtheater on 12 April 1991.

204. Rolf Michaelis, "Schwarze Revue," *Die Zeit*, 19 April 1991. For other reviews, see Otto F. Beer, "Taboris Wege zum Glück," *Süddeutsche Zeitung*, 15 April 1991; Gerhard Stadelmaier, "Furchtbar, herrlich, lieb," *Frankfurter Allgemeine Zeitung*, 15 April 1991; Paul Kruntorad, "Nur noch schlechtes Kabarett," *Frankfurter Rundschau*, 16 April 1991; Sigrid Löffler, "Die Trickkiste ist leer," *Die Weltwoche*, 18 April 1991; Hellmuth Butterweck, "Die Burg wird taborisiert," *Stuttgarter Zeitung*, 25 April 1991; Dieter Bandhauer, "Schade," *Falter* 16 (1991): 9. See also the following articles and interviews with Tabori preceding the premiere: Barbara Petsch, "Der Theater-Guru," *Die Presse*, 11 April 1991; Sibylle Fritsch, "Bibel und Babylon," *Profil*, 18 March 1991, p. 97; and Sibylle Fritsch, "Da streiten sich die Leut' herum," *Profil*, 8 April 1991, pp. 88–92.

205. The play, directed by Tabori, premiered at the Akademietheater on 22 June 1991. For reviews, see among others Gerhard Stadelmaier, "Schinder des Paradieses," *Frankfurter Allgemeine Zeitung*, 24 June 1991; Sibylle Wirsing, "Gott und Mensch in einem Boot," *Der Tagesspiegel*, 25 June 1991; Hans Haider, "Der Vater und der Sohn," *Basler Zeitung*, 28 June 1991; Michael Skasa, "Die Erschöpfung der Welt," *Die Zeit*, 28 June 1991; Paul Kruntorad, "Theatergold," *Frankfurter Rundschau*, 29 June 1991; Wolfgang Reiter, "Ein Atheist von Gottes Gnaden," *Falter* 26 (1991): 22; Sibylle Fritsch, "Vom Scheitern Gottes," *Die deutsche Bühne* 8 (1991): 14–16; Wolfgang Kralicek, "Die göttliche Komödie," *Theater Heute* 8 (1991): 4–6; and Werner Schulze-Reimpell, "Verzweiflung über den Zustand der Welt," *Allgemeine jüdische Wochenzeitung*, 4 June 1992.

206. See ms. bearing the date 22 August 1990, SAdK, Box 1.

207. Christof Nikolaus Schröder speculates on the meaning of names in *The*

Goldberg Variations in his M.A. thesis, "Aber was, wenn Gott auch nicht Gott ist?: Gott im zeitgenössischen Theater: George Taboris *Goldberg-Variationen* und andere Stücke."

208. "George Taboris letzter Wille," *Der Spiegel,* 12 September 1988.

209. Tabori participated as the narrator in Michael Verhoeven's film (based on Tabori's play) *Mutters Courage* (1996). He also participated in the film feature *Nach Ihnen, Herr Mandelbaum: George Tabori in Auschwitz,* which was shown on SAT 3 on 28 May 1994, to mark the occasion of his eightieth birthday. Cf. Pott and Schönert, "Tabori unter den Deutschen: Stationen einer authentischen Existenz?" in *Theater gegen das Vergessen,* ed. Bayerdörfer and Schönert, pp. 362–377. May 1999 saw the premiere of Tabori's *Purgatorium.*

210. See Wolf Biermann's "Laudatio für George Tabori," in *Tabori,* ed. Welker, pp. 313–317; and Tabori's reply entitled "Dieses peinliche Wort: Liebe," in ibid., pp. 318–320. For the full list of prizes, see Welker, *Tabori,* p. 349.

211. George Tabori, "Fragebogen," *Die Woche,* 10 May 1992.

212. For the role of chess in his life and in his theatre, see Welker, "Das Wort," in *Tabori,* ed. Welker, pp. 303–304; and Tabori, "Die einfachste Stimme, die ich kenne," in *Tabori,* ed. Gronius and Kässens, pp. 50–51.

213. Hanna Schygulla, "Dear George," in *Tabori,* ed. Welker, p. 107.

214. George Tabori, "Der alte Mann und was mehr," in *Betrachtungen,* p. 213.

215. Barrington Cooper, "Die-Fünf-Pfund-Note," in *Tabori,* ed. Welker, pp. 226–227. See also the contribution of his Munich-based Hungarian doctor, Lucia Gergely-Feimer, "Ärzte und Verrückte," pp. 194–195.

216. George Tabori, "Was mich ärgert," in *Betrachtungen,* pp. 273–274.

217. Trenkler, "Ich bereite mich," p. 12.

2. TOWARD A DANGEROUS THEATRE

1. George Tabori, "Tod am Nachmittag," in *Unterammergau,* p. 181.

2. Ibid., p. 183.

3. Program for *Verwandlungen,* Kammerspiele, Munich, 1977, no page.

4. Cf. *Bonner Rundschau,* 24 January 1974; and Christopher Müller, "Eklektische Mixtur," *Theater Heute* 7 (1972): 13–14.

5. George Tabori, letter to Rolf Michaelis, 8 April 1976, SAdK, Box 68.

6. See "George Tabori," in *Theatermacher,* ed. Wend Kässens and Jörg W. Gronius, p. 157. See also Jürgen Berger, "Vielleicht ende ich als Bühnenarbeiter," *Die Tageszeitung,* 24 May 1994.

7. Andres Müry, "Warum macht das deutsche Theater uns krank, Herr Tabori?" *Frankfurter Allgemeine Zeitung* (Magazine), 18 September 1987, pp. 106–107.

8. Unpublished notes to *Sigmunds Freude,* SAdK, Box 10, p. 2.

9. Karin Kathrein, "Eine andere Art von Rückkehr."

10. George Tabori, letter to Moritz Millar, 10 July 1978, SAdK, Box 72.

11. Kässens and Gronius, *Theatermacher,* p. 157.

12. George Tabori, "Hamlet in Blue," *Theatre Quarterly* 20 (1975–1976): 116–

132. Tabori also discusses the malady of the theatre in his articles "Bett und Bühne," "Spiel und Zeit," and "Verlustliste oder das große deutsche Theaterrätsel," all available in *Betrachtungen*.

13. Program for *Talk Show*, Bremen, 1976, p. 4.

14. Tabori, "Hamlet in Blue," pp. 118–119.

15. Sibylle Fritsch, "Perfektion ist Blasphemie," *Profil*, 14 June 1993, pp. 72–73. Also Jan Bielicki, "Macht doch, was ihr wollt!" *Süddeutsche Zeitung* (Magazine), 6 July 1990.

16. George Tabori, "Verliebte und Verrückte," in *Betrachtungen*, p. 87.

17. Cf. for instance Erwin Leiser, "George Tabori," *Frankfurter Allgemeine Zeitung* (Magazine), 9 October 1987; and Karena Niehoff, "In welcher Sprache träumst Du, George?" *Die Zeit*, 26 May 1989, p. 68.

18. Tabori, "Hamlet in Blue," p. 118.

19. Kässens and Gronius, *Theatermacher*, p. 170.

20. Tabori, "Hamlet in Blue," p. 119. Cf. "Das Wort ist eine heilige Waffe," in *Tabori*, ed. Welker, p. 300; and Tabori's interview with Sibylle Fritsch, "Nur im Gefühl liegt die Wahrheit," *Psychologie Heute* 2 (1994): 40–42.

21. Alexander Mitscherlich and Margarete Mitscherlich, *Die Unfähigkeit zu trauern*.

22. Tabori, "Hamlet in Blue," p. 130.

23. George Tabori, "Why Fritz?" (unpublished manscript, SAdK, Box 80, p. 6). Cf. "Spiel und Zeit," in *Betrachtungen*, pp. 17–18.

24. Tabori, "Hamlet in Blue," p. 130. See also his letter to Paul Tabori, 21 January 1941, SAdK, Box 35. This sentence is also the motto of his production *Talk Show* (1976).

25. Tabori, "Spiel und Zeit," in *Betrachtungen*, pp. 17–18.

26. Erwin Leiser, "Bei ihm muß ein König kein Mann sein," *Die Weltwoche*, 25 May 1989, pp. 65–66. See also "Unterammergau," p. 27.

27. Tabori, "Spiel und Zeit," p. 20.

28. Cf. Christopher D. Innes, *Avant Garde Theatre 1892–1992*, p. 182.

29. Tabori, "Unterammergau," p. 18.

30. George Tabori, "Lieber Lee," in *Betrachtungen*, p. 190. Tabori wrote about Brecht and his theatre also in "Bemerkungen über Brecht, Studien zur Theorie und Praxis des sozialistischen Theaters," supplement to *Theater der Zeit* 23 (1968): 14.

31. Tabori, "Lieber Lee," p. 188.

32. Cf. Steven Connor, *Postmodernist Culture: An Introduction to Theories of the Contemporary*, p. 141. Also Hans Bertens, *The Idea of the Postmodern: A History*, p. 76.

33. See, for instance, Patrice Pavis, "The Classical Heritage of Modern Drama: The Case of Postmodern Theatre," *Modern Drama* 1 (1986): 1–22.

34. Tabori, "Spiel und Zeit," p. 19.

35. George Tabori, "Tod am Nachmittag," in *Unterammergau*, p. 187.

36. Antonin Artaud, *Oeuvres complètes*, vol. 2, p. 19.

37. Tabori, "Spiel und Zeit," p. 16. See also Tabori's interview with Fritz Rad-

datz, "Den Tod zu überlisten," *Die Zeit* (Magazine), 13 November 1992, p. 54.

38. George Tabori, letter to Moritz Milar, 10 July 1978.

39. Antonin Artaud, *The Theatre and Its Double*, p. 77.

40. Tabori, "Verliebte und Verrückte," pp. 84–85.

41. Tabori, "Hamlet in Blue," p. 118.

42. George Tabori, "Warum am Theater?" in *Betrachtungen*, p. 67.

43. Tabori, "Why Fritz?" p. 4.

44. The speech entitled "Dieses peinliches Wort: Liebe" is printed in *Tabori*, ed. Welker, pp. 318–320.

45. Bardischewski and Martens, "George Tabori — Weltwanderer."

46. Tabori, "Tod am Nachmittag," p. 192.

47. Cf. George Tabori, "Bett und Bühne," in *Betrachtungen*, p. 11.

48. George Tabori, "Die Sucht des Sehens," in *Betrachtungen*, p. 97.

49. Tabori, "Unterammergau," p. 28.

50. Addressing the ideal of the poor theatre, Tabori sometimes mentions Alberto Giacometti, whose slim, unostentatious figures he describes as "three strokes to evoke the whole." See Tabori's letter to Samuel Beckett, 18 January 1981, SAdK, Box 78.

51. Cf. Brook's option for the Bouffes du Nord or Richard Schechner's theatre performances in a garage.

52. Rolf Ronzier, "Theater als Prozeß: Die Theaterarbeit George Taboris," vol. 1, p. 226.

53. Kässens and Gronius, *Theatermacher*, p. 159.

54. Tabori, "Unterammergau," p. 19.

55. George Tabori, letter to Moritz Milar, 10 July 1978. Cf. "Verliebte und Verrückte," p. 86.

56. I use the wording of actor Jochen Winter, "Energie der Angst," in his "Hommage an Tabori," unpublished manuscript. Cf. "Tod am Nachmittag," p. 189. For Tabori as playmaker, see, for instance, Peter von Becker, "Theaterarbeit mit George Tabori," *Theater Heute* 1 (1979): 50; and Jörn Rohwer, "Nach der Illusion der Unsterblichkeit," *Berliner Zeitung*, 15/16 August 1998.

57. Gundula Ohngemach, "George Taboris Theaterarbeit: Eine Analyse der Probenarbeit am Beispiel von *Jubiläum*," p. 67.

58. Ohngemach, *George Tabori*, p. 55.

59. Hanna Schygulla later worked with Tabori on Jean-Claude Carrière's *La seconde fois* (Vienna, 1988); cf. Ohngemach, *George Tabori*, pp. 103–107. See also Schygulla's contribution "Dear George," in *Tabori*, ed. Welker, p. 107.

60. Gert Voss, "Lichterloh Leidenschaft," in *Tabori*, ed. Welker, pp. 246–247.

61. Cf. David Garfield, *A Player's Place*, p. 150.

62. "André Müller im Gespräch mit Claus Peymann," in *Tabori*, ed. Welker, p. 242. Following this accusation, a dispute ensued between the two. See also Claus Peymann, "Die Welt in einer Anekdote," *Profil*, 16 May 1994.

63. George Tabori, "Psychologisches Theater," in *Tabori*, ed. Welker, p. 117.

64. Tabori, "Verliebte und Verrückte," p. 87.

65. Tabori said he had learned from Elia Kazan to restrain himself as a director, to resist the need to demonstrate to the actors, knowing that this paralyzes them. Von Becker, "Theaterarbeit mit George Tabori," p. 50.

66. Duglore Pizzini, "Arbeitsfreude statt Regie-Gewalttätigkeit," *Die Presse*, no date.

67. George Tabori, "Besprechung am ersten Probentag," in *Betrachtungen*, p. 39. Also: "A play without an actor is inconceivable, but acting without a play is" (*Betrachtungen*, p. 195).

68. Tabori, "Unterammergau," p. 9.

69. George Tabori, "Staats-Theater," in *Betrachtungen*, p. 122. See also Ursula Voss, "Hoffnungsselig liebender Timon," in *Tabori*, ed. Welker, p. 197.

70. George Tabori, "Marx Brothers in Zauberberg," in program for *Talk Show* (1976), p. 5

71. Tabori, program for *Talk Show*, p. 5

72. Tabori, "Hamlet in Blue," p. 118.

73. Lindfors, *Viveka... Viveca*, p. 218.

74. Sybille Fritsch, "Keine Zeit zu trauern," *Profil*, 23 July 1990.

75. Tabori, "Tod am Nachmittag," p. 187.

76. Ibid., p. 190. Tabori says he found variations on this idea in Zen, Blake, Proust, and Kafka as well as in Strasberg and Wilhelm Reich.

77. Hans Fröhlich, "My Lai und die Ästhetik," *Stuttgarter Nachrichten*, 26 August 1971.

78. George Tabori, "Rationalismus — Irrationalismus," in *Tabori*, ed. Welker, p. 102.

79. Ursula Höpfner, "Der Begriff der Authentizität aus der Sicht eines Theatermachers," SAdK, Box 91b, p. 14.

80. Müry, "Warum macht das deutsche Theater uns krank."

81. Tabori, "Why Fritz?" p. 5.

82. Kässens and Gronius, *Theatermacher*, p. 168.

83. Höpfner, "Authentizität."

84. George Tabori, letter to Hans-Reinhard Müller, 28 December 1979, SAdK, Box 72.

85. Michaelis, "Ein begeisterungsfähiger Skeptiker."

86. George Tabori, notes to *Sigmunds Freude*, p. 7.

87. Ohngemach, *George Tabori*, p. 39.

88. Tabori, "Hamlet in Blue," p. 126. George Tabori, "Warten auf Beckett," in *Betrachtungen*, p. 51.

89. Tabori, "Warten auf Beckett," p. 51.

90. George Tabori, letter to Hans-Reinhard Müller, 28 December 1979.

91. Tabori, "Verliebte und Verrückte," p. 85.

92. Tabori, "Hamlet in Blue," p. 125.

93. George Tabori, "On the Goodness of Theatre," SAdK, Box 62.

94. Tabori, "Hamlet in Blue," p. 127.

95. Tabori, "Spiel und Zeit," p. 20.

96. Tabori, *Unterammergau*, p. 37.

97. Detlef Jacobsen told me how Tabori burst out laughing when he heard of a

woman who teaches the "Tabori method" in a drama school in Germany. "I
never knew I had a method" was Tabori's reaction.

98. George Tabori, "Traum der Leidenschaft," in *Betrachtungen*, p. 195. See also
Ohngemach, *George Tabori*, p. 137.

99. "Der kleine Klick," in *Tabori*, ed. Welker, p. 224.

100. Bardischeski and Martens, "George Tabori — Weltwanderer."

101. Tabori, "Unterammergau," p. 9. Cf. Ekkehard Schall on this point in *The
Cambridge Companion to Brecht*, ed. Thomson and Sachs, p. 264.

102. Tabori, notes to *Sigmunds Freude*, p. 2.

103. Jennifer Kumiega emphasizes in her study *The Theatre of Grotowski*, p. 45, that
Grotowski "strongly resisted any attempt to categorize and 'package' the
results of his work into a method to be placed alongside those of Stanislavsky or Brecht." A similar attitude is shared by Joe Chaikin: "Chaikin's evolving thoughts about theatre do not add up to a totally coherent poetics on
theatrics," maintains Eileen Blumenthal in *Joseph Chaikin: Exploring at the
Boundaries of Theater*, pp. 38ff.

104. Tabori, letter to Moritz Milar, 10 July 1978.

105. Hans Haider and Verena Hoehne, "George Tabori," *du* 9 (1993): 66. See also
Kässens and Gronius, *Theatermacher*, p. 174.

106. Tabori, "Hamlet in Blue," p. 131.

107. Blumenthal, *Joseph Chaikin*, p. 39.

108. Tabori, "Hamlet in Blue," p. 118.

109. Jerzy Grotowski, *Towards a Poor Theatre*, p. 98.

110. Ibid., p. 57.

111. Grotowski speaks of a "box of tricks" in *Towards a Poor Theatre*, p. 218.

112. Kässens and Gronius, *Theatermacher*, p. 176.

113. Tabori, "Hamlet in Blue," p. 120. Cf. also Grotowski, *Towards a Poor Theatre*,
p. 50.

114. Müry, "Warum macht das deutsche Theater uns krank," p. 106.

115. Kässens and Gronius, *Theatermacher*, p. 174.

116. Kumiega, *The Theatre of Grotowski*, p. 116. Describing his own theatrics, German director Peter Stein says: "Distance and scepticism are for me the basis
of all work in the theatre. The fascinating part then comes in the dialectic
between distance and closeness" (Michael Patterson, *Peter Stein: Germany's
Leading Theatre Director*, p. 161).

117. Tabori, "Lieber Lee," p. 190.

118. Innes, *Avant Garde Theatre*, p. 180.

119. Grotowski, *Towards a Poor Theatre*, p. 85.

120. Tabori translated *Andorra* and was praised by Swiss playwright Max Frisch;
see Max Frisch, letter to Cheryl Crawford, 24 October 1962, SAdK, Box 63.
A few years earlier, he produced a stage version of Bernard Malamud's novel
The Assistant, " a little masterpiece about poor Jews in Brooklyn," as he wrote
to brother Paul Tabori, 7 March 1957, Box 35. See also Box 54 for various
versions of the adaptation.

121. Cf. Martin Esslin, *Bertolt Brecht*, p. 40.

3. THE DIALECTICS OF FREEDOM AND ORDER: TABORI'S THEATERLABOR

1. Cf. Innes, *Avant Garde Theatre*, pp. 125–192.
2. See "Lust und Wahrheit," in *Tabori*, ed. Welker, p. 76.
3. In the course of rehearsing in Bremen Tabori also directed Sławomir Mrożek's *Emigrants* in Bonn (premiere 12 June 1975) and his own dramatization of Kafka's *Metamorphosis* in the Münchner Kammerspiele (see chapter 4).
4. Marietta Eggmann recounts her experiences with Tabori in "Ein ungarischer Jude und eine Schweizer Schickse," in *Tabori*, ed. Welker, p. 81, as well as in "Ein massiver Einbruch von Realität," in Ohngemach, *George Tabori*, pp. 65–69.
5. Cf. "Lust und Wahrheit," in *Tabori*, ed. Welker, p. 77.
6. George Tabori, letter to Peter Stoltzenberg, 2 June 1977, SAdK, Box 74. Notably, during the protracted negotiations with the SED (Sozialistische Einheitspartei Deutschlands) about his Berliner Ensemble, Brecht complained about "the foul breath of provincialism." Cf. Carl Weber, "Brecht and the Berliner Ensemble — The Making of a Model," in *The Cambridge Companion to Brecht*, ed. Peter Thomson and Glendyr Sachs, p. 167.
7. Ohngemach, *George Tabori*, p. 58.
8. Detlef Jacobsen in a personal interview.
9. Ohngemach, *George Tabori*, p. 62.
10. Ibid., p. 69.
11. See "Ein Appell," *Theater Heute* 6 (1978): 16.
12. Peter von Becker, "Das Nachtspiel bis zum Morgengrauen," *Theater Heute* 6 (1978): 15.
13. Georg Hensel, "Die Last der toten Väter," *Frankfurter Allgemeine Zeitung*, 22 March 1978. See also comments on the closing of the lab in Mechthild Lange, "Der Vater war leider schon um die Ecke gebracht," *Frankfurter Rundschau*, 12 April 1978; and Kurt Lothar Tank, "Schöpferische Zerstörungslust," *Der Tagesspiegel*, 26 April 1978.
14. George Tabori in a conversation with Sibylle Fritsch, "Perfektion ist Blasphemie," *Profil*, 14 June 1993, pp. 72–73.
15. George Tabori in a conversation with Michaelis, "Ein begeisterungsfähiger Skeptiker," p. 32.
16. Quoted in Ohngemach, *George Tabori*, p. 84.
17. See the conversation about the rehearsal period in the program for Rudkin's *Afore Night Come*, Theater der Freien Hansestadt Bremen 1975, pp. 81–93.
18. Cf. Günter Einbrodt's sense memory experience with the skull in *Hamlet*, in Ohngemach, *George Tabori*, p. 101.
19. "Theaterarbeit mit George Tabori," *Theater Heute* 1 (1979): 47.
20. "Ach ja, die Hungerkunst!: Protokoll einer Inszenierung," in Program for Tabori's *Hungerkünstler*, p. 6.
21. Cf. Ohngemach, *George Tabori*, p. 75.

22. Cf. "Die einfachste Stimme, die ich kenne," in Gronius and Kässens, *Tabori*, p. 50.

23. Tabori, *Unterammergau*, p. 9.

24. Bertolt Brecht, *Über den Beruf des Schauspielers*, p. 28.

25. Tabori, "Hamlet in Blue," pp. 116–132.

26. George Tabori, "Notes to *Siegmunds* [*sic*] *Freude*," unpublished manuscript "for internal use only," July 1975, SAdK, Box 16. I am greatly indebted to Gustav Kiepenheuer Bühnenvertriebs GmbH for making this text available to me. Devine's maxim is mentioned by George Tabori in a letter to Beckett, 24 October 1980, SAdK, Box 78.

27. Ohngemach, *George Tabori*, p. 25.

28. See George Tabori, "Bacon and X," in *Betrachtungen*, pp. 91–93.

29. See "Theaterarbeit mit George Tabori." Tabori reports on his visit to the "Shakespeare's Memory" evening at the Schaubühne, directed by Peter Stein. He greatly admired the production, especially the research done for that eight-hour performance. Yet it soon became clear to him that his group could not really profit from such research and that it "had to make its own way."

30. Cf. program for *Hungerkünstler*, pp. 33ff.

31. Ohngemach, *George Tabori*, p. 98.

32. Protocol for rehearsals of *Hungerkünstler*, p. 7. Cf. Ohngemach, *George Tabori*, pp. 90ff.

33. Höpfner, "Authentizität," p. 9.

34. Horst W. Franke, letter to Senator Herbert Brückner, 16 May 1977, identification number 6403.

35. Höpfner, "Authentizität," pp. 10–11.

36. Ohngemach, *George Tabori*, p. 86.

37. Program for *Hamlet*, p. 3. Tabori referred to Chekhov's dictum that "one never finishes."

38. Detlef Jacobsen, "Wir brauchen sie: eine kleine Änderung," in *Tabori*, ed. Welker, p. 83. See also Tabori's letter to the group of 30 October 1976, SAdK, Box 74, following the premiere of *Talk Show*, in which he says: "first and foremost, have fun yourselves."

39. David Rudkin, letter to George Tabori entitled "Gedanken zum Stück," program for the production, p. 79.

40. Klaus Wagner, "Gruppenangst beim Äpfelpflücken," *Frankfurter Allgemeine Zeitung*, 1 April 1975. For other reviews, see Erich Emigholz, "Ein Ritualmord und warum es dazu kommt," *Bremer Nachrichten*, 27 March 1975; Ernst Goetsch, "Die Welt — ein Schlachthaus," *Nordwest-Zeitung*, 27 March 1975; Simon Neubauer, "Ritualmord an einem Außenseiter," *Weser Kurier*, 27 March 1975; Mathes Rehder, "Ein Tramp wird geschlachtet," *Hamburger Abendblatt*, 27 March 1975; and Henning Rischbieter, "Rudkins Vor der Nacht," *Theater Heute* 6 (1975): 15–16.

41. Wagner, "Gruppenangst."

42. The figure of the physically disabled has preoccupied Tabori time and again.

See, for example, the choice of Peter Radtke, in a wheelchair, for the leading male role in *M.* (1985) and in *Happy Days* (1986). Other examples from Tabori's own plays are Mitzi in *Jubilee* (1983) and Ruthi in *Weisman and Copperface* (1990).

43. This was the only production which took place outside the Concordia. Following this experience Tabori said in a conversation with Rolf Michaelis that "now is clear to me what I have always known, that I feel much better in the cellar than in one of those despicable opera-houses," *Theater Heute* 6 (1976): 32.

44. Rolf Michaelis, "Theater gegen Gewalt — Gewalt gegen Theater," *Theater Heute* 6 (1976): 33–38. Veronika Dorn was responsible in this production for the set and the costumes.

45. Rolf Ronzier, "Theater als Prozeß: Die Theaterarbeit George Taboris," vol. 2, p. 137.

46. Peter Iden, "Mord im Theater," *Frankfurter Rundschau*, 28 March 1977. Cf. also Ohngemach, *George Tabori*, pp. 86–87. For other reviews of the production, see Georg Hensel, "Lynchmord als Lustbarkeit," *Frankfurter Allgemeine Zeitung*, 28 March 1977; Jürgen Schmidt, "Beihilfe zum Mord," *Stuttgarter Nachrichten*, 30 March 1977; Kurt Lothar Tank, "Stakkato der Gewalt," *Der Tagesspiegel*, 6 April 1977; and Jens Wendland, "Depremierend klapprige Schaukel," *Stuttgarter Zeitung*, 6 April 1977.

47. Erich Emigholz, "Wie brave Kleinstädter zu Mördern werden können," *Bremer Nachrichten*, 28 March 1977.

48. Tabori, "Notes to *Siegmunds Freude*," p. 4.

49. Ohngemach, *George Tabori*, pp. 74–75.

50. Innes, *Avant Garde Theatre*, p. 175.

51. Erich Emigholz, "Traumarbeit," *Theater Heute* 1 (1976): 10ff.

52. Georg Hensel, "Seelentrip im Traumseminar," *Frankfurter Allgemeine Zeitung*, 11 December 1975. For other reviews, see Simon Neubauer, "Sitzungen beim Seelendoktor," *Weser Kurier*, 1 December 1975; Dietmar N. Schmidt, "Wenn die Küche mit dem Schlafzimmer spricht," *Frankfurter Rundschau*, 10 December 1975; Hans Berndt, "Menschen suchen ihre Mitte," *Mannheimer Morgen*, 11 December 1975; Karena Niehoff, "Heile, heile Segen aus beseelter Hand," *Süddeutsche Zeitung*, 15 December 1975; and Bernhard Häußermann, "Eine Seelen-Spielweise," *Hannoversche Allgemeine Zeitung*, 23 December 1975.

53. Hensel, "Seelentrip."

54. Tabori, "Notes to *Siegmunds Freude*," p. 1. See also Tabori's unpublished manuscript "Why Fritz?" p. 2.

55. Ronzier, "Theater als Prozeß," vol. 2, p. 80.

56. Tabori, "Notes to *Siegmunds Freude*," pp. 5–6.

57. See, for example, Dietmar N. Schmidt, "Die Küche spricht mit dem Schlafzimmer," *Südwest Presse*, 15 December 1975; Hans Berndt, "Menschen suchen ihre Mitte," *Mannheimer Morgen*, 11 December 1975; and Lothar Schmidt-Mühlisch, "Ach, Nachtigal, ick hör dir schon von janz weit trapsen," *Die Welt*, 4 July 1978.

58. Tabori, "Die Marx Brothers in Zauberberg," p. 2.

59. Tabori refers associatively to Heinrich Heine's "Matratzengruft."

60. Tabori, "Der alte Mann und was mehr," in *Betrachtungen*, p. 213.

61. John Webster, *The Duchess of Malfi*, ed. John Russell Brown (London: Methuen and Co., 1964), II.i.42.

62. For reviews of *Talk Show*, see Erich Emigholz, "Der Tod soll nun endgültig abgeschafft werden," *Bremer Nachrichten*, 25 October 1976; Klaus Wagner, "Totentänze in der Matratzengruft," *Frankfurter Allgemeine Zeitung*, 26 October 1976; Bernhard Häußermann, "Strapaze auf der Matratze," *Hannoversche Allgemeine Zeitung*, 27 October 1976; Kurt Lothar Tank, "Totentanztraining für Schauspieler," *Der Tagesspiegel*, 29 October 1976; Hainz Klunker, "Banalitäten aus der Matratzengruft," *Deutsches Allgemeines Sonntagsblatt*, 31 October 1976; Max Wieland, "Lachen, um zu leben," *Kieler Nachrichten*, 4 November 1976; and Gerd Jäger, "Das Schauspieltheater der Regisseure," *Theater Heute*, 12 (1976): 35–38.

63. The premiere took place without the official consent of Kafka's heirs. In a letter to Tabori, 2 August 1977, SAdK, Box 74, Dr. Maria Sommer writes: "I have trembled a little in the meantime, as I received an embarrassing query from London, from Kafka's heirs; they had read in the papers that the production was totally different from the manuscript they had read, and on top of it all apparently even bad."

64. The group performed the play later in a circus arena in Berlin (Mariannenplatz-Zelt) and in Munich.

65. In the second version there were only six.

66. Tabori, "Die Kannibalen: Zur europäischen Erstaufführung," in *Unterammergau*, pp. 38–39.

67. Erich Emigholz, "Tabori überzeugt als Grenzgänger des Theaters," *Bremer Nachrichten*, 25 June 1977. For other reviews, see Bernhard Häußermann, "Der Hunger als Regisseur," *Hannoversche Allgemeine Zeitung*, 15 June 1977; Jens Wieland, "Selbsterfahrungsversuche mit Kafka," *Süddeutsche Zeitung*, 16 June 1977; Hellmuth Karasek, "Bremer Theaterhunger," *Der Spiegel*, 20 June 1977; Klaus Kuntze, "Wohlschmeckendes Brot," *Frankfurter Rundschau*, 21 June 1977; Simon Neubauer, "Theaterlabor auf dem Holzweg?" *Weser Kurier*, 25 June 1977; and Georg Hensel, "Die Katze tut, was sie tut," *Frankfurter Allgemeine Zeitung*, 17 September 1977.

68. Tabori, "Hamlet in Blue," p. 129.

69. Ibid., p. 127. Cf. Tabori, *Unterammergau*, p. 37.

70. Peter von Becker, "Das Nachtspiel bis zum Morgen-Grauen," *Theater Heute*, 6 (1978): 12ff.

71. Tabori, "Wir sind keine Götter," in *Betrachtungen*, p. 205.

72. Tabori, "Hamlet in Blue," p. 128.

73. Ibid., p. 129.

74. Simon Neubauer, "Hamlet als Fleckerlteppich," *Weser Kurier*, 21 March 1978. For other reviews, see Erich Emigholz, "Taboris Hamlet soll uns das Trauern wieder lehren," *Bremer Nachrichten*, 21 March 1978; Ernst Goetsch, "Taboris Hamlet — nackt und neu," *Nordwest-Zeitung*, 23 March 1978; Jür-

gen Schmidt, "Von Gefühlen erschlagen," *Nürnberger Nachrichten*, 25 March 1978; Mechthild Lange, "Der Vater war leider schon um die Ecke gebracht," *Frankfurter Rundschau*, 12 April 1978; and Friedrich Luft, "Der Dänenprinz als Pop-Figur mit vielen Blessuren," *Die Welt*, 29 June 1978.

75. Georg Hensel, "Die Last der toten Väter," *Frankfurter Allgemeine Zeitung*, 22 March 1978.

76. Ohngemach, *George Tabori*, p. 91. See also "Ein Appell," *Theater Heute* 6 (1978): 16.

77. Welker, *Tabori*, p. 77.

4. KAFKA-OVERPAINT: THE *METAMORPHOSES* PERFORMANCE

1. Unless stated otherwise all references to and quotations from Kafka's prose are taken from J. A. Underwood's translation of Franz Kafka: *Stories 1904–1924*.

2. The entire speech is printed in Welker, *Tabori*, pp. 318–319.

3. Tabori, *Unterammergau*, p. 11.

4. These included presentations from all over the Continent, ranging from theatre and dance shows to concerts, films, puppet shows, and an exhibition.

5. George Tabori, "Frühstück," in *Betrachtungen*, pp. 220–226. The English original entitled "Breakfast," SAdK, Box 31, bears the date "1.5.1983." Tabori included this short prose piece in his play *Babylon Blues* (1991).

6. Cf. Koelbl, *Jüdische Portraits*, p. 237. Also Tabori, "Berliner Betten," in *Betrachtungen*, pp. 255–257.

7. Tabori, "Frühstück," p. 225.

8. George Tabori, "Besprechung am ersten Probentag," in *Betrachtungen*, p. 36. Cf. also "Was mich ärgert . . . ," in *Betrachtungen*, p. 274.

9. George Tabori, "Über Kafka," in *Tabori*, ed. Welker, p. 245.

10. George Tabori, "Vom Wesen des Glücks," in *Tabori*, ed. Welker, pp. 79–80.

11. Sander L. Gilman elucidates Kafka's complex feelings toward Judaism in *Franz Kafka: The Jewish Patient*. See also Lovis M. Wambach, *Ahasver und Kafka: Zur Bedeutung der Judenfeindschaft in dessen Leben und Werk* (Heidelberg: Winter, 1993); Karl E. Grözinger, Stéphane Moses, and Hans Dieter Zimmermann, eds., *Kafka und das Judentum* (Frankfurt: Jüdischer Verlag/Athenäum, 1987); Ritchie Robertson, *Kafka: Judaism, Politics, and Literature* (Oxford: Oxford University Press, 1981).

12. Franz Kafka, *Briefe 1902–1924*, in *Gesammelte Schriften*, edited by Max Brod, vol. 6, p. 404.

13. Tabori, *Unterammergau*, p. 26.

14. Kafka, *Briefe*, pp. 172–173.

15. Tabori explicitly speaks of the influence of Hasidism on his sense of humor. Cf. Tabori, "Marx Brothers in Zauberberg."

16. Bardischewski and Martens, "George Tabori — Weltwanderer," p. 23 .

17. "Like Kafka I hate construction," writes Tabori (*Unterammergau*, p. 19).

18. George Tabori, "Verwandlungen: Eine Improvisation frei nach Kafka," ms.,

October 1976. I am indebted to Gustav Kiepenheuer Bühnenvertriebs-GmbH, Berlin, for letting me use the unpublished play-text. The handwritten English manuscript of the production is in SAdK, Box 14.

19. Tabori told the press that 80 percent of the script was based on Kafka. Cf. Gerhard Pörtl, "Exorzimus auf Kafka komm raus," *Saarbrücker Zeitung*, 26 February 1977. Tabori also referred occasionally to other letters by Kafka as well as to his diary.

20. Cf. Sibylle Fritsch, "Kafka-Übermalungen," *Profil*, 4 May 1992, p. 100.

21. For a description and analysis of Beuys's interaction with the coyote, see Caroline Tisdall, *Joseph Beuys Coyote* (Munich: Thames and Hudson, 1979); Heiner Stachelhaus, *Joseph Beuys* (Düsseldorf: Claassen, 1987), pp. 209–211; and Uwe M. Schneede, ed., *Joseph Beuys: Die Aktionen* (Stuttgart: Hatje, 1994), pp. 330–353. Tabori was intrigued by the personality and the art of Joseph Beuys and entertains ambivalent feelings toward this controversial artist. He mentions Beuys in his parody "Die Wende," in *Betrachtungen*, p. 144, as well as in his slightly ironical article "Der Tod eines Kritikers," in *Betrachtungen*, p. 174. See also *Betrachtungen*, p. 89.

22. Cf. Colin Counsell, *Signs of Performance*, p. 221.

23. Tabori defined the presentation as a "Gruppen-Projekt" (Group-Project).

24. For the analysis of Beuys's aesthetics and art, see Götz Adriani, Winfried Konnertz, and Karin Thoms, eds., *Joseph Beuys* (Cologne: Dumont, 1994), and Stachelhaus, *Joseph Beuys*.

25. Veronika Dorn was responsible for the set and the costumes.

26. Tabori repeatedly experimented with close and open spaces, fences, and enclosures. See, for example, his production of David Rudkin's *Afore Night Come*.

27. The address "An die Schauspieler" was published in the program for the production.

28. Peter Dyckhoff, "Angstträume — frei nach Kafka," *Schleswig-Holsteinische Landeszeitung*, 25 February 1977.

29. Helmut Schödel, "Ein Rollensuchspiel," *Theater Heute* 4 (1977): 6–7.

30. Tabori also framed his productions of Jean-Claude Carrière's *La seconde fois* in 1988 and Beckett's *Endgame* (1998) as a rehearsal. The director's table was part of the set in the Carrière production, and at one point some of the people involved in the production came onstage.

31. Tabori, "Verwandlungen," p. 43; Kafka, *Briefe*, pp. 27–28.

32. Tabori relates Samsa's squeak to Kafka's wheezing as the result of his laryngeal cancer.

33. Georg Hensel, "Franz Kafkas Väter und Söhne," *Frankfurter Allgemeine Zeitung*, 11 March 1977.

34. Tabori, *Unterammergau*, p. 37.

35. Cf. Klaus Wagenbach, *Kafka*, p. 72.

36. Tabori often addresses this episode. See, for example, the preface to his play *Jubilee*.

37. Thomas Petz, "Gruppenbild mit Kafka," *Süddeutsche Zeitung*, 25 February 1977.

38. Armin Eichholz, "Familienbild mit Käfer," *Münchner Merkur*, 25 February 1977.

39. Tabori added to the two chief sources, *The Metamorphosis* and *In the Penal Colony*, *A Fasting-Artist*, which he previously presented as an independent production.

40. Gerhard Stadelmeier, "Vor den Vätern sterben die Käfer," *Frankfurter Allgemeine Zeitung*, 2 May 1992.

41. George Tabori, *Der Babylon-Blues oder Wie man glücklich wird, ohne sich zu verausgaben*, in *Theaterstücke*, vol. 2, p. 274.

5. WHAT GOES UNDER SO FABULOUSLY CANNOT BE LOST: TABORI'S *TITANIC*

1. Enzensberger's epic poem met with a controversial reception upon its publication in 1978. Some critics considered the poet to be a canny opportunist; others celebrated him as a Postmodernist. Cf. *Kindlers Neues Literatur Lexikon*, 22 vols. (Munich: Kindler, 1989), vol. 5, pp. 222–223. All references and quotations (in my own translation into English) from the text are based on the original edition (Frankfurt: Suhrkamp, 1978).

2. Hans Magnus Enzensberger, "Ein Souvenir vom Untergang der Titanic," in *Tabori*, ed. Welker, p. 110.

3. Enzensberger wrote the first version in Havana, Cuba, in 1969 and the second in Berlin, completing the work in 1977.

4. Tabori, "Verwandlungen," p. 43.

5. Carna Zacharias, "Angst vorm Ertrinken," *Abendzeitung*, 8 May 1980.

6. See, for example, Rainer Stephan, "Unangemessen angestrengt," *Frankfurter Rundschau*, 20 May 1980.

7. The set and costumes were designed by Veronika Dorn.

8. Thomas Thieringer, "Der Untergang," *Nürnberger Nachrichten*, 10 May 1980.

9. George Tabori, "Berlin Connection," in *Betrachtungen*, p. 47.

10. In an interview he gave Ellen Grebe, "Das Einmalige am Theater," *Nürnberger Nachrichten*, 24 January 1980, Tabori says: "This is a strangely apocalyptic time, one only has to follow the papers. . . . Despair, disappointment, misery all over. One can only manage if one challenges reality and says, 'I'll carry on.' This as a pronouncement is very important to me. Politically, in the broadest sense of the word, Enzensberger refers to it in his text on various levels."

11. Cf. Tabori's letter to Hans-Reinhard Müller, 28 December 1979, SAdK, Box 74. The joint presentation was shown in Berlin, 26 November 1980, and later in some other cities.

12. This is the subtitle of Enzensberger's text.

13. George Tabori, "Berlin Connection," in *Betrachtungen*, p. 47.

14. Andrzej Wirth, "Die Lust an der schwachen Lesung," *Theater Heute* 6 (1980): 10–13. See also Armin Eichholz, "Am 8. Mai war das ein Ding, als die Ti-

tanic unterging — mit sieben Leuten on the rocks," *Münchner Merkur*, 10 May 1980. The title of this chapter is taken from Eichholz's review.

15. The six were Ursula Höpfner, Brigitte Kahn, Günter Einbrodt, Klaus Fischer, Nico Grüneke, and Murray Levy. They were joined by Helmut Pick of the Kammerspiele.

16. George Tabori, letter to Hans-Reinhard Müller, 28 December 1978.

17. Ibid. The Cassavetes project never got off the ground. All three projects were intended as world premieres. Tabori maintained they shared a "thematic connection."

18. The production was also presented at the Akademie der Künste in Berlin and was taken up again in 1984 for the "Frankfurter Feste," which focused that year on the *Titanic* story. According to Rolf Ronzier, Tabori played with the idea of producing it again in his own Kreis-theatre in Vienna, but this never came to pass. See Ronzier, "Theater als Prozeß," vol. 2, p. 229.

19. For a descriptive critique, see Karena Niehoff, "Die Titanic auf dem Wannsee," *Der Tagesspiegel*, 2 February 1981.

20. Hans Magnus Enzensberger, "Souvenir," in *Tabori*, ed. Welker, p. 110.

21. Rehearsal notes of 1 February 1980 and 4 February 1980, printed as part of the program for the production, Kammerspiele, Munich, May 1980. Tabori's handwritten notes during the rehearsal period are in SAdK, Box 79b.

22. Stanley Walden, "Das Jucken, das nicht nachläßt," in *Tabori*, ed. Welker, p. 279.

23. On later occasions the aquarium was replaced by a bathtub. Tabori obtained the permission of the Society for the Prevention of Cruelty to Animals for the actors' plunging into the aquarium.

24. Walden, "Das Jucken," p. 297.

25. Personal belongings were an integral component here as in the lab's production of Kafka's *Fasting-Artist*.

26. Rehearsal notes, 14 April 1980.

27. Tabori's *Delirium* to texts by Enzensberger premiered at the Thalia Theater in Hamburg on 29 May 1994. For reviews, see, for example, anon., "Eine Pille täglich," *Der Spiegel*, 30 May 1994, pp. 197–199; C. Bernd Sucher, "Und er sah, daß es gut war," *Süddeutsche Zeitung*, 31 May 1994; Matthias Wegner, "Ihr irrt, wenn ihr lebt," *Frankfurter Allgemeine Zeitung*, 31 May 1994; Mechthild Lange, "Abendanzug mit Zwangsjacke," *Frankfurter Rundschau*, 3 June 1994; Werner Schulze-Reimpell, "Tabori verzaubert das Nichts," *Rheinischer Merkur*, 3 June 1994; and Robin Detje, "Theater schwänzen," *Die Zeit*, 10 June 1994.

6. PLAY IT AGAIN, SAM: STAGING BECKETT

1. George Tabori, "Aufs beste zu," *Die Zeit*, 5 January 1990. See also Tabori, "Samspeak," in *Betrachtungen*, pp. 63–66; and "Die Sprache liebkosen, küssen, beissen, lecken, saugen," *Die Woche*, 4 March 1993.

2. Tabori deliberately uses the English title of Beckett's play, entitled in French *Le dépeupleur*.

3. George Tabori, "Die einfachste Stimme, die ich kenne," in *Tabori*, ed. Gronius and Kässens, p. 49.

4. Ibid., p. 53. There are copies of four letters Tabori wrote to Beckett in SAdK, Box 78. They bear the dates 24 October 1980, 15 December 1980, 9 January 1981 (a letter which most likely was never sent), and 18 January 1981. "Thank you for your generous note, the nicest New Year's gift ever, quite undeserved," Tabori begins his letter of 18 January 1981.

5. Tabori described the meeting or, to be more precise, his fears and hopes prior to it in "Warten auf Beckett," in *Betrachtungen*, pp. 48–62.

6. Tabori, "Die einfachste Stimme," pp. 53–54.

7. Ibid., p. 50.

8. George Tabori, "Besprechung am ersten Probentag" in *Betrachtungen*, p. 37.

9. George Tabori, "Warten auf Beckett," in *Betrachtungen*, p. 54.

10. Ibid., p. 49.

11. George Tabori's letter to Beckett, 24 October 1980.

12. Following the prologue the theatrical collage included the following texts: *Act without Words I and II, Breath, Closed Place, Rough for Theater I and II, That Time, Eh Joe, Old Earth, I Gave Up before Birth, Not I*, and *Play*. See Tabori's "Continuity Notes, Nov. 24 [1980]," unpublished manuscript, SAdK, Box 78. Among the reviews of this production, the following are particularly valuable: Eva-Elisabeth Fischer, "Arena ohne Ausweg," *Süddeutsche Zeitung*, 6 December 1980; Georg Hensel, "Tabori inszeniert Beckett im Zirkus," *Frankfurter Allgemeine Zeitung*, 11 December 1980; Hannes S. Macher, "Menschendressur im Zirkus," *Rheinischer Merkur*, 12 December 1980; Helmut Schödel, "Auf der Suche," *Die Zeit*, 19 December 1980; anon., "Allerbeste Seelenqualen," *Der Spiegel*, 51 (1980): 167. Julian A. Garforth deals with Tabori's Beckett productions in his essay "George Tabori's Bair Essentials — A Perspective on Beckett Staging in Germany," in *Forum Modernes Theater* 1 (1994): 59–75.

13. The German motto reads: "Ich bin unglücklich, aber nicht unglücklich genug. Das ist mein Unglück." The last word could be understood as meaning both unhappiness and bad luck.

14. Later in the evening the trainer shouts from the arena: "You are incompetent! Dump him into a concentration camp!"

15. George Tabori, "Besprechung," in *Betrachtungen*, pp. 36–37.

16. Cf. Tabori, "Warten auf Beckett," p. 60.

17. "Allerbeste Seelenqualen."

18. Fischer, "Arena ohne Ausweg."

19. George Tabori, letter to Beckett, 15 December 1980.

20. Michael Simbruk, "Glück im Zylinder?" (unpublished manuscript written in the course of rehearsals). Simbruk was one of the participants in the production. Tabori told Ellen Grebe that he was the first to obtain Beckett's permission to stage the prose text. See Ellen Grebe, "Das Einmalige im Theater," *Nürnberger Nachrichten*, 24 January 1980.

21. George Tabori, letter to Beckett, 24 October 1980.

22. Tabori, "Besprechung," p. 31.

23. Tabori kept a copy of the prose text with ample notes he wrote in the margins. See SAdK, Box 78.

24. Alfred Alvarez, rpt. in Manuel Lichtwitz, ed., *Materialien zu Samuel Beckett "Der Verwaiser,"* p. 186.

25. Joachim Kaiser, "Höllenlokal für Becketts letzte Menschen," in *Materialien*, ed. Lichtwitz, pp. 60–61.

26. Tabori, "Besprechung," p. 32.

27. The two main reasons for it were the fact that the cultural department of the city of Munich refused to pay the high price requested by the management of the Atlas-Circus and Tabori's insistence on producing the play with no less than twenty actors.

28. Tabori, "Besprechung," p. 37.

29. For the differences between the three versions, see Ohngemach, *George Tabori*, pp. 30–33.

30. Tabori, "Besprechung," pp. 34 37.

31. Cf. Ohngemach, *George Tabori*, p. 33.

32. Tabori asks Beckett about the meaning of the three titles in his letter of 18 January 1981.

33. Cf. Tabori, unpublished manuscript which was distributed among the actors during the rehearsals.

34. Tabori, "Besprechung," p. 32. See also Ohngemach, *George Tabori*, p. 33.

35. Program for *The Lost Ones*, published on the occasion of the presentation in Berlin in 1981, p. 3.

36. See, for instance, *Jubilee* or the poem "Was mich ärgert, am meisten ärgert."

37. Program for the presentation in Berlin, p. 3.

38. Cf. Tabori, "Besprechung," p. 33.

39. Michael Erdmann, "Turm der lebenden Leichen," *Theater Heute* 8 (1981): 44–45. Other interesting reviews include Nina Hellenkemper and Pet Klöpges, "In Erwartung der Katastrophe," *Revue Köln*, 26 November 1981; and Ingrid Seidenfaden, "Ohne Zirkus, ohne Raum, ohne Geld," *Abendzeitung*, 14 March 1981. See also a television report about the production shown on WDR on 1 July 1981.

40. Geogre Tabori, unpublished notes on *Der Verwaiser*, SAdK, Box 78. See also Jochen Winter's account, "Rituale der Vergenglichkeit und der Liebe," in *Tabori*, ed. Welker, pp. 157–158.

41. In the Berlin version the text was read live by actor Günter Einbrodt, who sat in the middle of the acting area.

42. Michael Erdmann, "Turm der lebenden Leichen," *Theater Heute* 8 (1981): 44–45; program for *The Lost Ones*, p. 3.

43. Tabori, "Warten auf Beckett," p. 61.

44. Samuel Beckett, letter to Klaus Herm, 9 August 1984. Cf. James Knowlson, *Damned to Fame: The Life of Samuel Beckett*, p. 693. Unfortunately, there is no trace of Beckett's letters to Tabori at the Tabori Archive.

45. See Ohngemach, "Gespräch mit Thomas Holtzmann: Ein Herz und eine

Seele," in *George Tabori*, pp. 109–116. See also Tabori's notes on the play (8–9/1983) in SAdK, Box 17 and in Box 28.

46. George Tabori, "Eros und Empfindsamkeit," *Theater Heute* 11 (1989): 8.

47. Cf. Charlotte Nennecke, "Flüchtlingsgespräch statt Clownspiele," *Süddeutsche Zeitung*, 3 January 1984.

48. Joachim Kaiser, "Was man tut, wenn man nichts tut," *Süddeutsche Zeitung*, 7 January 1984. Among the many reviews of this production, see Armin Eichholz, "Ist das die Wende im Becketts Warte-Raum?" *Münsterländische Tageszeitung*, 7 January 1984; Ingrid Seidenfaden, "Der Küchenwecker sagt tick-tack," *Abendzeitung*, 7 January 1984; Hans Schwab-Felisch, "Was bleibt, ist Warten," *Frankfurter Allgemeine Zeitung*, 9 January 1984; Helmut Schödel, "Das Glück am Ende des Tunnels," *Die Zeit*, 13 January 1984; Barbara Schmitz-Burckhardt, "Man hätte ihnen endlos zuschauen mögen," *Frankfurter Rundschau*, 18 January 1984; Peter Iden, "Gesellschaft — was ist das?" *Frankfurter Rundschau*, 28 January 1984; Reinhard Baumgart, "Vorsicht, die Komödianten kommen," *Der Spiegel*, 30 January 1984; Peter von Becker, "Existenzchoreographien oder die Stunde der Komödianten," *Theater Heute* 3 (1984): 4–6; and Friedrich Luft, "Tragisches Spiel von lässiger Herrlichkeit," *Berliner Morgenpost*, 9 May 1984. See also Jonathan Kalb, *Beckett in Performance*, pp. 91–92.

49. In later performances the opening scene was changed. The acting area was empty, and the leading actors were summoned by their private names to enter. Holtzmann and Lühr entered with cups of coffee and sat down at the table.

50. Rolf May, "Das Warten lohnt," *Die Tageszeitung*, 7 January 1984.

51. George Tabori, "Die einfachste Stimme," in *Tabori*, ed. Gronius and Kässens, p. 49.

52. Schmitz-Burckhardt, "Man hätte ihnen endlos zuschauen mögen."

53. Iden, "Gesellschaft — was ist das?"

54. Tabori, "Warten auf Beckett," p. 51.

55. George Tabori, letter to Beckett, 24 October 1980.

56. Martin Esslin, "Towards the Zero of Language," in James Acheson and Kateryna Arthur, eds., *Beckett's Later Fiction and Drama*, p. 35.

57. Cf. George Tabori, "Berliner Betten," in *Betrachtungen*, p. 244.

58. Tabori in an interview published in the *Süddeutsche Zeitung*, 12 April 1986. For rehearsal work, see Bohn and Schröder, *Theater des Zorns*, pp. 54–56. Tabori's handwritten rehearsal notes are in SAdK, Box 28 and Box 78.

59. Tabori in an interview with the *Süddeutsche Zeitung*, 12 April 1986.

60. See, for instance, Joachim Kaiser, "Wie Tabori Beckett banalisiert," *Süddeutsche Zeitung*, 15 April 1986.

61. For instance, Armin Eichholz, "Respekt vor dem Mut zu solchen Fehlern," *Münchner Merkur*, 15 April 1986. For other valuable reviews, see Wolfgang Ignée, "Leben, das bessere Theater?" *Stuttgarter Zeitung*, 17 April 1986; Michael Skasa, "Im Bett: Beckett," *Die Zeit*, 18 April 1986; Wolfgang Müller-Funk, "Beckett — einmal psychoanalytisch," *Die Presse*, 23 April 1986; and Peter

von Becker, "Beckett spielen im Ehehöllenbett," *Theater Heute* 6 (1986): 55.

62. Cf. Michael Warton, "*Waiting for Godot* and *Endgame*: Theatre as Text," in *The Cambridge Companion to Beckett*, ed. John Pilling, p. 71.

63. Gerhard Stadelmaier, "Probieren geht über Beckett," *Frankfurter Allgemeine Zeitung*, 2 February 1998. For other reviews, see Uwe Mattheiss, "Du outrierst! — Da steht: elegisch," *Süddeutsche Zeitung*, 3 February 1998; Wolfgang Reiter, "Bloßes Spiel," *Neue Zürcher Zeitung*, 3 February 1998; and Michael Merschmeier, "Play It Again, George," *Theater Heute* 3 (1998): 12–13.

64. Gronius and Kässens, *Tabori*, p. 47.

65. Tabori, "Besprechung am ersten Probentag," p. 31.

7. *LOVERS AND LUNATICS*: A SHAKESPEARE COLLAGE

1. The productions are *The Merchant of Venice as Performed in Theresienstadt*, Berkshire Theatre Festival, 1966; *Hamlet*, Bremen, 1978; *"Ich wollte meine Tochter läge tot zu meinen Füßen und hätte die Juwelen in den Ohren": Improvisationen über Shakespeares Shylock*, Munich, 1978; *Verliebte und Verrückte*, Vienna, 1989; *Lears Schatten*, Bregenz and Vienna, 1989; *Othello*, Vienna, 1990; *Hamlet*, Vienna, 1990. At the height of the Waldheim affair in Austria, in 1989, Tabori considered staging *Measure for Measure*, foregrounding topical political issues, but he had to give up the plan. Following his eightieth birthday, he said there were two more Shakespeare plays he would like to direct: *Timon of Athens* and another production of *Lear*. One of Tabori's favorite sentence constructions (for instance, "Between the longing and the fulfillment there falls a shadow," *Betrachtungen*, p. 101) follows *Julius Caesar* II.i.63. See also *Betrachtungen*, p. 94. Finally, Tabori named his dog Gobbo, after *The Merchant of Venice*.

2. These include "Desdemona," "Measure for Measure," "Romeo," "Lear," "Tempest," "Richard and the Hebrews," "Shylock," "Ophelia," "Hamlet," "Cleopatra," and also "Oedipus," all under the heading "The Classics," SAdK, Box 29.

3. Paul Tabori, letter to George Tabori, 30 August 1953, SAdK, Box 35.

4. George Tabori, letter to Paul Tabori, no date, written in Roxbury, Conn., SAdK, Box 35.

5. George Tabori, letter to Paul Tabori, no date, written in Dennis, Mass., SAdK, Box 35.

6. Ibid.

7. George Tabori in the program for the *Verwandlungen* production, Kammerspiele, Munich, 23 February 1977.

8. George Tabori, "Es geht schon wieder los," in *Unterammergau*, p. 202.

9. Tabori, "Betrachtungen," p. 104.

10. George Tabori, "Künstler und Hexen," in *Tabori*, ed. Welker, p. 175. See also "Betrachtungen," p. 106.

11. Tabori, "Betrachtungen," p. 109.

12. Gunther Baumann, "Schlag' nach bei Shakespeare," *Wiener*, March 1989.

13. *Lovers and Lunatics* premiered at the Kreis on 14 March 1989. The performance was split after the premiere and shown on two consecutive evenings.

14. Michael Patterson, *Peter Stein: Germany's Leading Theatre Director*, p. 125.

15. Tabori, "Verliebte und Verrückte," p. 88.

16. Sibylle Fritsch, "Beziehungskisten," *Profil*, 14 March 1989, p. 88. Andreas Szalla was responsible for the set, Birgit Hutter for the costumes.

17. These included *A Midsummer Night's Dream, Richard III, As You Like It, Twelfth Night, Measure for Measure, Macbeth, Hamlet, Othello, Henry V, Troilus and Cressida, The Taming of the Shrew, Antony and Cleopatra, The Merchant of Venice*, and *Romeo and Juliet* as well as some of Shakespeare's sonnets. The episodes from *Othello* and *Henry V* were eventually taken out of the collage, though occasionally reincorporated in a later performance.

18. Tabori, "Verliebte und Verrückte," p. 88.

19. Sigrid Löffler, "Fool and Lover," *Profil*, 20 March 1989, p. 100.

20. "Fools for Love," *Wochenpresse*, 17 March 1989.

21. Fritsch, "Beziehungskisten."

22. Knitting is one of Höpfner's passions, and it was her suggestion to incorporate her hobby in the depiction of Lady Macbeth.

23. Cf. "Shakespeare-Collage Verliebte und Verrückte im Kreis," *Die Presse*, 2 March 1989.

24. Rolf Michaelis, "Verliebte und Verrückte," *Die Zeit*, 7 April 1989.

25. Cf. Fritsch, "Beziehungskisten." "Much of the misunderstanding and the pain in Shakespeare stems from the fact that the men do not listen or pay heed to what the women have to say," maintains Tabori in *Tabori*, ed. Welker, p. 225.

26. Fritsch, "Beziehungskisten."

27. Ludwig Plakolb, "Zehn 'Mille' für sechs Stunden," *Österreichische Nachrichten*, 16 March 1989. See also Paul Kruntorad, "Wie in der tiefsten Theaterprovinz," *Frankfurter Rundschau*, 1 April 1989.

8. *KING LEAR*: VARIATIONS

1. George Tabori, letter to Paul Tabori, no date, marked 1a, SAdK, Box 35 (to judge by the context, the letter dates back to his New York days in the early 1950s); and letter to Paul Tabori, August, no year, SAdK, Box 35.

2. George Tabori, "Cues for the Actors," manuscript, SAdK, Box 80. The German version was printed in the program for the production *Lears Schatten* in Bregenz, July 1988.

3. Cf. Baumann, "Schlag' nach bei Shakespeare."

4. George Tabori, "Cues." I would spell it "Mentsch," as Tabori obviously refers to the Yiddish, not the German meaning of the word.

5. Cf. Tabori's letter to Samuel Beckett, 24 October 1980, SAdK, Box 78.

6. George Tabori, "Der alte Mann und was mehr," in *Betrachtungen*, p. 214.

7. Tabori, "Betrachtungen," p. 111. Tabori also praises Brook's and Strehler's

"wonderful productions" of *Lear* and likewise mentions the Japanese film *Ran*. Cf. Tabori, "Cues."

8. Noteworthy also is the fact that around the same time, in 1989, the Kreis troupe staged Ronald Howard's *The Dresser*, a play which likewise revolves around the *Lear* fable.

9. Alfred Pfoser, "Stalin in Stöckelschuhen," *Salzburger Nachrichten*, 11 March 1988.

10. Klaus Reitz, "Zwei alte Männer spielen König Lear," *Mannheimer Morgen*, 4 June 1988. The world premiere of Gaston Salvatore's *Stalin* was directed by Herbert Sasse at the Schiller Theater in Berlin, 31 October 1987, and received mediocre to bad reviews.

11. Tabori, "Cues."

12. "Zwei wie Katz und Maus," *Wochenpresse*, 18 March 1988.

13. The set and costumes were designed by Marietta Eggmann.

14. Heinz Sichrovsky, "Kunst kämpft mit der Macht," *Neue Kronen Zeitung*, 11 March 1988.

15. Sibylle Fritsch, "Grenzgänger," *Profil*, 22 February 1988.

16. Sigmund Freud, "The Uncanny," in *The Collected Works*, vol. 12, p. 235.

17. Cf. Heinz Sichrovsky, "Shakespeare — unterm Seziermesser," *Kronen Zeitung*, 24 July 1989.

18. Tabori, "Cues."

19. Ibid.

20. Sigmund Freud, "Das Motiv der Kästchenwahl," in *Gesammelte Werke*, vol. 10, esp. pp. 26–36.

21. Cf. "Lange Schatten, wenig Licht," *Neue Zürcher Zeitung*, 25 July 1989; or Thomas Terry, "Ein doppelter, aber kein ganzer Lear," *Bühne*, September 1989.

22. See "Lears Schatten — Eine Übermalung," *Der Standard*, 19 September 1989.

23. Sibylle Fritsch, "Theater ist keine Pizzafabrik," *Profil*, 16 October 1989, p. 98; and Baumann, "Schlag' nach bei Shakespeare."

24. Sigrid Löffler, "Lear in Therapie," *Profil*, 25 September 1989.

25. Tabori, "Cues."

26. Löffler, "Lear in Therapie"; and Wolfgang Herles, "Das Herz auf der Zunge, den Apfel im Mund," *Der Standard*, 21 September 1989. Wolfgang Reiter speaks of a "Brechtian ascetics" in his review "Lear II," *Falter*, 29 September 1989.

27. Luise Czerwonatis designed the set, Birgit Hutter the costumes.

28. Hilde Haider-Pregler, "Archetypische Shakespeare-Bilder," *Wiener Zeitung*, 22 September 1989.

29. Tabori, "Cues."

30. Typical is Löffler, "Lear in Therapie." Among the positive reviews are Erich Demmer, "Wenn Macht zahnlos wird," *Abendzeitung*, 21 September 1989; Regina Doppelbauer, "Der greise Lear schreitet den Kreis seiner selbst und der Welt ab," *Tiroler Tageszeitung*, 21 September 1989; and Wolfgang Freitag, "Schattenbilder mächtiger Könige," *Die Presse*, 21 September 1989. Among

the negative evaluations of the performance are Andrea Amort, "Skizzen eines Themas," *Kurier*, 21 September 1989; and Reiter, "Lear II." Reiter was one of the very few critics who preferred the Bregenz version to the Vienna one. Cf. Wolfgang Reiter, "Die Probe als Aufführung," *Falter*, 2 August 1989.

31. Haider-Pregler, "Archetypische Shakespeare-Bilder."

9. *HAMLET*: ALL OVER AGAIN

1. Tabori used Heiner Müller's translation in Bremen and Erich Fried's rendering of the play in Vienna. His dramaturgical assistant in Vienna was Ursula Voss. Actors Ursula Höpfner, Detlef Jacobsen, Klaus Fischer, and Rainer Frieb participated in both productions.
2. Tabori, "Hamlet in Blue," p. 119.
3. Tabori's notes in the program for *Hamlet*, Vienna, 22 May 1990.
4. The set was designed by Luise Czerwonatis.
5. Paul Kruntorad, "Kein anderer Shakespeare," *Frankfurter Rundschau*, 29 May 1990.
6. Hilde Haider-Pregler, "Nur ein skizzenhafter Entwurf," *Wiener Zeitung*, 24 May 1990.
7. As in the Bremen version, the relationship between Hamlet and Horatio is a homoerotic one.
8. George Tabori, "Lächendes Rätsel," *Theater Heute* (Jahresband 1995): 123.
9. Tabori, "Hamlet in Blue," p. 123.
10. Wolfgang Reiter, "Solo für Hamlet," *Falter* 22 (1 June 1990): 12. See also Barbara Petsch, "Marathon für eine geniale Schauspielerin," *Die Presse*, 25 May 1990.

10. *OTHELLO*: THE TRIUMPH OF A DEFEATED MAN

1. Tabori, "Betrachtungen," p. 103.
2. Tabori in *Tabori*, ed. Welker, p. 318.
3. Karl-Ernst Herrmann was in charge of the set, Jorge Jara of the costumes.
4. Surprisingly, only two critics seem to have paid attention to her. Cf. Rolf Michaelis, "Eine Liebe nach dem Tod," *Die Zeit*, 19 January 1990; and Sibylle Fritsch, "Die großen Gefühle," *Profil*, 18 January 1990.
5. Rolf Michaelis also finds a political undertone, associating the Arabic figure with Palestinian Intifada women, "Eine Liebe."
6. George Tabori, "Es geht schon wieder los," in *Unterammergau*, p. 202.
7. George Tabori, "Das Theater ist ein Liebesakt," *Die Tageszeitung*, 24 January 1990.
8. "Der Mohr von Wien: Portrait: Gert Voss," *Zeit* (Magazine), 5 January 1990, pp. 7–8.

9. Wolfgang Höbel, "Der schwarze Bluff," *Der Spiegel,* January 1990 (exact date unknown).

10. Gerhard Stadelmaier, "Mensch Mohr oder Sterben ist geschmacklos," *Frankfurter Allgemeine Zeitung,* 12 January 1990.

11. "Im Clinch zerstörerischer Leidenschaften," *Neue Zürcher Zeitung,* 20 January 1990.

12. Tabori, "Betrachtungen," p. 101.

11. A BLACK MASS IN BERLIN: *THE CANNIBALS*

1. George Tabori, letter to Paul Tabori, 10 January [1970] and 29 December [1969], SAdK, Box 35.

2. The play, directed by Martin Fried and George Tabori, was premiered on 13 December 1969. The text was translated into German by Peter Sandberg. Whenever relying on the German version *Die Kannibalen,* I refer to *Theaterstücke,* vol. 1, pp. 1–74. Quotations and references to the English version are taken from *The Cannibals* in *The Theater of the Holocaust: Four Plays,* ed. Robert Skloot, pp. 201–265. An early single play edition was published by Davis-Poynter (London, 1974).

3. Directed by Martin Fried, the play was premiered with the American Place Theatre in New York on 17 October 1968. An earlier attempt to involve director Joe Chaikin in the production came to nothing. "I spoke briefly to Joe Chaikin on the phone," writes Wynn Handman to Tabori. "He has read the play several times, has great admiration for it, but seriously doubts his ability to fulfill it and does not wish to be thought as a director of it." Wynn Handman, letter to George Tabori, 14 July 1967, SAdK, Box 64. In a letter to Tabori, 16 October 1967, SAdK, Box 64, Chaikin explains his reservations about the play.

4. Walter Kerr, "Where Do You Draw a Line?" *New York Times,* 8 November 1968. For other reviews, see Clive Barnes, "Theater: The Cannibals," *Times,* 4 November 1968; Daphne Kraft, "Cannibals: Powerful," *Evening News,* 4 November 1968; John Lahr, "On Refusing to Swallow," *New York Free Press,* 7 November 1968; Robert Pasoli, "The Cannibals," *Village Voice,* 7 November 1968; R. B., "Ein Tollhaus in der Kirche," *Aufbau,* 8 November 1968; and Marilyn Stasio, "The Cannibals," *Cue,* 9 November 1968. Viveca Lindfors, Tabori's wife at that time, speaks of a "modest success" in her memoirs, *Viveka . . . Viveca,* p. 28. Dr. Maria Piscator, widow of director Erwin Piscator, was among the spectators who wrote to Tabori after attending the performance. "I must tell you that not in years have I been so fascinated and moved by any other play, here or abroad. I was literally shaken" (Maria Piscator, letter to George Tabori, 1 November 1968, SAdK, Box 49).

5. Lindfors, *Viveka,* p. 28.

6. Peter Münder, "Die Dummheit aller Dämonologien: George Taboris Romane," in *Tabori,* ed. Gronius and Kässens, p. 68.

7. Cf. Lindfors, *Viveka,* p. 223.

8. André Müller, "Ich habe mein Lachen verloren," *Die Zeit,* 6 May 1994.

9. Tabori, *Unterammergau,* p. 21.

10. See SAdK, Boxes 5, 49, 50, and 64.

11. George Tabori, letter to Paul Tabori, 22 October 1947, SAdK, Box 35.

12. T. V. Boardman, letter to George Tabori, 13 February 1948, SAdK, Box 81/12.

13. Dietmar N. Schmidt, "Aus Betroffenheit Kunst: Nathan, Shylock," in *Tabori,* ed. Welker, p. 106.

14. George Tabori in a radio interview with Bob Dworkin, CBS, 21 September 1947, SAdK, Box 57.

15. For instance, George Tabori, "Dieses peinliche Wort: Liebe," in *Tabori,* ed. Welker, p. 319; Tabori, *Unterammergau,* p. 11; and Tabori in notes to his production of *The Merchant of Venice* at the Berkshire Festival, USA, 1966 (ms. entitled "For B.H.") SAdK, Box 62. Here the sentence reads ". . . After you, Alphonse." Cf. the inclusion of this statement in *Cannibals,* p. 204 ("After you, sir") and p. 236 ("After you, gentlemen!").

16. Tabori, unpublished notes to *The Merchant of Venice,* SAdK, Box 62, p. 1. Tabori expressed the view that "Auschwitz was in a way the last Jewish gesture. . . . There are satisfactions in being a victim" (letter to Mr. Handman, 4 July 1967, SAdK, Box 67). By comparison, the militant Israel is "the end of Jewishness." Cf. also: "As long as one is the victim, one has in any case a certain moral integrity. The minute one stops being a victim, one becomes a perpetrator. Innocence is lost" (Tabori in an interview with Koelbl, *Jüdische Portraits,* p. 237).

17. See Sven Michaelsen, "Gipfeltreffen der Provokateure," *Stern* (26 May 1994): 70. Tabori mentions his visit to Auschwitz and says he desperately looked for the spirit of his father and failed to find it there, in that tourist-filled site. See also his "Kitsch in Auschwitz," in *Betrachtungen,* pp. 164–165; and "Geschmacksfrage," in *Betrachtungen,* pp. 158–159.

18. Wolfgang Roth, who had worked for Brecht, was in charge of the setting of both the American and the German productions.

19. Jörg Gronius, "Bitte zu Tisch," in *Tabori,* ed. Gronius and Kässens, p. 19.

20. Yosef Hayim Yerushalmi, *Zakhor: Jewish History and Jewish Memory,* p. 5.

21. George Tabori, "Es geht schon wieder los," in *Unterammergau,* p. 200.

22. Tabori, *Unterammergau,* p. 19.

23. Cf. Yerushalmi, *Zakhor,* p. 44.

24. George Tabori, "Die Kannibalen: Zur europäischen Erstaufführung," in *Unterammergau,* pp. 37–39. I refer to and quote from the original article entitled "Parricide," SAdK, Box 81/16.

25. Tabori, "Kannibalen," p. 37.

26. Jewish actor Michael Degen (born 1932) survived the war in a hiding place together with his mother. His father died in a concentration camp. Degen, who played the part of Uncle, later played the leading parts in Tabori's *Masada* (1988) and *Weisman and Copperface* (1990).

27. Tabori, *Unterammergau,* p. 23.

28. Tabori, "Kannibalen," p. 38.

29. Andrea Welker, "Das Wort is eine heilige Waffe," in *Tabori*, ed. Welker, p. 301.

30. Cf. Sigmund Freud, *Totem and Taboo*, translated and edited by James Strachey, pp. 174 ff.

31. George Tabori, "Parricide," Box 81/16. The German version, "Kannibalen," *Unterammergau*, p. 37, leaves out the first sentence.

32. Interestingly, Richard Schechner's 1969 production of *Makbeth* forefronted the image of the totemistic cannibal feasting. The motif of parricide recurs in many plays and prose texts by Tabori. See, for instance, his play *Peepshow*, the two productions of *Hamlet* (1978 and 1990), and his Kafka production *Unruhige Träume*.

33. In Müller's play three hungry German soldiers kill their comrade and consume him as a cannibalistic parody of the Last Supper.

34. Leah Hadomi, *Dramatic Metaphors of Fascism and Antifascism*, p. 84. For further interpretations of the play, see Brigitte Marschall, "Verstrickt in Geschichte(n): Im Würgegriff des Überlebenskampfes George Taboris," *Maske und Kothurn* 1–4 (1991): 311–325; Christian Klein, "Unter jedem Stein schläft ein Skorpion: Vom Familienroman zum Theaterstück: Der Fall von Georg [*sic*] Taboris *Die Kannibalen*," in *Ecritures de la mémoire* (*Cahiers d'Etudes Germaniques*), ed. Ingrid Haag and Michel Vanoosthuyse (1995): 167–177; Rachel Perets, "Vom Erhabenen ins Groteske —George Taboris *Die Kannibalen*," in *In der Sprache der Täter*, ed. Stephan Braese, pp. 117–136; Cf. also the ritualistic consumption of the Jewish victim as the Eucharist in Tabori's *My Mother's Courage*.

35. Tabori, *Cannibals*, 239, and *Kannibalen*, 44. Cf. for instance Job 2:12.

36. Only in the English version, *Cannibals*, 210 and 252.

37. Tabori maintains that Jewish religion is based on a dialogue with God and that this dialogue was disrupted through the Holocaust. See Koelbl, *Jüdische Portraits*, p. 236.

38. Tabori, *Cannibals*, 211 and 235. Cf. the priest and the German officer in white gloves in *My Mother's Courage*.

39. Tabori, "Kannibalen," p. 39.

40. Tabori also refers (in the English version only!) to Deuteronomy 14:7–21 (*Cannibals*, pp. 216–217).

41. Cf. Claude Lévi-Strauss, *The Raw and the Cooked*. See also Nick Fiddes, *Meat: A Natural Symbol* (London and New York: Routledge, 1991).

42. As for the name Puffi, Tabori writes in "Tod am Nachmittag" in (*Unterammergau*, p. 181) about Puffi Huszár, "the fattest actor in the world," who featured in the first movie he saw as a child.

43. Tabori, *Cannibals*, pp. 264–265. Cf. on cannibalism, Fiddes, *Meat*, pp. 121–131; W. Arens, *The Man-Eating Myth* (New York: Oxford University Press, 1979); Hedwig Röcklein, ed., *Kannibalismus und europäische Kultur* (Tübingen: G. Kimmerle, 1996); Frank Lestringant, *Cannibals* (Berkeley: University of California Press, 1997).

44. George Tabori, "Der Tod des Kritikers," in *Betrachtungen*, p. 175. In this essay

as well as in his "Les Gourmets," in *Betrachtungen*, pp. 149–150, cooking, and its adjunct eating, is the central metaphor in Tabori's discussion of theatre critics and their métier. Notably, Brecht spoke derogatively of the "culinary theatre," which offers nothing but shallow entertainment. Antonin Artaud had a similar name for it — "digestive" theatre. The eating/cooking metaphor is crucial to Tabori's "Ein Weihnachtsschmaus," in *Betrachtungen*, pp. 7–8.

45. Frederick S. Perls, *Ego, Hunger and Aggression: The Beginning of Gestalt Therapy*, p. 117.

46. George Tabori, "Es geht," in *Unterammergau*, p. 201.

47. Tabori, *Cannibals*, p. 254. Tabori comments on this sentence in relation to his father's identity in a letter to Viveca Lindfors, 10 April 1979.

48. Tabori, *Unterammergau*, p. 22.

49. Rolf Michaelis, "Ein Alptraumspiel," *Frankfurter Allgemeine Zeitung*, 15 December 1969.

50. Ohngemach, *George Tabori*, p. 51.

51. Jürgen Beckelmann, "Widersinniger Nachruhm," *Frankfurter Rundschau*, 17 December 1969, and "Unter Kannibalen im KZ," *Kölner-Stadt-Anzeiger*, 18 December 1969; and H. K., "Fleisch ist Fleisch," *Abendzeitung*, 22 December 1969. See also Friedrich Luft, "Schwarze Messe mit einer Gruppe aus dem Tartarus," *Die Welt*, 14 December 1969.

52. See Karena Niehoff, "Der Mensch lebt nicht vom Mensch allein," *Süddeutsche Zeitung*, 18 December 1969; and Dora Fehling, "Mit Kannibalen und Gespenstern," *Madame* (Munich, May 1970): 12–13. See also the controversy over the play and its implication in *Tribüne* 33 (1970): 3602–3661.

53. Fiddes, *Meat*, p. 90.

54. Tabori's attempts to find a British stage for *Cannibals* (before its premiere in New York) failed. Peter Hall, artistic director of the RSC, wrote: "It is a play that *must* be done but I think for us to do it would give it a bad start because our opinions and attitudes are already well known in this direction. . . . If we had not done 'The Representative' and 'The Investigation' and one or two other pieces asking the same sort of question, I think we would have gone for 'Cannibals' in a big way" (Peter Hall, letter to George Tabori, 25 April 1967, SAdK, Box 64). A discussion of the productions of Holocaust plays on the London stage, including *The Representative* and *The Investigation*, is available in Nicholas John White, "In the Absence of Memory? Jewish Fate and Dramatic Representation: The Production and Critical Reception of Holocaust Drama on the London Stage 1945–1989."

12. THE WOUND AND THE KNIFE: VARIATIONS ON SHYLOCK

1. George Tabori, "Es geht schon wieder los," in *Unterammergau*, p. 202.

2. See John Gross, *Shylock*, pp. 299–326.

3. Tabori in an interview with Sabine Durrant, "The Art of Darkness," *Independent* (London), October 1989. In the same interview Tabori expresses his

disappointment with Peter Hall's production of the play (with Dustin Hoffman as Shylock), primarily because Hall's production ignores the Holocaust.

4. George Tabori, "Ein Goi bleibt immer ein Goi . . . " in *Unterammergau*, p. 30.

5. Dan Diner, "Negative Symbiose: Deutsche und Juden nach Auschwitz," *Babylon: Beiträge zur jüdischen Gegenwart* 1 (1986): 9–20.

6. Tabori in an interview with Sabine Durrant.

7. See Tabori, "Es geht," 204.

8. George Tabori, "Spiel und Zeit," in *Betrachtungen*, p. 22.

9. Cf. Tabori's statement: "You are reminded by the others that you are a Jew," in Koelbl, *Jüdische Portraits*, p. 234. Elsewhere Tabori writes: "I would not be a Jew if the Germans hadn't reminded me of being one" (*Unterammergau*, p. 26).

10. Tabori, "Hamlet in Blue," p. 117. See Thomas Rothschild's discussion in "Die Wunde versteht das Messer," in *Text + Kritik* 133 (January 1997): 4–9.

11. Zadek's production, with Hans Mahnke as Shylock, premiered on 30 December 1972 in Bochum. See Mechthild Lange, *Peter Zadek* (Frankfurt/M.: Fischer Verlag, 1989), esp. pp. 54 and 47. Zadek first staged the play in Ulm in 1961, and again, for the third time, in Vienna in 1988. See Peter Zadek, *My Way: Eine Autobiographie, 1926–1969*, pp. 315–322. Critic Georg Hensel describes Zadek's unconventional and provocative interpretations in "Laudatio auf Peter Zadek," in *My Way*, pp. 548–549.

In a letter to Zadek, 9 August 1988, Tabori writes: "My feeling is that since the '*Schonzeit*' is over, this sort of self-criticism [he refers to the controversial British play *Perdition* by Jim Allen, 1987] can and will be easily abused by the audience. I think what 'Ghetto' has done and to a more modest degree my 'Cannibals' is for the time being enough to fill the black hole which gapes both in Germany as well as in Austria. Besides, you are doing the 'Merchant,' which is after all still the best play about anti-Semitism" (SAdK, Box 76/10).

12. Other productions included Thornton Wilder's *The Skin of Our Teeth*, directed by Arthur Penn, Beckett's *Waiting for Godot*, directed by Gene Frankel, and Robinson Jeffers's *The Cretan Women*, directed by Martin Fried, who subsequently accompanied Tabori in America and in Europe, acted as director or assistant-director of Tabori's plays, and was "always there to help George out of a directorial trouble," according to actor Detlef Jacobsen.

13. Lindfors, *Viveka . . . Viveca*, p. 251.

14. R. E. Krieger, "Merchant, Nazi Style," no place, no date, SAdK, Box 62.

15. Reuter Newsagency, "Shakespeare's Shylock in a Nazi Camp," no date, SAdK, Box 62.

16. The unidentified author reports in his typed manuscript, SAdK, Box 62, on "violent reactions in the audience; some walked out, some talked out loud, some demanded their money back, great numbers seemed deeply moved." Box 62 holds spectators' written reactions to the production, among them a lengthy report by Lucien Aigner, 1 August 1966, in which his verdict reads: " . . . it is a terrific idea, but the play is not yet written. . . . Pulled together

from the various elements, a hodge podge full of inconsistencies, contradictions, vagueness, symbolic hints in the Stockbridge production, it remains highly confusing."

17. Cf. Leon A. Jick, "The Holocaust: Its Use and Abuse within the American Public," *Yad Vashem Studies* 14 (1981): 303–318. For the production and reception of Holocaust drama in the United States, see Edward R. Isser, *Stages of Annihilation: Theatrical Representations of the Holocaust.*

18. Gross, *Shylock*, pp. 300–301.

19. Unidentified author, SAdK, Box 62, also contains handwritten notes made by Tabori in preparation for rehearsals and during the rehearsing period.

20. Tabori recalls that he had twenty actors at his disposal, each of whom got $200 per week. See Jan Strümpel, "Große Krise, kleine Krise, lustige Krise," in *Text + Kritik* 133 (January 1997): 54.

21. Lindfors recounts how "GT had found an old, yellow flyer advertising a performance of the play in Auschwitz by a group of inmates" (*Viveca*, p. 251). Again, I believe she confuses Auschwitz with Theresienstadt, where theatre shows and other cultural activities were allowed to take place.

22. A study of theatre productions in concentration camps, especially in Theresienstadt, is offered by Angela Esther Metzger, *Wahrheit aus Tränen und Blut: Theater in nationalsozialistischen Konzentrationslagern von 1933–1945* (Hagen: Erich Walter, 1996). See also Zdenek Lederer, *Ghetto Theresienstadt* (London: Goldstein, 1953; New York: Fertig, 1983); and Michael Patterson, "The Final Chapter: Theatre in the Concentration Camps of Nazi Germany," in *Theatre in the Third Reich — Essays on Theatre in Nazi Germany*, ed. Glen W. Gudberry, (Westport, Conn.: Greenwood Press, 1995), pp. 157–165.

23. These seminal questions were embedded in Jehoshua Sobol's play *Ghetto* (1984) and in Hanan Snir's production of *The Merchant of Venice* at the theatre in Weimar in 1995. The Israeli director Snir followed (unknowingly?) Tabori's model: only a few kilometers away from the Buchenwald concentration camp, the actors of the Weimar Theatre were Jewish prisoners who presented Shakespeare's play to a group of Nazi officers! A discussion of Sobol's play is offered by Freddie Rokem, "On the Fantastic in Holocaust Performance," in *Staging the Holocaust*, ed. Claude Schumacher, pp. 45–48.

24. Curiously, Tabori himself speaks of "only three weeks" (Strümpel, "Große Krise," p. 54). I believe Tabori refers to the actual rehearsal period on site, leaving out the workshop phase. Since the gradual development of the mise-en-scène is so essential in Tabori's theatre-making, I decided to elucidate it from its outset. The preparatory phase included also watching and discussing Alain Resnais's film *Night and Fog*.

25. Program notes for the Berkshire Theatre Festival, SAdK, Box 62.

26. Krieger, "Merchant Nazi Style."

27. Lindfors, *Viveca*, p. 252.

28. Ibid. According to Tabori, there were two versions of the final scene and both played on opening night: his version, "which was more in line with Shakespeare's intention" (in all likelihood the one Lindfors describes); and Arthur Penn's version, which evolved as Tabori "was awfully tired and asked

Penn to 'go ahead, direct it too.' In Penn's version the good one wins. Shylock kills the Nazi. An American ending then" (Strümpel, "Große Krise," p. 54).

29. Tabori, "Es geht wieder," p. 203.

30. George Tabori, "Ein Goi," in *Unterammergau*, p. 30.

31. Andrea Welker and Tina Berger, eds., *"Ich wollte meine Tochter läge tot zu meinen Füßen und hätte die Juwelen in den Ohren": Improvisationen über Shakespeares Shylock*, p. 70.

32. In his reply to Tabori, 31 March 1981, director and friend Joseph Losey writes: "Both Patricia and I were profoundly shocked about your report of anti-Semitism in West Germany, your threatening phone calls, etc. Of course, it's going on here, too. And I'm sure it is in the United States, but somehow it seems less sinister" (SAdK, Box 74).

33. George Tabori, "Zehn Gebote, Nachbars Kuh," *Theater Heute* (Jahrbuch 1992): 25.

34. Kirstin Martins's rehearsal notes in "Der Fels, der in der Mitte bricht," *Theater Heute* 1 (1979): 52–55.

35. Stanley Walden, "Ein paar Gedanken über Improvisationen," in *Tabori*, ed. Welker, pp. 103–104.

36. Critic Georg Hensel points out the mistake of attributing the ballad, which was composed in Munich around 1558, to Pepys, in "Shakespeare, Jazz und Judenhaß," *Frankfurter Allgemeine Zeitung*, 23 November 1978.

37. Walden, "Ein paar Gedanken," p. 103.

38. George Tabori, in Welker and Berger, *"Ich wollte,"* p. 70.

39. The cast list registers each actor as Shylock/real name/role (i.e., Antonio, Jessica, etc.). Last on the list is Shylock /Stanley Walden/Der Klesmer. Cf. Welker and Berger, *"Ich wollte,"* p. 20.

40. In addition to the notes made by Kirstin Martins, I was also assisted by the notes of Marietta Eggmann and Ernst Wiener, who were responsible for set and costumes. See Welker and Berger, *"Ich wollte,"* pp. 95–96.

41. Tabori, "Ein Goi," p. 29. Compare Aleida Assmann's discussion of Auschwitz as memory site in *Erinnerungsräume* (Munich: Beck, 1999), pp. 329–334.

42. Tabori used a raw piece of meat also for his *Hungerkünstler* (1977) and his staging of *Hamlet* (1978) in Bremen. See chapters 3 and 4.

43. Tabori describes how a piece of raw meat was passed on from one actor to the other until one of them tore it apart and gave each a piece to eat. At that point, according to Tabori, "we were close to the secret" ("Es geht schon wieder," in *Unterammergau*, pp. 204–205).

44. Martins, "Der Fels," p. 52.

45. Reik, *The Search Within*, p. 359.

46. See Brigitte Marschall, "Verstrickt in Geschichte(n)," pp. 311–325.

47. Tabori, "Dieses peinliches Wort: Liebe," p. 318.

48. Martins, "Der Fels," p. 53.

49. SAdK, Box 31. The letter bears no date, but is most likely to have been written shortly after the premiere.

50. Martins, "Der Fels," p. 55.

51. Welker and Berger, "*Ich wollte*," p. 94.

52. Hannes S. Macher, "Theater der Grausamkeit," *Trostberger Tagblatt*, 24–25 November 1978.

53. Peter Zadek also incorporated such jokes in his 1972 production of the play.

54. Peter von Becker, "Von Juden und Christen, von Vätern und Kindern," *Süddeutsche Zeitung*, 21 November 1978.

55. During the rehearsals Tabori suggested that the actors be the creators and destroyers of these puppets. "Take the puppets and dress them as your own Shylock, paint them, give them hair. Later, torture them, kill them" (Welker and Berger, "*Ich wollte*," p. 27). Zadek also included puppets in his 1972 production. Spectators could pierce the arm of a Shylock puppet.

56. Welker and Berger, "*Ich wollte*," p. 48.

57. Michael Krüger, "Menschen-Spiele," *Theater Heute* 2 (1979): 4.

58. Von Becker, "Von Juden."

59. Welker and Beger, "*Ich wollte*," p. 63. Here it actually says "Goj'sche Schickse," but a Schickse is by definition non-Jewish.

60. Tabori: "Shylock should physically feel the thousand-year-old pursuit of justice by his own people, that path of suffering" (Angie Dullinger, "Die Quälerei um ein Pfund Fleisch," *Abendzeitung*, 18 November 1978).

61. On this issue, see Sander L. Gilman, *Franz Kafka: The Jewish Patient* (New York: Routledge, 1995), and *The Jew's Body* (London and New York: Routledge, 1991). Circumcision also figures in Tabori's *Weisman and Copperface*.

62. Welker and Berger, "*Ich wollte*," p. 84.

63. Rüdiger Hacker, "Existentieller Realismus oder Gott mit Dir, Du Land der Bayern," in "*Ich wollte*," ed. Welker and Berger, p. 93.

64. Wend Kässens, "Sehen, was man nicht sehen will," in *Tabori*, ed. Gronius and Kässens, p. 38.

65. Beate Kayser, "Trauren — das schönste was passieren kann," *Abendzeitung*, 2 January 1979.

66. See Felix von Manteuffel's report in Welker and Berger, "*Ich wollte*," p. 98. The Jewish author Richard Chaim Schneider describes the reaction of Jewish spectators to the show (ibid., pp. 89–90).

67. Von Becker, "Von Juden." See also Dietmar N. Schmidt, "Was die Tradition eine Komödie nennt," *Frankfurter Rundschau*, 25 November 1978; Ingrid Seidenfaden, "Shylock und wir," *Hannoversche Allgemeine Zeitung*, 25 November 1978; Helmut Schödel, "Der dreizehnfache Shylock," *Die Zeit*, 1 December 1978.

68. Among the negative reviews are anon., "Das Streiflicht," *Süddeutsche Zeitung*, 22 November 1978; anon., "Shylock im Souterrain," *Die Welt*, 23 November 1978; and Hans Lehmann, "Die große Show von Antisemitismus," *Darmstädter Echo*, 8 December 1978.

69. Anon., "Shylock im Souterrain."

70. Tabori in his interview with Dullinger, "Die Quälerei."

71. Armin Eichholz, "Aufregende Nachtübung mit dreizehn Shylocks," *Münchner Merkur*, 21 November 1978.

72. See Volker Canaris, "Die ersten Juden, die ich kannte, waren Nathan und

Shylock," *Theater Heute* 2 (1973): 20–25. See also Maria Verch, "*The Merchant of Venice* on the German Stage since 1945," *Theatre History Studies* 5 (1985): 84–94, and Anat Feinberg, "Shylock," in *Antisemitismus: Vorurteile und Mythen*, ed. Julius H. Schoeps and Joachim Schlör, p. 125.

73. Tabori, "Es geht," pp. 199–200.

13. A MOCK FAIRY TALE: *MY MOTHER'S COURAGE*

1. The story, in German translation, was first published in Tabori, *Son of a Bitch: Erzählungen* (1981), pp. 5–30. The stage text, in German translation, is printed in Tabori, *Unterammergau*, pp. 139–177, and in Tabori, *Theaterstücke*, vol. 1, pp. 285–317. Whenever I refer to or quote from the play, I rely on Tabori's original manuscript in English, SAdK, Box 4, although I give the pagination according to the 1994 German edition. The play premiered at the Kammerspiele in Munich on 17 May 1979. Tabori also directed it as a radio play for RIAS Berlin in 1979. Austrian film producer Michael Verhoeven directed the film based on the story. The film, premiered in 1996, won both the Bavarian Film Prize in 1996 and a special award at the 1997 Jerusalem Film Festival. For English reviews of the film, see Annette Insdorf, "On Film, World War II Is Still a Moral Minefield," *New York Times*, 31 August 1997; and Philip French, "Take That Look Off My Face," *Observer* (London), 9 November 1997.

2. Prompted by her son George, Elsa Tabori wrote down her life story shortly after the war. She described in "three pages" her narrow escape from the gas chambers, where her husband, Cornelius, found his death. The manuscript was lost, and Tabori wrote his version of the case years later from memory, as he told Alfred Biolek on the television talk show *Boulevard Bio*, WDR, 20 February 1996.

3. Georg Hensel, "Scheue Verklärung einer Mutter," *Frankfurter Allgemeine Zeitung*, 19 May 1979; and Benjamin Henrichs, "Jüdischer Muttertag," *Die Zeit*, 1 June 1979.

4. Sibylle Fritsch, "Wiener Alpträume," *Illustrierte Neue Welt* 4 (1996): 10. During my conversation with him, Tabori spoke of "a crack" in his mother. "She used to be soft as cream, but after the war her chin was like a rock." The English version of the story (p. 6) speaks of "a petrified mother."

5. Koelbl, *Jüdische Portraits*, p. 236.

6. George Tabori, letter to Paul Tabori, 21 January 1949, SAdK, Box 35. In another letter, to his daughter Lena, no place, no date, Tabori writes: "I spent the evening with Mother. She was reminiscing of her concentration camp days. An SS guard once told her, 'You are nice. If you weren't Jewish, I'd talk to you.' Mother replied: 'If you weren't a Christian, I wouldn't be here to talk to.' I didn't realize she had wit."

7. Tabori in the program for the production of *My Mother's Courage*, Kammerspiele, Munich, 1979.

8. Klaus Colberg, "Der Massenmord und die Ausnahme," *Wiesbadener Tagblatt*, 26 May 1979.

9. Ursula Höpfner, "Der Begriff der Authentizität," ms., pp. 37–38, SAdK, Box 91b.

10. In a letter to his ex-wife Viveca Lindfors, 10 April 1979, SAdK, Box 74, Tabori suggests the impossibility of having two identical versions of a specific story and mentions in this connection *My Mother's Courage*, which he was rehearsing at the time.

11. Tabori to Alfred Biolek in *Boulevard Bio*; and Höpfner, "Authentizität," p. 36.

12. A number of critics spoke of the unnecessary duplication — the acting out of that which had already been recounted. See, for example, Peter von Becker, "Wie kompliziert war Elsa Tabori?" *Theater Heute* 7 (1979): 36–37. Cf. also Martin Kagel's analysis of the play in "Mit den Augen der Mutter: Über George Taboris *Mutters Courage*," in *Verkörperte Geschichtsentwürfe*, ed. Höyng, pp. 89–105.

13. For a short description of the filming, see Sandra Pott and Jörg Schönert, "Tabori unter den Deutschen: Stationen einer authentischen Existenz?" in *Theater gegen das Vergessen*, ed. Bayerdörfer and Schönert, pp. 372–377.

14. Von Becker, "Wie kompliziert?"

15. Hanna Schygulla in interview with Gundula Ohngemach, in Ohngemach, *George Tabori*, pp. 103–108, esp. p. 104. Schygulla, who considered both Tabori and Fassbinder revolutionary directors, wrote a poem in praise of Tabori entitled "Lieber George" ("Dear George"), in which she describes his personality, his *Weltanschauung*, and the experience of working with him in the theatre. See Welker, *Tabori*, p. 107.

16. The setting and costumes were designed by Marietta Eggmann and Ernst Wiener.

17. Stanley Walden, "Das Jucken, das nicht nachläßt," in *Tabori*, ed. Welker, p. 296. For a discussion of music in the production, see also Ronzier, "Theater als Prozeß," vol. 1, p. 210.

18. The Father, played by Helmut Pick, had no speaking part in Tabori's stage version.

19. Armin Eichholz, "Taboris Mutter kam nicht bis Auschwitz," *Münchner Merkur*, 19 May 1979.

20. Koelbl, *Jüdische Portraits*, p. 238.

21. George Tabori, "Heiterkeit der Verzweiflung," *Theater Heute* 4 (1991): 71, and "Spiel und Zeit," in *Betrachtungen*, p. 16.

22. "Gipfeltreffen der Provokateure," *Stern* 22 (26 May 1994): 63.

23. In the English version it is the Hungarian tale about Jancsi and Juliska; see English ms., p. 12.

24. Tabori, "Es geht," p. 204.

25. Ibid.

26. Tabori to Alfred Biolek in *Boulevard Bio*.

27. See Koelbl, *Jüdische Portraits*, p. 236. Tabori says he sees "the special style of the Holocaust in its scientific impartiality."

28. George Salmony, "Martyrium im roten Sand," *Abendzeitung*, 19/20 May 1979.

29. The actors first rehearsed another play by Tabori, namely *The 25th Hour*, but soon abandoned it in favor of *My Mother's Courage*. Cf. Ohngemach, *George Tabori*, p. 103.

30. For a discussion and analysis of the impact the film had on German viewers, see Peter Märthesheimer and Ivo Frenzel, eds., *Im Kreuzfeuer: Der Fernsehfilm Holocaust: Eine Nation ist betroffen* (Frankfurt: Fischer Verlag, 1979).

31. Daniel Menaker, letter to George Tabori, 12 October 1979, SAdK, Box 74.

14. THE DRY BONES OF MEMORY: *JUBILEE*

1. There are three versions of the play. The first is dated December 1982; the second is the one printed in *Theater Heute* 2 (1983); the third appeared in the series *Das neue Stück*, published upon the premiere by the Schauspielhaus Bochum (Programmbuch no. 41). For various manuscript versions of this play, see SAdK, Boxes 8, 18, and 77. I refer to *Theaterstücke*, vol. 2, pp. 49–86. The quotations are from the original English stage script, unless otherwise stated.

2. Tabori discusses the inability of the Germans to mourn the victims of the Holocaust and draws a distinction between melancholy and genuine grief in his essay "Hamlet in Blue," pp. 116–132. In February 1998 Tabori signed a petition against the planned Holocaust Memorial in Berlin.

3. Tabori, "Die Kannibalen," p. 38.

4. Kipphardt's *Bruder Eichmann* was premiered at the Residenztheater in Munich on 21 January 1983. Cf. my article "The Appeal of the Executive: Adolf Eichmann on the Stage," *Monatshefte* 78 (1986): 203–214; and Alexander Stillmark, "Heinar Kipphardt's *Brother Eichmann*," in *Staging the Holocaust*, ed. Claude Schumacher, pp. 254–266.

5. George Tabori in a letter to Kipphardt, July 1978, printed in Heinar Kipphardt, *Bruder Eichmann: Schauspiel und Materialien*, pp. 197–198.

6. Cf. Rainer Werner Fassbinder, "Philosemiten und Antisemiten," *Die Zeit*, 9 April 1976.

7. Alexander Mitscherlich and Margarete Mitscherlich, *Die Unfähigkeit zu trauern*.

8. Sigmund Freud, "Erinnern, Wiederholen und Durcharbeiten," in *Gesammelte Werke*, vol. 10, pp. 126–136.

9. The term is used by Jochen Winter in his "Hommage an Tabori," unpublished manuscript. Winter participated in several Tabori productions and wrote his short piece after the production of Beckett's *The Lost Ones* in Munich in 1981.

10. Tabori, "Es geht," p. 202. Cf. also Jerzy Grotowski's stipulation of the entire body as memory: "It is our skin which has not forgotten, our eyes which have not forgotten," in his *Towards a Poor Theatre*, p. 186. Also Elaine Scarry, *The Body in Pain: The Making and Unmaking of the World*, p. 4.

11. Tabori, "Es geht," p. 201.

12. R. Kill, "Die Opfer blicken zurück," *Rheinische Post*, 1 February 1983.

13. Cf. Claus Peymann, "Die Welt in eine Anekdote," *Profil*, 16 May 1994. See also Wend Kässens, "Die Scherze der Verzweiflung: Zur Prosa von George Tabori," in *Tabori*, ed. Gronius and Kässens, pp. 79–88, esp. p. 81.

14. Tabori, "Verliebte und Verrückte," p. 85.

15. See C. Bernd Sucher, "George Taboris Chuzpe," *Süddeutsche Zeitung*, 1 February 1983.

16. See Gundula Ohngemach's M.A. dissertation "George Taboris Theaterarbeit: Eine Analyse der Probenarbeit am Beispiel von *Jubiläum*." See also Stanley Walden, "Das Jucken, das nicht nachläßt," in *Tabori*, ed. Welker, p. 297.

17. Tabori originally intended to write further episodes for Brecht's play. For a discussion of Brecht's impact on *Jubilee* and its American production, see Susan Russell, "The Possibilities for Brechtian Theory in Contemporary Theatrical Practice: George Tabori's *Jubiläum*," in *Verkörperte Geschichtsentwürfe*, ed. Höyng, pp. 107–127.

18. Tabori, *Unterammergau*, p. 34.

19. Tabori's stage version of *The Great Inquisitor* was premiered in Munich on 29 January 1993.

20. Cf. Steven Connor, *Postmodernist Culture: An Introduction to the Theories of the Contemporary*, p. 143.

21. George Tabori, *Die Ballade vom Wiener Schnitzel*, in *Theater Heute* 5 (1996): 46–52; here p. 52.

22. See Sigmund Freud, *Totem and Taboo*, translated and edited by James Strachey, p. 72.

23. George Tabori, "Zehn Gebote, Nachbars Kuh," *Theater Heute* (Jahresband 1992): 25.

24. George Tabori, *Mein Kampf*, in *DramaContemporary: Germany*, ed. Carl Weber, p. 83.

25. George Tabori, "Vom Wesen des Glücks," in *Tabori*, ed. Welker, p. 80.

26. George Tabori, "Was mich ärgert, am meisten ärgert," in *Betrachtungen*, p. 274.

27. See also the report about the two prisoners who die through water, in *Jubilee*, p. 67.

28. Tabori, "Es geht," p. 201.

29. Cf. Ohngemach, "George Taboris Theaterarbeit," p. 40; or Gabriela Pagener, "Lachen und Grauen dicht beieinander," *Allgemeine jüdische Wochenzeitung*, 11 March 1983.

30. See Radtke's own account of his work with Tabori in *M. — Wie Tabori*, and his article "Täter und Opfer," in *Tabori*, ed. Welker, pp. 118–120.

31. George Tabori, "Warten auf Beckett," in *Betrachtungen*, p. 60. There is also an autobiographical touch to Tabori's preoccupation with physical impairment. His cousin Bela was an invalid (Tabori, "Ich habe ihn besiegt," *Der Spiegel* special issue 2 [1989]: 76); so was the daughter of Doctor S., whom Tabori helped to smuggle to Palestine (Tabori, "Berliner Betten," in *Betrachtungen*, pp. 248–249).

32. Tabori, "Notes to *Siegmunds Freude*," p. 5.

15. FROM PATHOS TO BATHOS: *MEIN KAMPF*

1. Palm and Voss, "... So viele ichs," in program for *Mein Kampf*, Burgtheater, Vienna, 6 May 1987, p. 128.

2. The play, which won the annual accolade of "Production of the Year," *Theater Heute* 13 (1987), enjoyed innumerable productions in German-speaking theatres as well as performances in Britain, France, and the USA. There were some 1,729 performances of the play on German speaking stages between the 1987/88 season and 1993/94, according to the statistics of the Deutscher Bühnenverein.

3. The text mentions no year. It reads "Vienna. Winter 19——." Hitler's unsuccessful attempt to be admitted to the Akademie für Bildende Künste (Academy of Art) in Vienna dates back to autumn 1907, followed by another application, similarly unsuccessful, in September 1908. For the historical account I have relied on Alan Bullock's *Hitler: A Study in Tyranny* and on Brigitte Hamann's fascinating study of Hitler's "formative" years in Vienna, *Hitlers Wien*. All English quotations from Tabori's *Mein Kampf* are taken from the original English text as reprinted in Carl Weber's anthology *Drama-Contemporary: Germany*, pp. 39–83. References and quotations from the German version of the play, translated by Ursula Grützmacher-Tabori, are from *Theaterstücke*, vol. 2, pp. 143–203.

4. The story, in German translation by Ursula Grützmacher-Tabori, is contained in George Tabori, *Meine Kämpfe*, pp. 1–99. The original English prose ms. is in SAdK, Box 8. For a comparison of the prose version and the play, see Sandra Pott, "Ecce Schlomo: *Mein Kampf*— Farce oder theologischer Schwank?" in *Theater gegen das Vergessen*, ed. Bayerdörfer and Schönert, pp. 248–269.

5. See title page in *Theaterstücke*, vol. 2, p. 143. I could not find a parallel subtitle in the various English drafts of the play. Nor does it appear in Carl Weber's edition.

6. Cf. Palm and Voss, " . . . So viele," p. 125. Tabori speaks of his play as a "theologischer Schwank." The German terms *Farce*, *Schwank* and *Posse* approximate the English "farce," although *Schwank* is primarily associated with simple and brief peasant romps, involving cuckolding and lacking realistic motivation. Cf. Hans-Peter Bayerdörfer, "Die Einakter-Gehversuche auf schwankhaftem Boden," in *Brechts Dramen: Neue Interpretationen*, ed. Walter Hinderer (Stuttgart: Reclam, 1984). Peter Höyng addressed this problem in "Immer spielt ihr und scherzt? Zur Dialektik des Lachens in George Taboris *Mein Kampf*: Farce," in *Verkörperte Geschichtsentwürfe*, ed. Höyng, pp. 129–149.

7. Gregory Dobrov, "The Dawn of Farce: Aristophanes," in *Farce*, ed. James Redmond, p. 15. For studies of this dramatic genre, see also Eric Bentley, *The Life of the Drama*, chapter 7; Albert Bermel, *Farce: A History from Aristophanes to Woody Allen* (New York: Simon and Schuster, 1982); Anthony Caputi, *Buffo: The Genius of Vulgar Comedy* (Detroit: Wayne State University Press, 1978); and Jessica Milner Davis, *Farce* (London: Methuen, 1978).

8. Christopher Balme, "Grotesque Farce in the Weimar Republic," in *Farce*, ed.

Redmond, p. 181. Prominent among these avant-garde experimentations with "farce" are plays by Eugene Ionesco, Samuel Beckett, Harold Pinter, and other dramatists who are associated with Martin Esslin's notion of the Theatre of the Absurd.

9. Davis, *Farce*, p. 93.

10. Cf. Palm and Voss, "... So viele," p. 130.

11. George Tabori, "Ich habe ihn besiegt," *Spiegel*, special issue 2 (1989): 76.

12. Andres Müry, "Es ist mein Hitler. Ist Hitler in mir," *Rheinischer Merkur*, 29 April 1988.

13. Michael Merschmeier, *"Mein Kampf*: Taboris theologischer Schwank," *Theater Heute* 7 (1987): 12.

14. George Tabori, "Exposing the Naked Truth," in the *Guardian*, 2 September 1989. Tabori uses the term not in a Postmodernist sense, but in the sense of exposure or, as he suggests, the Hebrew *gilui* (revelation), which he wrongly names "gala."

15. Merschmeier, *"Mein Kampf,"* p. 11.

16. Frau Death and Hitler depart at the end of Tabori's production, climbing the staircase arm in arm, as she refers to "the beginning of a wonderful friendship" (*Mein Kampf*, 82).

17. George Tabori, "Der Sollyjupp unter uns," *Profil*, 23 March 1992, p. 94.

18. Tabori, "Hamlet in Blue," p. 117.

19. The topos of the ugly Jew, the infector, is prominent in anti-Semitic literature. See Gilman, *The Jew's Body*; and John Efron, "Der reine und der schmutzige Jude," in *Der schejne Jid*, ed. Sander L. Gilman, Robert Jütte, and Gabriele Kohlbauer-Fritz, pp. 75–85. A soul mate to Shlomo Herzl is Master Zvi, a *Talmid chacham*, Tabori's alter-ego in *Babylon Blues*. Cf. the prologue to the play, *Theaterstücke*, vol. 2, pp. 245–248.

20. Peter von Becker speaks of "Mein Kampf or Mein Faust" in his critique of the production, "Herzl und Hitler," *Die Zeit*, 15 May 1987. Albert Goldman recognizes the infatuation of the Schlemiel Jew with the blonde American as a topos in Jewish American comedy. See his essay "Laughtermakers," in *Jewish Wry*, ed. Sarah Blacher Cohen, p. 81.

21. George Tabori, "Die Macht des Wortes," *Süddeutsche Zeitung*, 28/29 November 1992.

22. For instance, *Mein Kampf*, 58 and 68. Cf. Adolf Hitler, *Mein Kampf*, translated by James Murphy (London: Hurst and Blackett, 1939), pp. 59, 60, and 273.

23. See Thomas Rothschild's review "Hitler in Wien," *Die Deutsche Bühne* 7 (1987): 28–30, in which the production is evaluated in the context of actual events. Tabori himself holds ambivalent sentiments toward the Viennese capital, in which he settled in 1987. Vienna is the setting of a number of his later plays and the subject of a short prose piece, "Wiener Blut," in *Betrachtungen*, pp. 75–77, in which he describes himself as the alibi-Jew in the Austrian metropolis that is "hell." A year after the premiere of Tabori's *Mein Kampf*, Thomas Bernhard's provocative *Heldenplatz* raised a political storm. See Jeanette R. Malkin, "Thomas Bernhard, Jews, Heldenplatz," in *Staging the Holocaust*, ed. Claude Schumacher, pp. 281–297.

24. George Tabori in an interview with Sabine Durrant, "The Art of Darkness," *Independent* (London), 1989.

25. Hitler got an old black overcoat from the Hungarian-Jewish old-clothes dealer Alan Neumann, whom he met at the hostel. Bullock, *Hitler*, p. 34.

26. Cf. Randall Stevenson, "Acts without Words," *Times Literary Supplement*, 1–7 September 1989, p. 946.

27. In Christopher Hampton's stage version of Steiner's text, Hitler holds a twenty-minute-long monologue, which, as the reviews of the London premiere reported, gained him the sympathy of the audience. Steiner was apparently aware of this problem and said he relied on the intelligence and proper judgment of each and every spectator. See George Steiner, "Who Do You Think You Are Kidding, Dr. Gilbert?" *Times* (London), 11 March 1982.

28. Albert Speer recalls that "Hitler had no humor: he liked laughing but it was always at the expense of others" (Speer, *Inside the Third Reich*, translated by Richard and Clara Winston [London: Weidenfeld and Nicolson, 1970]), p. 123.

29. See Steven Lipman's *Laughter in Hell: The Use of Humor during the Holocaust*.

30. Cf. Anat Feinberg, "Das Laterndl in London 1939–1945," *German Life and Letters* 37:3 (1984): 211–217.

31. Lipman, *Hell*, p. 233. Best-selling author Ephraim Kishon wrote a satire of Hitler, *Mein Kamm oder die Locke auf der Glatze* (My Comb or the Curl on My Bald Head), in 1945, while he was hiding in Budapest. The novel was first published more than fifty years later, in Germany in 1997.

32. Milton Meltzer, *Never to Forget: The Jews of the Holocaust*, p. 87.

33. Lipman, *Hell*, p. 72. See also the innumerable Hitler jokes included in the book.

34. In his 1966 production of *The Merchant of Venice as Performed in Theresienstadt*, Tabori presented the Prince of Aragon as a sarcastic parody of Hitler.

35. Weber, editor's note, in *DramaContemporary*, p. 40.

36. Gundula Leni Ohngemach, "Die Wahrheit des Drehorgelspielers," in *Deutsches Drama der 8oer Jahre*, ed. Richard Weber, pp. 107–119.

37. It is tempting to speculate on the onomastics of this figure, who is the namesake of the Bohemian aristocrat who founded the library of ancient manuscripts in Prague. Lefkowitz is a common Jewish name; a joke told during the Holocaust recounts how the Jew Lefkowitz told the German police they should not count on him. Cf. Lipman, *Hell*, p. 139. There is a Lupowitz in the English version of *Cannibals*, which was changed in the German version into Katz.

38. Moskowitz and Lupowitz feature in Tabori's "Die hohe Kunst des Nichtseins."

39. Cf. Shakespeare, *All's Well That Ends Well*, II.i.108.

40. Bentley, *The Life of the Drama*, p. 248.

41. George Tabori, "Warten auf Beckett," in *Betrachtungen*, p. 54.

42. Samuel Beckett, *Waiting for Godot* (London: Faber and Faber 1965), p. 9; also p. 59. Cf. *Mein Kampf*, pp. 42 and 55.

43. George Tabori, "Waiting for Beckett," in *Betrachtungen*, p. 54.
44. Beckett, *Godot*, p. 39.
45. Interestingly, there are also echoes of the pair AA and XX of Mrożek's *Emigrants*, which Tabori directed in Bonn in 1975. AA, the intellectual among the two, speaks of his work, but, as it turns out, does not write it at all.
46. This joke was left out of the German version. Cf. Beckett, *Godot*, p. 11.
47. *Mein Kampf*, 42. See the reference to the cock also on p. 55, and Hitler referring to Shlomo as Judah, p. 60.
48. Only in the German version, p. 182. Cf. Leah Hadomi's discussion of the Christian motif in *Dramatic Metaphors of Fascism and Antifascism*, pp. 79–95.
49. Andrea Kunne discusses the relationship of Tabori's text to the Old and New Testament in "Die Apokalypse als 'Farce' in George Taboris *Mein Kampf*," in *Literatur und politische Aktualität*, ed. Elrud Ibsch and Ferdinand van Ingen, pp. 283–297.
50. The episode from Talmud Yerushalmi is included in Micha Yosef Ben Gurion, ed., *Zfunot ve-agadot* (Hebrew; Tel Aviv: Am Oved, 1956) p. 160. I am indebted to Professor Reuven Kritz and Professor Dov Noy for helping me trace the source.
51. The popular song "Wien, nur Du allein" (Vienna, Only You) features in a number of Tabori's plays and productions, among them *The Ballad of the Wiener Schnitzel* and *The Last Night in September*.
52. Marietta Eggmann was responsible for the setting, Gisela Köster for the costumes.
53. Stanley Walden, "Das Jucken, das nicht nachläßt," in *Tabori*, ed. Welker, p. 298.
54. Merschmeier, *"Mein Kampf,"* pp. 11–12.
55. Tabori, "Marx Brothers in Zauberberg," p. 2. Elsewhere Tabori speaks of the "joke as a Hungarian form of expression"; see Bardischewski and Martens, "George Tabori — Weltwanderer," p. 3.
56. George Tabori in an interview with Peter von Becker, "Zeuge des Jahrhunderts," in *Tabori*, ed. Welker, p. 254, and in an interview with Durrant, "The Art of Darkness."
57. This is the original English title of his article "Die Heiterkeit der Verzweiflung," *Theater Heute* 4 (1991): 71.
58. Palm and Voss, " . . . So viele," p. 128.
59. Maurice Samuel, *The World of Sholem Aleichem*.
60. For studies of Jewish humor, see, for example, Cohen, *Jewish Wry*; Chaim Bermant, *What's the Joke: A Study of Jewish Humor through the Ages* (London: Weidenfeld and Nicolson, 1986); Martin Grotjahn, *Beyond Laughter: Humor and the Subconscious*; Heda Jason, "The Jewish Joke: The Problem of Definition," *Southern Folklore Quarterly* 31 (1967): 48–54; Israel Knox, "The Traditional Roots of Jewish Humor," *Judaism* 12 (1964–1965): 327–333; Salcia Landman, "On Jewish Humour," *Jewish Journal of Sociology* 4 (1962): 193–204; Elliott Oring, "The People of the Joke: On the Conceptualization of a Jewish Humor," *Western Folklore* 42 (1983): 261–271; Reik, *Jewish Wit*; Kurt

Schlesinger, "Jewish Humor as Jewish Identity," *International Review of Psycho-Analysis* (1979): 1–14.

61. Reik, *Jewish Wit*, p. 27.
62. The joke, quoted in Lipman, *Hell*, p. 140, was also found in Emil Dorian's diary in occupied Romania.
63. Freud, *Jokes and Their Relation to the Unconscious*; and George Tabori, "Das Wort ist eine heilige Waffe," in *Tabori*, ed. Welker, p. 303. Tabori suggests elsewhere (*Unterammergau*, p. 22) that humor is the Jewish contribution to civilization.
64. George Tabori, "Spiel und Zeit," in *Betrachtungen*, p. 18. Cf. also "Die Heiterkeit der Verzweiflung": " I do not believe that laughter is inferior to tears or reflection. It is a healing reaction."
65. Tabori, "Notes to *Siegmunds Freude*," p. 5.
66. Cf. Joseph Boskin, "Beyond *Kvetching* and *Jiving*: The Thrust of Jewish and Black Folkhumor," in Cohen, *Jewish Wry*, pp. 60–61.
67. Cf. Salcia Landmann, ed., *Jüdische Witze*, pp. 70–71.
68. Freud, *Jokes and Their Relation to the Unconscious*, p. 122.
69. Grotjahn, *Beyond Laughter*.
70. Only in the German version! *Theaterstücke*, vol. 2, pp. 155–156. This is based on the well-known Jewish joke about the bride (or, alternatively, the bridegroom) who is lame, blind, ugly, poor, etc., and yet a jewel. Cf. Also Sander L. Gilman, "Die Rasse ist nicht schön — Nein, wir Juden sind keine hübsche Rasse," in "*Der schejne Jid*," ed. Gilman, Jütte, and Kohlbauer-Fritz, p. 57.
71. Among these repetitions: "in small doses" (*Mein Kampf*, 52, 58); "which Leonardo?" (57) and "which Christ?" (65); "sounds better" (46).
72. Similar concerns were recently voiced upon the screening of the prizewinning film *La vita è bella* (Life Is Beautiful) by Roberto Benigni, arguably Europe's most famous comic actor — a film in comic vein that takes place, in part, in a concentration camp. See a report on the film and the involved problematics in Daniel Kotzin, "A Clown in the Camps," *Jerusalem Report*, 26 October 1998, pp. 40–45; and Linda Holt, "If All This Were Nothing But a Joke," *Times Literary Supplement*, 12 March 1999, p. 20.
73. Tabori, *Unterammergau*, p. 24.
74. George Tabori, "Staats-Theater," in *Betrachtungen*, p. 128.
75. Paul Kruntorad, "Eine Hitler-Farce," *Frankfurter Rundschau*, 19 May 1987.
76. Rothschild, "Hitler in Wien." The same view is held for instance by Lothar Sträter, "Auf wienerische Art mit Entsetzen Scherz getrieben," *Badische Neueste Nachrichten*, 12 May 1987; and Rainer Weber, "Ecce Shlomo," *Der Spiegel* 20 (1987): 273. See also Wend Kässens, "Kein anderer als Tabori kann und darf es sich leisten, jenen millionenfachen Mord der Faschisten als eine böse Groteske zu zeichnen," in *Tabori*, ed. Gronius and Kässens, p. 25.
77. Bentley, *The Life of the Drama*, p. 232.
78. Peter Kemp, "The Sick Joke," *Independent* (London), 6 October 1990.

79. Konrad Paul Liessmann, "Die Tragödie als Farce: Anmerkungen zu George Taboris *Mein Kampf*," in *Text und Kritik* 133 (January 1997): 85.

CONCLUDING REMARKS

1. George Tabori, "Don in Himmel," in *Betrachtungen*, p. 265.
2. Erwin Leiser, "George Tabori und der Baum der Erkenntnis," in *Tabori*, ed. Welker, p. 215.
3. Werner Schulze-Reimpell, "Vom Provocateur zum Medienstar: Die Umwege des Dramatikers und Regisseurs George Tabori," in *Text + Kritik* 133 (January 1997): 16.
4. George Tabori, "Die Kannibalen: Zur europäischen Erstaufführung," in *Unterammergau*, p. 37.
5. Cf. my study *Wiedergutmachung im Programm: Jüdisches Schicksal im deutschen Nachkriegsdrama*. Reference to Tabori's work is made explicitly on pp. 56ff. I likewise discuss Tabori's contribution in my article "Jewish Playwrights in the Postwar German Theater Begin to Break the Taboos Associated with German-Jewish Relations and the Holocaust," in *Yale Companion to Jewish Writing and Thought*, ed. Sander L. Gilman and Jack Zipes (New Haven: Yale University Press, 1997), pp. 648–654. See also Iwona Uberman's "Auschwitz im Theater der 'Peinlichkeit': George Taboris Holocaust-Stücke im Rahmen der Theatergeschichte seit dem Ende der 60er Jahre."
6. George Tabori, "Die Heiterkeit der Verzweiflung," *Theater Heute* 4 (1991): 71.
7. Jörg W. Gronius, "Bitte zu Tisch," in *Tabori*, ed. Gronius and Kässens, pp. 9–24.
8. Thomas Rothschild, "Die Wunde versteht das Messer: Juden auf Taboris Bühne," in *Text + Kritik* 133 (January 1997): 4–9.
9. Hartmut Krug, "Zirkus um die Zauberflöte," in *Die Tageszeitung*, 17 August 1998.
10. Cf. Sandra Pott and Jörg Schönert, "Tabori unter den Deutschen: Stationen einer 'authentischen Existenz'?" in *Theater gegen das Vergessen*, ed. Hans-Peter Bayerdörfer and Jörg Schönert, p. 348.
11. Konrad Paul Liessmann, "Der Versöhnungskünstler," in *Tabori*, ed. Welker, pp. 237–240.
12. See Rothschild, "Die Wunde versteht das Messer," p. 9.
13. Elisabeth Loibl, in *Der Standard*, 15 March 1989.
14. This is the title of Peter von Becker's television documentation on Tabori, ZDF, 1991; printed in *Tabori*, ed. Welker, pp. 248–256.
15. Yerushalmi, *Zakhor*, p. 98. See also Saul Friedländer, ed., *Probing the Limits of Representation: Nazism and the "Final Solution"*; Claude Schumacher, ed., *Staging the Holocaust: The Shoah in Drama and Performance*; and Alvin H. Rosenfeld, ed., *Thinking about the Holocaust: After Half a Century*.

BIBLIOGRAPHY

PRIMARY SOURCES

Tabori's Published Works

Beneath the Stone the Scorpion. London: Boardman, 1945. Boston: Houghton Mifflin Company, 1945.

Companions of the Left Hand. London: Boardman, 1946. Boston: Houghton Mifflin Company, 1946.

Original Sin. London: Boardman, 1947. Boston: Houghton Mifflin Company, 1947.

The Caravan Passes. London: Boardman, 1951. New York: Appleton-Century-Crofts, 1951.

The Emperor's Clothes. New York: Samuel French, 1953.

Flight into Egypt. New York: Dramatists Play Service, 1953.

The Journey. New York: Bantam, 1958.

The Good One. New York: Permabooks, 1960.

Brecht on Brecht: An Improvisation. New York: Samuel French, 1967.

The Cannibals. London: Davis-Poynter, 1974.

Son of A Bitch: Erzählungen. Translated by Ursula Grützmacher-Tabori and Peter Sandberg. Munich and Vienna: Hanser, 1981. (Includes the stories "Mutters Courage," "Insomnia," "Weisman und Rotgesicht," and "Son of a Bitch.")

Unterammergau oder die guten Deutschen. Translated by Ursula Grützmacher-Tabori, Ursula Menck-Adriani, and Peter Sandberg. Frankfurt: Suhrkamp, 1981.

The Cannibals. In *The Theatre of the Holocaust: Four Plays,* edited by Robert Skloot, pp. 197–265. Madison: University of Wisconsin Press, 1982.

Jubiläum. Translated by Ursula Grützmacher-Tabori. *Theater Heute* 2 (1983): 36–42.

Spiele: Peepshow, Pinkville, Jubiläum. Translated by Ursula Grützmacher-Tabori, Peter Hirche, and Volker Ludwig, with a foreword by Peter von Becker. Cologne: Prometh, 1984.

Meine Kämpfe. Translated by Ursula Grützmacher-Tabori. Munich and Vienna: Hanser, 1986. (Includes the stories "Mein Kampf," "Erste Nacht, letzte Nacht," and "Pffft oder Der letzte Tango am Telefon.")

Mein Kampf: Farce. Translated by Ursula Grützmacher-Tabori. *Theater Heute* 7 (1987): 26–36.

Betrachtungen über das Feigenblatt: Handbuch für Verliebte und Verrückte. Translated by Ursula Grützmacher-Tabori. Munich and Vienna: Hanser, 1991.

Die Goldberg Variationen. Translated by Ursula Grützmacher-Tabori. *Theater Heute* 6 (1991): 34–42.

Theaterstücke. 2 vol. Translated by Ursula Grützmacher-Tabori, Peter Hirche, and Peter Sandberg, with an introduction by Peter von Becker. Munich and Vienna: Hanser, 1994.

Die Ballade vom Wiener Schnitzel. Translated by Ursula Grützmacher-Tabori. *Theater Heute* 5 (1996): 46–52.

Mein Kampf: Farce. In *DramaContemporary: Germany*, edited by Carl Weber, pp. 39–83. Baltimore: Johns Hopkins University Press, 1996.

Tabori's Essays and Articles

"Bemerkungen über Brecht." In *Studien zur Theorie und Praxis des sozialistischen Theaters, Theater der Zeit*, Beilage 23 (1968): 14.

"Hamlet in Blue." *Theatre Quarterly* 20 (1975–1976): 116–132.

"Statt des Urschreis das Urkichern." *Theater Heute* 5 (1983): 30.

"Ein Schulterzucken, ein Lächeln und eine Hand, die zittert." *Süddeutsche Zeitung*, 29 November 1984.

"Brief an Heinar Kipphardt." In Heinar Kipphardt, *Bruder Eichmann: Schauspiel und Materialien*, pp. 197–198. Reinbek: Rowohlt, 1986.

"Eros und Empfindsamkeit." *Theater Heute* 11 (1989): 8–9.

"Hoffend das Scheitern akzeptieren." *Die Weltwoche*, 28 December 1989.

"Ich habe ihn besiegt." *Der Spiegel*, special issue 2 (1989): 76.

"Vorwort." In Bernd Uhlig, *Theater und Photographie*, pp. 8–9. Berlin: Artland, 1989.

"Aufs beste zu." *Die Zeit*, 5 January 1990.

"Auf der Suche nach der verlorenen Schonzeit." *Theater Heute* 1 (1991): 55.

"Auf der Wippe." *Theater Heute* 6 (1991): 63.

"Die Heiterkeit der Verzweiflung." *Theater Heute* 4 (1991): 71.

"Eiskalte Engel, adieu." *Theater Heute* 5 (1991): 71.

"Kunst und Kaiser." *Theater Heute* 2 (1991): 71.

"Kurzklassiker für Bildungsbürger." *Theater Heute* (Jahresband 1991): 6–7.

"Mother of All Battles." *Theater Heute* 3 (1991): 63.

"Bon Voyage." In *Wären die Wände zwischen uns aus Glas: Jüdische Lyrik aus Österreich*, edited by Peter Daniel, Johannes Diethart, and Herbert Kuhner, pp. 126–127. Vienna: Verlag der Apfel, 1992.

"Der unheimliche Clown: Lobrede auf Gert Voss." *Theater Heute* 12 (1992): 2.

"Dieses peinliche Wort: Liebe. Rede zum Georg-Büchner-Preis 1992." *Die Zeit*, 16 October 1992. Rpt. in *Tabori*, edited by Andrea Welker, pp. 318–320.

"Es ist schön, alt zu sein." In *Wir wollen nicht ohne Hoffnung leben: Texte und Beiträge anläßlich des 85. Geburtstages von Hans Mayer*, edited by Michael Lewin, pp. 122–123. Vienna: Schriften der Internationalen Erich-Fried-Gesellschaft für Literatur und Sprache, 2, 1992.

"Protest einer ewig jungen Sau." *Die Zeit*, 10 January 1992.

"Where Have All the Flowers Gone?" *Theater Heute* 6 (1992): 12.

"Zehn Gebote, Nachbars Kuh." *Theater Heute* (1992): 25.

"Die Sprache liebkosen, küssen, beißen, lecken, saugen." *Die Woche*, 4 March 1993.

"Katastrophale Auskünfte eines Asylanten." *Der Standard*, 18 October 1993.

"Nachwort." In Keith Johnstone, *Improvisation und Theater*, pp. 361–363. Berlin: Alexander, 1993.

"Auschwitz-Lüge." *Die Woche*, 11 May 1994.

"Der Mohr hat seine Schuldigkeit getan: O. J. Simpson — Theater und Tribunal." *Theater Heute* 11 (1995): 1.

"Ein deutscher Alptraum." *Theater Heute* 2 (1995): 2.

"Lächelndes Rätsel." *Theater Heute* (Jahresband 1995): 123.

"Der Kuß." *Theater Heute* 2 (1996): 36.

"Rauchverbot im Paradies." *Die Woche*, 20 September 1996.

"Wie sollen Kritiker jemanden beschreiben, der keine Kuh ist?" In *Gert Voss: Ich würd' gern wissen, wie man ein Geheimnis spielt*, edited by Hans-Dieter Schütt, pp. 58–61. Berlin: Schwarzkopf and Schwarzkopf, 1997.

"Bertolt Brecht." *Frankfurter Allgemeine Zeitung* (Bilder und Zeiten), 7 February 1998.

Tabori's Published Interviews and Conversations

Baumbauer, Frank. "Gehören diese Huster zum Stück?" *Süddeutsche Zeitung*, 6 November 1998.

Becker, Peter von. "Diese große Lebensreise." *Theater Heute* 5 (1994): 8–17.

———. "Theaterarbeit mit George Tabori: Der Weg vom Bremer *Hamlet* zum Münchner *Shylock*: Gespräch mit Tabori und Ensemblemitgliedern." *Theater Heute* 1 (1979): 47–51.

Becker, Peter von, and Ursula Voss. "Solche Begegnungen habe ich mein Leben lang gefürchtet und mir gewünscht." *Theater Heute* 5 (1990): 16–18.

Berger, Jürgen. "Vielleicht ende ich als Bühnenarbeiter." *Die Tageszeitung*, 24 May 1994.

Bohn, Emmanuel. "Zwischen Identitäten — Liga und Erfahrungsraum." *Theater des Zorns und der Zärtlichkeit*, edited by Emmanuel Bohn and Siegmar Schröder, pp. 53–68. Bielefeld: Theaterlabor Bielefeld e. V., 1988.

"Die Marxs [*sic*] Brothers im Zauberberg." In program for *Talk Show*, Bremen, October 1976, pp. 2–3.

Dworkin, Bob. "Meet the Author." CBS, 21 September 1947.

Ernst, Michael. "Ich fühle mich überall als Fremdling." *Wochenpost*, 24 November 1994.

Fischer, Eva-Elisabeth. "Das Mitleid der Opfer." *Süddeutsche Zeitung*, 24–26 December 1984.

"Fragebogen." *Die Woche*, 6 May 1993.

Fritsch, Sibylle. "Ich bin ein Fremder." *Profil*, 16 May 1994.

———. "Keine Zeit zu trauern." *Profil*, 23 July 1990, pp. 76–77.

———. "Nur im Gefühl liegt die Wahrheit." *Psychologie Heute* 2 (1994): 40–42.

———. "Perfektion ist Blasphemie." *Profil*, 14 June 1993, pp. 72–73.

"George Tabori, Ich beende meine Regietätigkeit." *News*, 28 March 1996, p. 140.

Grebe, Ellen. "Das Einmalige am Theater." *Nürnberger Nachrichten*, 24 January 1980.

"Gute Dichter gehen fremd." *Der Spiegel*, 1 June 1992, p. 271.

Haider, Hans, and Verena Hoehne. "George Tabori." *du* 9 (1993): 64–66.

Hofmann, Gunter. "Baader-Meinhof, das ist schon Legende." *Die Zeit,*
7 February 1986.

Kagel, Martin. "Brecht Files: Conversation with George Tabori." In *The Brecht
Yearbook.* Berlin: Theater der Zeit, 1997.

Kässens, Wend, and Jörg W. Gronius. "George Tabori." In *Theatermacher,*
pp. 157–174. Frankfurt: Athenäum, 1987.

Koelbl, Herlinde. "Georges [sic] Tabori." In *Jüdische Portraits: Photographien und
Interviews,* pp. 234–238. Frankfurt: Fischer, 1989.

Kranz, Dieter. "Hinter jedem Scherz steckt eine kleine Katastrophe: Gespräch
mit George Tabori." *Sonntag* 17 (1990).

Löffler, Sigrid. "Der Claus ist kein Gentleman." *Profil,* 6 June 1988, pp. 87–88.

Loibl, Elisabeth, and Armin Thurnher. "Kein Beruf für Erwachsene, aber eine
Lebensrettung." *Falter* 10 (1985): 8–9.

Michaelis, Rolf. "Ein begeisterungsfähiger Skeptiker." *Theater Heute* 6 (1976):
29–33.

Michaelsen, Sven. "Gipfeltreffen der Provokateure: Gespräch mit George
Tabori und Claus Peymann." *Stern,* 26 May 1994, pp. 62–70.

Müller, André. "Ich habe mein Lachen verloren." *Die Zeit,* 6 May 1994.

Müry, Andres. "Warum macht das deutsche Theater uns krank, Herr Tabori?"
Frankfurter Allgemeine Zeitung (Magazine), 18 September 1987.

Neumann, Tanja. "Das Theater ist ein Liebesakt." *Die Tageszeitung,* 24 January
1990.

Palm, Reinhard, and Ursula Voss. ". . . So viele Ichs, so viele Figuren." In
program for *Mein Kampf,* Vienna, Burgtheater, 6 May 1987, pp. 117–130.
Partly rpt. as "Es ist das große Welttheater, jedes Leben." *Theater Heute*
7 (1987): 24–27.

Petsch, Barbara. "Unbehaust glücklich." *Die Presse,* 20 August 1994.

Raddatz, Fritz J. "Den Tod zu überlisten." *Die Zeit* (Magazine), 13 November
1992.

Renk, Herta-Elisabeth. "Das Sein bestimmt das Spielen." *Praxis Deutsch,*
76 (1987): 16–17.

Rohwer, Jörn. "Nach der Illusion der Unsterblichkeit." *Berliner Zeitung,*
15/16 August 1998.

Rötzer, Florian. "Die plötzliche Eruption des Realen." *Die Tageszeitung,*
2 February 1985.

Schaper, Rüdiger, and Peter Laudenbach. "Generationenwechsel?
Degenerationwechsel!" *Tip* 12 (1998): 91–92.

Schutt, Hans-Dieter. "Wir sind pausenlos mit dem Verrat beschäftigt. Wir alle!"
Neues Deutschland, 14 July 1993.

Thieringer, Thomas. "Von Übermalungen und Utopien." *Süddeutsche Zeitung,*
29 January 1993.

Thuswaldner, Anton. "George Tabori." In *Verflechtungen: Literatur und Musik,*
edited by Reinhard Kannonier and Charlotte Liedl, pp. 194–198. Linz:
Grosser, 1994.

Trenkler, Thomas. "Ich bereite mich auf den Tod vor." *Musik und Theater*
10 (1997): 10–15.

Witte, Karsten. "Kasperl, Käfig und Kommerz." *Frankfurter Rundschau*, 18 February 1986.

"Wo liegen auf der Bühne die Grenzen des unbürgerlichen Erotischen?" *Guckloch* (May 1984).

SECONDARY SOURCES

Documentation and Studies of Tabori's Plays and Theatre

Bayerdörfer, Hans-Peter, and Jörg Schönert, eds. *Theater gegen das Vergessen: Bühnenarbeit und Drama bei George Tabori.* Tübingen: Niemeyer, 1997.

Becker, Peter von. "Die Stücke — ein Leben." In *George Tabori, Theaterstücke*, vol. 1, pp. vii–xxi. 2 vols. Munich and Vienna: Hanser, 1994.

Braese, Stephan. "Rückkehr zum Ort der Verbrechen: George Tabori in Deutschland." In *Das Politische im literarischen Diskurs*, ed. Sven Kramer, pp. 32–55. Studien zur deutschen Gegenwartsliteratur. Opladen: Westdeutscher Verlag, 1996.

Dahlke, Karin. "Denn Witze sind nichts anderes als überrumpelte Katastrophen: George Taboris Theater der Peinlichkeit." In *Frag-mente* 46 (1994): 29–58.

Feinberg, Anat. "The Taboos Must Be Broken: George Tabori's Mourning Work in *Jubiläum*." In *Staging the Holocaust*, edited by Claude Schumacher, pp. 267–280. Cambridge: Cambridge University Press, 1998.

Feinberg-Jütte, Anat. "The Task Is Not to Reproduce the External Form, But to Find the Subtext: George Tabori's Productions of Samuel Beckett Texts." *Journal of Beckett Studies* 1–2 (1992): 95–115.

Garforth, Julian A. "George Tabori's Bair Essentials — A Perspective on Beckett Staging in Germany." *Forum Modernes Theater* 1 (1994): 59–75.

Gronius, Jörg W., and Wend Kässens, eds. *Tabori.* Frankfurt: Athenäum, 1989.

Hadomi, Leah. "The Historical and the Mythical in Tabori's Plays." *Forum Modernes Theater* 1 (1993): 3–6.

Harth, Dietrich. "Gestörtes Einvernehmen: Die antiritualistischen Holocaust-Spiele George Taboris und Joshua Sobols." In *Bilder des Holocaust*, edited by Manuel Köppen and Klaus R. Scherpe, pp. 13–28. Vienna: Böhlau, 1997.

Hensel, Georg. "George Tabori: Zwischen den Nationen." In *Spielplan*, vol. 2, pp. 1078–1083. 2 vols. Munich: List, 1992.

Hentschel, Kerstin. "Die Theaterarbeit George Taboris." M.A. diss., University of Erlangen, Nuremberg, 1989.

Höpfner, Ursula. "Der Begriff der Authentizität aus der Sicht eines Theatermachers: Ein Intensiv-Interview und seine Auswirkung." Unpub. ms. No date.

Höyng, Peter, ed. *Verkörperte Geschichtsentwürfe: George Taboris Theaterarbeit.* Tübingen: Francke Verlag, 1998.

———. "George Tabori's 'Brecht on Brecht' Production: A Success Story." *Brecht Yearbook* 24 (1999): 97–107.

Isser, Edward R. "Contaminated by Death: The Theatre of Tabori and Szajna."

In *Stages of Annihilation: Theatrical Representations of the Holocaust*, pp. 124–133. Madison amd Teaneck: Fairleigh Dickinson University Press, 1997.

Janz, Rolf-Peter. "Witz und Grauen: Zu einigen Theaterstücken George Taboris." In *Wechsel der Orte: Studien zum Wandel des literarischen Geschichtsbewußtseins — Festschrift für Anke Bennholdt-Thomsen*, ed. Irmela von der Lühe and Anita Runge, pp. 346–354. Göttingen: Wallstein, 1997.

Kagel, Martin. "Geschichte und Versöhnung: Anmerkungen zu George Taboris Erzählung 'Mutters Courage' und seinem jüdischen Western 'Weisman und Rotgesicht." *Jahrbuch für Internationale Germanistik* 1 (1996): 40–55.

Klein, Christian. "Unter jedem Stein schläft ein Skorpion: Vom Familienroman zum Theaterstück: Der Fall von Georg [*sic*] Taboris *Die Kannibalen.*" *Ecritures de la mémoire, Cahiers d'Etudes Germaniques* 29, edited by Ingrid Haag and Michel Vanoosthuyse (1995): 167–177.

Kubat, Violetta. "Tabori für die Schule: Etappen eines Lernprozesses." M.A. diss., Hochschule für Künste, Berlin, December 1991.

Kunne, Andrea. "Die Apokalypse als 'Farce' in George Taboris *Mein Kampf.*" In *Literatur und politische Aktualität*, edited by Elrud Ibsch and Ferdinand van Ingen, pp. 283–297. Amsterdam: Rodopi, 1993.

Kurzenberger, Hajo. "Katzelmacher, Toubabs, Judenärsche, Mongolenzombis, schmierige Rothäute: Über Fremdenhaß, Kolonialismus und Minderheitenkonflikte in Dramen von Fassbinder, Koltès und Tabori." In *Interkulturelles Theater und Theaterpädagogik*, edited by Hajo Kurzenberger and Frank Matzke, pp. 48–65. Hildesheim: Universität Hildesheim, Medien und Theater, 1994.

Marschall, Brigitte. "Verstrickt in Geschichte(n): Im Würgegriff des Überlebenskampfes George Taboris." *Maske und Kothurn* 1–4 (1991): 311–325.

Ohngemach, Gundula. *George Tabori*. Frankfurt: Fischer, 1989.

———. "George Taboris Theaterarbeit: Eine Analyse der Probenarbeit am Beispiel von *Jubiläum.*" M.A. diss., Ludwig-Maximilians-Universität, Munich, 1983.

Ohngemach, Gundula Leni. "Die Wahrheit des Drehorgelspielers." In *Deutsches Drama der 8oer Jahre*, edited by Richard Weber, pp. 107–119. Frankfurt: Suhrkamp, 1992.

Perets, Rachel. "Vom Erhabenen ins Groteske — George Taboris *Die Kannibalen.*" In *In der Sprache der Täter: Neue Lektüren deutschsprachiger Nachkriegs- und Gegenwartsliteratur*, edited by Stephan Braese, pp. 117–136. Opladen: Westdeutscher Verlag, 1998.

Radtke, Peter. *M. — Wie Tabori: Erfahrungen eines behinderten Schauspielers*. Zurich: Pendo, 1987.

Ronzier, Rolf. "Theater als Prozeß: Die Theaterarbeit George Taboris." M.A. diss., Freie Universität Berlin, 1988.

Rothschild, Thomas. "Jüdische Anarchisten: Notizen zu George Tabori und Thomas Brasch." *Die Neue Gesellschaft/Frankfurter Hefte* 3 (1990): 259–264.

Russell, Susan. "Beyond All Tears: The Holocaust Plays of George Tabori." M.A. diss., University of Wisconsin, 1989.

Sander, Marcus. "Peinliche Erinnerung: George Taboris theatrale Darstellungen des Holocaust." *Die Neue Gesellschaft/Frankfurter Hefte* 7 (1996): 634–639.

Schröder, Christof Nikolas. "Aber was, wenn Gott auch nicht Gott ist? Gott im zeitgenössischen Theater: George Taboris *Goldberg-Variationen* und andere Stücke." M.A. diss., Ruprecht-Karls-Universität, Heidelberg, 1997.

Scott-Prelorentzos, Alison. "Plus c'est la même chose, plus ça change! George Tabori's *Nathans Tod*, nach Lessing." In *Analogon Rationis: Festschrift für Gerwin Marahrens zum 65. Geburtstag*, edited by Marianne Henn and Christoph Lorey, pp. 49–71. Edmonton: University of Alberta Press, 1994.

Simbruk, Michael. "Non-sense oder Der letzte Akt." Munich: Selbstverlag, 1983.

Strümpel, Jan. "George Tabori." In *Kritisches Lexikon zur deutschsprachigen Gegenwartsliteratur*, edited by Heinz Ludwig Arnold. Munich: Edition Text, 1995.

———. *Vorstellungen vom Holocaust: George Taboris Erinnerungs-Spiele*. Göttingen: Wallstein, 2000. (Ph.D. diss., Georg-August-Universität, Göttingen, 1998).

Text + Kritik 133: George Tabori. Munich: Edition Text, 1997.

Thunecke, Jörg. "Farce oder Volksstück? Eine Untersuchung der Theaterversion von George Taboris *Mein Kampf*." *Modern Austrian Literature* 3–4 (1993): 247–272.

Uberman, Iwona. "Auschwitz im Theater der 'Peinlichkeit': George Taboris Holocaust-Stücke im Rahmen der Theatergeschichte seit dem Ende der 6oer Jahre." Munich: Dissertationsverlag NG Kopierladen, 1995.

Welker, Andrea, ed. *George Tabori: Dem Gedächtnis, der Trauer und dem Lachen gewidmet*. Weitra: Bibliothek der Provinz, 1994.

Welker, Andrea, and Tina Berger eds. *"Ich wollte meine Tochter läge tot zu meinen Füßen und hätte die Juwelen in den Ohren": Improvisationen über Shakespeares Shylock, Dokumentation einer Theaterarbeit*. Munich and Vienna: Hanser, 1979.

Wießner, Stefan. "Taboris Goldberg Variationen in Wien." M.A. diss., Freie Universität Berlin, 1993.

Articles on Tabori

Bardischewski, M., and K. Martens. "George Tabori — Weltwanderer." Süddeutscher Rundfunk, Stuttgart, 18 October 1987.

Becker, Peter von. "Liebe und Lachen — nach Auschwitz." *Theater Heute* 6 (1991): 28–31.

———. "Offene Wunde und bittersüße Medizin." *Der Spiegel*, 22 May 1989, pp. 242–245.

Bielicki, Jan. "Macht doch, was ihr wollt!" *Süddeutsche Zeitung* (Magazine), 6 July 1990, pp. 30–31.

Biermann, Wolf. "Ein Kampf mit falschem Leben und echter Kunst." *Frankfurter Allgemeine Zeitung*, 12 October 1992. Rpt. in *Tabori*, ed. Welker, pp. 313–317.

Böhm, Gotthard. "Rattenfänger von Alsergrund." *Bühne* 4 (1987): 6–10.

Durrant, Sabine. "The Art of Darkness." *Independent*, October 1989.

Emigholz, Erich. "Lernen, wie man sich unterscheidet." *Theater Heute* 9 (1975): 20–23.

Fischer, Eva-Elisabeth. "Menschen im Zylinder: Zwei Monate in der Theatergruppe von George Tabori." *Süddeutsche Zeitung*, 4–5 July 1981.

Fritsch, Sibylle. "Da streiten sich die Leut' herum." *Profil*, 8 April 1991, pp. 88–92.

―――. "Der Sollyjupp unter uns." *Profil*, 23 March 1992, p. 94.

―――. "George für Alle." *Profil*, 11 May 1987, pp. 79–82.

―――. "It's Not My Cup of Tea." *Die deutsche Bühne* 9 (1997): 12.

―――. "Konzept Katharsis." *Profil*, 18 May 1987, pp. 76–77.

―――. "Theater ist keine Pizzafabrik." *Profil*, 16 October 1989, pp. 97–98.

Godard, Colette. "George Tabori: Un Humour Sauvage." *Le Monde*, 10 September 1992.

"Hamlets Geburtswehen." *Thüringische Landeszeitung* ("Treff"-Supplement), 5 May 1990.

Hensel, Georg. "Aus Katastrophen etwas Hilfreiches machen." *Frankfurter Allgemeine Zeitung*, 19 May 1984.

―――. "Shakespeare, Jazz und Judenhaß." *Frankfurter Allgemeine Zeitung*, 23 November 1978.

Hofkemeler, Jörg. "Gespräch über die Probenarbeit zu Rudkins *Vor der Nacht*." Program for *Vor der Nacht*, Bremen, March 1975, pp. 81–93.

Jäger, Gerd. "Das Schauspieltheater der Regisseure." *Theater Heute* 12 (1976): 31–36.

Jütte, Anat. "Der Zauberer mit der jugendlichen Seele." *Allgemeine jüdische Wochenzeitung*, 14 October 1988.

Kainz, Wilfried. "George Tabori." *Wien Wann Was Wo* 1 (1988): 8–13.

Kässens, Wend. "Was ist an Tabori so faszinierend?" *Der Tagesspiegel*, 5 May 1992.

Kirchner, Ignaz. "George Tabori wird 80." *Süddeutsche Zeitung*, 24 May 1994.

Leiser, Erwin. "Beim ihm muß ein König kein Mann sein." *Die Weltwoche*, 25 May 1989.

―――. "George Tabori." *Frankfurter Allgemeine Zeitung* (Magazine), 9 October 1987.

―――. "Kunst darf alles." *Musik und Theater* 3 (1986): 8–13.

―――. "Taboris Kreis hat sich nun geschlossen." *Die Weltwoche*, 26 July 1990.

―――. "Was ist, wenn Gott nicht Gott ist?" *Die Weltwoche*, 17 February 1994.

Lindfors, Viveca. *Viveka . . . Viveca*. Stockholm: Bonniers, 1978. New York: Everest House, 1981.

Löffler, Sigrid. "Fragen an die Väter." *Deutsches Allgemeines Sonntagsblatt*, 4 October 1987.

―――. "Katastrophen-Witze, todtraurige Chuzpe." *Freitag*, 27 May 1994.

―――. "Taboris Träume." *Theater Heute* 12 (1988): 5–8.

Marin, Marcel. "Verliebter Verrückter." *Esslinger Zeitung*, 17–18 November 1990.

Martins, Kirstin. "Der Fels, der in der Mitte bricht." *Theater Heute* 1 (1979): 52–55.

May, Rolf. "Der alte Mann und das jüngste Theater." *Westermanns Kulturmagazin* 2 (1987): 50–55.

Merschmeier, Michael. "Dem Theater Beine Machen!" (conversation with Stanley Walden). *Theater Heute* 6 (1992): 21–24.

Müry, Andres. "Ich habe nur die Neugier des Möchtegern-Arztes." *Die Weltwoche*, 29 October 1987. Also published as "Es ist mein Hitler. Ist Hitler in mir" in *Rheinische Merkur*, 29 April 1988.

Neumann, Robert. "George Taboris *Die Kannibalen.*" *Tribüne* (1970): 3602–3606.

Niehoff, Karena. "In welcher Sprache träumst Du, George?" *Die Zeit*, 22–26 May 1989.

Petsch, Barbara. "Der Theater-Guru." *Die Presse*, 11 April 1991.

Peymann, Claus. "Die Welt in einer Anekdote." *Profil*, 16 May 1994, p. 50.

Pizzini, Duglore. "Arbeitsfreude statt Regie-Gewalttätigkeit." *Die Presse*, no date.

Reich, Richard. "Vorsicht Kalauer!" *Neue Zürcher Zeitung*, 25 May 1994.

Schneider, Richard Chaim. "Grenzgänger auf der Bühne." *Die Zeit*, 16 December 1988.

Spengler, Tilman. "Ein Zauberer bleibt Lehrling." *Die Woche*, 19 May 1994.

Stadelmaier, Gerhard. "Fürst des Feigenblatts." *Frankfurter Allgemeine Zeitung*, 24 May 1994.

———. "Lebensspiel: Büchner-Preis für Tabori." *Frankfurter Allgemeine Zeitung*, 22 May 1992.

Stoltzenberg, Peter. "Nur kein Theater." *Frankfurter Rundschau*, 24 May 1994.

Sucher, C. Bernd. "Provokateur der Liebe." *Süddeutsche Zeitung*, 24–25 May 1989.

Thieringer, Thomas. "Ein Theaterlabor in der Porzellangasse: George Tabori und sein Wiener Kreis." *Süddeutsche Zeitung*, 28 April 1987.

Wagener, Sybil. "Der Dramatiker George Tabori." *Bühnenkunst* 4 (1990): 81–86.

Weichinger, Robert. "Soso, die ganze Welt?" *Die Presse*, 21 May 1994.

Weninger, Franz. "Theatererwartungen: G. Tabori." *Disput*, no date, pp. 12–18.

"Wie ein Stadttheater-Ensemble mit der Regel bricht." *Theater Heute* (1974 Jahresband): 70–71.

Wille, Franz. "Du sollst dir kein Bildnis machen? — Überlegungen zu *Schindlers Liste*, George Taboris Dramen und dem ersten Stück von Rainer Werner Fassbinder." *Theater Heute* 5 (1994): 4–5.

Wirsing, Sibylle. "Du bist ein Dichter, Willie, ein wahrer Dichter." in *Der Tagesspiegel*, 22–23 May 1994.

General

Acheson, James, and Kateryna Arthur. *Beckett's Later Fiction and Drama*. London: Macmillan, 1987.

Aronson, Arnold. "Postmodern Design." *Theater Journal* 43 (1991): 1–13.

Artaud, Antonin. *Oeuvres complètes*. 26 vols. Paris: Gallimard, 1956–1994.

———. *The Theatre and Its Double*. Translated by Victor Corti. London: Calder and Boyars, 1970.

Bakhtin, Mikhail. *Rabelais and His World*. Translated by Helene Iswolsky. Cambridge: Cambridge University Press, 1968.

Beckett, Samuel. *The Complete Dramatic Works*. London: Faber and Faber, 1986.
———. *Waiting for Godot*. London: Faber and Faber, 1965.
Bentley, Eric. *The Life of the Drama*. London: Methuen, 1965.
Bertens, Hans. *The Idea of the Postmodern: A History*. London and New York: Routledge, 1995.
Billeter, Erika. *Paradise Now: Ein Bericht in Wort und Bild*. With photos by Dölf Preising. Bonn, Munich, and Vienna: Rütten und Loening, 1968.
Biner, Pierre. *The Living Theatre*. New York: Horizon Press, 1972.
Blumenthal, Eileen. *Joseph Chaikin: Exploring at the Boundaries of Theatre*. Cambridge and New York: Cambridge University Press, 1984.
Brecht, Bertolt. *Gesammelte Werke*. Vols. 15–17 (Schriften zum Theater) of 20 vols. Frankfurt: Suhrkamp, 1981.
———. *Über den Beruf des Schauspielers*. Frankfurt: Suhrkamp, 1981.
Breznitz, Shlomo. *Memory Fields: The Legacy of a Wartime Childhood in Czechoslovakia*. Tel Aviv: Am Oved, 1993. New York: Alfred A. Knopf, 1993.
Brook, Peter. *The Empty Space*. Harmondsworth: Penguin, 1968.
———. *The Shifting Point*. New York: Harper and Row, 1987.
Bullock, Alan. *Hitler: A Study in Tyranny*. 1952. Revised ed. Harmondsworth: Penguin, 1962.
Calandra, Denis. *New German Dramatists*. New York: Grove Press, 1983.
Canaris, Volker. "Die ersten Juden, die ich kannte, waren Nathan und Shylock." *Theater Heute* 2 (1973): 20–25.
Caute, David. *Joseph Losey: A Revenge on Life*. London and Boston: Faber and Faber, 1994.
Chaikin, Joseph. *The Presence of the Actor: Notes on the Open Theater*. New York: Atheneum, 1972.
Cohen, Sarah Blacher, ed. *Jewish Wry: Essays on Jewish Humor*. Bloomington: Indiana University Press, 1987.
Connor, Steven. *Postmodernist Culture: An Introduction to Theories of the Contemporary*. Oxford and New York: Basil Blackwell, 1989.
Counsell, Colin. *Signs of Performance*. London and New York: Routledge, 1996.
Davis, Jessica Milner. *Farce*. London: Methuen, 1978.
Diner, Dan. "Negative Symbiose: Deutsche und Juden nach Auschwitz." *Babylon: Beiträge zur jüdischen Gegenwart* 1 (1986): 9–20.
Enzensberger, Hans Magnus. *Der Untergang der Titanic*. Frankfurt: Suhrkamp, 1978.
Eörsi, István. *Tage mit Gombrowicz*. Translated by Hans Skirecki. Leipzig: Kipenheuer, 1997.
Esslin, Martin. *Artaud*. London: Calder, 1976.
———. *Bertolt Brecht*. New York and London: Columbia University Press, 1969.
Fassbinder, Rainer Werner. "Philosemiten und Antisemiten." *Die Zeit*, 9 April 1976.
Feinberg, Anat. "Abiding in a Haunted Land: The Issue of Heimat in Contemporary German-Jewish Writing." *New German Critique* 70 (1997): 161–181.

————. "Das Laterndl in London 1939–1945." *German Life and Letters* 37 : 3 (1984): 211–217.

————. "Der permanente Ruhestörer: Juden in der deutschen Nachkriegsliteratur." In *Conditio Judaica, Antisemitismus und deutschsprachige Literatur vom Ersten Weltkrieg bis 1933/38*, edited by Hans-Otto Horch and Horst Denkler, part 3, pp. 380–387. Tübingen: Niemeyer, 1993.

————. *Wiedergutmachung im Programm: Jüdisches Schicksal im deutschen Nachkriegsdrama*. Cologne: Prometh, 1988.

Feinberg-Jütte, Anat. "Shylock." In *Antisemitismus: Vorurteile und Mythen*, edited by Julius H. Schoeps and Joachim Schlör, pp. 119–126. Munich: Piper, 1995.

Fiddes, Nick. *Meat: A Natural Symbol*. London and New York: Routledge, 1991.

Freud, Sigmund. *Collected Works*. 24 vols. London: Hogarth Press, 1935.

————. *Gesammelte Werke*. 18 vols. Frankfurt: S. Fischer, 1978.

————. *Jokes and Their Relation to the Unconscious*. Translated and edited by James Strachey with a biographical introduction by Peter Gay. New York and London: W. W. Norton, 1989.

————. *Totem and Taboo*. Translated and edited by James Strachey with a biographical introduction by Peter Gay. New York and London: W. W. Norton, 1989.

Friedländer, Saul. *Reflections of Nazism: An Essay on Kitsch and Death*. Translated by Thomas Weyr. New York: Harper and Row, 1982.

————, ed. *Probing the Limits of Representation: Nazism and the "Final Solution."* Cambridge, Mass.: Harvard University Press, 1992.

Garfield, David. *A Player's Place: The Story of the Actors Studio*. New York: Macmillan, 1988.

Gilman, Sander L. *Franz Kafka: The Jewish Patient*. New York: Routledge, 1995.

————. *The Jew's Body*. New York and London: Routledge, 1991.

Gilman, Sander L., Robert Jütte, and Gabriele Kohlbauer-Fritz, eds. *"Der schejne Jid": Das Bild des "jüdischen Körpers" in Mythos und Ritual*. Vienna: Picus, 1998.

Gross, John. *Shylock*. London: Chatto and Windus, 1992.

Grotjahn, Martin. *Beyond Laughter: Humor and the Subconscious*. New York: McGraw-Hill, 1957.

Grotowski, Jerzy. *Towards a Poor Theatre*. Edited by Eugenio Barba with a preface by Peter Brook. London: Methuen, 1986.

Hadomi, Leah. *Dramatic Metaphors of Fascism and Antifascism*. Tübingen: Niemeyer, 1996.

Hamann, Brigitte. *Hitlers Wien*. Munich: Piper, 1996.

Hartman, Geoffrey, ed. *Holocaust Remembrance: The Shapes of Memory*. Oxford: Blackwell, 1994.

Hayman, Ronald. *Artaud and After*. Oxford: Oxford University Press, 1977.

————, ed. *The German Theatre: A Symposium*. London: Wolff, 1975.

Innes, Christopher D. *Avant Garde Theatre 1892–1992*. London and New York: Routledge, 1993.

————. *Modern German Drama: A Study in Form*. Cambridge and London: Cambridge University Press, 1979.

Jenisch, Jakob, ed. *Das Schauspielerseminar Lee Strasberg*. Bochum: Schauspielhaus Bochum, 9–22 January 1978.

Kafka, Franz. *Briefe 1902–1924*. In *Gesammelte Schriften*, vol. 6, edited by Max Brod. 10 vols. Frankfurt: S. Fischer, 1965–1970.

—————. *Stories 1904–1924*. Translated and edited by J. A. Underwood. London: Abacus, 1995.

Kalb, Jonathan. *Beckett in Performance*. Cambridge: Cambridge University Press, 1989.

Kipphardt, Heinar. *Bruder Eichmann: Schauspiel und Materialien*. Reinbek: Rowohlt, 1986.

Knowlson, James. *Damned to Fame: The Life of Samuel Beckett*. London: Bloomsbury, 1996.

Kumiega, Jennifer. *The Theatre of Grotowski*. London: Methuen, 1985.

Landmann, Salcia, ed. *Jüdische Witze*. Munich: DTV, 1963. Rpt. 1994.

Lange, Mechthild. *Peter Zadek*. Frankfurt: Fischer, 1989.

Leftwich, Joseph, ed. *Great Yiddish Writers of the Twentieth Century*. Northvale, N.J.: J. Aronson, 1987.

Lévi-Strauss, Claude. *The Raw and the Cooked*. Translated by John Weightman and Doreen Weightman. London: Cape, 1970.

Lichtwitz, Manuel. *Materialien zu Samuel Beckett "Der Verwaiser."* Frankfurt: Suhrkamp, 1980.

Lipman, Steven. *Laughter in Hell: The Use of Humor during the Holocaust*. North Vale, N.J., and London: Aronson, 1991.

Malkin, Jeanette R. *Memory Theatre and Postmodern Drama*. Ann Arbor: University of Michigan Press, 1999.

Mann, Thomas. *Tagebücher 1946–1948*. Edited by Inge Jens. Frankfurt: S. Fischer, 1989.

Märthesheimer, Peter, and Ivo Frenzel, eds. *Im Kreuzfeuer: Der Fernsehfilm "Holocaust": Eine Nation ist betroffen*. Frankfurt: Fischer, 1979.

Meltzer, Milton. *Never to Forget: The Jews of the Holocaust*. New York: Harper and Row, 1976.

Mitscherlich, Alexander, and Margarete Mitscherlich. *Die Unfähigkeit zu trauern*. Munich: Piper, 1967.

Patterson, Michael. *German Theatre Today: Postwar Theatre in West and East Germany, Austria and Northern Switzerland*. London: Pitman Publishing, 1976.

—————. *Peter Stein: Germany's Leading Theatre Director*. Cambridge and New York: Cambridge University Press, 1981.

Pavis, Patrice. "The Classical Heritage of Modern Drama: The Case of Postmodern Theatre." *Modern Drama* 29 (1986): 1–22.

Perls, Frederick S. *Ego, Hunger and Aggression: The Beginning of Gestalt Therapy*. New York: Vintage Books, 1969.

Pilling, John, ed. *The Cambridge Companion to Beckett*. Cambridge: Cambridge University Press, 1994.

Poggioli, Renato. *The Theory of the Avant Garde*. Cambridge, Mass.: Belknap Press of Harvard University, 1968.

Redmond, James, ed. *Farce*. Cambridge: Cambridge University Press, 1988.

Reik, Theodor. *Jewish Wit.* New York: Gamut Press, 1962.

————. *The Search Within.* New York: Jason Aronson, 1974.

Rice, Elmer. *The Living Theatre.* London: W. Heinemann, 1960.

Roose-Evans, James. *Experimental Theatre: From Stanislavski to Peter Brook.* London: Routledge, 1989.

Rosenfeld, Alvin H., ed. *Thinking about the Holocaust: After Half a Century.* Bloomington and Indianapolis: Indiana University Press, 1997.

Samuel, Maurice. *The World of Sholem Aleichem.* New York: Vintage Books, 1943.

Scarry, Elaine. *The Body in Pain: The Making and Unmaking of the World.* New York: Oxford University Press, 1985.

Schumacher, Claude, ed. *Staging the Holocaust: The Shoah in Drama and Performance.* Cambridge: Cambridge University Press, 1998.

Skloot, Robert. *The Darkness We Carry: The Drama of the Holocaust.* Madison: University of Wisconsin Press, 1988.

Steiner, George. *The Portage to San Cristobal of A.H.* London and Boston: Faber and Faber, 1981.

Strasberg, Lee. *A Dream of Passion: The Development of the Method.* Edited by Evangeline Morphos, 1987. Rpt. New York: Penguin, 1987.

————. *Ein Traum von Leidenschaft: Die Entwicklung der "Methode."* Translated by Reinhard Kaiser with a foreword by George Tabori. Munich: Schirmer-Mosel, 1988.

————. *Schauspielen und das Training des Schauspielers: Beiträge zur "Method."* Translated and edited by Wolfgang Wermelskirch. Berlin: Alexander, 1994.

Tabori, Cornelius (Kornél). *My Occult Diary.* Translated and edited by Paul Tabori. London: Rider and Co., 1951.

Tabori, Paul. *The Anatomy of Exile: A Semantic and Historical Study.* London: Harrap, 1972.

————. *Restless Summer: A Personal Record.* London: Sylvan Press, 1946.

Thomson, Peter, and Glendyr Sachs. *The Cambridge Companion to Brecht.* Cambridge and New York: Cambridge University Press, 1994.

Wagenbach, Klaus. *Kafka.* Reinbek: Rowohlt, 1964.

White, Nicholas John. "In the Absence of Memory? Jewish Fate and Dramatic Representation: The Production and Critical Reception of Holocaust Drama on the London Stage 1945–1989." Ph.D. diss., City University, London, August 1998.

Wiles, Timothy J. *The Theater Event: Modern Theories of Performance.* Chicago: University of Chicago Press, 1980.

Williams, David. *Peter Brook: A Theatrical Casebook.* London: Methuen, 1988.

Yerushalmi, Yosef Hayim. *Zakhor: Jewish History and Jewish Memory,* 1982. Rpt. with a new preface. Seattle: University of Washington, 1996.

Zadek, Peter. *My Way: Eine Autobiographie, 1926–1969.* Cologne: Kiepenheuer und Witsch, 1998.

INDEX

STUDIES IN THEATRE HISTORY AND CULTURE